Object-Oriented Programming in C++

Object-Oriented Programming in C++

Nabajyoti Barkakati

A Division of Macmillan Computer Publishing
11711 North College, Carmel, Indiana 46032 USA

To Leha, Ivy, Emily, and Ashley

International Standard Book Number: 0-672-22800-9
Library of Congress Catalog Card Number: 91-60443

Publisher: *Richard K. Swadley*
Publishing Manager: *Joseph B. Wikert*
Managing Editor: *Neweleen Trebnik*
Senior Editor: *Rebecca Whitney*
Manuscript Editor: *Lynn Brown, Brown Editorial Service*
Production Editor: *Katherine Stuart Ewing*
Technical Editor: *Les Dye*
Cover Artist: *Dan Armstrong*
Production Assistance: *Jeff Baker, Brad Chinn, Martin Coleman, Sandy Grieshop, Dennis Clay Hager, Louise Shinault*
Indexers: *Jill Bomaster, Johnna VanHoose*

Printed in the United States of America

Overview

Contents

Preface

Slowly but inexorably, object-oriented programming (OOP) is becoming the method of choice for software design, and with it, C++, the language of choice among programmers. Loosely speaking, OOP is a new way of organizing software that is based on real-world objects. Although OOP techniques can be applied in any language (C, for instance), a language such as C++ that is designed to support OOP makes it easier to implement the OOP techniques. Although the use of OOP does not impart anything to a finished software product that the user can see, the software developer can gain substantial advantages by using OOP, especially in large software projects. Because OOP allows the software to remain close to the conceptual, higher-level model of the real-world problem, the programmer can manage the complexity better than an approach that requires mapping the problem to fit the features of the language.

C++ is a superset of C with features designed to support OOP. C++ was developed in the early 1980s by Bjarne Stroustrup of AT&T Bell Laboratories. He created C++ while he was enhancing C to support efficient event-driven simulation programs. His inspiration came from the language Simula67, which supported the concept of a *class*. AT&T made many improvements to this initial language before releasing it commercially for the first time in 1985. Since then, C++ has continued to evolve, with AT&T controlling the releases.

In the beginning, AT&T supplied a translator called cfront for converting C++ programs into C, which were then compiled using a C compiler. By the time Release 1.2 of AT&T's C++ was available, C++ compilers such as the one from Zortech, Inc., were becoming available for PCs and workstations. AT&T released C++ 2.0 in 1989 and followed it promptly with Release 2.1, a maintenance release. Today, C++ translators and compilers are available on a wide variety of systems, including MS-DOS PCs, Apple Macintoshes, and all UNIX systems.

A good indication of the popularity of C++ and OOP is the large number of books published on these two topics. However, most of the books suffer from one or more drawbacks. Those that cover object-oriented design principles do not pay much attention to C++. The ones that are designed to teach C++ do not adequately describe OOP. Up to now, programmers have had to go through at least two or three books to learn OOP and C++. There is a definite need for a single source of information for these two topics.

Object-Oriented Programming in C++ is designed to answer the needs of C programmers learning C++ and OOP. This book teaches OOP and C++ and, at the same time, serves as a reference guide to the C++ programming language. It includes in-depth tutorials that gently introduce you to OOP and show you how to apply these techniques in C++.

The book features

- extensive tutorials on the basic concepts of object-oriented programming.
- discussion of data abstraction, inheritance, and polymorphism.
- a step-by-step introduction to the features of C++ such as classes and virtual functions that support OOP.
- complete coverage of the latest release of AT&T's C++.
- discussions of how C++ differs from ANSI standard C.
- detailed examples showing how to use OOP techniques.
- descriptions of the different approaches to building a library of reusable classes in C++.
- coverage of object-oriented software design principles.
- real-world examples of using C++ class libraries in applications meant for Microsoft Windows 3.0 and the X Window System.
- a glossary of OOP terminology.
- A minireference to the C++ programming language, especially its keywords.

Instead of going through a litany of syntactical details, *Object-Oriented Programming in C++* uses many short sample programs to illustrate OOP techniques. Features of C++ are always presented in the context of an OOP concept that the feature supports.

Although the descriptions of OOP and C++ rely on generic AT&T C++, *Object-Oriented Programming in C++* also includes coverage of commercial class libraries that are useful for building real-world applications. Specifically, this book describes M++, C++/Views, and InterViews toolkits—sets of classes that you can use in your applications. Additionally, you will find examples of writing Microsoft Windows programs in C++.

It is easy to get overwhelmed by the new syntax of C++ and the details of how everything fits together in a program that uses an object-oriented design. However, with a grasp of the fundamentals of OOP and with the help of C++ class libraries, you will find it relatively easy to employ OOP techniques in your applications. I sincerely hope that *Object-Oriented Programming in C++* will get you started on your way to harnessing the full power of object-oriented techniques and C++.

Acknowledgments

I am grateful to Joe Wikert for suggesting the idea of this book—a single source of information for C programmers interested in learning both C++ and object-oriented programming. Thanks to Joe for not only suggesting the idea but also for getting me started on this project and seeing it through to its successful completion.

Thanks to Nan Borreson of Borland International for providing me the beta copies of the Borland C++ 2.0 compiler. Thanks also to Bob Swarm of Zortech for sending me a copy of Zortech C++ Version 2.1. Barbara LoFranco of The Santa Cruz Operations was kind enough to send me a copy of SCO C++ as soon as it was released—thus making it possible to write Chapter 15 and test some of the examples under SCO C++. The folks at SCO, especially Barbara LoFranco and Allen Ginzburg, helped me immensely by providing copies of Open Desktop Personal System and Open Desktop Development System so that I could use the X Window System, Motif, and SCO C++.

For the chapter on C++ class libraries, I needed some sample libraries. Les Dye of Dyad Software and Jim Schwarz of CNS came through with *M++* and *C++/Views*, respectively. Thanks to both of you for helping me out. Les Dye deserves a second round of thanks for the technical review of the manuscript.

Production of a book like this always involves many dedicated professionals doing their part behind the scenes. I would like to give my heartfelt thanks to each and every one involved in turning my raw manuscript into this well-edited, beautifully packaged book. In particular, thanks to Lynn Brown of Brown Editorial Service for the thorough editing of the manuscript and to Kathy Ewing for managing the production.

Of course, there would be no reason for this book if it were not for the C++ programming language. For this, I have Bjarne Stroustrup, the principal author of C++, to thank.

Finally, my greatest thanks go to my wife Leha for her patience and understanding and for taking care of everything while I stayed glued to my PCs. I can't imagine how she managed, because our daughter Ashley was born midway through this book project. As I wrap up the book, Ashley is already hard at work encouraging me with her smiles, while her older sisters Ivy and Emily are tracking my progress and counting the days to the deadline. Thanks for being there!

Nabajyoti Barkakati

Trademarks

All terms mentioned in this book that are known to be trademarks or service marks are listed below. In addition, terms suspected of being trademarks or service marks have been appropriately capitalized. SAMS cannot attest to the accuracy of this information. Use of a term in this book should not be regarded as affecting the validity of any trademark or service mark.

Ada is a registered trademark of the U.S. Department of Defense.

Apple, MacApp, and Macintosh are registered trademarks and AppleTalk is a trademark of Apple Computer, Inc.

AT&T is a registered trademark of American Telephone and Telegraph Company.

BSD is a trademark of University of California, Berkeley.

Borland and Borland C++ are registered trademarks and Turbo Assembler, Turbo C++, and Turbo Profiler are trademarks of Borland International, Inc.

C++/Views is a trademark of CNS, Inc.

CompuServe is a registered trademark of CompuServe, Inc.

dbXtra is a trademark of SCO Canada, Inc.

DEC is a registered trademark and DECnet, Ultrix, VAX, VAXstation II/GPX, VAX/VMS, and VMS are trademarks of Digital Equipment Corporation.

Dyad and M++ are trademarks of Dyad Software Corporation.

Eiffel is a registered trademark of Interactive Software Engineering, Inc.

Ethernet is a trademark of Xerox Corporation.

Helvetica and Times are trademarks of Linotype Company.

Hewlett-Packard and HP are registered trademarks of Hewlett-Packard Company.

IBM, IBM PC, IBM XT, IBM AT are registered trademarks and OS/2 and Presentation Manager are trademarks of International Business Machines.

Intel is a registered trademark and Intel 8088, 8086, 80186, 80286, 80386, 80486, i860, 8087, 80287, and 80387 are trademarks of Intel Corporation.

Microsoft, MS-DOS, and XENIX are registered trademarks of Microsoft Corporation.

Motif, OSF, and OSF/Motif are trademarks of Open Software Foundation, Inc.

Motorola MC68000 is a trademark of Motorola, Inc.

Objective-C and Software-IC are registered trademarks of The Stepstone Corporation.

Open Desktop and SCO are registered trademarks and the Santa Cruz Operation is a trademark of The Santa Cruz Operation, Inc.

OPEN LOOK and System V are trademarks of AT&T.

PostScript is a registered trademark of Adobe Systems, Inc.

Simula67 is a trademark of Simula AS.

Smalltalk-80 is a trademark of ParcPlace Systems.

Software Through Pictures is a registered trademark of Interactive Development Environments, Inc.

SPARCstation, Sun, Sun-3, Sun-4, Sun Microsystems, Sun Workstation, and SunOS are registered trademarks of Sun Microsystems, Inc.

TEKTRONIX is a registered trademark of Tektronix, Inc.

Times Roman is a trademark of Monotype Corporation.

UNIX is a registered trademark of UNIX System Laboratories, Inc.

Whitewater Resource Toolkit is a trademark of The Whitewater Group.

X Window System is a trademark of The Massachusetts Institute of Technology.

Zinc and Zinc Interface Library are trademarks of Zinc Software, Inc.

Zortech is a trademark of Zortech, Inc.

Introduction

*O*bject-Oriented Programming in C++ is an intermediate-level book that introduces you to the basic concepts of object-oriented programming (OOP) and shows you how to apply OOP techniques using the C++ programming language. This book assumes that you already know the C programming language. The goal is to assist you, the C programmer, in becoming familiar with the terminology of OOP and to show you how various features of C++ support OOP.

To this end, *Object-Oriented Programming in C++* focuses on the basic concepts of OOP, how OOP helps you handle changes in software requirements easily, and how C++ supports OOP. This book also covers programming with the *iostream* I/O library and shows how to call C functions from C++, organize C++ class libraries, and use commercially available C++ class libraries. Once you have mastered the basics of OOP, C++, and C++ class libraries, *Object-Oriented Programming in C++* moves on to the subject of developing realistic applications in C++. The book includes sample programs for MS-DOS, Microsoft Windows, and the X Window System. Figures are used to illustrate concepts and show the inheritance hierarchies of classes.

Although *Object-Oriented Programming in C++* includes a reference section on the C++ programming language, it is *not* a complete reference for C++. This book's goal is to show you how to use C++ to create and use objects, not simply to present the language definition for compiler writers.

What You Need

To make the best use of this book, you should have access to a system with a C++ compiler. That way, you can test the example programs as you progress through the book. For those using MS-DOS PCs, the latest versions of Borland C++ or Zortech C++ fits the bill perfectly. On Intel 80386 PCs running UNIX System V, The Santa Cruz Operation's SCO C++ is a possible choice. For most other UNIX systems, C++ compilers are available directly from the system's vendor. If your system does not have a C++ compiler, you may be able to find a copy of Free Software Foundation's GNU C++ (g++) that works on your system.

Of course, if you want to use C++ to develop applications for Microsoft Windows or the X Window System, you will need some additional items. Chapters 14 and 15 describe what you need to use C++ for Microsoft Windows and X applications, respectively.

All examples in this book were tested with Borland C++ 2.0 on two systems: a 1985 vintage 6-MHz IBM PC-AT and an Intel 80386-based ISA (Industry Standard

Architecture) PC with 8MB of memory, a 150MB hard disk, and a VGA display. Many examples were also tested using Zortech C++ version 2.1. (I could not use Zortech C++ for many examples, because Zortech C++ 2.1 lacks the *iostream* library required by the examples.) When needed, I ran SCO Open Desktop (which includes UNIX System V/386 Release 3.2, X version 11 Release 3, and OSF/Motif version 1.0) on the 80386 system. All the examples should compile and link on most systems without any change. They do require the *iostream* library, however.

Conventions Used in This Book

Object-Oriented Programming in C++ uses a simple notational style. All listings are typeset in a `monospace` font for ease of reading. All file names, function names, variable names, and keywords appearing in text are also in the same `monospace` font. The first occurrence of new terms and concepts is in *italic*. Notes, which appear in boxes, explain terms and concepts that appear in the text nearby.

How to Use This Book

If you are a newcomer to C++, you should read the book from front to back. The sample programs usually build on classes introduced in earlier chapters. For example, a sample program in Chapter 13 might need classes that are presented in Chapter 8. If you read the chapters in order, you will be aware of this and be able to understand the examples easily.

There are five parts in the book. The first four parts comprise 16 chapters. Part I includes three chapters that explain the basic concepts of object-oriented programming (OOP). Part II has six chapters that describe how to use the features of C++ that support OOP. Part III includes three chapters that show how to organize C++ class libraries and how to use commercially available libraries. Part IV consists of four chapters that present realistic applications for MS-DOS and Microsoft Windows. Part IV also describes the InterViews toolkit that you can use to develop applications for the X Window System. The final part, Part V, is a collection of four appendixes that include a glossary and a list of C++ compilers and libraries, as well as the comprehensive index to the book.

From this quick overview, you can decide whether you want to skip any of the parts. For example, if you are already familiar with the basic terminology of OOP, you can skip Part I and go straight to Part II. On the other hand, if you know how C++ supports OOP and want to start using C++ in realistic applications, you can skip Parts I through III and start with Chapter 13. To help you decide how to best use the book, the following sections describe the chapters in greater detail.

Part I: Learning Object-Oriented Programming

This part of the book introduces you, the prospective C++ programmer, to the basic concepts of object-oriented programming: data abstraction, inheritance, and polymorphism. Examples in C illustrate how you can apply these concepts in practice. You will see the same examples in C++ and see how an object-oriented language simplifies the use of OOP techniques. At this point you do not have to know C++, but you will be asked to go along with the assumption that everything will be explained in later chapters. The final chapter in Part I describes the process of designing software the "object-oriented" way. Part I includes

> Chapter 1: Basics of Object-Oriented Programming
> Chapter 2: C++ and Object-Oriented Programming
> Chapter 3: Object-Oriented Software Design

Part II: Learning C++

Part II teaches the C++ programming language from the perspective of OOP. Chapter 4 provides a brief review of ANSI standard C and a summary of the new features of C++. This chapter serves as a refresher on C and gives a complete overview of C++. Chapter 5 shows how to use the predefined stream classes in the iostream library to perform I/O. The next four chapters explain how various facilities of C++ are used to define, create, and manipulate objects. These chapters show the use of C++ features such as classes, inheritance, and virtual functions. Part II also covers overloading of functions and operators. The chapters in Part II include

> Chapter 4: C++ and ANSI Standard C
> Chapter 5: Predefined Classes in C++
> Chapter 6: Building Objects with Classes
> Chapter 7: Defining Operations on Objects
> Chapter 8: Using Inheritance in C++
> Chapter 9: Virtual Functions and Polymorphism

Part III: Applying OOP Techniques in C++

Part III introduces you to the idea of building and using libraries of C++ classes. This part explains how to use C libraries in C++ programs. Chapter 11 describes some strategies for building C++ class libraries. The last chapter in this part summarizes the capabilities of two representative commercial class libraries and discusses how the programmer can supplement in-house libraries with these commercial offerings. Part III includes the following chapters:

Part IV: Developing Applications in C++

Part IV is devoted to illustrating how to use C++ class libraries in realistic applications. Chapter 13 starts with the basic building blocks for a Forms package—software that you use to create, store, and display forms. Because the user interface benefits the most from an OOP approach, the next chapter focuses on building the user interface for the Forms software under Microsoft Windows. Chapter 15 describes the InterViews toolkit which you can use to create applications that use the X Window System. Chapter 16 covers a number of advanced topics, such as exception-handling and templates that are being considered for addition to the C++ programming language. Part IV includes the following chapters:

Part V: Appendixes and Index

Part V starts with a glossary of terms used in OOP. This is followed by Appendix B which serves as a minireference for the C++ programming language. It includes reference entries for the keywords. Appendix C is a list of currently available C++ compilers and class libraries. Appendix C also includes information on how to obtain these libraries. Appendix D provides a summary of the standard ANSI C library. You will find the prototypes of all standard C library routines here.

How to Contact the Author

If you have any questions or suggestions, or if you want to report any errors, please feel free to contact me either by mail or through electronic mail. Here is how:

- Write to LNB Software, Inc., 2005 Aventurine Way, Silver Spring, MD 20904
- If you have access to an Internet node, send E-mail to:

  `naba@grebyn.com`

- If you use CompuServe, specify the following as SEND TO:

  `>INTERNET:naba@grebyn.com`

- From MCIMAIL, specify the following when sending mail:

  ```
  EMS: INTERNET
  MBX: naba@grebyn.com
  ```

Please do not phone, even if you happen to come across my telephone number. Instead, drop me a letter or send an E-mail message, and you are guaranteed a prompt reply.

How to Get the Source Code on Disk

For your convenience, the complete source code for the programs in *Object-Oriented Programming in C++* is available on MS-DOS disks. Use the order form at the back of the book to request your copy. If the form is missing, send $30 (money order or check in U.S. funds drawn on a U.S. bank) to

LNB Software, Inc.
2005 Aventurine Way
Silver Spring, MD 20904

Foreign orders, please add $6 for shipping and handling. Maryland residents, please add sales tax. Please specify diskette size ($5\frac{1}{4}$ inch or $3\frac{1}{2}$ inch).

Part One

Learning Object-Oriented Programming

## Chapter 1

Basics of Object-Oriented Programming

Since the early days of computing, programmers have looked for ways to manage the complexity of programming computers. Because a computer's central processing unit (CPU) works by fetching and executing simple instructions from memory, early computer programs were a sequence of such machine instructions that had to be loaded into memory through a set of switches or through a numeric keypad.

Assembly language improved the situation by enabling us to use mnemonic names for the machine instructions and symbolic names for memory locations. A translator called the *assembler* converts assembly language programs into machine code. Assemblers soon started providing special commands or directives that allowed programmers to group basic data items into structures with assigned names. With a program's tasks broken down into procedures and data organized into structures, assembly language provided reasonable programming facilities. However, the close connection between assembly language and the machine code means that assembly language forces you to think of the program in terms of the machine instructions that the underlying CPU can execute.

Higher-level languages such as FORTRAN, BASIC, Pascal, and C largely eliminate the close ties to the CPU's machine instructions by providing standard data types such as integers, floating-point numbers, and character strings that can be used in expressions and statements—each of which is translated by a *compiler* into many machine instructions. Most recent applications are written in a combination of these high-level languages and some assembly language. The accepted programming style has been to organize related data items using programming constructs such as Pascal RECORDs or C structs and then treat the resulting block of data as a single unit. Once the data structures are laid out, the application is written as a collection of procedures that manipulate these structures.

Although the traditional "design the data structures and write the functions to manipulate them" approach to programming has served us well, there is no denying that the complexity of software is increasing in keeping with more powerful computer hardware. With ever-increasing hardware capabilities such as faster CPUs, better graphics, and easier networking, users have come to expect software to have greater functionality. Users now routinely expect programs to include features such as a window-based graphical user interface, transparent access to data stored in mini- or mainframe computers, and the ability to work in a networked environment. Faced with this complexity, more programmers are starting to use *object-oriented programming (OOP)*. OOP is a new way of organizing code and data that promises increased control over the complexity of the software development process.

Object-oriented programming is nothing new; its underlying concepts are *data abstraction*, *inheritance*, and *polymorphism* (defined later in the chapter). All three have been around for quite some time (for example, in languages such as Simula67 and Smalltalk). What is new is the increasing interest in OOP among programmers in general, and C programmers in particular. One of the reasons is the popularity of the C++ programming language, which many programmers see as the successor to C, the current language of choice among software developers. C++ improves C by introducing several new programming constructs that directly support object-oriented techniques. If you are a C programmer, you will find it reasonably easy to learn the syntax of C++, but you have to reorient your thinking if you want to use object-oriented techniques in your programs.

The best way to learn C++ is to understand the basic concepts of OOP and see how C++ supports it. This book explains OOP through examples and, at the same time, teaches the C++ programming language—its features and how they relate to OOP. Chapter 1 starts by explaining basic OOP terminology. Examples show how you can apply object-oriented techniques in C. Chapter 2 gives you a bird's eye view of C++ from the perspective of OOP and revisits the examples of Chapter 1, this time in C++. Such revised views are intended to illustrate how an object-oriented programming language such as C++ makes it easy to apply object-oriented methods. The final chapter of Part I, Chapter 3, gives an overview of some techniques of designing software the "object-oriented" way.

What Is Object-Oriented Programming?

The term *object-oriented programming (OOP)* is widely used, but experts cannot seem to agree on its exact definition. However, most experts agree that OOP involves defining *abstract data types (ADT)* representing complex real-world or abstract objects and organizing your program around the collection of ADTs with an eye toward exploiting their common features. The term *data abstraction* refers to the process of defining ADTs; *inheritance* and *polymorphism* refer to the mechanisms that enable you to take advantage of the common characteristics of the ADTs—the *objects* in OOP. This chapter further explores these terms later.

> The term *abstract data type*, or *ADT* for short, refers to a programmer-defined data type together with a set of operations that can be performed on that data. It is called *abstract* to distinguish it from the fundamental built-in C data types such as int, char, and double. In C, you can define an ADT using typedef and struct and implementing the operations with a set of functions. As you will learn soon, C++ has much better facilities for defining and using ADTs.
>
> By the way, this book uses notes like this to explain terms and concepts that appear in the text.

Before you jump into OOP, take note of two points. First, OOP is only a method of designing and implementing software. Use of object-oriented techniques does not impart anything to a finished software product that the user can see. However, as a programmer implementing the software, you can gain significant advantages by using object-oriented methods, especially in large software projects. Because OOP enables you to remain close to the conceptual, higher-level model of the real-world problem you are trying to solve, you can manage the complexity better than with approaches that force you to map the problem to fit the features of the language. You can take advantage of the modularity of objects and implement the program in relatively independent units that are easier to maintain and extend. You can also share code among objects through inheritance.

The second point is that OOP has nothing to do with any programming language, although a programming language that supports OOP makes it easier to implement the object-oriented techniques. As you will see shortly, with some discipline, you can use objects in C programs.

Procedure-Oriented Programming

Before you get into OOP, take a look at conventional procedure-oriented programming in a language such as C. Using the procedure-oriented approach, you view a problem as a sequence of things to do. You organize the related data items into C structs and write the necessary functions (procedures) to manipulate the data and, in the process, complete the sequence of tasks that solve your problem. Although the data may be organized into structures, the primary focus is on the functions. Each C function transforms data in some way. For example, you may have a function that calculates the average value of a set of numbers, another that computes the square root, and one that prints a string. You do not have to look far to find examples of this kind of programming—C function libraries are implemented this way. Each function in a library performs a well-defined operation on its input arguments and returns the transformed data as a return value. Arguments may be pointers to data that the function directly alters or the function may have the effect of displaying graphics on a video monitor.

An Example in C

For a concrete illustration of procedure-oriented programming, consider the following example. Suppose you want to write a computer program that handles geometric shapes such as rectangles and circles. The program should be able to draw any shape and compute its area. Here is a conventional approach to writing this program.

As shown in Figure 1.1, you can break down the tasks of the program into two procedures: one to draw a shape and the other to compute its area. Call each function with a single argument: a pointer to a data structure that contains a shape's pertinent information, such as coordinates of a circle's center and its radius. For each geometric shape, it is easy to define an appropriate structure, but how do you reconcile these different structures into a single one? After all, the functions need a pointer to a single data structure.

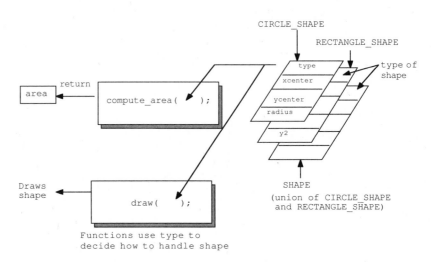

Fig. 1.1. C data and procedures for handling geometric shapes.

In such cases, a common technique is to combine the different structures into a single one using a C `union` with an additional integer flag to indicate the exact shape being handled by the `union`. In keeping with common C coding style, you should define these data types in a header file, `cshapes.h`, as shown in Listing 1.1. The resulting data type, `SHAPE`, is graphically illustrated in Figure 1.1.

The data structure for each shape is essentially a block of memory. Because the members of a C `union` all share the same block of memory, you need a way to determine which member is valid at any time. Listing 1.1 does this by declaring the first field in the union SHAPE to be a short integer denoting the type of the shape. Knowing the type, you can access the right structure in the union to extract information about the shape. The code in Listing 1.2 shows how the structures in the SHAPE union are used.

Listing 1.1. cshapes.h—Definition of data types for shapes.

```
/*----------------------------------------------------------*/
/*  File: cshapes.h
 *
 *  Define data types for manipulating geometric shapes
 *  in C.
 */
#ifndef CSHAPES_H     /* Used to avoid including file twice */
#define CSHAPES_H

#define T_CIRCLE    1
#define T_RECTANGLE 2

/* Define each individual shape's data structure */

typedef struct CIRCLE_SHAPE
{
    short   type;    /* Type of shape (T_CIRCLE)      */
    double  x, y;    /* Coordinates of center         */
    double  radius;  /* Radius of circle              */
} CIRCLE_SHAPE;

typedef struct RECTANGLE_SHAPE
{
    short   type;    /* Type of shape (T_RECTANGLE)   */
    double  x1, y1;  /* Coordinates of the corners    */
    double  x2, y2;
} RECTANGLE_SHAPE;

/* Now define a union of the two structures */

typedef union SHAPE
{
    short           type;       /* Type of shape      */
    CIRCLE_SHAPE    circle;      /* Data for circle    */
    RECTANGLE_SHAPE rectangle;   /* Data for rectangle*/
} SHAPE;
```

```
/* Function prototypes */

double compute_area(SHAPE *p_shape);
void   draw_shape(SHAPE *p_shape);

#endif  /* #ifndef CSHAPES_H  */
```

Once the data structures are defined, you can start writing the functions to operate on the data. In fact, as required by ANSI standard C, the header file cshapes.h already includes the *prototypes* for the functions compute_area and draw_shape. Listing 1.2 shows the implementation of these functions. The functions are straightforward: A switch statement is used to handle each shape individually.

To keep the program simple, this example does not actually go into the steps involved in displaying the shapes on a particular graphics device. The draw function simply prints the name of the shape and its location and size. The compute_area function uses a standard formula to compute the area and return the result.

Listing 1.2. cshapes.c—Functions for geometric shapes.

```
/*---------------------------------------------------------------*/
/*  File: cshapes.c
 *
 *  C functions to operate on geometric shapes.
 */
#include <stdio.h>
#include <cshapes.h>
#include <math.h>


/*---------------------------------------------------------------*/
/* c o m p u t e _ a r e a
 * Compute the area of the shape and return the area
 */
double compute_area(SHAPE *p_shape)
{
    double area;

/* Handle each shape according to its type */
    switch(p_shape->type)
    {
        case T_CIRCLE:
            area = M_PI * p_shape->circle.radius
                        * p_shape->circle.radius;
            break;
```

```
        case T_RECTANGLE:
            area = fabs(
                (p_shape->rectangle.x2 - p_shape->rectangle.x1) *
                (p_shape->rectangle.y2 - p_shape->rectangle.y1));
            break;

        default: printf("Unknown shape in 'compute_area'!\n");
    }
    return area;
}
/*-------------------------------------------------------------*/
/* d r a w
 * "Draw" a shape (print information about shape)
 */
void draw(SHAPE *p_shape)
{
/* Handle each shape according to its type */
    printf("Draw: ");
    switch(p_shape->type)
    {
        case T_CIRCLE:
            printf("Circle of radius %f at (%f, %f)\n",
                    p_shape->circle.radius,
                    p_shape->circle.x, p_shape->circle.y);
            break;

        case T_RECTANGLE:
            printf("Rectangle with corners:"
                    " (%f, %f) at (%f, %f)\n",
                    p_shape->rectangle.x1,
                    p_shape->rectangle.y1,
                    p_shape->rectangle.x2,
                    p_shape->rectangle.y2);
            break;

        default: printf("Unknown shape in 'draw'!\n");
    }
}
```

You can test these functions with the simple program, stest1.c, shown in Listing 1.3. This program defines an array of two shapes and initializes them. Then it computes the area of each shape and "draws" the shapes. In a more realistic implementation, you might include utility functions such as create_circle and create_rectangle to dynamically allocate and initialize a SHAPE union and return a pointer to it.

Listing 1.3. stest1.c—Program to test shape-manipulation functions.

```c
/*----------------------------------------------------------*/
/*  File:  stest1.c
 *
 *  Program to test shape-handling functions of Listing 1.2.
 *  Compile and link with file shown in Listing 1.1.
 */
#include <stdio.h>
#include <cshapes.h>

int main()
{
    int i;
    SHAPE s[2];

/* Initialize the shapes */

/* A 40 x 20 rectangle with lower left corner at (80, 30) */
    s[0].type = T_RECTANGLE;
    s[0].rectangle.x1 = 80.0;
    s[0].rectangle.y1 = 30.0;
    s[0].rectangle.x2 = 120.0;
    s[0].rectangle.y2 = 50.0;

/* A circle at (200.0, 100.0) of radius 50.0 units */
    s[1].type = T_CIRCLE;
    s[1].circle.x = 200.0;
    s[1].circle.y = 100.0;
    s[1].circle.radius = 50.0;

/* Compute areas . . . */
    for(i = 0; i < 2; i++)
        printf("Area of shape[%d] = %f\n", i,
                                    compute_area(&s[i]));

/* Draw shapes . . . */
    for(i = 0; i < 2; i++) draw(&s[i]);
    return 0;
}
```

You can build the stest1 program by compiling and linking the files shown in Listings 1.2 and 1.3. Use any ANSI standard-compliant C compiler to compile the files. When you run stest1, it produces the following output:

```
Area of shape[0] = 800.000000
Area of shape[1] = 7853.981634
Draw: Rectangle with corners: (80.000000, 30.000000) at (120.000000, 50.000000)
Draw: Circle of radius 50.000000 at (200.000000, 100.000000)
```

Even though this example is somewhat simple and contrived, it does embody the general style of procedure-oriented programming in C. Data structures are designed first. Then procedures are written to manipulate the data. Different types of related data (such as the geometric shapes circle and rectangle) are handled by switch statements.

Adding a New Shape

To see one of the problems of conventional procedure-oriented programming, consider what happens when you want your program to handle another type of geometric shape—say, triangles. To do this, you have to go through the following steps:

Step 1: Define a data structure for triangles. If you choose to represent the triangle by the coordinates of its vertices, you might add the following structure to the file cshapes.h (Listing 1.1):

```
#define T_TRIANGLE  3

typedef struct TRIANGLE_SHAPE
{
    short   type;      /* Type of shape (T_TRIANGLE)   */
    double  x1, y1;    /* Coordinates of the corners   */
    double  x2, y2;
    double  x3, y3;
} TRIANGLE_SHAPE;
```

Step 2: Add a new member to the SHAPE union to reflect the addition of the new shape:

```
typedef union SHAPE
{
    short           type;      /* Type of shape      */
    CIRCLE_SHAPE    circle;     /* Data for circle    */
    RECTANGLE_SHAPE rectangle;  /* Data for rectangle*/
    TRIANGLE_SHAPE  triangle;   /* Data for triangle */
} SHAPE;
```

Step 3: In the file cshapes.c (Listing 1.2), add code in the functions compute_area and draw to handle triangles. Specifically, you have to add additional case statements in the `switch` statement in each function. For example, the additional fragments of code are as follows:

```
/* In the compute_area function */

 double compute_area(SHAPE *p_shape)
{
    double area;

/* Handle each shape according to its type */
    switch(p_shape->type)
    {
        .
        .
        .
        case T_TRIANGLE:
        {
            double x21, y21, x31, y31;

            x21 =  p_shape->triangle.x2 - p_shape->triangle.x1;
            y21 =  p_shape->triangle.y2 - p_shape->triangle.y1;
            x31 =  p_shape->triangle.x3 - p_shape->triangle.x1;
            y31 =  p_shape->triangle.y3 - p_shape->triangle.y1;

            area = fabs(y21 * x31 - x21 * y31) / 2.0;
        }
        break;
        .
        .
        .

    }

/*-----------------------------------------------------------------*/
/* In function: draw() */
void draw(SHAPE *p_shape)
{
    printf("Draw: ");
    switch(p_shape->type)
    {
        .
        .
        .
        case T_TRIANGLE:
            printf("Triangle with vertices: "
                    "(%f, %f) (%f, %f) (%f, %f)\n",
                    p_shape->triangle.x1, p_shape->triangle.y1,
                    p_shape->triangle.x2, p_shape->triangle.y2,
                    p_shape->triangle.x3, p_shape->triangle.y3);
            break;
```

.
.
```
        }
}
```
Step 4: You can now test operations on the triangle shape. For example, you can define a triangle shape and use it as follows:

```
        SHAPE s;
        s.type = T_TRIANGLE;
        s.triangle.x1 = 100.0;
        s.triangle.y1 = 100.0;
        s.triangle.x2 = 200.0;
        s.triangle.y2 = 100.0;
        s.triangle.x3 = 150.0;
        s.triangle.y3 = 50.0;
    /* Compute area */
        printf("Area of triangle = %f\n", compute_area(&s));

    /* Draw the triangle . . . */
        draw(&s);
```

The reason for going through this exercise is to point out the types of changes you have to make when a new data type—a new *object*—has to be added to an existing program written in conventional procedure-oriented style. Notice that you have to edit working code—the switch statements in the compute_area and draw functions—when you want to handle triangles in addition to the rectangles and circles that the program was originally designed to accept. If this were a realistic program with many files, a change such as this would have required you to edit switch statements in most of the files.

As you will see next, the object-oriented approach avoids this problem by keeping data structures together with functions that operate on them. This approach effectively localizes the changes that become necessary when you decide to add a new object to your program. This is one of the benefits of OOP.

OOP Terminology

As mentioned earlier, there are three basic concepts underlying OOP:

- Data Abstraction
- Inheritance
- Polymorphism

Individually, these concepts have been known and used before, but their use as the foundation of OOP is new.

Data Abstraction

To understand data abstraction, consider the file I/O routines in the C run-time library. These routines enable you to view the file as a stream of bytes and to perform various operations on this stream by calling the file I/O routines. For example, you can call fopen to open a file, fclose to close it, fgetc to read a character from it, and fputc to write a character to it. This abstract model of a file is implemented by defining a data type named FILE to hold all relevant information about a file. The C constructs struct and typedef are used to define FILE. You will find the definition of FILE in the header file stdio.h. You can think of this definition of FILE, together with the functions that operate on it, as a new data type just like C's int or char.

To use the FILE data type, you do not have to know the C data structure that defines it. In fact, the underlying data structure of FILE can vary from one system to another. Yet, the C file I/O routines work in the same manner on all systems. This is possible because you never access the members of the FILE data structure directly. Instead, you rely on a functions and macros that essentially hide the inner details of FILE. This is known as *data hiding*.

Data abstraction is the process of defining a data type, often called an *abstract data type (ADT)*, together with the principle of data hiding. The definition of an ADT involves specifying the internal representation of the ADT's data as well as the functions to be used by others to manipulate the ADT. Data hiding ensures that the internal structure of the ADT can be altered without any fear of breaking the programs that call the functions provided for operations on that ADT. Thus, C's FILE data type is an example of an ADT (see Figure 1.2).

Objects, Classes, and Methods

In OOP, you create an *object* from an ADT. Essentially, an ADT is a collection of variables together with the functions necessary to operate on those variables. The variables represent the information contained in the object, whereas the functions define the operations that can be performed on that object. You can think of the ADT as a template from which specific instances of objects can be created as needed. The term *class* is often used for this template. Consequently, class is synonymous with an ADT. In fact, C++ provides the class declaration precisely for the purpose of defining an ADT—the template from which objects are created. The ADT is a template for objects in the sense that creating an object involves setting aside a block of memory for the variables of that object.

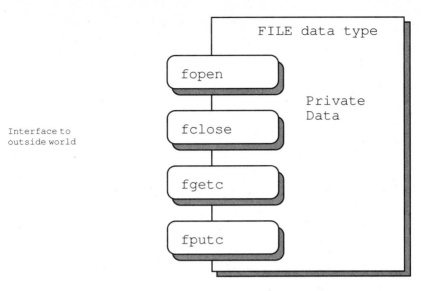

Fig. 1.2. C's FILE type as an example of ADT.

The functions that operate on an object are known as *methods*. This term comes from the object-oriented language Smalltalk. The methods define the behavior of an object. In C++, methods are called the *member functions* of the class.

Another common term of OOP originated in Smalltalk—the idea of sending messages to an object, causing it to perform an operation by invoking one of the methods. In C++, you do this by calling the appropriate member function of the object. For objects implemented in C, you can *send a message* by calling a function that accepts a pointer to a data structure representing the ADT's internal structure. Of course, the function must be capable of handling the operation you want. For instance, C's file I/O routines accept a pointer to the FILE structure as an argument. The file I/O routines use that pointer to identify the file with which the I/O operation is to be performed.

Inheritance

Data abstraction does not cover an important characteristic of objects. Real-world objects do not exist in isolation. Each object is related to one or more other objects. In fact, you can often describe a new kind of object by pointing out how the new object's characteristics and behavior differ from that of a class of objects that already exists. This is what you do when you describe an object with a sentence such as: *B is just like A, except that B has . . ., and B does. . . .* Here you are defining objects of type *B* in terms of those of type *A*.

This notion of defining a new object in terms of an old one is an integral part of OOP. The term *inheritance* is used for this concept, because you can think of one class of objects inheriting the data and behavior from another class. Inheritance imposes a hierarchical relationship among classes in which a child class inherits from its parent. In C++ terminology, the parent class is known as the *base class*; the child is the *derived class*.

Multiple Inheritance

A real-world object often exhibits characteristics that it inherits from more than one type of object. For instance, on the basis of eating habits, an animal may be classified as a carnivore; other ways of classification place it in a specific family, such as the bear family. When modeling a corporation, you may want to describe a technical manager as someone who is an engineer as well as a manager. An example from the programming world is a full-screen text editor. It displays a block of text on the screen and also stores the text in an internal buffer so that you can perform operations such as insert a character and delete a character. Thus, you may want to say that a text editor inherits its behavior from two classes: a *text buffer* class and a *text display* class that, for instance, manages an 80-character by 25-line text display area.

These examples illustrate *multiple inheritance*—the idea that a class can be derived from more than one base class. Many object-oriented programming languages do not support multiple inheritance, but C++ does.

Polymorphism

In a literal sense, *polymorphism* means the quality of having more than one form. In the context of OOP, polymorphism refers to the fact that a single operation can have different behavior in different objects. In other words, different objects react differently to the same message. For example, consider the operation of addition. For two numbers, addition should generate the sum. In a programming language that supports OOP, you should be able to express the operation of addition by a single operator, say, +. When this is possible, you can use the expression $x+y$ to denote the sum of x and y, for many different types of x and y: integers, floating-point numbers, and complex numbers, to name a few. You can even define the + operation for two strings to mean the concatenation of the string.

Similarly, suppose a number of geometrical shapes all respond to the message, *draw*. Each object reacts to this message by displaying its shape on a display screen. Obviously, the actual mechanism for displaying the object differs from one shape to another, but all shapes perform this task in response to the same message.

Polymorphism helps by enabling you to simplify the syntax of performing the same operation on a collection of objects. For example, by exploiting polymorphism, you can compute the area of each geometrical shape in an array of shapes with a simple loop like this:

```
/* Assume "shapes" is an array of shapes (rectangles, circles,
 * and so on) and "compute_area" is a function that computes
 * the area of a shape
 */
for (i = 0; i < number_of_shapes; i++)
    area_of_shape = shapes[i].compute_area();
```

This is possible because regardless of the exact geometrical shape, each object supports the `compute_area` function and computes the area in a way appropriate for that shape.

OOP in C

Once you know the basic concepts of OOP, it is not difficult to implement them in a C program *provided* you have somehow identified the objects and what they do. Deciding how to organize your software around objects—physical or abstract—falls under the topic of object-oriented analysis and design. Chapter 3 briefly discusses some methods for object-oriented design. The remainder of this chapter uses the geometric shapes as an example and shows one way to handle the shapes using object-oriented techniques.

Defining Objects in C

To illustrate the use of OOP techniques in C, consider the example of geometrical shapes introduced earlier in this chapter to explain procedural programming. The task is to write a computer program that handles geometric shapes such as rectangles and circles. The program should be able to draw any shape and compute its area.

To implement the program using objects, the first task is to work out the details of how to support message-handling and inheritance. Figure 1.3 gives an overview of the data structures you can use to implement the objects.

An easy way to handle messages is to assign each message an identifier (ID). You can associate each message ID with the pointer to a function that handles the message. To maintain this association, you can use a data structure such as the following MESSAGE structure:

```
typedef struct MESSAGE
{
    int   message_id;           /* Message identifier         */
    int   (*message_handler)(); /* Function to handle message */
} MESSAGE;
```

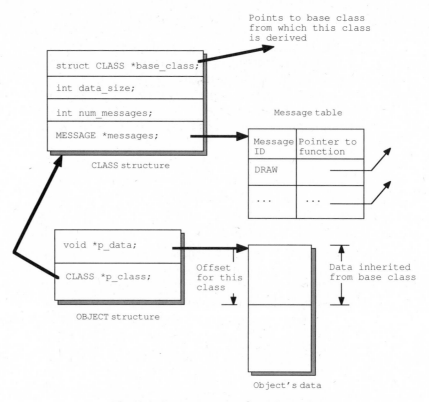

Fig. 1.3. Data structures for OOP in C.

With this definition of MESSAGE, a program can handle messages for a class by maintaining an array of MESSAGE structures (you can think of this as a table of messages). To exploit inheritance, each class data structure needs a pointer to the base class. This pointer will be NULL for a class that is not derived from anyone. Thus, a possible declaration of the CLASS data structure is as follows:

```
typedef struct CLASS
{
    struct CLASS *base_class;  /* Pointer to "base" class */
    int          data_size;    /* Size of instance's data */
    int          num_messages; /* Number of messages      */
    MESSAGE      *messages;    /* Table of messages       */
} CLASS;
```

Later on, you will see utility functions for sending messages to objects. That function will handle messages by searching the messages array for an entry with a matching message ID and calling the function whose pointer is stored in that entry. Inheritance is implemented by sending unprocessed messages to the base class through the base_class pointer.

Because the CLASS structure has only one base class, this implementation does not support multiple inheritance. If you want multiple inheritance, you have to make room for more than one base class, perhaps through an array of pointers in place of the lone base_class pointer in the CLASS structure.

The CLASS structure has the facilities for handling messages sent to an object, but it has no room for the object's data. This is because each object has its own data. In other words, a single copy of the class structure can serve all the objects of that class, but each object must have room for its own data. You can handle this by defining a data structure specifically meant to hold the instance-specific data of an object:

```
typedef struct OBJECT
{
    void   *p_data;  /* Data for an instance of the object */
    CLASS  *p_class; /* Pointer to the class structure      */
} OBJECT;
```

As you can see, this OBJECT data structure holds a pointer to its data and pointer to its class so that messages can be processed by consulting the message table in the class. The function responsible for creating an object also allocates room for the object's data and saves the pointer in the p_data field of the OBJECT structure. The data_size variable in the CLASS structure represents the number of bytes of memory needed for an object's data.

The file shapeobj.h shown in Listing 1.4 declares the necessary data structures and functions to this scheme of implementing objects in C.

Listing 1.4. shapeobj.h—Definition of shapes in example of OOP in C.

```
/*  File: shapeobj.h
 *
 *  Header file with definitions of shapes for
 *  an example of object-oriented programming in C.
 *
 */

#if !defined(SHAPEOBJ_H)
#define SHAPEOBJ_H

#include <stdio.h>
#include <stdlib.h>      /* For memory allocation routines      */
```

```c
#include <stdarg.h>     /* For variable number of arguments   */
#include <math.h>

typedef struct MESSAGE
{
    int   message_id;           /* Message identifier          */
    int  (*message_handler)(); /* Function to handle message */
} MESSAGE;

typedef struct CLASS
{
    struct CLASS *base_class;   /* Pointer to "base" class */
    int          data_size;    /* Size of instance's data */
    int          num_messages; /* Number of messages        */
    MESSAGE      *messages;     /* Table of messages         */
} CLASS;

typedef struct OBJECT
{
    void   *p_data;  /* Data for an instance of the object */
    CLASS  *p_class; /* Pointer to the class structure      */
} OBJECT;

/* Define some messages */
#define   ALLOCATE_DATA 1
#define   DRAW          2
#define   COMPUTE_AREA  3

/* Functions to create objects */

OBJECT *new_circle(double x, double y, double radius);
OBJECT *new_rectangle(double x1, double y1,
                      double x2, double y2);

/* Utility functions to handle messages */

int send_message(OBJECT *p_obj, int msgid, ...);
int class_message(CLASS *p_class, OBJECT *p_obj, int msgid,
                  va_list argp);
void *allocate_memory(size_t bytes);
int  get_offset(CLASS *p_class);

#endif /* #if !defined(SHAPEOBJ_H) */
```

Implementing Geometrical Shapes

To illustrate the use of these structures, we implement two shapes: circle and rectangle. Because each shape has to draw itself and compute its area, we move these functions to a common base class called `generic_shape`. Figure 1.4 shows the inheritance hierarchy of shapes.

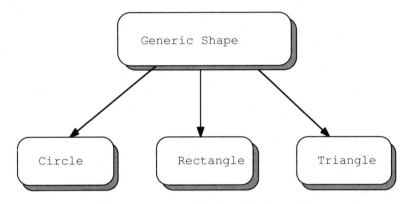

Fig. 1.4. Inheritance hierarchy of geometric shapes.

Listings 1.5, 1.6, and 1.7 show the implementation of the generic shape, the circle, and the rectangle, respectively. If you study the listings, you will notice that each file includes a CLASS structure properly initialized with a message table, a pointer to the base class, if any, and the size of the data structure of each instance of that class. The circle and rectangle classes include functions that you can call to create an instance of each.

Listing 1.5. `anyshape.c`—Implementation of a generic shape class.

```
/*  File: anyshape.c
 *
 *  This is the generic "shape" class.
 *  Data and functions common to all shapes appear here.
 *
 */
#include <shapeobj.h>

static int allocate_data(OBJECT *p_obj, va_list argp);

static MESSAGE messages[] =
{
    ALLOCATE_DATA,  allocate_data
};
```

```
/* The "class" data structure */

CLASS generic_shape =
{
    NULL,                             /* No base class      */
    0,                                /* No common data     */
    sizeof(messages)/sizeof(MESSAGE), /* How many messages */
    messages                          /* Message table      */
};

/*-----------------------------------------------------------*/
/* a l l o c a t e _ d a t a
 * Allocate memory for an object's data
 */
static int allocate_data(OBJECT *p_obj, va_list argp)
{
    CLASS  *p_class;
    int    size = 0;

/* Determine sum of instance data sizes for each class in the
 * hierarchy of this object
 */
    for(p_class = p_obj->p_class, size = 0;
        p_class != NULL; p_class = p_class->base_class)
            size += p_class->data_size;

/* Allocate the necessary number of bytes */
    p_obj->p_data = allocate_memory(size);

    return 1;
}
```

For example, to create a circle, you call the `new_circle` function (see Listing 1.6) with the coordinates of the center and radius as arguments. This function allocates an OBJECT structure, sends a message to the base class for allocating the instance data, and returns a pointer to the newly allocated OBJECT structure.

Listing 1.6. o_circle.c—Implementation of the circle class.

```
/*  File: o_circle.c
 *
 *  This is the circle class of shapes.
 */
```

```c
#include <shapeobj.h>

typedef double *P_DOUBLE;

typedef struct CIRCLE_DATA
{
    double  x, y;     /* Coordinates of center */
    double  radius;   /* Radius of circle      */
} CIRCLE_DATA;

extern CLASS generic_shape; /* The base class */

static int compute_area(OBJECT *p_obj, va_list argp);
static int draw(OBJECT *p_obj, va_list argp);

static MESSAGE messages[] =
{
    COMPUTE_AREA,  compute_area,
    DRAW,          draw
};

/* The "class" data structure */

CLASS circle_class =
{
    &generic_shape,                      /* Pointer to base class */
    sizeof(CIRCLE_DATA),                 /* Data for circles      */
    sizeof(messages)/sizeof(MESSAGE),    /* Number of messages    */
    messages                             /* The message table     */
};

static int circle_offset = -1;  /* Offset to circle's data    */
/*-------------------------------------------------------------*/
/* n e w _ c i r c l e
 * Create an instance of a circle and initialize it
 */
OBJECT *new_circle(double x, double y, double radius)
{
    OBJECT    *p_obj;
    CIRCLE_DATA *p_data;
```

```c
    p_obj = (OBJECT *) allocate_memory(sizeof(OBJECT));
    p_obj->p_class = &circle_class;

/* Send message to allocate memory for data */
    send_message(p_obj, ALLOCATE_DATA, 0);

/* Get offset to circle-specific data */
    if(circle_offset < 0)
        circle_offset = get_offset(&circle_class);
    p_data = (CIRCLE_DATA *)((char *)p_obj->p_data +
                                    circle_offset);

    p_data->x = x;
    p_data->y = y;
    p_data->radius = radius;

    return(p_obj);
}
/*------------------------------------------------------------------*/
/* c o m p u t e _ a r e a
 * Compute area of circle. Arguments expected:
 * pointer to a double where answer is returned
 */
static int compute_area(OBJECT *p_obj, va_list argp)
{
    int         status = 0;
    double      *p_area;
    CIRCLE_DATA *p_data;

/* Set up the pointer to circle's data */
    p_data = (CIRCLE_DATA *)((char *)p_obj->p_data +
                            circle_offset);
/* Get pointer to double where answer is to be returned */
    p_area = va_arg(argp, P_DOUBLE);
    if(p_area != NULL)
    {
        *p_area = M_PI * p_data->radius * p_data->radius;
        status = 1;
    }
    return(status);
}
/*------------------------------------------------------------------*/
/* d r a w
 * Draw the circle (for now, just print a message);
```

```
 * does not expect any arguments
 */
static int draw(OBJECT *p_obj, va_list argp)
{
    CIRCLE_DATA    *p_data;

/* Set up the pointer to circle's data */
    p_data = (CIRCLE_DATA *)((char *)p_obj->p_data +
                            circle_offset);
    printf("Draw: Circle of radius %f at (%f, %f)\n",
            p_data->radius, p_data->x, p_data->y);

    return 1;
}
```

Allocating an Object's Data

When programmers develop a framework for OOP in C, one of the tricky problems is the allocation of an object's data. Suppose you are allocating the data structure for an object whose class inherits from a base class. In our current implementation, the data for the base class and the derived class are laid out in a single block, with one following the other. Each class can access its data, provided it knows the offset of the start of its data in this block of memory. Figure 1.5 graphically illustrates the layout of data for a derived class and a base class.

For the geometric shapes, the allocation of the data block is handled by the allocate_data function in the generic shape class (see Listing 1.5). This function figures out the amount of storage needed by adding the sizes of data blocks for all classes in the hierarchy and then allocates the data. When an object must access its data, for instance in the new_circle function of Listing 1.6, it gets the offset to its data structure by calling a utility function named get_offset.

Listing 1.7. o_rect.c—Implementation of the rectangle class.

```
/*  File: o_rect.c
 *
 *  This is the rectangle class of shapes.
 */

#include <shapeobj.h>

typedef double *P_DOUBLE;

typedef struct RECTANGLE_DATA
```

```
{
    double  x1, y1;  /* Coordinates of the corners    */
    double  x2, y2;
} RECTANGLE_DATA;

extern CLASS generic_shape; /* The base class         */

static int compute_area(OBJECT *p_obj, va_list argp);
static int draw(OBJECT *p_obj, va_list argp);

static MESSAGE messages[] =
{
    COMPUTE_AREA,  compute_area,
    DRAW,          draw
};

/* The "class" data structure */

CLASS rectangle_class =
{
    &generic_shape,                     /* Pointer to base class */
    sizeof(RECTANGLE_DATA),             /* Data for rectangles   */
    sizeof(messages)/sizeof(MESSAGE),   /* Number of messages    */
    messages                            /* The message table     */
};

static int rectangle_offset = -1; /* Offset to rectangle's data*/
/*-------------------------------------------------------------*/
/* n e w _ r e c t a n g l e
 * Create an instance of a rectangle and initialize it
 */
OBJECT *new_rectangle(double x1, double y1, double x2, double y2)
{
    OBJECT    *p_obj;
    RECTANGLE_DATA *p_data;

    p_obj = (OBJECT *) allocate_memory(sizeof(OBJECT));
    p_obj->p_class = &rectangle_class;

/* Send message to allocate memory for data */
    send_message(p_obj, ALLOCATE_DATA, 0);
```

```
/* Get offset to rectangle-specific data */
    if(rectangle_offset < 0)
        rectangle_offset = get_offset(&rectangle_class);
    p_data = (RECTANGLE_DATA *)((char *)p_obj->p_data +
                                        rectangle_offset);

    p_data->x1 = x1;
    p_data->y1 = y1;
    p_data->x2 = x2;
    p_data->y2 = y2;

    return(p_obj);
}
/*-----------------------------------------------------------*/
/* c o m p u t e _ a r e a
 * Compute area of a rectangle. Arguments expected:
 * pointer to a double where answer is returned
 */
static int compute_area(OBJECT *p_obj, va_list argp)
{
    int           status = 0;
    double        *p_area;
    RECTANGLE_DATA    *p_data;

/* Set up the pointer to rectangle's data */
    p_data = (RECTANGLE_DATA *)((char *)p_obj->p_data +
                            rectangle_offset);
/* Get pointer to double where answer is to be returned */
    p_area = va_arg(argp, P_DOUBLE);
    if(p_area != NULL)
    {
        *p_area = fabs((p_data->x2 - p_data->x1) *
                        (p_data->y2 - p_data->y1));
        status = 1;
    }
    return(status);
}
/*-----------------------------------------------------------*/
/* d r a w
 * Draw the rectangle (for now, just print a message);
 * does not expect any arguments
 */
static int draw(OBJECT *p_obj, va_list argp)
```

```
{
    RECTANGLE_DATA   *p_data;

/* Set up the pointer to rectangle's data */
    p_data = (RECTANGLE_DATA *)((char *)p_obj->p_data +
                            rectangle_offset);
    printf("Draw: Rectangle with corners: "
          "(%f, %f) at (%f, %f)\n",
          p_data->x1, p_data->y1,
          p_data->x2, p_data->y2);
    return 1;
}
```

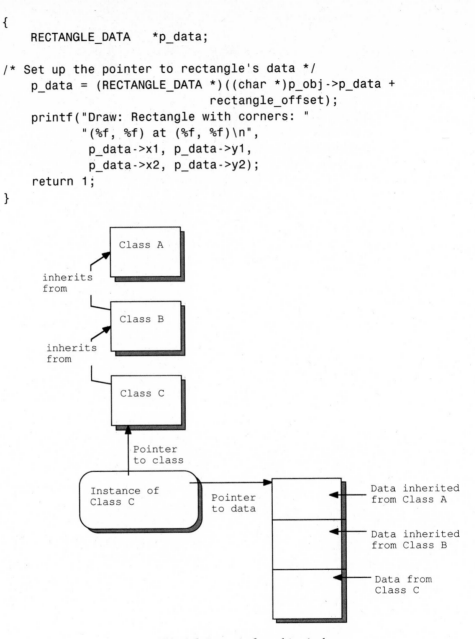

Fig. 1.5. Layout of an object's data.

Utility Functions

Because C does not directly support the notion of sending messages to objects, you have to devise your own means of doing so. For the messaging scheme used in our approach, you can accomplish the job by writing a set of utility functions that invoke the appropriate function in response to a message. Listing 1.8 presents the file `ooputil.c`, which defines a number of utility functions to help implement OOP in C. You may want to study the `send_message` function (Listing 1.8) to see how messages are dispatched to an object's class and how any message that is not handled by a class is passed up the class hierarchy.

Listing 1.8. `ooputil.c`—Utility functions for OOP in C.

```
/*   File: ooputil.c
 *
 *   Utility routines for example of OOP in C.
 *
 */

#include <shapeobj.h>

/*-----------------------------------------------------------------*/
/* s e n d _ m e s s a g e
 * Process message sent to an object by passing it to its class
 */
int send_message(OBJECT *p_obj, int msgid, ...)
{
    int     status;
    va_list argp;
    va_start(argp, msgid);
    status = class_message(p_obj->p_class, p_obj, msgid, argp);
    va_end(argp);
    return(status);
}
/*-----------------------------------------------------------------*/
/* c l a s s _ m e s s a g e
 * Search through message table for a specific message and
 * call the "message handler" if found
 */
int class_message(CLASS *p_class, OBJECT *p_obj, int msgid,
                  va_list argp)
{
    int i, status;
```

```
    if(p_class == NULL) return 0;

    if(p_class->messages != NULL)
    {
        for(i = 0; i < p_class->num_messages; i++)
            if(p_class->messages[i].message_id == msgid)
            {
                return ((*p_class->messages[i].message_handler)
                                               (p_obj, argp));
            }
/* If message not handled, send it to the base class */
        status = class_message(p_class->base_class, p_obj,
                                 msgid, argp);

    }
    return(status);
}
/*----------------------------------------------------------------*/
/* a l l o c a t e _ m e m o r y
 * Allocate memory; check for failure to allocate
 */
void *allocate_memory(size_t numbytes)
{
    void *ptr;
    if((ptr = calloc(1, numbytes)) == NULL)
    {
        fprintf(stderr, "Error allocating %d bytes of memory."
                "Exiting...", numbytes);
        exit(1);
    }
    return(ptr);
}
/*----------------------------------------------------------------*/
/* g e t _ o f f s e t
 * An instance's data is the concatenation of data of
 * all classes in its hierarchy; this function computes
 * the offset to the beginning of data for a specific class
 */
int  get_offset(CLASS *p_class)
{
    CLASS *p_ct;
    int size = 0;
/* Traverse class hierarchy up to "root" class and add up the
 * sizes of data belonging to each class
 */
```

```
    for(p_class = p_class->base_class;
        p_class != NULL;
        p_class = p_class->base_class) size += p_class->data_size;

    return size;
}
```

Using the Shapes

Once the framework for C-based OOP is in place, it is simple to create the shapes and use them. For example, to create a circle of radius 50 centered at the point (100, 100), you use the following:

```
    OBJECT *circle1;

/* Create a circle at (100, 100) with radius = 50 */
    circle1 = new_circle(100.0, 100.0, 50.0);
```

You can compute the area of this circle by sending it a COMPUTE_AREA message and passing it the arguments expected by this message as follows:

```
    double area;
    send_message(circle1, COMPUTE_AREA, &area);
    printf("Area of circle = %f\n", area);
```

The file stestobj.c in Listing 1.9 shows an example that uses the circle and rectangle shapes. To build the executable for this example, you have to compile and link the following files:

1. stestobj.c (Listing 1.9)

2. ooputil.c (Listing 1.8)

3. anyshape.c (Listing 1.5)

4. o_circle.c (Listing 1.6)

5. o_rect.c (Listing 1.7)

Listing 1.9. stestobj.c—Main function for testing the shape objects.

```
/*-----------------------------------------------------------*/
/*  File: stestobj.c
 *
 *  Test C-based OOP implementation of geometric shapes.
 */
```

```
#include <shapeobj.h>

int main(void)
{
    int     i;
    double area;
    OBJECT *shapes[3];

/* Create some shapes */
    shapes[0] = new_circle(100.0, 100.0, 50.0);
    shapes[1] = new_rectangle(100., 150., 200., 100.);

/* Compute the area of the shapes */
    for(i = 0; i < 2; i++)
    {
        send_message(shapes[i], COMPUTE_AREA, &area);
        printf("Area of shape [%d] = %f\n", i, area);
    }

/* "Draw" the shapes */
    for(i = 0; i < 2; i++)
        send_message(shapes[i], DRAW);

    return 0;
}
```

Adding a New Shape Object

Earlier, this chapter discussed a procedural implementation of the geometric shapes, showing the steps that were needed to handle a new shape such as a triangle. To help you see how OOP helps reduce the ripple effect of change, consider the addition of a triangle shape to the shape objects. Here are the steps:

1. Prepare a new file—let us call it o_triang.c—that defines the data and the functions for the triangle shape. Listing 1.10 shows a sample implementation of o_triang.c.

That's it! All you have to do is write a single module implementing the new object. Once you have done this, you can use the new shape in your programs (of course, you have to compile o_triang.c and link with it to build the program). For example, you can create a triangle, compute its area, and draw it as follows:

```
        OBJECT *t;
        double area;

    /* Create a triangle */
        t = new_triangle(100.,100., 200.,100., 150.,50.);

    /* Compute its area */
        send_message(t, COMPUTE_AREA, &area);
            printf("Area of triangle = %f\n", area);
        }

    /* "Draw" the triangle */
        send_message(t, DRAW);
```

Clearly, OOP techniques make it very easy to add new capabilities to the program because you do not need to modify existing code, only the new modules with code necessary to support the new objects.

Listing 1.10. o_triang.c—Implementation of a triangle shape.

```
/*-------------------------------------------------------------*/
/*  File: o_triang.c
 *
 *  This is the triangle class of shapes.
 */

#include <shapeobj.h>

typedef double *P_DOUBLE;

typedef struct TRIANGLE_DATA
{
    double  x1, y1;  /* Coordinates of the corners */
    double  x2, y2;
    double  x3, y3;
} TRIANGLE_DATA;

extern CLASS generic_shape; /* The base class       */

static int compute_area(OBJECT *p_obj, va_list argp);
static int draw(OBJECT *p_obj, va_list argp);

static MESSAGE messages[] =
{
    COMPUTE_AREA,  compute_area,
```

```
        DRAW,              draw
};

/* The "class" data structure */

CLASS triangle_class =
{
    &generic_shape,                        /* Pointer to base class */
    sizeof(TRIANGLE_DATA),                 /* Data for triangles    */
    sizeof(messages)/sizeof(MESSAGE),  /* Number of messages    */
    messages                               /* The message table     */
};

static int triangle_offset = -1;   /* Offset to triangle's data */
/*----------------------------------------------------------------*/
/* n e w _ t r i a n g l e
 * Create an instance of a triangle and initialize it
 */
OBJECT *new_triangle(double x1, double y1, double x2, double y2,
                     double x3, double y3)
{
    OBJECT    *p_obj;
    TRIANGLE_DATA *p_data;

    p_obj = (OBJECT *) allocate_memory(sizeof(OBJECT));
    p_obj->p_class = &triangle_class;

/* Send message to allocate memory for data */
    send_message(p_obj, ALLOCATE_DATA, 0);

/* Get offset to triangle-specific data */
    if(triangle_offset < 0)
        triangle_offset = get_offset(&triangle_class);
    p_data = (TRIANGLE_DATA *)((char *)p_obj->p_data +
                                       triangle_offset);
    p_data->x1 = x1;
    p_data->y1 = y1;
    p_data->x2 = x2;
    p_data->y2 = y2;
    p_data->x3 = x3;
    p_data->y3 = y3;

    return(p_obj);
}
```

```
/*-------------------------------------------------------------*/
/* c o m p u t e _ a r e a
 * Compute area of triangle. Arguments expected:
 * pointer to a double where answer is returned
 */
static int compute_area(OBJECT *p_obj, va_list argp)
{
    int             status = 0;
    double          *p_area;
    TRIANGLE_DATA   *p_data;

/* Set up the pointer to triangle's data */
    p_data = (TRIANGLE_DATA *)((char *)p_obj->p_data +
                            triangle_offset);
/* Get pointer to double where answer is to be returned */
    p_area = va_arg(argp, P_DOUBLE);
    if(p_area != NULL)
    {
        double x21, y21, x31, y31;

                x21 =  p_data->x2 - p_data->x1;
                y21 =  p_data->y2 - p_data->y1;
                x31 =  p_data->x3 - p_data->x1;
                y31 =  p_data->y3 - p_data->y1;

        *p_area = fabs(y21 * x31 - x21 * y31) / 2.0;
        status = 1;
    }
    return(status);
}
/*-------------------------------------------------------------*/
/* d r a w
 * Draw the triangle (for now, just print a message).
 * Does not expect any arguments
 */
    static int draw(OBJECT *p_obj, va_list argp)
    {
        TRIANGLE_DATA    *p_data;

    /* Set up the pointer to triangle's data */
        p_data = (TRIANGLE_DATA *)((char *)p_obj->p_data +
                                triangle_offset);
```

```
        printf("Draw: Triangle with vertices: "
                       "(%f, %f) (%f, %f) (%f, %f)\n",
                 p_data->x1, p_data->y1,
                 p_data->x2, p_data->y2,
                 p_data->x3, p_data->y3);
        return 1;
    }
```

Problems with OOP in C

Although you can define data structures to implement objects in C, there are several problems with practicing OOP in C:

- A basic tenet of OOP is that you must access and manipulate the object's data by calling functions provided by that object. This ensures that the internal implementation details of the object stay hidden from the outside world, enabling you to change these details without affecting other parts of the program. Although object-oriented languages enforce this principle of data hiding, implementing object-oriented techniques in a C program requires the programmer to exercise discipline, because C does not prohibit code that directly accesses members of an object's data structure.

- You are responsible for ensuring that the data structures of an object are laid out properly to support data inheritance from base classes. You have to write utility functions to allow an object to access its data properly.

- The programmer has to devise a scheme to invoke methods of objects in response to messages. Inheritance of behavior also requires support functions for properly dispatching messages.

Despite these problems, the modularity and localization of change afforded by OOP is worth the trouble, even if you have to write your object-oriented programs in C. Of course, as you will see in Chapter 2, OOP becomes much easier if you use a programming language such as C++ that supports the basic necessities of object-orientation: data abstraction, inheritance, and polymorphism.

Summary

Object-oriented programming (OOP) relies on three basic concepts: data abstraction, inheritance, and polymorphism.

Data abstraction refers to the ability to define abstract data types or ADTs (essentially, user-defined data types) that encapsulate some data together with a set of well-defined operations. Such user-defined data types can represent objects in software. The term *class* refers to the template from which specific instances of objects are created. Objects perform specific actions in response to messages (which may be implemented by function calls).

Inheritance is the mechanism that enables one object to behave just like another, except for some modifications. Inheritance implies a hierarchy of classes with *derived* classes inheriting behavior from *base* classes. In the context of software, inheritance promotes the sharing of code and data among classes.

Polymorphism refers to the fact that different objects react differently to the same message.

In particular, OOP refers to a new way of organizing your program using a collection of objects whose classes are organized in a predefined hierarchy with a view to sharing code and data through inheritance.

A comparison of two implementations of an example—one using procedural approach and the other using OOP—shows that the object-based organization enhances the modularity of the program by placing related data and functions in the same module. This makes it easier to accommodate changes in an object-based program than in a procedural one. Although you can implement object-oriented techniques in a procedural programming language such as C, it is easier when the language has the features necessary to support OOP.

Further Reading

As a topic, object-oriented programming is still in the evolutionary stage, with its very definition a subject of debate among experts. Still, the basic concepts of OOP have been covered in many books and journal articles. Here is a short list of references that can help you learn more about OOP. Note that Chapter 2 has further references that cover OOP as well as C++.

Bertrand Meyer's book[1] has a good description of the object-oriented approach. For a high-level overview of object-oriented concepts, terminology, and software, consult the recent books by Setrag Khosafian and Razmik Abnous[2] and Ann Winblad, Samuel Edwards, and David King.[3]

Other good sources of information on recent developments in OOP include the proceedings of the annual Object-Oriented Programming Systems, Languages, and Applications (OOPSLA) conference sponsored by the Association for Computing Machinery and the *Journal of Object-Oriented Programming* published bimonthly by SIGS Publications, Inc. of New York.

1. Bertrand Meyer, *Object-Oriented Software Construction* (Hertfordshire, Great Britain: Prentice-Hall International [UK] Ltd., 1988), 552 pages.

2. Setrag Khosafian and Razmik Abnous, *Object Orientation: Concepts, Languages, Databases, User Interfaces* (New York: John Wiley & Sons, 1990), 448 pages.

3. Ann L. Winblad, Samuel D. Edwards, and David R. King, *Object-Oriented Software* (Reading, Mass.: Addison-Wesley, 1990), 309 pages.

## Chapter 2

C++ and Object-Oriented Programming

Chapter 1 provides an overview of OOP terminology and shows how to implement the object-oriented techniques in a procedure-oriented language such as C. However, the example shown in Chapter 1 clearly illustrates several problems with using OOP in C:

- Information hiding is not enforced by the language.

- Message-passing has to be implemented by the programmer.

- Implementing inheritance requires the programmer to devise clever schemes.

Consider, for instance, C's FILE data type. Although it can be thought of as an object, the file I/O functions are not closely tied to the FILE data type. Also, the internal details of the FILE data type are not really hidden, because C has no way of stopping you from accessing the members of the FILE data structure. When writing object-oriented software in C, you can achieve information hiding only through self-discipline—you and others working on the software have to agree not to directly access the contents of data structures that are supposed to be hidden.

Basically, although it is possible to use OOP techniques in C, the lack of built-in support for OOP requires extra work to enforce the principles of data abstraction and to set up the mechanisms for inheritance and polymorphism. C++, on the other hand, was designed with OOP in mind. C++ was built by adding to C certain features that ease the task of implementing objects. This chapter describes these features and illustrates the ease of OOP in C++ by reimplementing the first chapter's example of geometric shapes.

This chapter will not completely describe all the features of C++. Instead, it provides an overview of the features that are necessary for object-oriented programming. In particular, this chapter does not get into the syntactical details of C++. Chapters 4 through 9 will again cover all aspects of C++ in detail. Of course, you can supplement this book's coverage of C++ and OOP by consulting one or more of the references listed at the end of this chapter.

C++ was developed in the early 1980s by Bjarne Stroustrup of AT&T Bell Laboratories. He created C++ while adding features to C to support efficient event-driven simulation programs. His inspiration came from the language Simula67, which supported the concept of a `class`. AT&T made many improvements to this initial language before releasing it commercially for the first time in 1985. Since then, C++ has continued to evolve with AT&T controlling the releases.

In the beginning, AT&T supplied a translator called `cfront` for converting C++ programs into C, which were then compiled using a C compiler. By the time release 1.2 of AT&T's C++ became available, C++ compilers such as the one from Zortech, Inc. were becoming available for PCs and workstations. AT&T released C++ 2.0 in 1989 and followed it promptly with release 2.1.

The X3J16 committee of the American National Standards Institute (ANSI) is currently in the process of drafting a standard specification for the C++ programming language based on the reference manual for AT&T C++ Release 2.1 and the ANSI standard for C (*ANSI X3.159–1989–Programming Language C*) which was adopted in late 1989.

Object-Oriented Programming in C++

Chapter 1 mentioned that there are three basic concepts underlying OOP: *data abstraction, inheritance,* and *polymorphism.* To recollect, here is how these concepts help OOP:

- Data abstraction helps you to tie data and functions together, which effectively defines a new data type with its own set of operations. Such a data type is called an *abstract data type (ADT)*, also referred to as a *class*.

- Inheritance enables you to organize the classes in a hierarchy so that you can place common data and functions in a base class from which other classes can inherit them (see Figure 2.1).

- Polymorphism helps you keep your programs conceptually simple by enabling you to call the same function to perform similar tasks in all classes in a hierarchy.

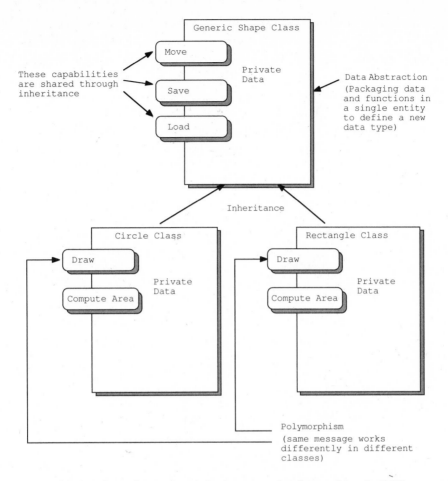

Fig. 2.1. Data abstraction, inheritance, and polymorphism in OOP.

C++ includes features to support each of these concepts.

Data Abstraction in C++

In C, an abstract data type such as FILE, for instance, is declared by a construct such as this:

```
typedef struct
{
    char     *buf;   /* Buffer for file I/O      */
    unsigned flags;  /* Flags to indicate status */
```

```
    .                /* Other internal variables    */
    .
} FILE;              /* This is the FILE data type */
```

The operations on FILE will be separate functions that take a pointer to a FILE structure as an argument. C++ introduces the class construct to augment C's struct. Using class, you could define the File data type, equivalent to C's FILE, as shown in Listing 2.1.

Listing 2.1. file.h—A data type for file I/O.

```
/*  File: file.h
 *
 *  A File class for file I/O.
 */
#if !defined(FILE_H)
#define FILE_H

#include <stdio.h>    // For C file I/O function declarations

class File
{
    FILE    *fp;    // C stream
//  . . .           // Other internal variables

public:
    File(const char *name,              // Constructor
        const char *open_mode);
    ~File();                            // Destructor
    size_t read(const size_t howmany,   // Read from file
                const size_t elem_size, // into buffer
                void *buffer);
    size_t write(const size_t howmany,  // Write buffer to
                const size_t elem_size, // file
                const void *buffer);
};                                      // Note the semicolon
#endif
```

C++ recognizes the standard C comments that start with the characters /* and end after the characters */. Additionally, C++ treats as a comment everything following the characters // up to the end of the line. You can use the C format for comments spanning multiple lines, whereas the new style is convenient for single-line comments.

As a C programmer (especially if you know ANSI C), you should find most coding of Listing 2.1 familiar, but do not be concerned if you understand little of this; the rest of this chapter will explain it in greater depth. Also, Chapters 4 through 9 of this book cover the C++ features again, in detail. In particular, Chapter 4 provides an overview of ANSI C and compares it with C++.

The `const` keyword used to prefix the name of a variable indicates that the contents of the variable must not be modified by the program. Similarly, if a function's argument is pointer and if that pointer is declared to be `const`, the function cannot modify the contents of the location referenced by that pointer.

Listing 2.1 assumes that the `File` class will provide a higher-level abstraction for file I/O, but it will use C's file I/O functions for the actual work. That is why there is a pointer to a `FILE` in the class. As you will see later, this `FILE` pointer is set up when an instance of the `File` class is created.

If you examine the declaration of the class `File` (Listing 2.1), you can see that it looks very much like C's `struct` except for the ANSI C-style declaration of several functions following the `public:` keyword. These functions, called *member functions*, operate on the data items being encapsulated in the class. The data items in the class declaration are called *member variables*. The significance of the `public:` keyword is that all member functions and variables appearing after the keyword are accessible to other parts of the program. The initial members of the class that appear before the `public:` keyword are considered *private*. Such private variables and functions are not accessible to any function other than those declared within the class. The C++ compiler enforces this rule and gives an error message if any outside function refers to the private members of any class.

When you define a class in C++, you are defining a new, possibly complex, data type. The compiler hides the internal details of this data type to the outside world. The only way the outside functions can access the data is through the public member functions. Thus, the `class` construct enables you to implement data abstraction and promotes modularity.

C++ continues to support ANSI C's `struct` keyword. In fact, C++ expands the definition of `struct` by allowing inclusion of member functions. In C++, the only difference between a `class` and a `struct` is that the contents of a `struct` are always public.

Defining the Member Functions for `File`

When declaring a class, you declare its member functions but do not define all of them. Typically, you define the member functions in a separate file. That way, you can think of the header file with the class declaration as a specification of the interface to the class, whereas the module with the function definitions is its implementation. Ideally, if the interface is defined clearly enough, programmers using the class need not know the details of the implementation. For the `File` class, we plan to call standard C file I/O functions to implement the member functions. This can be done in a straightforward manner, as shown in Listing 2.2.

Note that this book uses `.cpp` as the file extension for C++ source files. Header files have the `.h` extension, as they do in C.

You do need to be aware of one operator—the scope resolution operator, which is denoted by a pair of colons (`::`). When defining the member functions, you use the scope resolution operator to indicate the class with which the function is associated. Thus, the notation `File::read` identifies `read` as a member function of the class `File`. You can also use the scope resolution operator without a class name to indicate a globally defined function or variable. For example, the following code shows how you can differentiate between a globally defined `int` variable and a local one with the same name:

```
int AllDone;        // Variable visible throughout file

void AnyFunction(void)
{
    int AllDone;   // Local variable with same name
    AllDone = 1;   // Refers to local variable

    if(::AllDone) // This refers to the global "AllDone"
        DoSomething();
}
```

The same approach can be used to call a global function in a member function of the same name.

Listing 2.2. `file.cpp`—Definition of member functions of the `File` class.

```
/*------------------------------------------------------------*/
/*  File: file.cpp
 *
 *  Illustrate data encapsulation in C++.
 */
#include <file.h>
/*------------------------------------------------------------*/
// Constructor—opens a file
File::File(const char *name, const char *open_mode)
{
    fp = fopen(name, open_mode);
}
```

```
/*------------------------------------------------------------*/
// Destructor—closes file
File::~File()
{
    if(fp != NULL) fclose(fp);
}
/*------------------------------------------------------------*/
size_t File::read(const size_t howmany,     // Read from file
                  const size_t elem_size,   // into buffer
                  void *buffer)
{
    if(fp != NULL)
        return(fread(buffer, elem_size, howmany, fp));
    else
        return 0;
}
/*------------------------------------------------------------*/
size_t File::write(const size_t howmany,    // Write buffer to
                   const size_t elem_size,  // file
                   const void *buffer)
{
    if(fp != NULL)
        return(fwrite(buffer, elem_size, howmany, fp));
    else
        return 0;
}
```

Constructors and Destructors

Note that the File class has a member function named File and another named ~File. The two member functions are, respectively, called the *constructor* and *destructor* of the class. The C++ compiler calls a constructor, if one is defined, whenever an instance of a class is created. You can use the constructor to handle any specific requirements for initializing objects of a class. For example, if an object needs extra storage, you can allocate memory in the constructor. In the File class, the constructor calls fopen to open the file. Note that the constructor function always has the same name as that of the class.

You can also define a *destructor* function for a class, if there is any need to clean up after an object is destroyed (for example, if you want to free memory allocated in the constructor). The C++ compiler calls the destructor function of a class whenever it needs to destroy an instance of that class. The destructor has the same name as the class except for a tilde (~) prefix. Thus, the destructor function for the class File is ~File(). Note that in the File class, we simply close the file that was opened by the constructor.

Using the File Class

An instance of the `File` class can be defined and its member functions are accessed just like a C `struct`. For example, to define an instance of the `File` class named `f1` and call its `read` function, you would write:

```
// Open file named "test.dat" for reading
File    f1("test.dat", "rb");
char    buffer[128];
size_t bytes_read;
//...
bytes_read = f1.read(128, sizeof(char), buffer);
```

For a more meaningful example, consider the small program shown in Listing 2.3. It uses the `File` class to copy the contents of one file to another by reading from one and writing to the other.

Listing 2.3. Program to copy from one file to another.

```
/*--------------------------------------------------------------*/
/*  Main function to copy file "test.dat" to "copy.out."
 */
void main(void)
{
// Open files . . .
    File f1("test.dat", "rb");
    File f2("copy.out", "wb");

    char    buffer[512];
    size_t count;

// Read a chunk from one file and write it to the other . . .
    while((count = f1.read(512, sizeof(char), buffer)) != 0)
    {
        f2.write(count, sizeof(char), buffer);
    }
}
```

Inheritance in C++ Classes

When declaring a class, you can also indicate whether it inherits from any other classes. On the first line of the `class` declaration, you place a colon (`:`) followed by a list of base classes from which this class inherits. For example, suppose you want to declare the `circle_shape` class which is derived from a generic `shape` class. In this case, the first line of the declaration of the `circle_shape` class looks like this:

```
class circle_shape: public shape
{

// Declare member variables and member functions . . .

}
```

Here, the `shape` class is the *base* class and `circle_shape` is the *derived* class. The keyword `public` preceding `shape` signifies that any public member variables and functions of `shape` will be accessible to the `circle_shape` class.

Polymorphism and Dynamic Binding

C++ provides a way to override a function defined in a base class with one defined in a derived class. Another feature of C++ is that you can use pointers to a base class to refer to objects of a derived class. The combination of these two features enables you to implement polymorphic behavior in C++ classes.

Here is how. Suppose you have a base class called `shape` that encapsulates data and functions common to other classes of shapes, such as `circle_shape` and `rectangle_shape`, which are derived from the `shape` class. One of the functions is `draw`, which draws the shape. Because each shape is drawn differently, the base class defines the `draw` function with the `virtual` keyword:

```
class shape
{
public:
    virtual void draw(void) const{ }
// Other member functions . . .
};
```

The `virtual` keyword tells the C++ compiler that the `draw` function defined in the base class is to be used only if the derived classes do not define it. In this case, the base class defines `draw` to be a "do nothing" function.

In a derived class, you can override this definition simply by supplying a function with the same name, like this:

```
class circle_shape: public shape
{
// Private data . . .
public:
// Other member functions . . .
    virtual void draw(void) const;
};
```

Later on you have to actually define the draw function for the circle_shape class. You can do the same for the rectangle_shape class. Once this is done, you can apply the same member function to instances of different classes and the correct draw function will be called:

```
// Create instances of circle_shape and rectangle_shape
circle_shape c1(100.,100.,50.);
rectangle_shape r1(10.,20.,30.,40.);

c1.draw();   // "draw" from "circle_shape" class is called
r1.draw();   // "draw" from "rectangle_shape" class is
called
```

Although this is polymorphic behavior, it is not as interesting, because the C++ compiler (and you) can determine, by studying the code, exactly which function should be called. In fact, this case is referred to as the *static binding* of virtual functions, because the compiler can determine the function to be called at compile-time.

The more interesting case is that of *dynamic binding* when a virtual function is invoked through a pointer to an object and the type of the object is not known during compilation. This is possible because C++ enables you to use a pointer to a base class to refer to an instance of a derived class. For example, suppose you want to create a number of shapes (the new operator used to create the shapes is described later in this chapter), store them in an array, and draw them. Here is how you might do it:

```
int i;
shape *shapes[2];    // Array of pointers to base class

// Create some shapes and save the pointers
    shapes[0] = new circle_shape(100., 100., 50.);
    shapes[1] = new rectangle_shape(80., 40., 120., 60.);

// Draw the shapes
    for(i = 0; i < 2; i++) shapes[i]->draw();
```

Notice how we can simply loop through the pointers to the shapes and call the draw member function of each object. Because draw is a virtual function, the actual draw function that gets called at run-time depends on the type of shape that the pointer shapes[i] references. If shapes[i] points to an instance of a circle_shape, then the circle_shape::draw() function is called. On the other hand, if shapes[i] points to an instance of rectangle_shape, the draw function of rectangle_shape is called. At run-time, the pointers in the shapes array can point to any instance of the classes derived from the base class shape. Thus, the actual function being called varies according to shape's pointer type determined at run-time. That is why this style of virtual function call is called *dynamic binding*.

Geometric Shapes in C++

To illustrate how C++'s object-oriented features help you write object-oriented programs, consider the example of geometric shapes from Chapter 1, which presented a C-based implementation of the shape objects. Here we will rewrite that example in C++. You will notice that the code is much more compact, because we no longer need additional C utility routines to support the implementation of objects.

The Shape Classes

The first step in implementing the geometric shapes in C++ is to define the classes. As in the C version of the program (see Chapter 1), we start with an abstract base class called `shape`. This class is abstract because we never create any instance of this class. It is used to encapsulate data and functions common to all derived classes, thus promoting inheritance and polymorphism (through the `virtual` keyword, which is explained later). As shown in Figure 2.2, all other shapes are derived from this base class. See the file `shapes.h` (Listing 2.4) for the actual declaration of the classes.

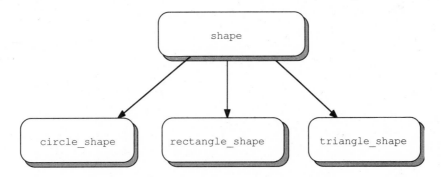

Fig. 2.2. A class hierarchy for geometric shapes.

Listing 2.4. `shapes.h`—Classes of geometric shapes in C++.

```
/*-------------------------------------------------------------*/
/*  File: shapes.h
 *
 *  C++ header file with definitions of geometrical shapes.
 */
```

```
#if !defined(SHAPES_H)
#define SHAPES_H

#include <stdio.h>
#include <math.h>

// Define an abstract shape class—"abstract"—because we
// do not create any instances of this class; it's there
// to encapsulate common data and functions to be shared
// by all shapes

class shape
{
// In this case, we do not have any data,
// only member functions
public:
    virtual double compute_area(void) const
    {
        printf("Not implemented\n");
        return 0.0;
    }
    virtual void draw(void) const{ }
};

// Define the "circle" class

class circle_shape: public shape
{
private:
    double x, y;    // Coordinates of center
    double radius; // Radius of circle
public:
    circle_shape(double x, double y, double radius);
    virtual double compute_area(void) const;
    virtual void draw(void) const;
};

// Define the "rectangle" class

class rectangle_shape: public shape
{
private:
    double x1, y1;  // Coordinates of opposite corners
    double x2, y2;
```

```
public:
    rectangle_shape(double x1, double y1, double x2, double y2);
    double compute_area(void) const;
    void draw(void) const;
};
```

```
#endif  // #if !defined(SHAPES_H)
```

The header file `shapes.h` declares the member functions of the classes, but usually the definitions are placed in separate modules. For smaller functions, you can define a function directly in the body of the class, as we have done for the `compute_area` function in the `shape` class.

> Use the `const` keyword after the arguments in the declaration of a member function if that member function does not modify any of the member variables. This tells the compiler that it is safe to apply this member function to a `const` instance of this class. For instance, the following is permissible, because `compute_area` is a `const` member function:
>
> ```
> // Define a const circle
> const circle_shape c1(100.0, 100.0, 50.0);
> double area = c1.compute_area();
> ```

Circle and Rectangle Classes

Listings 2.5 and 2.6 show the implementation of the classes `circle_shape` and `rectangle_shape`, respectively. Each class is implemented in its own file, just as you would do for a larger project. You implement a class by defining its member functions. In this example, each class has two member functions: `draw` and `compute_area`. The definition of each member function looks like a standard C function except for the scope resolution operator `::` used to indicate the class to which that function belongs. For example, the `compute_area` function of the `circle_shape` class is defined as follows;

```
double circle_shape::compute_area(void) const
{
    return (M_PI * radius * radius);
}
```

Listing 2.5. `circle.cpp`—C++ implementation of the `circle_shape` class.

```
/*---------------------------------------------------------*/
/*  File:  circle.cpp
```

```
 *
 *  Definition of the "circle" class of shapes in C++.
 */

#include <shapes.h>

/*----------------------------------------------------------*/
circle_shape::circle_shape(double xc, double yc, double r)
{
    x = xc;
    y = yc;
    radius = r;
}

/*----------------------------------------------------------*/
double circle_shape::compute_area(void) const
{
    return (M_PI * radius * radius);
}

/*----------------------------------------------------------*/
void circle_shape::draw(void) const
{
    printf("Draw: Circle of radius %f centered at (%f, %f)\n",
            radius, x, y);
}
```

**Listing 2.6. `rect.cpp`—C++ implementation of the
`rectangle_shape` class.**

```
/*----------------------------------------------------------*/
/*  File:  rect.cpp
 *
 *  Definition of the "rectangle" class of shapes in C++.
 */

#include <shapes.h>

rectangle_shape::rectangle_shape(double xul, double yul,
                                 double xlr, double ylr)
{
    x1 = xul;
    y1 = yul;
```

```
    x2 = xlr;
    y2 = ylr;
}


/*------------------------------------------------------------*/
double rectangle_shape::compute_area(void) const
{
    return fabs( (x1-x2) * (y1-y2) );
}


/*------------------------------------------------------------*/
void rectangle_shape::draw(void) const
{
    printf("Draw: Rectangle with corners (%f, %f) (%f, %f)\n",
            x1, y1, x2, y2);
}
```

Using the Shape Classes

Listing 2.7 shows a sample C++ program, `shapetst.cpp`, that creates instances of circle and rectangle shapes and tests their member functions. To build the executable of this program, compile and link the following files:

1. `shapetst.cpp` (Listing 2.7)

2. `circle.cpp` (Listing 2.5)

3. `rect.cpp` (Listing 2.6)

   Each of these files needs the header file `shapes.h` shown in Listing 2.4.

   The sample program exploits dynamic binding of virtual functions by storing pointers to different types of shapes in an array and invoking the member functions of the appropriate class through the pointer. This is a good example of how dynamic binding and polymorphism is used in C++ programs.

   The `delete` operator used to deallocate the shapes is explained in a later section.

Listing 2.7. `shapetst.cpp`—A C++ program to test the "shape" classes.

```
/*------------------------------------------------------*/
/*  File: shapetst.cpp
 *
 *  Program to test the "shape" classes.
 */

#include <shapes.h>
```

```
int main(void)
{
    int i;
    shape *shapes[3];

// Create some shapes
    shapes[0] = new circle_shape(100., 100., 50.);
    shapes[1] = new rectangle_shape(80., 40., 120., 60.);

// Compute the areas
    for(i = 0; i < 2; i++)
    {
        printf("Area of shape [%d] = %f\n", i,
                shapes[i]->compute_area());
    }

// Draw the shapes
    for(i = 0; i < 2; i++) shapes[i]->draw();

// Destroy the shapes
    delete shapes[0];
    delete shapes[1];

    return 0;
}
```

Adding a New Shape Class

How would you add a new shape such as a triangle to the classes that already exist? With an object-oriented program, it is quite simple to accomplish. Here are the steps:

1. Add declaration of a `triangle_shape` class to the header file `shapes.h` (Listing 2.4), defined as follows:

```
// Define the "triangle" class

class triangle_shape: public shape
{
private:
    double x1, y1;   // Coordinates of the corners
    double x2, y2;
    double x3, y3;
```

```
        public:
            triangle_shape(double x1, double y1,
                            double x2, double y2,
                            double x3, double y3);
            double compute_area(void) const;
            void draw(void) const;
        };
```

2. Define the member functions of the `triangle_shape` class in a separate file. Listing 2.8 shows the file `triangle.cpp`, which defines the functions.

   Once these two steps are done, you can begin using the `triangle_shape` class in your program. However, you do have to compile and link your program with the file `triangle.cpp` (Listing 2.8). For example, you can write code such as this:

```
int i;
shape *shapes[3];

// Create some shapes
    shapes[0] = new circle_shape(100., 100., 50.);
    shapes[1] = new rectangle_shape(80., 40., 120., 60.);
    shapes[2] = new triangle_shape(100.,100., 200.,100.,150.,50.);

// Compute the areas
    for(i = 0; i < 3; i++)
    {
        printf("Area of shape [%d] = %f\n", i,
                shapes[i]->compute_area());
    }
```

Listing 2.8. `triangle.cpp`—C++ implementation of the `triangle_shape` class.

```
/*------------------------------------------------------------*/
/*  File:  triangle.cpp
 *
 *  Definition of the "triangle" class of shapes in C++.
 */

#include <shapes.h>

/*------------------------------------------------------------*/
triangle_shape::triangle_shape(double xa, double ya,
                double xb, double yb, double xc, double yc)
```

```
{
    x1 = xa;
    y1 = ya;
    x2 = xb;
    y2 = yb;
    x3 = xc;
    y3 = yc;
}

/*--------------------------------------------------------------*/
double triangle_shape::compute_area(void) const
{
    double area, x21, y21, x31, y31;
    x21 =   x2 - x1;
    y21 =   y2 - y1;
    x31 =   x3 - x1;
    y31 =   y3 - y1;
    area = fabs(y21 * x31 - x21 * y31) / 2.0;
    return (area);
}

/*--------------------------------------------------------------*/
void triangle_shape::draw(void) const
{
    printf("Draw: Triangle with corners at\n"
           "       (%f, %f) (%f, %f) (%f, %f)\n",
           x1, y1, x2, y2, x3, y3);
}
```

Creating Objects at Run-Time

We have not mentioned one important feature of C++: the ability to create instances of a class at run-time. In C, you use memory allocation routines such as `calloc` or `malloc` to dynamically allocate data. These functions return a pointer to the allocated data. When you no longer need the data, you can reclaim the memory by calling `free` with the pointer as the argument. C++ provides the operators `new` and `delete` to create and destroy objects, respectively. Listing 2.7 illustrates how to use the `new` operator to create the geometric shapes and how `delete` is used to destroy them. Like `calloc` or `malloc`, `new` also returns a pointer to the newly created instance of the class. Unlike `malloc`, which returns a generic pointer (`void *`) that you have to cast to the type of your data, new returns a pointer to the correct data type. Additionally, new automatically calls the constructor of the class to initialize the new instance.

Summary

Object-oriented programming is easier to practice if the programming language supports the basic necessities of OOP: data abstraction, inheritance, and polymorphism. C++ was developed from C by adding precisely the kind of features that support OOP. It provides the class construct to define abstract data types, the virtual keyword to allow polymorphic functions, and includes the syntax necessary to indicate inheritance relationship between a derived class and one or more base classes.

C++'s class construct is similar to C's struct but has many more features. In particular, using class you can define the operations on the object—instances of a class—via member functions and operators. A C++ program manipulates objects by calling the member functions only. This enhances the modularity of programs, because you are free to change the internal representation of objects without affecting other parts of a program.

Further Reading

C++ and object-oriented programming are steadily gaining popularity and the number of books and articles on these topics reflect this trend. Here is a short list of resources that will help you learn more about C++ and object-oriented programming.

Most books on C++ cover the topic of object-oriented programming. Among the recent books, the one by Keith Gorlen, Sanford Orlow, and Perry Plexico[1] does a good job of teaching data abstraction and OOP using C++. Much of their book shows how to exploit reusable software components from class libraries such as the NIH Class Library, which was developed by the authors.

For historical reasons, you might want a copy of Bjarne Stroustrup's 1986 book[2] on C++, because this was the first published definition of the language. On the other hand, for an official description of the current status of C++, you would want a copy of the annotated reference manual[3] (often referred to as the *ARM*) by Margaret Ellis and Bjarne Stroustrup. The annotations in this book can help you understand the motivation behind the choices made during the design and improvement of the C++ programming language.

Bjarne Stroustrup's article[4] describes object-oriented programming from the point of view of a C++ programmer. The book by Mark Mullin[5] is also worth noting because it covers object-oriented techniques with a single, large-scale example in C++. Jerry Smith's book[6] is another one that covers the design and implementation of a single program, in this case a text window-based editor.

There is a host of other books[7-14] that cover the C++ programming language, occasionally with some insights into OOP, but mostly focusing on the features of the language without any particular emphasis on object-orientation.

To keep up with recent developments on how others are using C++ and how the ANSI standard for C++ is progressing, you should consult journals such as *The C++ Report* published 10 times a year by SIGS Publications, New York, and *The C++ Journal*, a quarterly publication of The C++ Journal, Inc. of Port Washington, N.Y.

1. Keith E. Gorlen, Sanford M. Orlow, and Perry S. Plexico, *Data Abstractions and Object-Oriented Programming in C++* (Chichester, West Sussex, England: John Wiley & Sons Ltd., 1990), 424 pages.

2. Bjarne Stroustrup, *The C++ Programming Language* (Reading, Mass.: Addison-Wesley, 1986), 336 pages.

3. Margaret A. Ellis and Bjarne Stroustrup, *The Annotated C++ Reference Manual* (Reading, Mass.: Addison-Wesley, 1990), 457 pages.

4. Bjarne Stroustrup, "What Is Object-Oriented Programming?" *IEEE Software* 5, No. 3 (May 1988), pp. 10–20.

5. Mark Mullin, *Object-Oriented Program Design with Examples in C++* (Reading, Mass.: Addison-Wesley, 1989), 329 pages.

6. Jerry D. Smith, *Reusability & Software Construction: C & C++* (New York: John Wiley & Sons, 1990), 559 pages.

7. Bruce Eckel, *Using C++* (Berkeley, Calif.: Osborne McGraw-Hill, 1989), 638 pages.

8. Stanley B. Lippman, *C++ Primer* (Reading, Mass.: Addison-Wesley, 1989), 474 pages.

9. Richard S. Wiener and Lewis J. Pinson, *An Introduction to Object-Oriented Programming and C++* (Reading, Mass.: Addison-Wesley, 1988), 285 pages.

10. Ira Pohl, *C++ for C Programmers* (Redwood City, Calif.: Benjamin/Cummings, 1989), 256 pages.

11. Stephen C. Dewhurst and Kathy T. Stark, *Programming in C++* (Englewood Cliffs, N.J.: Prentice-Hall, 1989), 239 pages.

12. Tony L. Hansen, *The C++ Answer Book* (Reading, Mass.: Addison-Wesley, 1990), 588 pages.

13. Keith Weiskamp and Bryan Flamig, *The Complete C++ Primer* (San Diego, Calif.: Academic Press, 1990), 541 pages.

14. John Berry, *The Waite Group's C++ Programming* (Indianapolis, Ind.: Howard W. Sams, 1988), 397 pages.

## Chapter 3

Object-Oriented Software Design

Chapters 1 and 2 explained OOP terminology and showed you how to implement a simple program using an object-oriented approach. However, for any real-world problem, you have to design the software—identify the objects and their interrelationships—*before* you can write any code to implement the objects in an object-oriented language such as C++. In fact, this early part of the software development process—the analysis and design phases—is much harder than the actual coding because there are no well-defined, step-by-step methods for accomplishing the job. The best you can do is to learn about the prevailing practices in object-oriented analysis and design and adapt them to your problem.

This chapter provides a summary description of some of the current ideas in this field. However, the chapter does not attempt complete coverage of object-oriented design. To learn more about object-oriented analysis and design methods, consult one or more of the readings listed at the end of this chapter.

Software Engineering Trends

Books on software engineering show the traditional lifecycle of software development in the form of a waterfall (see Figure 3.1), in which the development process follows a rigid sequence from analysis to design and to implementation and testing. Based on that waterfall process, here is an oversimplified view of the sequence of activities that constitute software development:

1. You begin development with the *analysis phase* by analyzing what the software must do and arriving at a complete, detailed description of the software's behavior in response to the possible set of inputs. You work with potential users of the software to find a definitive answer to the question: *What does the software do?* The result of this step is a set of requirements for the software.

2. Next comes the *design phase*, during which you decide how to do what the user wants. Here your goal is to map the user's real-world description of the software into algorithms and data that can be implemented in a programming language. Typically, you might follow a *top-down approach* and repeatedly decompose the software's functions into a sequence of progressively simpler functions that are eventually implemented in the implementation phase.

3. In the *implementation phase* you define the data structures and write the code to implement the functions that were identified in the design. Finally, you have to test the software to verify that it conforms to the original specification as much as possible.

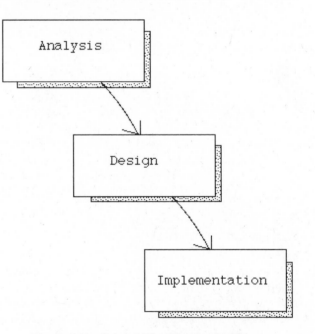

Fig. 3.1. Traditional lifecycle of software.

Prevailing Methods

Although there is no single, clear-cut, step-by-step approach to designing software, there are well-known methods and tools for accomplishing the analysis and design phases of the process.

Among the analysis methods, the most popular is *structured analysis*, attributed to Tom DeMarco, who built on prior work by Ed Yourdon and Larry Constantine. Structured analysis is concerned with the way data flows through the system. It generates a *data flow diagram (DFD)* and two textual descriptions: a *data dictionary* and a *minispecification*. The DFD is a diagramming notation that depicts the flow of data through the system and identifies the processes that manipulate the data. The data dictionary describes the data shown in the DFD, whereas the minispecification describes, in plain English, how the data is processed by each process. As an example, consider the problem of querying a database and printing a sorted list of the items retrieved by the database. Figure 3.2 shows a grossly simplified data flow diagram for this task. The diagram shows the major processes (functions), with arrows indicating the data being passed between functions.

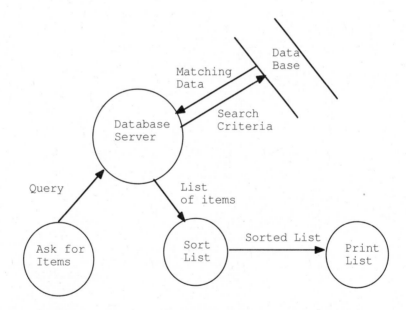

Fig. 3.2. Data flow diagram (DFD) for querying a database.

Another type of diagram for representing a software system is the *structure chart* introduced by Larry Constantine in the 1970s as a replacement for flowcharts of earlier years. The structure charts are quite similar to the flowcharts, and they provide a notational means to represent the behavior of the system being implemented. As shown in Figure 3.3, a structure chart starts with a single top-level module represented by a rectangle. That module represents the overall function of the system. From that topmost module, arrows fan out to subordinate modules that the topmost module invokes. The subordinate modules, in turn, invoke other modules. Thus, the structure looks like an organization chart, reflecting the top-down nature of the design. Each arrow emanating from one module to another represents a function call as well as a data transfer. In an actual structure chart, a label next to each arrow identifies the data being transferred. There are other symbols as well that indicate a program's control flow, such as `if` statements and loops. Many commercially available computer-aided software engineering (CASE) tools support structure charts with symbols similar to those originally suggested by Larry Constantine.

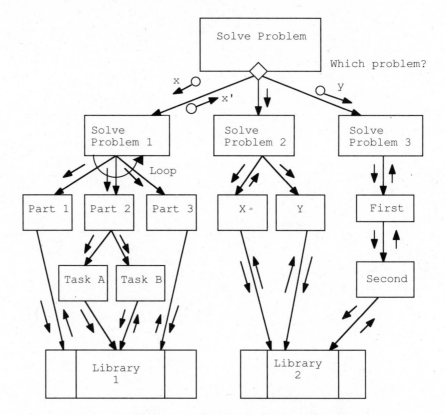

Fig. 3.3. A typical structure chart.

The design phase of the traditional development cycle is rather loosely defined. The goal of design is to refine the data flow diagrams and map the data into data structures using facilities of the programming language (for example, `struct` in C) that you will use to implement the software. Procedures are then defined to implement the modules that manipulate the data. The distinction between the analysis and design phases are often blurred and, usually, there are several iterations before you arrive at a design for the software.

Problems with the Top-Down Approach

There are several problems with the top-down approach so prevalent in structured techniques. As Bertrand Meyer[4] points out, top-down design

- does not allow for evolutionary changes in software.

- characterizes the system as having a single top-level function, which is not always true (in Meyer's words: "Real systems have no top").

- gives functions more importance than data, thus ignoring important characteristics of the data.

- hampers reusability, because submodules are usually written to satisfy the specific needs of a higher-level module.

Object-Oriented Approach

In any realistic software project, postimplementation changes are all but inevitable. Also, the real nature of the human creative process is inherently evolutionary. Because we learn as we go along, our usual approach to a new programming task is to go through an iterative process of analyzing the problem, implementing it, and then refining the design. In other words, we develop *prototypes* or working models of the software. Grady Booch[2] calls this the strategy of "analyze a little, design a little." He qualifies this by stating that it does not mean that you should design by trial and error. Instead, Booch advocates a design process that proceeds with a series of prototypes, each modeling an important aspect of the system and each selected with an eye toward arriving at the complete functionality as the collection of prototypes grows.

The emerging object-oriented design (OOD) techniques reflect the evolutionary aspect of software development. The steps of analysis, design, and implementation are still necessary, but the separation between them is blurred. Also, the approach in each phase is more closely tied to the *objects* in the real-world problem being solved. The remainder of this chapter briefly discusses several ways of using object-oriented techniques in the software development process.

Object-oriented programming (OOP) refers to the implementation of programs using objects, preferably in an object-oriented programming language such as C++. Although this book focuses on OOP using C++, the analysis and design phases of the software development process are even more important. *Object-oriented analysis (OOA)* refers to methods of specifying the requirements of the software in terms of real-world objects—their behavior and their interactions. *Object-oriented design (OOD)*, on the other hand, turns the software requirements into specifications for objects and derives class hierarchies from which the objects can be created. OOD methods usually use a diagramming notation to represent the class hierarchy and to express the interaction among objects.

Finding Objects Using Structured Analysis Tools

As illustrated in Chapters 1 and 2, at the implementation level, object-orientation means encapsulating data structures with related functions and using the notion of "message-passing" (which may very well be implemented by function calls) to accomplish the tasks of a program. The question in object-oriented design is how to find the objects. For those already familiar with structured analysis, the answer may be in using the results of structured analysis to find the objects to be implemented using OOP techniques. This approach can be exploited by commercial software developers who are trying to introduce object-oriented technology but have already invested in CASE tools that employ top-down analysis and design.

A *class* is the template that defines the data and functions common to a set of objects. Each *object* is an instance of its class. A *class library* is a collection of classes, usually meant for some related tasks such as displaying objects or storing them on disk.

Figure 3.4 illustrates the steps for a simplified example of finding the objects for an *index card file*. Each card stores a name, address, and phone number. Conventional structured analysis will model the card file as follows:

1. Identify the requirements of the card filing system. In this case, the system must be capable of creating a new card deck, adding or deleting a card, finding a card, and saving cards in a disk-resident database.

2. Translate the requirements into a top-down structure in which the topmost module enables the user to pick one of several choices: create a new deck, save it, add a card, delete a card, or find a card. Each choice is

handled by separate modules. The analysis also identifies the data items and how they are processed. Typically, you will use libraries of functions for specialized tasks such as displaying a card or organizing the deck of cards as a database.

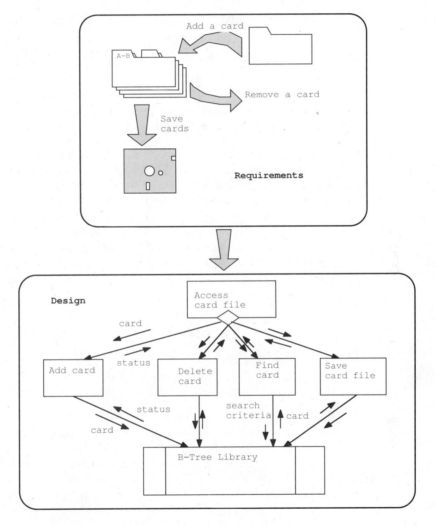

Fig. 3.4. Designing a card file.

You can use existing CASE tools in performing the analysis to determine the functional breakdown of the system and identify the necessary data items (from the data dictionary, for instance). At this point, instead of using the CASE tool to design the system, you can try to identify the objects from the data and the functions. For the card file, here is a partial description of how you might do this:

- Note that cards are manipulated by most modules identified by structured analysis. Thus, each *card* should be an object in the system. In C++ terminology, you might decide to define an `IndexCard` class, for instance, to encapsulate the data and functions necessary to model an index card.

- Because a card file is a collection of cards, there should be a way to maintain such a collection. You might use a container class (a class designed to hold objects) or simply use an array of `IndexCard` objects for this.

- Each card has several strings to hold information such as the name and address. For this, you can use a `String` class that enables you to handle each string as an object. When a new card is created, you can create the necessary string objects.

- You can choose from among three options for obtaining the database that will store the cards. You can design a complete set of classes, implementing a database in an object-oriented manner. You can buy a commercially available library of classes and use it. Lastly, you can directly call functions from the programming interface to a commercial database that does not follow an object-based design. The problem with the last approach is that embedding calls to a database in the `IndexCard` class, for instance, couples the card class too tightly to a specific database.

As you can see, the process of identifying the objects can be quite complicated, even for a relatively simple example such as the card file. Even so, there are some general guidelines for identifying the classes:

- Look for data and related functions that operate on the data. Group them into a class.

- If a class seems too specific, try to derive it from a more general-purpose class. The idea is to look for similarities among classes and to create a hierarchy in which the common features are in a base class. For example, instead of implementing a circle and a rectangle shape, first define a generic shape class, then derive circle and rectangle classes from that generic shape. That way, a new shape, such as a triangle, can be derived easily from the same base.

- Use a *bottom-up approach* to design libraries of basic classes such as strings and collections. For example, if you design a database for the card file, it can be a general-purpose database class that can be reused in other projects as well.

- Avoid embedding in a class any code for displaying an object or storing it to the disk. Instead, use a separate class library for these tasks.

Unfortunately, as fuzzy as these guidelines are for identifying objects and their interrelationships, the material in most of the references listed at the end of this chapter is not any more specific. Luckily, this situation is bound to improve, because object-oriented design is the current topic of choice among many researchers and new design methods are gradually beginning to emerge. The following discussions summarize some important ideas that can help you gain insight into designing object-oriented software.

Notation for Objects

Diagrams are an essential part of any design, and object-oriented design is no exception. Unfortunately, there is no standard notation for representing objects and their interactions. Authors of books[2,3,4] on object-oriented techniques have used their own notations to denote objects. Recently other suggested notations have appeared in computer journals.[8,9] Of these, Wasserman, Muller, and Pircher[8] have based their notation on a combination of structure charts and the notation that Booch[1,2] uses for *Ada packages*—modules in the Ada programming language. Figure 3.5 shows a subset of Wasserman's notation that is adequate for representing objects. The notation developed by Wasserman and colleagues is used in a design technique termed *object-oriented structured design (OOSD)*, which forms the basis of a useful design tool named *Software Through Pictures* developed and marketed by Interactive Development Environments, Inc.

Hybrid Design Methods

One trouble with using structured analysis as a basis for object-oriented design is that the two approaches use radically different grouping of the functions in the system. As Bailin[7] points out, structured analysis groups functions together if, as a group, they constitute a higher-level function. On the other hand, object-oriented analysis groups functions together on the basis of the data they operate on. Thus, in object-oriented approach, all functions operating on the same class of data fall in the same group.

This, however, does not mean that structured analysis is not useful. In fact, according to Larry Constantine,[10] one of the pioneers of the structured approach, it may be more useful and even practical to use a mix of top-down functional analysis together with object-orientation. Here are three possible scenarios:

- *An object-oriented system with top-down functional decomposition applied to each object's methods:* You decompose the system into interacting objects, either by identifying the objects from the output of a CASE tool or by using one of the methods discussed later in the chapter. Then, you apply top-down structured analysis techniques to design the object's internal methods (member functions in C++ terminology). In this case, outwardly, the system appears object-oriented, but inside each object there may be a small hierarchy of functions designed in a top-down manner (see Figure 3.6).

- *A top-down hierarchy of functions controlling the system that employs object-oriented modules for its functionality:* As you can see from Figure 3.7, in this case you design the system using a top-down approach, but you implement the modules by using a set of interacting objects.

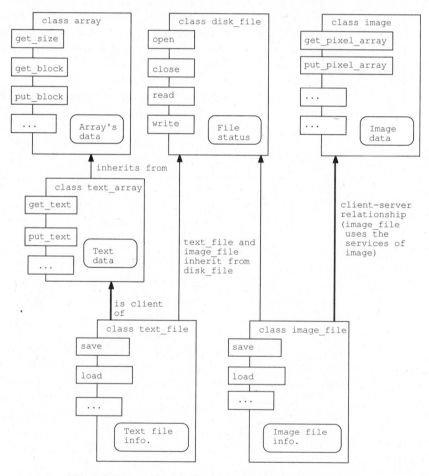

Fig. 3.5. Notations for objects and their interactions.

- *An object-oriented system built on a traditional library of functions:* This is a common case when you are building an object-oriented system using the facilities of a conventional library of functions such as *Xlib*— the C function library for the X Window System. As illustrated in Figure 3.8, the objects call functions from the library to do their work, but the application is built on the objects.

Using Physical Metaphors: The Desktop

One way to design software is to find the right physical metaphor for the problem. The metaphor refers to something tangible onto which you can map various features of the software you are designing. For example, the user interface in Apple Macintosh computers uses the *desktop metaphor*. You are supposed to view the display as a desktop containing folders and files of all information laid out like paper. You can shuffle these "papers" around, keeping in view the one you are currently using. To use a document, you simply open it and the right application gets started. The desktop metaphor is extended to the point that there is even a trashcan where you discard files and folders that you no longer need. As with a real-world trashcan, you have to empty this trashcan before the items are actually deleted from the system's disk.

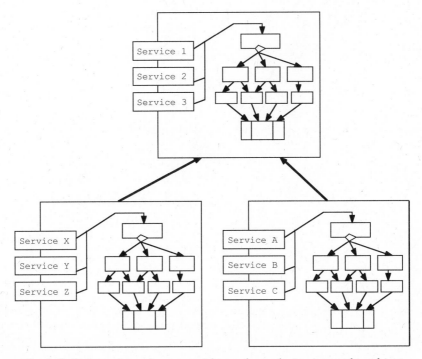

Fig. 3.6. Object-oriented system with top-down design internal to objects.

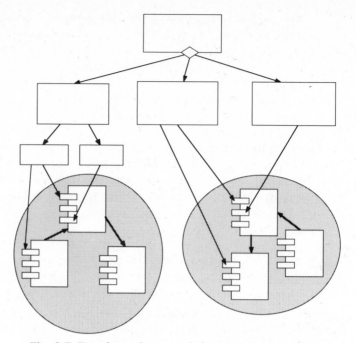

Fig. 3.7. Top-down design with functionality from objects.

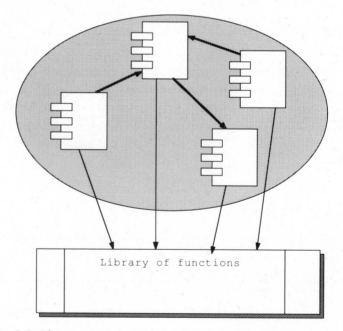

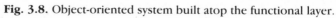

Library of functions

Fig. 3.8. Object-oriented system built atop the functional layer.

The advantage of using such physical metaphors is that your job as a designer becomes simple. Your software simply implements the features of the chosen metaphor. You do not necessarily have to use an object-oriented approach to exploit a metaphor, but physical metaphors lend themselves more readily to object-oriented organization. After all, the objects in the software can be the direct counterparts of the objects that are part of the physical metaphor.

The idea of using electronic circuits as a metaphor may seem natural for simulating actual integrated circuits (ICs), but you can use this metaphor to build user interfaces. In fact, the idea of software packaged as ICs was first used by Brad Cox,[3] who also coined the term *Software-IC*. Suppose you are using a windowing system such as the X Window System to implement a user interface. Here is a rough idea of how you might use the electronic circuit metaphor (see Figure 3.9) to implement the user interface:

- Think of each window as an IC with a number of input and output pins.

- Provide "connector" objects and functions to connect one pin to another. Use a linked list of connectors to handle multiple connections at a pin.

- Allow signals to be sent from output pins to input pins. This means that you need signal objects. Signals arriving at an input pin can be handled by calling a function inside the IC.

- As the user provides input with mouse or keyboard, send signals out on appropriate pins to perform the task requested by the user.

Depending on your application, this can turn out to be a useful metaphor. For example, you might exploit such a metaphor in an application with which the user interactively builds a graphical user interface. With such a metaphor, the user can select individual user interface components and connect their input and output pins to build the interface. You could provide some means for exercising the interface and, when the user is satisfied, allow generation of code that implements the interface.

Separation of Responsibilities

Earlier the chapter alluded to the idea of keeping classes free of unnecessary details such as how to display an object or how to save it to a file. You should define separate classes for handling chores such as display and file storage, because doing so will enable you to

- reuse the display and storage classes in other projects.

- easily change the way an object is stored or displayed.

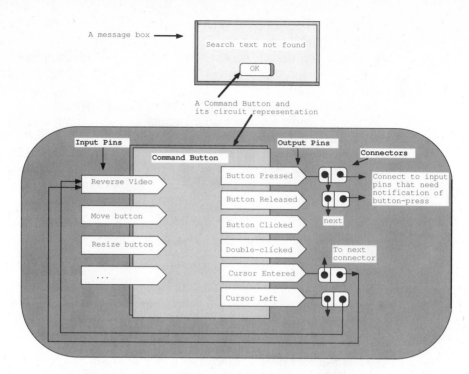

Fig. 3.9. Electronic circuit metaphor for user interfaces.

Real systems invariably have a clear separation between the internals of a system and its user interface. For example, all cars have a similar interface regardless of the number of cylinders or type of fuel being used. This idea has been exploited in Smalltalk-80's user interface.

Model-View-Controller (MVC) Architecture of Smalltalk-80

As Figure 3.10 shows, Smalltalk-80 user interfaces consist of three separate layers:

1. The *application layer* or the *model* implements the application's functionality. All application-specific code is in this layer.

2. The *presentation layer* or the *view* implements the mechanisms for presenting various aspects of the application layer to the user. In a graphical user interface, the view provides the windows.

3. The *virtual terminal layer* or the *controller* handles the user's interactions with the application. This is a graphics library that hides device dependence but presents a device independent interface to the presentation layer.

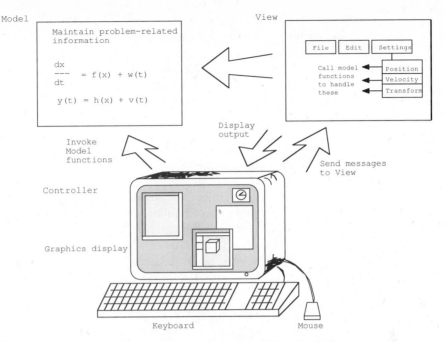

Fig. 3.10. MVC architecture of Smalltalk-80.

The Model-View-Controller (MVC) architecture does an excellent job of separating the responsibilities of the objects in the system. The application-specific details are insulated from the user interface. Also, the user interface itself is broken down into two parts, with the presentation handled by the view and the interaction by the controller.

Each Smalltalk-80 application consists of a model and an associated view-controller pair. Figure 3.11 shows the usual interactions in Smalltalk-80's MVC architecture. The controller accepts the user's inputs and invokes the appropriate function from the model to perform the task requested by the user. When the work is done, the function in the model sends messages to the view and controller. The view updates the display in response to this message, accessing the model for further information, if necessary. Thus, the model has a view and a controller, but it never directly accesses any of them. The view and controller, on the other hand, access the model's functions and data, when necessary.

Influence of the MVC Architecture

Many commercially available programming environments and libraries are influenced by Smalltalk-80's MVC architecture. Consider, for instance, the *MacApp* class library, which provides all the components necessary to build a standard user interface for any Macintosh application. MacApp uses an architecture similar to MVC. MacApp's TApplication class is the controller that manages interactions with the user, TView is responsible for displaying the view, and TDocument provides the hooks for implementing the application's model. The TDocument class is also responsible for reading the application's data from, and writing it to, the disk. Toolkits like MacApp are often called *frameworks*, because they essentially provide all the components for skeletal programs that can be easily fleshed out into complete applications.

Another example is Stepstone Corporation's ICpak 201 Graphical User Interface Library, which is also modeled after Smalltalk-80's MVC architecture and is meant for use with the Objective-C language, created by Brad Cox.[3] The ICpak 201 library uses the metaphor of an artist building an animated sequence using transparent sheets of acetate. The artist cuts sheets of acetate, draws on them, positions them in layers, and moves each illustration in relation to the others to achieve the effect of animation. ICpak 201 also provides the facilities for creating a complete image by drawing individual layers and arranging them as necessary.

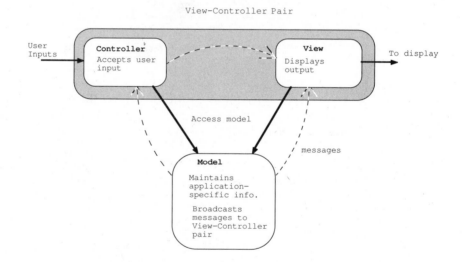

Fig. 3.11. Interactions among model, view, and controller in Smalltalk-80.

Applying the Principle of Separation

In practice, how do you apply the principle of separation of responsibilities? To illustrate, consider the design of a time-series analysis package. A *time series* is a sequence of measurements representing how a physical variable, such as the temperature or the number of cars at an intersection, varies with time. A *time-series analysis* includes tasks such as computing the mean and variance or, perhaps, applying a Fast Fourier Transform (FFT). The FFT is a mathematical operation that breaks down the time series into a number of components, each varying at a specific periodic rate. Of course, you would also want to store time series in files and load them into your program for analysis. Additionally, as shown in Figure 3.12, the user of this time-series analysis package should also be able to view a signal as an *x-y* plot or as a column of data.

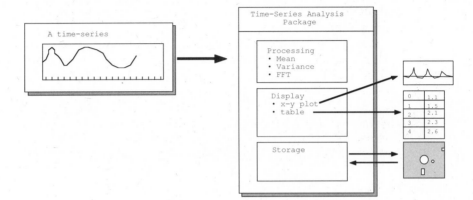

Fig. 3.12. A time-series analysis package.

Clearly, the program needs a class `time_series` to represent the time series. Using the philosophy of the MVC architecture, you can organize the classes for the package so that the `time_series` class does not have to know how to store data to disk or display a plot on the video monitor. As shown in Figure 3.13, you can delegate the tasks of storage and display to two separate classes.

To handle the task of saving a time series to a disk-based file, you might start with a top-level class `disk_file` that knows how to open and close a file as well as read from and write to a file. You can then derive a class `time_series_file` that knows how to store a time series in a file (see Figure 3.13). The `time_series_file` class is only concerned with the representation of a time series in a file. It does not have to know anything about the internal details of the actual `time_series` class. Of course, the `time_series_file` class has to ask the `time_series` class to provide it with specific components of the time series that it is saving to the disk.

You can handle displaying of time series by a scheme similar to that used for saving a time series to a disk file. You might start with a `windowed_display` class that can use an underlying display system, such as the X Window System or Microsoft Windows, and provide basic drawing functions. Derive from this a `time_series_display` class that handles the actual display of a time series in a window. You might want to provide different ways of displaying a time series, for instance, as a graph or as a table of values. You can handle this by developing separate classes `time_series_graph` and `time_series_table`, for example, to handle such needs (see Figure 3.13).

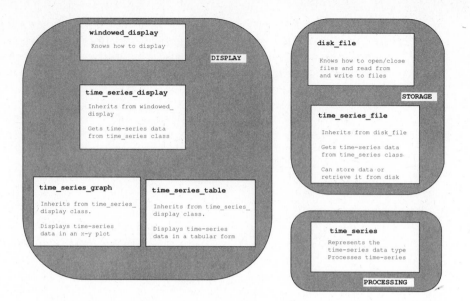

Fig. 3.13. Separation of responsibilities in a time-series analysis package.

Responsibility-Driven Design

In their recent book,[5] Rebecca Wirfs-Brock, Brian Wilkerson, and Lauren Wiener present what they call a *responsibility-driven design method* for object-oriented software. This terminology is used because the authors model the software as a collection of collaborating objects, each with specific responsibilities. Collaboration refers to one class of objects using the facilities of another. The objects are modeled by a *client-server* relationship, in which a client class makes a request to have a specific task performed by the server.

This section briefly describes responsibility-driven design because it appears to be a promising new approach for object-oriented design. For further information on this approach, consult the book by Wirfs-Brock and colleagues.

Design Phases

The responsibility-driven design is broken down into two phases:

1. *Exploratory phase*. Here you discover the classes required to model the application, divide up the system's total responsibility, and delegate the appropriate responsibilities to the classes. You also identify the collaborations among the classes.

2. *Analysis phase*. The purpose of this phase is to refine the design created during the exploratory phase. Here you move the common responsibilities to the base classes so that code is reused as much as possible. You group classes that work closely together. In fact, you can think of a group of classes as a single entity—a *subsystem*. In the analysis phase, you also derive complete specifications of the classes and determine the message protocols to be used by client-server pairs.

The Design Tools

The responsibility-driven design suggests the use of index cards to record the classes, responsibilities, and collaborations. This simple tool was first used by Beck and Cunningham,[13] and some call these *CRC cards* because they are used to record *c*lasses, *r*esponsibilities, and *c*ollaborations. Responsibility-driven design uses two sets of index cards: one for recording information about a class (see Figure 3.14) and the other for recording information about a subsystem (see Figure 3.15).

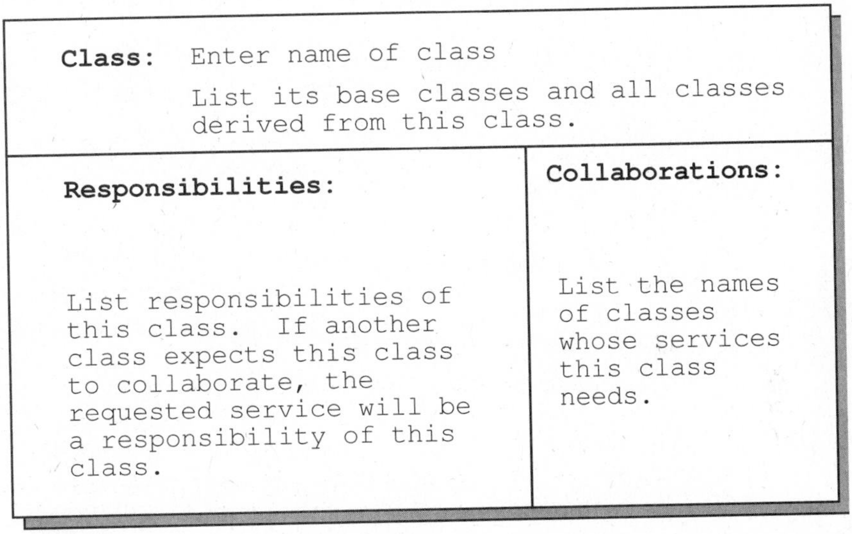

Class:	Enter name of class
	List its base classes and all classes derived from this class.

Responsibilities:	**Collaborations:**
List responsibilities of this class. If another class expects this class to collaborate, the requested service will be a responsibility of this class.	List the names of classes whose services this class needs.

Fig. 3.14. Layout of an index card used to record information about a class.

Other diagrams used by this approach include the following:

- Hierarchy graphs that show how the classes inherit from one another (see Figure 3.16).

- Venn diagrams, a common tool for showing the intersection and union of sets, are employed in responsibility-driven design to indicate how responsibilities of classes overlap (see Figure 3.17). This helps you identify responsibilities that should be elevated to a base class.

- Collaborations graphs show the relationships between client and server classes. Figure 3.18 illustrates this notation.

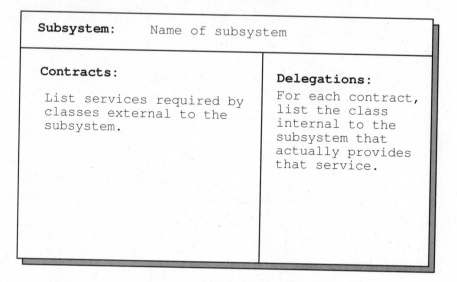

Fig. 3.15. Layout of an index card used to record information about a subsystem.

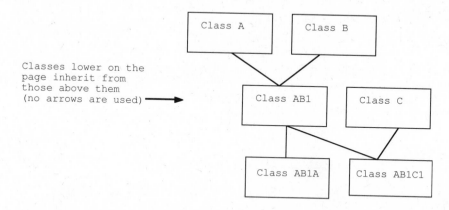

Fig. 3.16. A hierarchy graph.

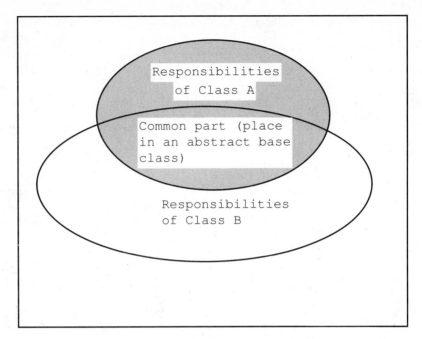

Fig. 3.17. Venn diagram of responsibilities.

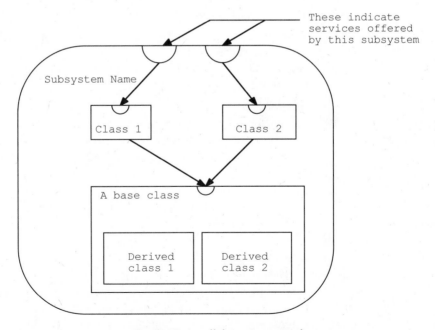

Fig. 3.18. A collaborations graph.

Step-by-Step Design

Because this is a design process, you should have available the results of the analysis phase—the specified requirements for the software. You start the design process by studying the requirements to identify the objects that have to be modeled by the software. The high-level outline of the design process is as follows:

1. *Identify the classes, their responsibilities, and collaborations*. Record these on index cards. When you look for classes, focus on any physical or conceptual object in the system and give preference to categories of objects. Introduce abstract base classes—classes from which no instances are ever created but that serve as repositories of common code and data. Write down a descriptive purpose for each class and use these descriptions to determine the responsibilities and collaborations of the classes. This step is iterative, because you might discover missing classes as you begin recording the information of a class. Discard any class that stands alone—it does not collaborate with others, nor do others collaborate with it.

2. *Determine class hierarchies and draw hierarchy graphs*. Draw Venn diagrams of the responsibilities to help factor out common responsibilities.

3. *Draw collaborations graphs*. Identify subsystems by looking for classes that are strongly dependent on each other.

4. *Determine how the client classes will use the services offered by the server classes*. In the context of C++, this will mean defining the member functions of a class and deciding how many forms of a member function (determined by the type and number of arguments) are necessary to fulfill the responsibilities of the class.

5. *Write down the design specifications*. You should specify ones for each class, subsystem, and contract to be honored by the classes.

Summary

Although object-oriented programming focuses on implementing programs using object-oriented concepts, you have to identify the objects before you can use OOP for implementation. This crucial part of the software development process is handled by the analysis and design phases. Analysis identifies the requirements of the software; design provides the specifications for the data and functions that are eventually implemented. So far, analysis and design have been the domain of structured techniques that were originated and popularized by the pioneers of the technique such as Tom DeMarco, Larry Constantine, and Ed Yourdon.

More recently, the focus has shifted from structured methods to object-oriented techniques. Proponents of the object-oriented approach claim that working with objects is easier, because objects appear naturally when you describe the underlying physical problem you are solving in the software. Also, use of objects in all phases of the development cycle—analysis, design, and implementation—helps you to create smooth transitions from one step to another and to meet the requirements better.

Once you identify the objects and their interactions, you have to find the classes—the templates from which objects are created. The classes should be organized in a hierarchy, with common functions and data stored in the base class from which other classes can inherit. Although there is no step-by-step approach that works in all situations, there are many heuristic guidelines available for proceeding with the design. For instance, classes should be designed to handle a well-defined task. Distinct responsibilities demand distinct classes. The Model-View-Controller architecture of Smalltalk-80 is an example that meets this goal. If you find a physical metaphor for your problem, you can exploit it just as the Apple Macintosh user interface mimics a desktop.

A promising new approach is the responsibility-driven design technique suggested by Rebecca Wirfs-Brock, Brian Wilkerson, and Lauren Wiener. Their model of software is a collection of objects with well-defined responsibilities that get the job done through collaborations. The initial exploratory step of this method involves identifying the classes, determining their responsibilities and collaborations, and recording them on index cards. Later, in the detailed analysis phase, you group related classes into subsystems and organize the classes into hierarchies to factor out common responsibilities. The collaboration refers to one class using the capabilities of another and is modeled as a client-server transaction—one class requesting service from another.

Further Reading

Despite a recent surge in books and articles about object-oriented design, this topic remains an elusive one to grasp. Because no single approach works for all problems, most descriptions of object-oriented design are, of necessity, a collage of case studies and extrapolations based on the experience. Basically, you have to go through various examples before you arrive at a set of guidelines for the software design approach that suits a specific problem. Here is a selection of reading material to help you achieve that goal. Although this is a short list, each of these sources will, in turn, provide you with numerous other references on object-oriented design.

Grady Booch[1] describes object-oriented design in his 1983 book on the Ada programming language. In his 1990 book,[2] he presents a more refined description of the incremental and iterative nature of object-oriented software design.

Brad Cox,[3] the originator of the Objective-C language, describes his view of object-oriented programming in a 1986 book. He promotes the idea of packaging software in modular units that he calls *Software-ICs* (software integrated circuits).

Bertrand Meyer,[4] author of an object-oriented language named *Eiffel*, describes object-oriented design as supported by the Eiffel language. One of his ideas is the notion of *programming by contract*—the idea that for correct operation, a software module and its consumers must, in some way, formally express the rights and obligations of each side.

The recent book[5] by Rebecca Wirfs-Brock, Brian Wilkerson, and Lauren Wiener presents a detailed example of object-oriented design using a responsibility-driven approach. The authors' idea is to identify the classes, their responsibilities, and their collaborators. In this approach, you lay out the design on a set of index cards, called CRC cards (where CRC stands for class, responsibility, and collaboration). This appears to be a promising step-by-step approach to object-oriented design of software.

The September 1990 issue of *Communications of the ACM*[6]—the flagship magazine of the Association for Computing Machinery—is a special issue on object-oriented design. Consult this issue for a good assortment of articles on the object-oriented approach. In another article in the May 1989 issue of this journal, Sidney Bailin[7] presents a method for specifying the requirements for object-oriented software.

Notational schemes are another important tool, because they permit you to express your design in a concise yet descriptive manner. Although Booch,[2] Meyer,[3] and Cox[4] have all used some form of notation in their books, there is no universally accepted convention. For a sampling of some proposed notational schemes, see the recent journal articles.[8,9]

Another interesting idea is to mix conventional function-oriented design with object-oriented concepts in a hybrid design strategy. Larry Constantine,[10] one of the pioneers of structural techniques, discusses such an approach in an article.

For a description of Smalltalk-80's Model-View-Controller (MVC) architecture, see Adele Goldberg's recent article.[11] For another good discussion of the MVC model as well as some other examples of practical applications of object-oriented methods, see the compendium of essays edited by Lewis Pinson and Richard Wiener.[12]

Beck and Cunningham's article[13] describes the use of index cards to record initial class designs. This tool is used by Wirfs-Brock[5] and colleagues in their responsibility-driven design approach.

The recent book[14] by James Rumbaugh and his colleagues at the General Electric Research and Development Center in Schenectady, New York is another recommended source of material on object-oriented modeling and design. This book covers the entire development life cycle—analysis, design, and implementation—using a graphical notation and methodology developed by the authors.

1. Grady Booch, *Software Engineering with Ada* (Redwood City, Calif.: Benjamin/Cummings, 1991), 600 pages.

2. Grady Booch, *Object-Oriented Design with Applications* (Redwood City, Calif.: Benjamin/Cummings, 1991), 600 pages.

3. Brad Cox, *Object-Oriented Programming—An Evolutionary Approach* (Reading, Mass.: Addison-Wesley, 1986), 287 pages.

4. Bertrand Meyer, *Object-Oriented Software Construction* (Hertfordshire, Great Britain: Prentice-Hall International [UK] Ltd., 1988), 552 pages.

5. Rebecca Wirfs-Brock, Brian Wilkerson, and Lauren Wiener, *Designing Object-Oriented Software* (Englewood Cliffs, N.J.: Prentice-Hall, 1990), 360 pages.

6. *Communications of the ACM*, Special Issue on Object-Oriented Design, Volume 33, No. 9, September 1990, pages 38–159.

7. Sidney C. Bailin, "An Object-Oriented Requirements Specification Method," *Communications of the ACM* 32, No. 5 (May 1989), pp. 608–623.

8. Anthony I. Wasserman, Peter A. Pircher, and Robert J. Muller, "The Object-Oriented Structured Design Notation for Software Design Representation," *Computer* 23, No. 3 (March 1990), pp. 50–63.

9. Meilir Page-Jones, Larry L. Constantine, and Steven Weiss, "Modeling Object-Oriented Systems: The Uniform Object Notation," *Computer Language* 7, No. 10 (October 1990), pp. 69–87.

10. Larry L. Constantine, "Objects, Functions, and Program Extensibility," *Computer Language* 7, No. 1 (January 1990), pp. 34–54.

11. Adele Goldberg, "Information Models, Views, and Controllers," *Dr. Dobb's Journal* (July 1990), pp. 54–61.

12. Lewis J. Pinson and Richard S. Wiener, eds., *Applications of Object-Oriented Programming* (Reading, Mass.: Addison-Wesley, 1990), 222 pages.

13. K. Beck and H. Cunningham, "A Laboratory for Teaching Object-Oriented Thinking," *Proceedings of OOPSLA 1989*, New Orleans, October 1989, pp. 1–6.

14. James Rumbaugh, Michael Blaha, William Premerlani, Frederick Eddy, and William Lorensen, *Object-Oriented Modeling and Design* (Englewood-Cliffs, N.J.: Prentice-Hall, 1991), 512 pages.

Part Two

Learning C++

Chapter 4: C++ and ANSI Standard C

Chapter 5: Predefined Classes in C++

Chapter 6: Building Objects with Classes

Chapter 7: Defining Operations on Objects

Chapter 8: Using Inheritance in C++

Chapter 9: Virtual Functions and Polymorphism

C++ and ANSI Standard C

$\mathbf{T}$he first part of this book introduced the terminology of object-oriented programming, explained the basic concepts, and presented a simple example to illustrate how OOP makes it easier to handle unanticipated changes in a program. The last chapter of Part I, Chapter 3, described some commonly used methods for designing object-oriented software.

This part of the book, Chapters 4 through 9, provides complete details of the C++ programming language—explaining its syntax and showing how to use its features to write object-oriented programs. However, before getting into C++ in earnest, you should become familiar with the recently adopted ANSI standard for the C programming language, because certain seemingly new features of C++ are already in ANSI C. Therefore, this chapter starts with a summary description of ANSI C followed by a bird's-eye view of C++. The chapter ends with a discussion of the differences between C++ and ANSI C.

Overview of ANSI Standard C

In late 1989, the C programming language went through a significant transition. That's when the American National Standards Institute (ANSI) adopted a standard for C, referred to as the ANSI X3.159 1989, which defines not only the C language but also the standard header files, standard libraries, and the behavior of the C preprocessor. Prior to the ANSI standard, the C language as defined by Kernighan and Ritchie's 1978 book was the de facto standard—one that often goes by the name *K&R C*. As for library, the de facto standard was the C library in UNIX. ANSI C changes this by clearly specifying all aspects of C: the language, the preprocessor, and the library.

Because C++ existed and continued to evolve as C was being standardized during the period 1983 through 1989, many features that appeared in C++ also found their way into ANSI C. Therefore, if you know ANSI C, you will already be familiar with many C++ constructs. This section briefly describes ANSI C.

Structure of a C Program

As shown in Figure 4.1, a typical C program is organized into one or more *source files,* or modules. Each file has a similar structure, with comments, preprocessor directives, declarations of variables and functions, and their definitions. You will usually place each group of related variables and functions in a single source file. Some files are simply a set of declarations that are used in other files through the #include directive of the C preprocessor. These files are usually referred to as *header files* and have names ending with the .h extension. In Figure 4.1, the file shapes.h is a header file that declares common data structures and functions for the program.

```
                                shapes.h
/* File: shapes.h
 * Header file for data structures
 */
#ifndef _SHAPES_H
#define _SHAPES_H

enumshape_type(T_CIRCLE,T_RECTANGLE);
typedef struct RECTANGLE
{
    double x1, y1, c2, y2;
} RECTANGLE;
typedef struct CIRCLE
{
    double xc, yc, radius;
} CIRCLE;
typedef struct SHAPE
{
    enum shape_type type;
    union
    {
        RECTANGLE r;
```

```
                                shapes.c
/* File: shapes.c
 * Compute area of shapes
 */
#include <math.h>
#include <shapes.h>

doublecompute_area(SHAPE*p_s)
{
    switch(p_s->type)
    {
        case T_CIRCLE:
        {
            CIRCLE *p_c = &(p_s->u.c);
            return M_PI * p_c->radius *
p_c->radius;
        }
        case T_RECTANGLE:
        {
```

```
                                shapetst.c
/* File: shapetst.c
 * Main program to test shapes.c
 */
#include <stdio.h>
#include <shapes.h>

int main(void)
{
    SHAPE s;
    CIRCLE *p_c = &(s.u.c)
    s.type = T_CIRCLE;
    p_c->radius = 50.0;
    p_c->xc = p_c->yc = 100.0;
```

Fig. 4.1. Source files of a C program.

Another file, shapes.c, defines the functions, and a third file, shapetst.c, implements the main function. This is the function where the execution of a C program begins. Files with names ending in .c are the source files in which you define the functions needed by your program. Although Figure 4.1 shows only one function in each source file, in typical programs the source file contains definitions for many functions.

You have to compile and link the source files to create an executable program. The exact steps for building programs from C source files depends on the compiler and the operating system. You can find this information in your compiler's documentation.

A *declaration* specifies how to interpret a symbol. A *definition*, on the other hand, actually creates a variable or a function. Definitions cause the compiler to set aside storage for data or code, but declarations do not. For example,

```
int x, y, z;
```

is a definition of three integer variables, but

```
extern int x, y, z;
```

is a declaration indicating that the three integer variables are defined in another source file.

Within each source file, the components of the program are laid out in a standard manner. As shown in Figure 4.2, the typical components of a C source file are as follows:

1. The file starts with some comments that describe the purpose of the module and provide some other pertinent information, such as the name of the author and revision dates. In ANSI C, comments start with a /* and end after a */ pair.

2. Commands for the preprocessor, known as *preprocessor directives*, follow the comments. The first few directives are typically for including header files and defining constants.

3. Next come declarations of variables and functions that are to be visible throughout the file. In other words, the names of these variables and functions may be used in any of the functions in this file. Here you also define variables needed within the file. Use the static keyword as a prefix when you want to confine the visibility of the variables and functions to this module only. On the other hand, the extern keyword indicates that the items you are declaring are defined in another file.

4. The rest of the file includes definitions of functions. Inside a function's body, you can define variables that are local to the function and that exist only while the function's code is being executed.

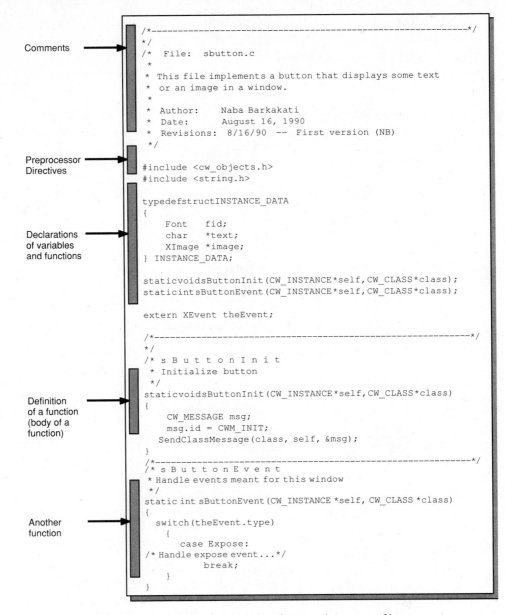

Comments

Preprocessor
Directives

Declarations
of variables
and functions

Definition
of a function
(body of a
function)

Another
function

```c
/*--------------------------------------------------------------*/
*/
/*  File:  sbutton.c
 *
 * This file implements a button that displays some text
 * or an image in a window.
 *
 * Author:    Naba Barkakati
 * Date:      August 16, 1990
 * Revisions: 8/16/90 -- First version (NB)
 */

#include <cw_objects.h>
#include <string.h>

typedefstructINSTANCE_DATA
{
    Font    fid;
    char   *text;
    XImage *image;
} INSTANCE_DATA;

staticvoidsButtonInit(CW_INSTANCE*self,CW_CLASS*class);
staticintsButtonEvent(CW_INSTANCE*self,CW_CLASS*class);

extern XEvent theEvent;

/*--------------------------------------------------------------*/
*/
/* s B u t t o n I n i t
 * Initialize button
 */
staticvoidsButtonInit(CW_INSTANCE*self,CW_CLASS*class)
{
    CW_MESSAGE msg;
    msg.id = CWM_INIT;
    SendClassMessage(class, self, &msg);
}
/*--------------------------------------------------------------*/
/* s B u t t o n E v e n t
 * Handle events meant for this window
 */
static int sButtonEvent(CW_INSTANCE *self, CW_CLASS *class)
{
  switch(theEvent.type)
    {
      case Expose:
/* Handle expose event...*/
        break;
    }
}
```

Fig. 4.2. Layout of a typical C source file.

Here is a list of all the keywords of ANSI C:

```
auto        double      int         struct
break       else        long        switch
case        enum        register    typedef
char        extern      return      union
const       float       short       unsigned
continue    for         signed      void
default     goto        sizeof      volatile
do          if          static      while
```

The keywords const, enum, void, and volatile are new in ANSI C.

ANSI C Escape Sequences and Trigraphs

In C, you can insert nonprintable characters such as a tab in strings by using an *escape sequence*—a sequence of characters that starts with a backslash. For example, tab and newline are represented by the sequences \t and \n, respectively. ANSI C has enlarged the set of escape sequences. Table 4.1 lists the escape sequences supported in ANSI C.

Table 4.1. ANSI C Escape Sequences.

Sequence	Name	Interpretation or Action
\a	alert	Rings bell
\b	backspace	Moves backward one space
\f	form feed	Moves to the beginning of next page
\n	new-line	Moves to beginning of next line
\r	carriage return	Moves to beginning of current line
\t	horizontal tab	Moves to next tab position on this line
\v	vertical tab	Moves to next vertical tab position
\\	backslash	\
\'	single quote	'
\"	double quote	"

continues

Table 4.1. continued

Sequence	Name	Interpretation or Action
\?	question mark	?
\<octal digits>	octal constant	Depends on printer or terminal
\x<hexadecimal digits>	hexadecimal	Depends on printer or terminal

ANSI C also introduces the concept of *trigraph sequences* that programmers use to enter certain important characters from keyboards that do not have them (non-English keyboards may not have these characters). Each three-character trigraph sequence begins with a pair of question marks, ??, followed by a third character. For example, if a keyboard does not have a backslash \, a programmer can use the trigraph ??/ to enter it in a C program. Table 4.2 lists the nine trigraph sequences available in ANSI C.

Table 4.2. ANSI C Trigraph Sequences.

Trigraph	Translation
??(	[
??/	\
??)	]
??'	^
??<	{
??!	¦
??>	}
??-	~
??=	#

Preprocessor Directives

Preprocessing refers to the first step in translating or *compiling* an ANSI C file from this high-level language into machine instructions. Traditionally, a separate program named the *C preprocessor* was used for this task. Although the ANSI standard does not require a separate preprocessor, most C compilers provide a distinct preprocessor.

The preprocessor processes the source file and acts on preprocessor directives embedded in the program. These directives begin with the # character. Usually the compiler automatically invokes the preprocessor before beginning compilation, but most compilers give you the option of invoking the preprocessor alone. There are three major capabilities of the preprocessor that you can use to make your programs modular, readable, and easier to customize:

- You can use the #include directive to insert the contents of a file into your program. This enables you to place common declarations in one location and use them in all source files through file inclusion. The result is a reduced risk of mismatches between declarations of variables and functions in separate program modules.

- Through the #define directive, you can define macros that enable you to replace one string with another. You can use the #define directive to give meaningful names to numeric constants, thus improving the readability of your source files.

- Directives such as #if, #ifdef, #else, and #endif enable you to compile selected portions of your program. You can use this feature to write source files with code for two or more systems but compile only those parts that apply to the computer system you are currently writing for. With this strategy you can maintain multiple versions of a program using a single set of source files.

Including Files

You can write modular programs by exploiting the #include directive. The C preprocessor can keep commonly used declarations in a single file that you can insert in other source files as needed. ANSI C supports three forms of the #include directive. As a C programmer, you are familiar with the first two forms:

```
#include <stdio.h>
#include "winobj.h"
```

You use the first form of the #include directive to read in the contents of a file—in this case the standard C header file, stdio.h, from the default location where all the header files reside. This default usually is the directory /usr/include in UNIX systems. You can use the second form, which encloses the file name in double quotation marks, when the file being included (such as winobj.h) is in the current directory. The exact conventions for locating the file being included depend on the compiler.

ANSI C provides a third way of specifying the name of the file in the #include directive: through a macro. The following example illustrates how this might be done:

```
/* The following was introduced in ANSI C */

#ifdef SYSV
    #define  SYSTEM_DEFINES  "/usr/local/sysvdef.h"
#else
    #define  SYSTEM_DEFINES  "/usr/local/bsddef.h"
#endif

#include SYSTEM_DEFINES
```

This example uses the #ifdef and #define directives (to be described later in the chapter) to set the symbol SYSTEM_DEFINES to the name a file to be included depending on the definition of the symbol SYSV.

Defining Macros

By defining a macro, you can define a symbol (a *token*) to be equal to some C code and use that symbol wherever you want to use the code in your program. When the source file is preprocessed, every occurrence of a macro's name is replaced with its definition. A common use of this feature is to define a symbolic name for a numerical constant and use the symbol instead of the numbers in your program. This improves the readability of the source code, because with a descriptive name, you are not left guessing why a particular number is being used in the program. You can define such macros in a straightforward manner using the #define directive as follows:

```
#define PI          3.14159
#define GRAV_ACC    9.80665
#define BUFSIZE     512
```

Once these symbols are defined, you can use PI, GRAV_ACC, and BUFSIZE instead of the numerical constants throughout the source file.

The capabilities of macros, however, go well beyond replacing a symbol for a constant. Macros can accept parameters and replace each occurrence of a parameter with the value provided for it when the macro is used in a program. Thus, the code resulting from the expansion of a macro can change depending on the parameter you provide when using the macro.

For example, the following macro accepts a parameter and expands to an expression designed to calculate the square of the parameter:

```
#define square(x) ((x)*(x))
```

If you use square(z) in your program, it becomes ((z)*(z)) after the source file is preprocessed. This macro is essentially equivalent to a function that computes the square of its arguments. You do not, however, have the overhead of calling a function, because the expression generated by the macro is placed directly in the source file.

When the preprocessor expands a macro, it replaces each parameter with the one you provide when using the macro. If you are not careful in defining the macro, you can end up with code that does something completely different from what you intended. For example, if you were to define square(x) as x*x, a macro invocation of the form square(a+b) would expand to a+b*a+b, which is certainly not the square of a+b. However, with square(x) defined as ((x)*(x)), square(a+b) will result in ((a+b)*(a+b)), which gives you the correct result. The moral is that you should use parentheses liberally when you define a macro with parameters.

An interesting new feature of the ANSI C preprocessor is the *token-pasting* operator denoted by the ## pair of characters. Using this operator you can append one token to another and create a third valid token. The following scenario demonstrates how you might use this feature: Suppose you have two types of data files, and an integer at the beginning of the file identifies each type. File type 1 uses the hexadecimal constant 0x4d4d; type 2 has 0x4949 in the first two bytes. In your program to read these files, you want to refer to the type with a macro of the form Type(n), where n would be either 1 or 2. Here is how you can use the token-pasting operator ## to define the Type(n) macro:

```
#define TYPE1    0x4d4d
#define TYPE2    0x4949
#define Type(n) TYPE##n
```

With this definition, when the preprocessor expands the macro Type(2), it replaces n with 2 and generates the string TYPE##2 that, after interpretation of the token-pasting operator, becomes the token TYPE2. The preprocessor finds that TYPE2 is defined to be 0x4949 and uses that as the replacement for the macro Type(2).

Another new feature of the ANSI C preprocessor is the *stringizing* operator, which makes a string out of any parameter with a # prefix by putting that parameter in quotes. Suppose you want to print out the value of certain variables in your program. Instead of calling the printf function directly, you can define a utility macro that will do the work for you. Here is how you might write the macro:

```
#define Trace(x)        printf(#x" = %d\n", x)
```

Then, to print out the value of a variable named current_index. for instance, you can simply write this:

```
Trace(current_index);
```

When the preprocessor expands this, it generates the following statement:

```
printf("current_index"" = %d\n", current_index);
```

At this point another new feature of ANSI C becomes relevant. ANSI C also stipulates that adjacent strings will be concatenated. Applying this rule, the macro expansion becomes the following:

```
printf("current_index = %d\n", current_index);
```

This is exactly what you would have written to print the value of the current_index variable.

Conditional Directives

You can use *conditional directives* such as #if, #ifdef, #ifndef, #else, #elif, and #endif to control which parts of a source file get compiled and under which conditions. With this feature, you maintain a single set of source files that can be selectively compiled with different compilers and in different environments. Another common use is to insert printf statements for debugging that are compiled only if a symbol named DEBUG is defined. Conditional directives start with #if, #ifdef, or #ifndef, followed by zero or more #elif directives. Next comes an optional #else, followed by an #endif directive that marks the end of that conditional block.

Here are some common ways of using conditional directives. To include a header file only once, you can use the following:

```
#ifndef __PROJECT_H
#define __PROJECT_H
/* Declarations to be included once */
/* . . . */

#endif
```

The following prints a diagnostic message during debugging (when the symbol DEBUG is defined):

```
#ifdef DEBUG
    printf("In read_file: bytes_read = %d\n", bytes_read);
#endif
```

The following example shows how you can include a different header file depending on the version number of the software directives. To include a header file only once, you can use the following:

```
#if CPU_TYPE == 8086
    #include <real_mode.h>
#elif CPU_TYPE == 80386
    #include <prot_mode.h>
#else
    #error Unknown CPU type.
#endif
```

The #error directive is used to display error messages during preprocessing.

Other Directives

Several other preprocessor directives are meant for miscellaneous tasks. For example, you can use the #undef directive to remove the current definition of a symbol. The #pragma is another special-purpose directive that you can use to convey information to the C compiler. Preprocessor directives that begin with #pragma are known as *pragmas*, and they are used to access special features of a compiler and as such they vary from one compiler to another.

ANSI standard C compilers maintain several predefined macros (see Table 4.3). Of these, the macros __FILE__ and __LINE__, respectively, refer to the current source file name and the current line number being processed. You can use the #line directive to change these. For example, to set __FILE__ to "file_io.c" and __LINE__ to 100, you would say this:

```
#line 100 "file_io.c"
```

Table 4.3. Predefined Macros in ANSI C.

Macro	Definition
__DATE__	This is a string containing the date when you invoked the C compiler. It is of the form "MMM DD YYYY" (for example, "Oct 26 1990").
__FILE__	This expands to a string containing the name of the source file.
__LINE__	This is a decimal integer whose value is the line number within the current source file.
__STDC__	This macro expands to the decimal constant 1 to indicate that the C compiler conforms to the ANSI standard.
__TIME__	This string gives you the time when you started compiling the source file. It is of the form "HH:MM:SS" (for example, "21:59:45").

Declaration and Definition of Variables

In C, you have to either define or declare all variables and functions before you use them. The definition of a variable specifies the following:

- Its *visibility*, which indicates exactly where the variable can be used (is it defined for the whole file or only in a function).

- Its *lifetime*, which determines whether the variable exists temporarily (for example, a local variable in a function) or permanently (as long as the program is running).

- Its *type* and, where allowed, its initial value. For example, an integer variable x initialized to 1 is defined as follows:

```
int  x = 1;
```

If a variable you are using happens to be defined in another source file, you simply declare the variable with an extern keyword like this:

```
extern int message_count;
```

You must have at least one source file in which this variable is defined without the extern qualifier. When the program is built, the linker will resolve all references to the message_count variable and make sure that they all use the same variable.

Basic Types

C has four basic data types: char and int are for storing characters and integers, and float and double are for floating-point numbers. The ANSI standard specifies only the minimum range of values that each type must be able to represent. The exact number of bytes used to store each type of data may vary from one compiler to another. For example, ANSI C requires that the size of an int be at least 2 bytes, which is what most MS-DOS C compilers provide. Most UNIX C compilers, on the other hand, use 4 bytes for an int. Most systems use a single byte for a char. Common sizes for float and double are 4 and 8 bytes, respectively. You can define variables of these basic data types in a straightforward manner:

```
char   c;
int    i, j, bufsize;
float  volts;
double mean, variance;
```

C can expand the basic data types into a much larger set when the programmer uses the long, short, and unsigned qualifiers as prefixes. The long and the short qualifiers are size modifiers. For example, a long int is *at least* 4 bytes long in ANSI C, as opposed to the minimum size of 2 bytes for a short. The size of an int is system-dependent, but it is guaranteed to be at least as large as a short.

The unsigned qualifier is for int and char types only. Normally, each of these types hold negative as well as positive values. This is the default signed form of these data types. You can use the unsigned qualifier when you want the variable to hold positive values only. Here are some examples of using the short, long, and unsigned qualifiers:

```
unsigned char   mode_select, printer_status;
short           record_number; /* Same as "short int"           */
long            offset;        /* Same as "long int"            */
unsigned        i, j, msg_id;  /* Same as "unsigned int"        */
unsigned short  width, height; /* Same as "unsigned short int" */
unsigned long   file_pos;      /* Same as "unsigned long int"  */
long double     result;
```

Note that when the short, long, and unsigned qualifiers are used with int types, you can drop the int from the declaration. Also, ANSI C enables you to extend the double data type with a long prefix.

The exact sizes of various data types and the ranges of values they can store depend on the C compiler you use. ANSI C requires that these limits be defined in the header files <limits.h> and <float.h>. You can examine these files in your system to determine the sizes of basic data types that your C compiler supports.

Enumerations

ANSI C introduces the enum data type, which you can use to define your own enumerated list—a fixed set of named integer constants. For example, you can declare a Boolean data type named BOOLEAN using enum as follows:

```
/* Declare an enumerated type named BOOLEAN */
      enum BOOLEAN {false = 0, true = 1, stop = 0, go = 1,
                    off = 0, on = 1};

/* Define a BOOLEAN called "status" and initialize it */
      enum BOOLEAN status = stop;
```

This example first declares BOOLEAN to be an enumerated type. The list within the braces shows the *enumeration constants* that are valid values of an enum BOOLEAN variable. You can initialize each constant to a value of your choice, and you can have several constants that use the same value. In this example, the constants false, stop, and off are set to 0, and true, go, and on are initialized to 1. The example then defines an enumerated BOOLEAN variable named status, which is initially set to the constant stop.

Structures, Unions, and Bit-fields

In C, you use struct to group related data items together and refer to the group with a name. For example, the declaration of a structure to hold variables of a queue might look like this:

```
/* Declare a structure */
struct QUEUE
{
    int  count;      /* Number of items in queue      */
    int  front;      /* Index of first item in queue */
    int  rear;       /* Index of last item in queue   */
    int  elemsize;   /* Size of each element of data */
    int  maxsize;    /* Maximum capacity of queue     */
    char *data;      /* Pointer to queued data        */
};

/* Define two queues (data storage area not allocated yet) */
struct QUEUE rcv_q, xmit_q;
```

The elements inside the QUEUE structure are called its *members*. You can access the members by using the member selection operator (.). For instance, rcv_q.count refers to the count member of the rcv_q structure.

A union is like a struct, but instead of grouping related data items together as struct does, a union allocates storage for several data items starting at the same location. Thus, all members of a union share the same storage location. You can use unions to view the same data item in different ways. Suppose you are using a compiler that supports 4-byte longs and you want to be able to access the 4 individual bytes of a long integer. Here is a union that helps you to accomplish this:

```
union
{
    long  file_type;
    char  bytes[4];
} header_id;
```

With this definition, header_id.file_type refers to the long integer, and header_id.bytes[0] is the first byte of that long integer.

In C, you can also define structures that contain groups of bits packed into an int. These *bit-fields* are useful for manipulating selected bits in an integer and are often used when accessing hardware devices, such as disk drive controllers and serial ports. You can think of a bit-field as a structure whose members are bits. The declaration of a bit-field is like any other structure, except for the syntax used to indicate the size of each group of bits. For example, in the IBM PC, the text display memory uses a 16-bit cell for each character: the least significant 8 bits for the character's ASCII code and the other 8 for attributes such as foreground and background colors. A 16-bit bit-field describing this layout might be the following:

```
struct TEXT_CELL
{
    unsigned  c:8, fg_color:4, bg_color:3, blink_on:1;
};
```

This bit-field definition assumes that the compiler packs the bit-fields from least-significant bit to the most significant. The exact order of the bits in a bit-field depends on the compiler.

Arrays

An *array* is a collection of one or more identical data items. You can declare arrays of any type of data, including structures and types defined by typedef. For example, to define an array of 80 characters, you write the following:

```
char    string[80];
```

The characters in the string array occupy successive storage locations, beginning with location 0. Thus, string[0] refers to the first character in this array, and string[79] is the last one. You can define arrays of other data types and structures similarly:

```
struct Customer                    /* Declare a structure       */
{
    int  id;
    char first_name[40];
    char last_name[40];
};

struct Customer customers[100]; /* Define array of structures */
int             index[64];      /* An array of 64 integers    */
```

You can also define multidimensional arrays. For example, to represent an 80-column by 25-line text display, you can use a two-dimensional array as follows:

```
unsigned char text_screen[25][80];
```

Each item of text_screen is an array of 80 unsigned chars, and text_screen contains 25 such arrays. In other words, the two-dimensional array is stored by laying out one row after another in memory. You can use expressions such as text_screen[0][0] to refer to the first character in the first row and text_screen[24][79] to refer to the last character of the last row of the display screen. Higher-dimensional arrays are defined similarly:

```
float coords[3][2][5];
```

This defines coords as a three-dimensional array of three data items. Each item is an array of two arrays, each of which, in turn, is an array of five float variables. Thus, you interpret a multidimensional array as "arrays of arrays."

Pointers

A *pointer* is a variable that can hold the address of any type of data except a bit-field. For example, if p_i is a pointer to an integer variable, you can define and use it as follows:

```
/* Define an int pointer and an integer */
   int *p_i, count;

/* Set pointer to the address of the integer "count" */
   p_i = &count;
```

In this case, the compiler will allocate storage for an int variable count and a *pointer to an integer* p_i. The number of bytes necessary to represent a pointer depends on the underlying system's addressing scheme. You should not use a pointer until it contains the address of a valid object. The example shows p_i being initialized to the address of the integer variable count using the & operator, which provides the address of a variable. Once p_i is initialized, you can refer to the value of count with the expression *p_i, which is read as the "contents of the object whose address is in p_i."

Pointers are useful in many situations, an important one being the dynamic allocation of memory. The standard C libraries include functions such as malloc and calloc that you can call to allocate storage for arrays of objects. After allocating memory, these functions return the starting address of the block of memory. Because this address is the only way to reach that memory, you have to store it in a variable capable of holding an address—a pointer. Suppose you allocate memory for an array of 50 integers and save the returned address in p_i. Now you can treat this block memory as an array of 50 integers with the name p_i. Thus, you can refer to the last element in the array as p_i[49], which is equivalent to *(p_i+49).

Similarly, ANSI C treats the name of an array as a pointer to the first element of the array. The difference between the name of an array and a pointer variable is that the array's name is a constant without any explicit storage necessary to hold the address of the array's first element, whereas the pointer is an actual storage location capable of holding the address of any data.

In addition to storing the address of dynamically allocated memory, pointers are also commonly used as arguments to functions. When a C function is called, all of its arguments are passed by value—that is, the function gets a copy of each argument, not the original variables appearing in the argument list of the function call. Thus, a C function cannot alter the value of its arguments. Pointers provide a way out. To change the value of a variable in a function, you can pass it a pointer to the variable, and the function can alter the value through the pointer.

Type Definitions

Through the typedef keyword, C gives you the convenience of assigning a new name to an existing data type. You can use the typedef facility to give meaningful names to data types used in a particular application. For example, a graphics application might declare a data type named Point as follows:

```
/* Declare a Point data type */
    typedef struct Point
    {
        short x;
        short y;
    } Point;

/* Declare PointPtr to be pointer to Point types */
    typedef Point *PointPtr;

/* Define some instances of these types and initialize them */
    Point    a = {0, 0};
    PointPtr  p_a = &a;
```

As shown by the Point and PointPtr types, you can use typedef to declare complex data types conveniently.

Type Qualifiers: const and volatile

ANSI C introduces two new keywords, const and volatile, that you can use as qualifiers in a declaration. The const qualifier in a declaration tells the compiler that the particular data object must not be modified by the program. This means the compiler must not generate code that might alter the contents of the location where that data item is stored. On the other hand, volatile specifies that the value of a variable may be changed by factors beyond the control of the program. You can use both keywords on a single data item to mean that although the item must not be modified by your program, it may be altered by some other process.

The const and volatile keywords always qualify the item immediately to their right. The information provided by the const and the volatile qualifiers is supposed to help the compiler optimize the code it generates. For example, suppose the variable block_size is declared and initialized as follows:

```
const int block_size = 512;
```

In this case, the compiler need not generate code to load the value of block_size from memory. Instead it can use the value 512 wherever your program uses block_size. Now suppose you added volatile to the declaration and changed it as follows:

```
volatile const int block_size = 512;
```

This says that the contents of `block_size` may be changed by some external process. Therefore, the compiler cannot optimize away any reference to `block_size`. You may have to use such declarations when you refer to an I/O port or video memory, because these locations can be changed by factors beyond the control of your program.

Expressions

An *expression* is a combination of variables, function calls, and operators that result in a single value. For example, here is an expression whose value is the number of bytes needed to store the null-terminated string (an array of `char`s with a zero byte at the end), `str`:

```
(strlen(str) * sizeof(char) + 1)
```

This expression involves a function call, `strlen(str)`, and the operator `sizeof` as well as a multiplication sign (*) and an addition symbol (+).

ANSI C has a large number of operators, and they are an important part of expressions. Table 4.4 summarizes the operators in ANSI C.

Table 4.4. Summary of ANSI C Operators.

Name of Operator	Syntax	Result
Arithmetic Operators		
Add	x+y	Adds x and y.
Subtract	x-y	Subtracts y from x.
Multiply	x*y	Multiplies x and y.
Divide	x/y	Divides x by y.
Remainder	x%y	Computes the remainder of x divided by y.
Preincrement	++x	Increments x before use.
Postincrement	x++	Increments x after use.
Predecrement	--x	Decrements x before use.
Postdecrement	x--	Decrements x after use.
Minus	-x	Negates the value of x.
Plus	+x	Maintains value of x unchanged.
Relational and Logical Operators		
Greater than	x>y	Value is 1 if x exceeds y, else 0.
Greater than or equal to	x>=y	Value is 1 if x exceeds or equals y, else 0.

Name of Operator	Syntax	Result
Less than	x<y	Value is 1 if y exceeds x, else 0.
Less than or equal to	x<=y	Value is 1 if y exceeds or equals x, else 0.
Equal to	x==y	Value is 1 if x equals y, else 0.
Not equal to	x!=y	Value is 1 if x and y are unequal, else 0.
Logical NOT	!x	Value is 1 if x is 0, else 0.
Logical AND	x&&y	Value is 0 if either x or y is 0.
Logical OR	x¦¦y	Value is 0 if both x and y are 0.

Assignment Operators

Name of Operator	Syntax	Result
Assignment	x=y	Puts value of y into x.
Compound assignment	x O= y	Equivalent to x = x O y where O is one of the +-*/% >> & ^ ¦ operators.

Data Access and Size Operators

Name of Operator	Syntax	Result
Subscript	x[y]	Selects the y-th element of array x.
Member selection	x.y	Selects member y of structure (or union) x.
Member selection	x->y	Selects member named y from a structure or union whose address is x.
Indirection	*x	Contents of location whose address is x.
Address of	&x	Address of data object named x.
Sizeof	sizeof(x)	Size (in bytes) of data object named x.

Bitwise Operators

Name of Operator	Syntax	Result
Bitwise NOT	~x	Changes all 1s to 0s and 0s to 1s.
Bitwise AND	x&y	Result is bitwise AND of x and y.
Bitwise OR	x¦y	Result is bitwise OR of x and y.
Bitwise exclusive OR	x^y	Result has 1s where corresponding bits of x and y differ.

continues

Table 4.4. continued

Name of Operator	Syntax	Result
Left shift	x<<y	Shifts the bits of x to the left by y bit positions. Fills 0s in vacated bit positions.
Right shift	x>>y	Shifts the bits of x to the right by y bit positions. Fills 0s in vacated bit positions.

Miscellaneous Operators

Name of Operator	Syntax	Result
Function call	x(y)	Result is value returned (if any) by function x which is called with argument y.
Type cast	(type)x	Converts value of x to type whose name appears in parentheses.
Conditional	z?x:y	If z is not 0, evaluates x, else evaluates y.
Comma	x,y	First evaluates x, then y

Operator Precedence

Typical C expressions consist of several operands and operators. When writing complicated expressions, you have to be aware of the sequence in which the compiler evaluates the operators. For example, a program uses an array of pointers to integers defined as follows:

```
typedef int *IntPtr;   /* Use typedef to simplify declarations */
IntPtr  iptr[10];      /* An array of 10 pointers to int        */
```

Now suppose you encounter the expression *iptr[4]. Does this refer to the value of the int whose address is in iptr[4], or is it the fifth element from the location whose address is in iptr? In other words, is the compiler going to evaluate the subscript operator ([]) before the indirection operator (*), or will the compiler evaluate them the other way around? To answer questions such as these, you need to know the *precedence*, or order of application, of the operators. Table 4.5 summarizes ANSI C's precedence rules. The table shows the operators in order of decreasing precedence. The operators with highest precedence—those that are applied first—are shown first. The table also shows the *associativity* of operators—the order in which operators at the same level are evaluated.

Getting back to the question of interpreting *iptr[4], a quick look at Table 4.5 tells you that the [] operator has precedence over the * operator. Thus, when the compiler processes the expression `*iptr[4]`, it evaluates `iptr[4]` first and then applies the indirection operator, resulting in the value of the `int` whose address is in `iptr[4]`.

Table 4.5. Precedence and Associativity of ANSI C Operators.

Operator Group	Operator Name	Notation	Associativity
Postfix	Subscript	`x[y]`	Left to right
	Function call	`x(y)`	
	Member selection	`x.y`	
	Member selection	`x->y`	
	Postincrement	`x++`	
	Postdecrement	`x--`	
Unary	Preincrement	`++x`	Right to left
	Predecrement	`--x`	
	Address of	`&x`	
	Indirection	`*x`	
	Plus	`+x`	
	Minus	`-x`	
	Bitewise NOT	`~x`	
	Logical NOT	`!x`	
	Sizeof	`sizeof x`	
	Type cast	`(type)x`	
Multiplicative	Multiply	`x*y`	Left to right
	Divide	`x/y`	
	Remainder	`x%y`	
Additive	Add	`x+y`	Left to right
	Subtract	`x-y`	
Shift	Left shift	`x<<y`	Left to right
	Right shift	`x>>y`	
Relational	Greater than	`x>y`	Left to right
	Greater than or equal	`x>=y`	
	Less than	`x<y`	
	Less than or equal	`x<=y`	

continues

Table 4.5. continued

Operator Group	Operator Name	Notation	Associativity
Equality	Equal to	x==y	Left to right
	Not equal to	x!=y	
Bitwise AND	Bitwise AND	x&y	Left to right
Bitwise XOR	Bitwise exclusive OR	x^y	Left to right
Bitwise OR	Bitwise OR	x¦y	Left to right
Logical AND	Logical AND	x&&y	Left to right
Logical OR	Logical OR	x¦¦y	Left to right
Conditional	Conditional	z?x:y	Right to left
Assignment	Assignment	x=y	Right to left
	Multiply assign	x *= y	
	Divide assign	x /= y	
	Remainder assign	x %= y	
	Add assign	x += y	
	Subtract assign	x -= y	
	Left shift assign	x <<= y	
	Right shift assign	x >>= y	
	Bitwise AND assign	x &= y	
	Bitwise XOR assign	x ^= y	
	Bitwise OR assign	x ¦= y	
Comma	Comma	x,y	Left to right

Statements

You use statements to represent the actions to be performed by C functions and to control the flow of execution in the C program. A *statement* consists of keywords, expressions, and other statements. Each statement ends with a semicolon.

A special type of statement, the *compound statement*, comprises a group of statements enclosed in a pair of braces ({...}). The body of a function is a compound statement. Also known as *blocks*, such compound statements can have local variables.

The following alphabetically describes the types of statements available in ANSI C.

break Statement

You use the break statement to jump to the statement following the innermost do, for, switch, or while statement. It is also used to exit from a switch statement. The following example uses break to exit a for loop:

```
for(i = 0; i < ncommands; i++)
{
    if(strcmp(input, commands[i]) == 0) break;
}
```

case Label

The case statement marks labels in a switch statement. The following is an example:

```
switch (interrupt_id)
{
    case XMIT_RDY:
        transmit();
        break;

    case RCV_RDY:
        receive();
        break;
}
```

Compound Statement or Block

As mentioned earlier, the compound statement or block is a group of declarations followed by statements, all enclosed in a pair of braces ({...}). The body of a function and the block of code following an if statement are some examples of compound statements. In the following example, the declarations and statements within the braces constitute a compound statement:

```
if(theEvent.xexpose.count == 0)
{
    int i;
/* Clear the window and draw the figures
 * in the "figures" array
 */
    XClearWindow(theDisplay, dWin);
    if(numfigures > 0)
```

```
                for(i=0; i<numfigures; i++)
                    draw_figure(theDisplay, dWin,
                                theGC, i);
    }
```

continue Statement

The continue statement begins the next iteration of the innermost do, for, or while statement in which it appears. You can use continue when you want to skip an iteration of the loop.

For example, to add the numbers from 1 to 10, excluding 5, you can use a for loop that skips the body when the loop index (i) is 5:

```
    for(i=0, sum=0; i <= 10, i++)
    {
        if(i == 5) continue;    /* Exclude 5 */
        sum += i;
    }
```

default Label

You use default as the label in a switch statement to mark code that will be executed when none of the case labels match the switch expression.

do Statement

The do statement together with a while forms iterative loops of the kind:

```
    do
        statement
        while(expression);
```

where the statement (usually a compound statement) is executed until the expression in the while statement evaluates to 0. The expression is evaluated after each execution of the statement. Thus a do..while block always executes at least once. For example, to add the numbers from 1 to 10, you can use the following do statement:

```
    sum = 0;
    do
    {
        sum += i;
```

```
        i++;
    }
    while(i <= 10);
```

Expression Statements

These are statements that are evaluated for their side effects. Some examples are calling a function, assigning a value to a variable, and incrementing a variable. Here are some examples:

```
printf("Hello, World!\n");
i++;
num_bytes = length * sizeof(char);
```

for Statement

Use the for statement to execute a statement zero or more times based on the value of an expression. The syntax is as follows:

```
for (expr_1; expr_2; expr_3) statement
```

where the expr_1 is evaluated once at the beginning of the loop, and the statement is executed until the expression expr_2 evaluates to 0. The third expression, expr_3, is evaluated after each execution of the statement. The expressions expr_1 and expr_3 are optional. Here is an example that uses a for loop to add the numbers from 1 to 10:

```
for(i=0, sum=0; i <= 10; sum += i, i++);
```

In this example, the actual work of adding the numbers is being done in the third expression. The statement controlled by the for loop is a null statement (a lone ;).

goto Statement

The goto statement transfers control to a statement label. Here is an example that prompts the user for a value and repeats the request if the value is not acceptable:

```
ReEnter:
    printf("Enter offset: ");
    scanf(" %d", &offset);
    if(offset < 0 || offset > MAX_OFFSET)
    {
```

```
                printf("Bad offset: %d Please reenter:\n",
                        offset);
                goto ReEnter;
        }
```

if Statement

You can use the `if` statement to test an expression and execute a statement only when the expression is nonzero. An `if` statement has the following form:

```
if ( expression )   statement
```

The statement following the `if` is executed only if the expression in parentheses evaluates to a nonzero value. That statement is usually a compound statement. The following is an example:

```
if(mem_left < threshold)
{
    Message("Low on memory! Close some windows.\n");
}
```

if..else Statement

This is a form of the `if` statement together with an `else` clause. The statement has the following syntax:

```
if ( expression )
        statement_1
else
        statement_2
```

where `statement_1` is executed if the expression within the parentheses is nonzero. Otherwise, `statement_2` is executed. This example uses `if` and `else` to pick the smaller of two variables:

```
if ( a <= b)
        smaller = a;
else
        smaller = b;
```

Null Statement

This statement, represented by a solitary semicolon, does nothing. You use null statements in loops when all processing is done in the loop expressions rather than in the body of the loop. For example, to locate the 0 byte marking the end of a string, you might use the following:

```
char str[80] = "Test";
int i;

for (i=0; str[i] != '\0'; i++)
                            ;   /* Null statement */
```

return Statement

The return statement stops executing the current function and returns control to the calling function. The syntax is as follows:

```
return expression;
```

where the value of the expression is returned as the value of the function.

switch Statement

The switch statement performs a multiway branch depending on the value of an expression. It has the following syntax:

```
switch (expression)
{
    case value1:
        statement_1
        break;
    case value2:
        statement_2
        break;
        .

        .

        .
    default:
        statement_default
}
```

If the `expression` being tested by `switch` evaluates to `value1`, `statement_1` is executed. If the `expression` is equal to `value2`, `statement_2` is executed. The value is compared with each `case` label and the statement following the matching label is executed. If the value does not match any of the `case` labels, the `block statement_default` following the `default` label is executed. Each statement ends with a `break` statement that separates the code of one case label from another. Following is a `switch` statement that calls different routines depending on the value of an integer variable named `cmd`:

```
switch (cmd)
{
    case 'q':
        quit_app(0);

    case 'c':
        connect();
        break;

    case 's':
        set_params();
        break;

    case '?':
    case 'H':
        print_help();
        break;

    default:
        printf("Unknown command!\n");
}
```

while Statement

The `while` statement is used in the following form:

```
while (expression) statement
```

where the `statement` is executed until the `expression` evaluates to 0. A `while` statement evaluates the expression before each execution of the statement. Thus, a `while` loop executes the statement zero or more times. Here is a `while` statement for copying one array to another:

```
i = length;
while (i >= 0)  /* Copy one array to another */
```

```
      {
            array2[i] = array1[i];
            i--;
      }
```

Functions

Functions are the building blocks of C programs. A *function* is a collection of declarations and statements. Each C program has at least one function: the `main` function. The execution of a C program begins with `main`. The ANSI C library is also mostly functions, although there are quite a few macros.

Function Prototypes

In ANSI C, you should declare a function before using it. (If you do not declare a function, the compiler creates a declaration for you; this declaration may not match the actual function definition.) The function declaration tells the compiler the type of value the function returns and the number and type of arguments it takes. Most C programmers are accustomed to declaring functions only when they return a value other than an `int`, because that is how Kernighan and Ritchie's definition of C works. For example, in the old UNIX C library, the memory allocation function `calloc` used to return a pointer to a `char` (as you will see soon, the ANSI C version of `calloc` returns a `void` pointer).

Thus, an old-style C program that uses `calloc` would include the following declaration:

```
char *calloc();
```

You can continue to use this in ANSI C, but you can also declare a function as a complete *function prototype*, showing the return type as well as a list of arguments. The `calloc` function in the ANSI C library returns a `void` pointer and accepts two arguments, each of type `size_t`. This type is an unsigned integer of sufficient size to hold the value of the `sizeof` operator. Thus, the ANSI C prototype for `calloc` is as follows:

```
void *calloc(size_t, size_t);
```

which shows the type of each argument in the argument list. You can also include an identifier for each argument and write the prototype as follows:

```
void *calloc(size_t num_elements, size_t elem_size);
```

In this case the prototype looks exactly like the first line in the definition of the function, except that you stop short of defining the function and end the line with a semicolon. With well-chosen names for arguments, this form of prototype can provide a lot of information about the function's use. For example, one look at the prototype of `calloc` should tell you that its first argument is the number of elements to allocate, and the second one is the size of each element.

Prototypes also help the compiler to check function arguments and to generate code that may use a faster mechanism for passing arguments. From the prototype, the compiler can determine the exact number and type of arguments to expect. Therefore, it can catch any mistakes you might make when calling a function, such as passing the wrong number of arguments (when the function takes a fixed number of arguments) or passing the wrong type of argument to a function.

The `void` Type

What do you do when a function does not return anything or when it does not accept any parameters? To handle these cases, ANSI C provides the `void` type, which is useful for declaring functions that return nothing and for describing pointers that can point to any type of data. For example, you can use the `void` return type to declare a function such as `exit` that does not return a value:

```
void exit(int status);
```

On the other hand, if a function does not accept any formal parameters, its list of arguments is represented by a `void`:

```
FILE *tmpfile(void);
```

The `void` pointer is useful for functions that work with blocks of memory. For example, when you request a certain number of bytes from the memory allocation routine `malloc`, you can use these locations to store any data that fits the space. In this case, the address of the first location of the allocated block of memory is returned as a `void` pointer. Thus, the prototype of `malloc` is as follows:

```
void *malloc(size_t numbytes);
```

Functions with Varying Numbers of Arguments

If a function accepts a variable number of arguments, you can indicate this by using an ellipsis (. . .) in place of the argument list. However, you have to list at least one argument before the ellipsis. A good example of such functions is the `printf` family of functions defined in the header file `<stdio.h>`. The prototypes of these functions are as follows:

```
int fprintf(FILE *stream, const char *format, ...);
int printf(const char *format, ...);
int sprintf(char *buffer, const char *format, ...);
```

As you can see, after a list of required arguments, the variable number of arguments is indicated by an ellipsis.

The ANSI C Library

The ANSI standard for C defines all aspects of C: the language, the preprocessor, and the library. The prototypes of the functions in the library as well as all necessary data structures and preprocessor constants are defined in a set of standard header files. Table 4.6 lists the standard header files, including a summary of their contents. (See Appendix D for a list of macros and declarations in each header.)

Table 4.6. Standard Header Files in ANSI C.

Header file	Purpose
assert.h	Defines the assert macro. Used for program diagnostics.
ctype.h	Declares functions for classifying and converting characters.
errno.h	Defines macros for error conditions, EDOM and ERANGE, and the integer variable errno where library functions return error code.
float.h	Defines the range of values that can be stored in floating-point types.
limits.h	Defines the limiting values of all integer data types.
locale.h	Declares the lconv structure and the functions necessary for customizing a C program to a particular locale.
math.h	Declares the math functions and the HUGE_VAL macro.
setjmp.h	Defines the setjmp and longjmp functions that can transfer control from one function to another without relying on normal function calls and returns. Also defines the jmp_buf data type used by setjmp and longjmp.
signal.h	Defines symbols and routines necessary for handling exceptional conditions.

continues

Table 4.6. continued

Header file	Purpose
stdarg.h	Defines the macros that provide access to the unnamed arguments in a function that accepts a varying number of arguments.
stddef.h	Defines the standard data types ptrdiff_t, size_t, wchar_t, the symbol NULL, and the macro offsetof.
stdio.h	Declares the functions and data types necessary for input and output operations. Defines macros such as BUFSIZ, EOF, NULL, SEEK_CUR, SEEK_END, and SEEK_SET.
stdlib.h	Declares many utility functions such as the string conversion routines, random number generator, memory allocation routines, and process control routines (such as abort, exit, and system).
string.h	Declares the string manipulation routines such as strcmp and strcpy.
time.h	Defines data types and declares functions that manipulate time. Defines the types clock_t and time_t, and the tm data structure.

Features of C++

In Chapter 2, you encountered a small but important subset of C++ that specifically supports object-oriented programming. There are many more features of C++ that may not directly support OOP but are nevertheless necessary for writing complete programs. Many of these features match what is in ANSI C, but there are many differences, some small, between the two.

The rest of this chapter provides a quick overview of C++'s features that differ from those of ANSI standard C. The chapter ends with a discussion of cases in which things that used to work one way in C no longer work similarly or, in a few cases, do not work at all in C++. The coverage of the topics in this section is sparse, because these topics will be covered again in Chapters 5 through 9.

New Features for Functions in C++

As in C, C++ programs are composed of functions. C++ introduces several new requirements to make functions efficient and safe to use. The first change is the use of prototypes for functions. A *prototype* is a function declaration, complete with a list of arguments that the function accepts. Although you can use prototypes in ANSI C, they are not mandatory.

In C++, you *must* declare a function before using it. You can either use a prototype or define the function before it is called.

Default Arguments

Another improvement to functions in C++ is that you can specify the default values for the arguments when you provide a prototype for a function. For example, if you are defining a function named `create_window` that sets up a window (a rectangular region) in a graphics display and fills it with a background color, you may opt to specify default values for the window's location, size, and background color, as follows:

```
// A function with default argument values
// Assume that Window is a user-defined type

Window create_window(int x = 0, int y = 0, int width = 100,
                     int height = 50, int bgpixel = 0);
```

With `create_window` declared this way, you can use any of the following calls to create new windows:

```
Window w;

// The following is same as: create_window(0, 0, 100, 50, 0);
w = create_window();

// This is same as: create_window(100, 0, 100, 50, 0);
w = create_window(100);

// Equivalent to create_window(30, 20, 100, 50, 0);
w = create_window(30, 20);
```

As you can see from the examples, it is impossible to give a nondefault value for the `height` argument without specifying the values for x, y, and `width` as well, because `height` comes after them and the compiler can only match arguments by position. In other words, the first argument you specify in a call to `create_window` always matches x, the second one matches y, and so on. Thus, you can leave only trailing arguments unspecified.

Overloaded Function Names

In C++ you can have several functions with the same name as long as their argument lists differ. When this happens, the function's name is said to be *overloaded*. You can use overloading to give a meaningful name to related functions that perform the same task. For example, take the case of evaluating the absolute value of numbers. The ANSI C library includes three functions for this purpose: abs for int arguments, labs for long, and fabs to get the absolute value of a double. In C++, you can use the name abs for all three versions and declare them as follows:

```
int    abs(int x);
long   abs(long x);
double abs(double x);
```

Then, you can use the functions as follows:

```
int i, diff = -2;
long offset;
double x;

i = abs(diff);            // abs(int)    called
offset = abs(-21956L);  // abs(long)   called
x = abs(-3.55);          // abs(double) called
```

The C++ compiler selects the correct function by comparing the types of arguments in the call with those that are specified in the function's declaration.

When you overload functions in C++, you have to ensure that the number and type of arguments of all overloaded versions are different. C++ does not allow overloading of functions that differ only in the type of return value. Thus, you cannot overload functions such as double compute(int) and float compute(int), because their argument lists are identical.

Inline Functions

Inline functions are like preprocessor macros, because the compiler substitutes the entire function body for each inline function call. The inline functions are provided to support efficient implementation of OOP techniques in C++. Because OOP approach requires extensive use of member functions, the overhead of function calls can hurt the performance of a program. For smaller functions, you can use the inline specifier to avoid the overhead of function call.

On the surface, inline functions look like preprocessor macros, but the two differ in a crucial aspect. Unlike the treatment of macros, the compiler treats inline functions as true functions. To see how this can be an important factor, consider the following example. Suppose you have defined a macro named multiply as follows:

```
#define multiply(x,y) (x*y)
```

If you were to use this macro as follows:

```
x = multiply(4+1,6);   // You want the product of 4 + 1 and 6
```

By straightforward substitution of the `multiply` macro, the preprocessor will transform the right-hand side of this statement into the following code:

```
x = (4+1*6);
```

This evaluates to 10 instead of the result of multiplying (4 + 1) and 6, which should have been 30. Of course, you know that the solution is to use parentheses around the macro arguments, but consider what happens when you define an inline function exactly as you defined the macro:

```
#include <stdio.h>

// Define in-line function to multiply two integers

inline int multiply(int x, int y)
{
    return(x * y);
}

// An overloaded version that multiplies two doubles

inline double multiply(double x, double y)
{
    return(x * y);
}

main()
{
    printf("Product of 5 and 6 = %d\n", multiply(4+1,6));
    printf("Product of 3.1 and 10.0 = %f\n",
           multiply(3.0+.1, 10.0));
}
```

When you compile and run this program, it correctly produces the following output:

```
Product of 5 and 6 = 30
Product of 3.1 and 10.0 = 31.000000
```

As you can see from this example, inline functions never have the kind of errors that plague ill-defined macros. Additionally, because inline functions are true functions, you can overload them and rely on the compiler to use the correct function based on the argument types.

Because the body of an inline function is duplicated wherever that function is called, you should use inline functions only when the functions are small in size. A good example of inline functions appears in the definition of the `complex` class, which is distributed with most C++ compilers and appears in the header file `<complex.h>`.

friend Functions

C++ introduces another new keyword—the `friend` specifier—to help you implement OOP techniques efficiently. The rules of data encapsulation in a class are such that only member functions can access the private data of a class. Of course, a class can provide special member functions that can return the values of its private variables, but this approach may be too inefficient in some cases. In such cases, you may want to allow a nonmember function to directly access data private to the class. You can do this by declaring that nonmember function within the class with the `friend` access specifier.

For example, suppose you want to define a nonmember function add to add two complex numbers. The following program illustrates how you might use `friend` functions to accomplish this. Note that this is a simplistic definition of a complex class meant to show how `friend` functions work. A much more complete definition of the complex class appears in `<complex.h>`.

```
#include <stdio.h>

class complex
{
    float real, imag;
public:
    friend complex add(complex a, complex b);
    friend void print(complex a);
    complex() { real = imag = 0.0;}
    complex(float a, float b) { real = a; imag = b;}
};

complex add(complex a, complex b)
{
    complex z;
    z.real = a.real + b.real;
    z.imag = a.imag + b.imag;
    return z;
}
```

```
void print(complex a)
{
    printf(" (%f + i %f)\n", a.real, a.imag);
}

main()
{
    complex a, b, c;
    a = complex(1.5, 2.1);
    b = complex(1.1, 1.4);

    printf("Sum of ");
    print(a);
    printf("and");
    print(b);

    c = add(a,b);

    printf(" = ");
    print(c);
}
```

This program uses the friend functions add and print to add two complex numbers and display the results. When you execute this program, it generates the result:

```
Sum of  (1.500000 + i 2.100000)
and (1.100000 + i 1.400000)
 =  (2.600000 + i 3.500000)
```

Reference Types as Arguments

The add function of the previous section has a drawback that stems from the way C passes arguments to functions. C passes arguments by value. This means that when you call a function with some arguments, the values of the arguments are copied to a special area of memory known as the *stack*. The function uses these copies for its operation. To see the effect of *call by value*, consider the following code:

```
void twice(int a)
{
    a *= 2;
}
.

.
int x = 5;
```

```
    // Call the "twice" function
       twice(x);

       printf("x = %d\n", x);
```

You will find that this program prints 5 as the value of x, not 10, even though the function twice multiplies its argument by 2. This is because the function twice receives a copy of x and whatever changes it makes to that copy are lost on return from the function.

In C, the only way you can change the value of a variable through a function is by explicitly passing the address of the variable to the function. For example, to double the value of a variable, you can write the function twice as follows:

```
       void twice(int *a)
       {
           *a *= 2;    // Double the value
       }
           .
           .
           .
       int x = 5;

    // Call "twice" with the address of x as argument
       twice(&x);

       printf("x = %d\n", x);
```

This time, the program prints 10 as the result. Thus, you can pass pointers to alter variables through a function call, but the syntax is messy. In the function, you have to dereference the argument by using the * operator.

C++ provides a way of passing arguments by reference by introducing the concept of a *reference*, which is the idea of defining an alias or alternative name for any instance of data. The syntax is to append an ampersand (&) to the name of the data type. For example, if you have the following:

```
   int i = 5;
   int *p_i = &i;   // A pointer to int initialized to point to i
   int &r_i = i;    // A reference to the int variable i
```

then you can use r_i anywhere you would use i or *p_i. In fact, if you write this:

```
    r_i += 10;   // adds 10 to i
```

i will change to 15, because r_i is simply another name for i.

Using reference types, you can rewrite the function named twice to multiply an integer by 2 in a much simpler manner:

```
    void twice(int &a)
    {
        a *= 2;
    }
    .

    .
    int x = 5;
// Call "twice" argument automatically passed by reference
    twice(x);

    printf("x = %d\n", x);
```

As expected, the program prints 10 as the result, but it looks a lot simpler than trying to accomplish the same task using pointers.

Another reason for passing arguments by reference is that when classes are passed by value, there is the overhead of copying objects to and from the stack. Passing a reference to an object avoids this unnecessary copying and allows an efficient implementation of OOP. This brings us back to the example in the previous discussion of friend functions. Once you know about references, you would want to rewrite that small complex class as follows:

```
#include <stdio.h>

class complex
{
    float real, imag;
public:
    friend complex add(const complex &a, const complex &b);
    friend void print(const complex &a);
    complex() { real = imag = 0.0;}
    complex(float a, float b) { real = a; imag = b;}
};

complex add(const complex &a, const complex &b)
{
    complex z;
    z.real = a.real + b.real;
    z.imag = a.imag + b.imag;
    return z;
}

void print(const complex &a)
{
    printf(" (%f + i %f)\n", a.real, a.imag);
}
```

You can use the class in the same manner as its old version. If you look carefully, you will notice that to pass arguments by reference, you simply add an & after the data type of the argument, thus changing all complex to complex& (you can have a space between the type and &). We have also added a const prefix to the arguments to emphasize that the functions add and print must not alter their arguments.

Overloaded Operators

Just as C++ permits you to define several functions with the same name but varying arguments, it also permits you to redefine the meaning of operators such as + – * / % += –= for any class. In other words, you can overload the meaning of operators. Because a class is a new abstract data type, such overloaded operators give you the ability to define operations on this data.

For example, instead of writing an add function to add two complex variables, you can define the + operator to perform addition for the complex class shown earlier. Using friend functions and const reference types, you might define the + operator as follows:

```
class complex
{
    float real, imag;
public:
    friend complex operator+(const complex &a, const complex
&b);

    complex() { real = imag = 0.0;}
    complex(float a, float b) { real = a; imag = b;}
};

complex operator+(const complex &a, const complex &b)
{
    complex z;
    z.real = a.real + b.real;
    z.imag = a.imag + b.imag;
    return z;
}
```

As you can see from the example, defining the operator is just like defining a function except for a special syntax for the name of the function—the name is the symbol of the operator with the operator keyword as prefix.

After you define a + operator for the complex class, you can use it just as you would normally use the + operator for other data types:

```
complex a, b, c;
a = complex(1.5, 2.1);
b = complex(1.1, 1.4);

c = a+b;      // Add two complex numbers a and b
```

Data Declarations in C++

In ANSI C, you cannot mix declarations with the statements of a program. You have to declare all variables at the beginning of a block. C++ does not distinguish between a declaration and other statements and permits you to declare variables anywhere. Thus, in C++, you can write this code:

```
#include <stdio.h>
#include <string.h>
.
.
void convert_string(char *s)
{
    if(s == NULL) return;
    int length = strlen(s);
    .
    .
    for(int i = 0; i <= length; i++)
    {
// Convert characters in the string . . .
    }
}
```

This feature of C++ is handy because you can declare a variable when needed and initialize it immediately. The program is more readable, because the variable is declared and initialized close to where it is actually used.

Another interesting feature of C++ is that you can start using the name of a struct as soon as its definition is started. In C, when you have to define structures containing pointers to its own type, you typically use constructs like this:

```
typedef struct node
{
    struct node *prev; /* Pointer to previous node */
    struct node *next; /* Pointer to next node     */
    void        *info; /* Other members of struct  */
} node;

node *top_node;          /* Define a node */
```

In C++, the same code becomes much simpler:

```
struct node
{
    node *prev; // Pointer to previous node
    node *next; // Pointer to next node
    void *info; // Other members of struct
} node;

node *top_node; // Define a node
```

As you can see, the name of a `struct` can be used inside the definition of the `struct` itself.

How C++ Differs from C

Although C++ proponents often blithely state that C++ is a superset of C, especially ANSI standard C, there are a small number of features in ANSI C that do not work quite the same way in C++. This section is a summary description of the differences.

New Reserved Keywords

To support object-oriented programming, C++ introduced 15 new keywords in addition to those reserved by ANSI C. You have to avoid use of these reserved words in C programs that you want to compile with a C++ compiler:

asm	friend	private	this
catch	inline	protected	throw
class	new	public	virtual
delete	operator	template	

You will encounter most of these keywords in the rest of this book. Some—like `catch`, `template`, and `throw`—are not yet in widespread use, but they are reserved in anticipation of new features being added to the language. The `template` keyword will be used to allow the definition of families of types or functions. Mechanisms for handling exceptions will use the `catch` and `throw` keywords.

Function Prototypes

In ANSI C, if a function does not have a prototype, the compiler assumes that the function returns an integer. C++ strictly enforces the prototypes and generates an error if you use a function without first declaring it. Thus, C++ gives an error when compiling the following old-style C program :

```
main()
{
    printf("Hello, World!\n"); // Allowed in C but not in C++
                               // C++ needs prototype before use
}
```

Of course, in ANSI C, you can remedy this by simply including <stdio.h>, which declares the printf function. You can also get another type of error from old-style C code where functions are declared only when they do not return an int. For example, many C programs declare and use malloc as follows:

```
char *malloc();
int  *raw_data;

raw_data = (int *) malloc(1024);
```

This code generates an error in C++, because C++ interprets empty argument lists differently from the way ANSI C interprets them. In ANSI standard C, an empty argument list in a function's declaration means that the function takes zero or more arguments, but C++ considers a function declaration with an empty argument list to be equivalent to the following:

```
char *malloc(void);
```

When C++ encounters the call, malloc(1024), it produces an error message, because it finds an argument where it expects none.

const Variables

C++ requires you to initialize const variables when you declare them; ANSI C does not. Thus, you can use

```
const buflen;       // OK in ANSI C but not in C++
```

in ANSI C, but in C++, you must write

```
const buflen = 512; // OK in C++ as well as ANSI C
```

where 512 happens to be the value of buflen. Another interesting property of const variables in C++ is that const integers can be used as subscripts and in any constant expression. This is possible because C++ requires const variables to be initialized during declaration. Thus, the compiler always knows the value of a const integer. This enables you to have the following:

```
const buflen = 512;
char  buffer[buflen];   // Allowed in C++ but not in ANSI C
```

Because const integers declared this way are full-fledged variables, you should use them wherever you need constants. In other words, in C++, instead of writing this:

```
#define   EOF       -1
#define   maxlen 128
#define   Pi        3.14159

char one_line[maxlen];      // Define an array to hold a line
```

you should write this:

```
const EOF = -1;             // This is a const int by default
const maxlen = 128;
const double Pi = 3.14159; // This is a floating-point constant

char one_line[maxlen];      // Define an array to hold a line
```

Names declared with #define are not typed, but names declared with const have type. This information can help the compiler detect errors such as calling a function with arguments of the wrong type.

void *Pointers*

ANSI C allows pointers of type void * to be assigned to any other pointer as well as any pointer to be assigned to a pointer of type void *. C++ does not allow assignment of a pointer of type void * to any other pointer without an explicit cast. The following example illustrates the difference:

```
void *p_void;
int  i, *p_i;

p_void = &i;            /* Allowed in both C and C++      */
p_i = p_void;           /* Allowed in C but not in C++    */
p_i = (int *)p_void; /* Cast makes it OK to use in C++ */
```

Initialization of Character Arrays

In ANSI C, you can initialize an array of three characters with the following:

```
char name[3] = "C++"; // Allowed in ANSI C but not in C++
```

After the initialization, the array elements name[0], name[1], and name[2] will be set to C, +, and +, respectively. However, C++ does not allow this type of initialization, because the array does not have room for the terminating null character. In C++, if you need to set up the name array as you did in C, you have to rewrite the initialization as follows:

```
char name[3] = {'C', '+', '+'}; // Allowed in both C and C++
```

Of course, the following initialization is valid in both C and C++, but this sets up a 4-byte array with the last byte set to a null character:

```
char name[] = "C++"; // Allowed in both C and C++
```

sizeof *Operator*

In ANSI C, the size of a character constant such as the expression sizeof('Q') will evaluate to the same value as sizeof(int). But C++ correctly evaluates this to sizeof(char).

Also, in ANSI C, the size of an enum variable is same as sizeof(int). In C++, it will be the size of an integral type, not necessarily sizeof(int).

Scope of enums

In ANSI C, the list of constants appearing in an enum are known throughout the file. C++ considers the constants in an enum to be local to a class or a struct and known only to member and friend functions of the class. For example, the following code is allowed in C++ but not in ANSI C:

```
struct finite_state_machine
{
    enum state{init, reset, end};
// . . .
}

int init(int state);  // Another variable name state is
                      // allowed in C++ but not in ANSI C
```

If a class declares an enum, functions outside the class can refer to the enumerated constants by explicitly qualifying the name using the scope resolution operator.

As an example, suppose you want to refer to the enumerated constant init, which is defined in the class named finite_state_machine. You have to use the notation finite_state_machine::init to access this constant.

Restriction on goto

ANSI C enables you to jump into a block of code, skipping over the declarations and initializations that may appear at the beginning of the block. C++ does not allow this. Here is an example:

```
    goto Start;    // OK in ANSI C but not in C++
// . . .
    {
        int  x = 4, y = 8;
        Node t1;          // This could be a class
        char buf[10];

    Start:
// . . .
    }  // Class destructors are called before leaving block
```

Although jumping into a block is a questionable practice in C, such jumps are almost always bound to be fatal in a C++ program. This is because C++ calls constructors for any class objects created at the beginning of a block, and it calls the corresponding destructors when the block ends. Allowing a jump into the middle of a block would mean that there may be calls to destructors for which there were no matching calls to constructors. Typically, that would be a fatal error for the program.

Summary

C++ was created by extending C with features that are designed to support object-oriented programming. C++'s support for OOP comes through the class and struct constructs, the concepts of overloading functions and operators, and virtual functions. Many features of the C++ language, such as function prototypes and the void and enum types, have been incorporated into ANSI standard C, officially known as ANSI X3.159 1989. Because many syntactical details of C++ are similar to those of ANSI C, a knowledge of ANSI C is helpful when you write programs in C++. This chapter provided a quick overview of ANSI C.

Although C++ compilers accept most ANSI C programs, there are certain constructs in ANSI C that behave differently in C++. You have to avoid inclusion of the new reserved keywords and for the strict enforcement of the function prototypes in C++.

Further Reading

There are many books on C, and all recent books cover the ANSI standard for C. If you are familiar with C as defined in Kernighan and Ritchie's original book[1] and want to learn about the changes wrought by the ANSI standardization of C, you can get the second edition of Kernighan and Ritchie.[2]

If you need a concise reference guide to the ANSI C language and the standard library, you will find *The Waite Group's Essential Guide to ANSI C*[3] handy. This book summarizes the ANSI C keywords and describes each function in the standard C library. Another good reference guide is the one by P. J. Plauger and Jim Brodie.[4] Stephen Kochan's book[5] provides a gentle yet thorough introduction to ANSI C language.

For C++, consult the references listed in Chapter 2. Of the books listed there, Stanley Lippman's primer[6] gives a good introduction to C++.

1. Brian W. Kernighan and Dennis M. Ritchie, *The C Programming Language*, First Edition (Englewood Cliffs, N.J.: Prentice-Hall, 1978), 228 pages.

2. Brian W. Kernighan and Dennis M. Ritchie, *The C Programming Language*, Second Edition (Englewood Cliffs, N.J.: Prentice-Hall, 1988), 261 pages.

3. Nabajyoti Barkakati, *The Waite Group's Essential Guide to ANSI C* (Carmel, Ind.: Howard W. Sams & Company, 1988), 243 pages.

4. P. J. Plauger and Jim Brodie, *Standard C* (Redmond, Wash.: Microsoft Press, 1989), 217 pages.

5. Stephen G. Kochan, *Programming in ANSI C* (Carmel, Ind.: Hayden Books, 1988), 450 pages.

6. Stanley B. Lippman, *C++ Primer* (Reading, Mass.: Addison-Wesley, 1989), 474 pages.

## Chapter 5

Predefined Classes in C++

From Chapter 4, you have an overview of the C++ programming language and how it relates to ANSI standard C. Before you start using C++ to define your own classes, this chapter gets you started with the `iostream` class library that is included with most C++ compilers, including Release 2.0 of the AT&T C++ Language System. This library is C++'s equivalent of C's `stdio` library, which includes the `printf` and `scanf` family. This chapter explains the structure of the classes that form the basis of the `iostream` library and shows how to use these classes for various types of input/output (I/O).

C++ I/O Library

Like C, C++ has no built-in facilities for I/O. Instead, you must rely on a library of functions for performing I/O. In ANSI C, the I/O functions are a part of the standard library, but C++ does not have any standard library yet. Of course, you can call the ANSI C library routines in C++, but for I/O, C++ release 2.0 provides an alternative to `printf` and `scanf`. C++ release 2.0 comes with the `iostream` library, which handles I/O through a class of objects. The following sections will describe simple usage of the `iostream` library and explain the class hierarchy that constitutes the library.

> Prior to release 2.0, C++ programmers used the stream I/O library declared in the header file `<stream.h>`. In C++ release 2.0, the `stream` library has been redesigned and introduced as the `iostream` I/O library, whose basic capabilities are declared in `<iostream.h>`. The `iostream` library is source-code compatible with the older `stream` package. Thus, existing C++ source files that use the `stream` library will compile and work in C++ release 2.0.

Stream I/O in C++

As a programmer learning OOP, you may want to delve into the details of the classes in the `iostream` library, but you do not have to know much about these classes to use the library for simple I/O. To begin with, you should be familiar with the concept of a stream and know the names of the predefined streams. The idea of a stream—a sequence of bytes—features prominently in UNIX and C. As a C programmer, you have heard the term *stream* in connection with ANSI C's file I/O functions that are prototyped in the header file `<stdio.h>`. A *stream* serves as an abstract model of I/O devices such as a disk file, the keyboard, the video display, or even a buffer in memory. In ANSI C, each stream has an associated `FILE` structure that holds the state of the stream and such data items as the buffer used for buffered I/O.

> *Buffered I/O* refers to the use of a block of memory as a temporary storage area for the bytes being read from or written to the stream. ANSI C's stream I/O routines as well as C++'s `iostream` library use a buffer to hold data in transit to and from a stream. For example, in a buffered read operation from a disk file, a fixed size chunk of bytes is read from the disk into a buffer having the same size. The routines requesting data from the file actually read from the buffer. When the buffer has no more characters left, it is automatically refilled by a disk read operation. A similar sequence occurs when you write to a file. Buffered I/O operations are efficient because they minimize time-consuming read/write operations with the disk. Note that you can turn off the buffering.

Each ANSI C stream is identified by the pointer to its associated `FILE` structure. You get back this pointer when you open the stream by calling the `fopen` function—in OOP terminology, this is equivalent to creating the stream object. Not all streams have to be explicitly opened, however. When your C program starts, three streams are already opened for you and need not be opened explicitly. These streams, identified by `stdin`, `stdout`, and `stderr`, are used to get input from the keyboard, display output, and display error messages, respectively. The `scanf` function reads from `stdin`, whereas `printf` sends its output to `stdout`. The `fscanf` and `fprintf` functions can handle I/O with streams that you open.

The C++ `iostream` library is an object-oriented implementation of the abstraction of a stream as a flow of bytes from a source (producer) to a sink (consumer). As you will see later, the `iostream` library includes input streams (`istream` class), output streams (`ostream` class), and streams (`iostream` class) that can handle both input and output operations. The `istream` class provides the functionality of `scanf` and `fscanf`, and `ostream` includes capabilities similar to those of `printf` and `fprintf`. Like the predefined C streams `stdin`, `stdout`, and `stderr`, the `iostream` library includes four predefined streams:

- `cin` is an input stream connected to the standard input. It is analogous to C's `stdin`.

- `cout` is an output stream connected to the standard output and is analogous to `stdout` in C.

- `cerr` is an output stream set up to provide unbuffered output to the standard error device. This is the same as C's `stderr`.

- `clog` is like `cerr`, but it is a fully buffered stream like `cin` and `cout`.

Later on, you will see how to assign other streams to these identifiers so that you can redirect I/O to a different file or device.

Using `iostream`

To use the `iostream` library, your C++ program must include the header file `<iostream.h>`. This file contains the definitions of the classes that implement the stream objects and provides the buffering. The file `<iostream.h>` is analogous to `<stdio.h>` in ANSI C.

Instead of defining member functions that perform I/O, the `iostream` library provides an operator notation for input as well as output. It uses C++'s ability to overload operators and defines `<<` and `>>` as the output and input operators, respectively. Figure 5.1 illustrates how these operators work with the `cin` and `cout` streams.

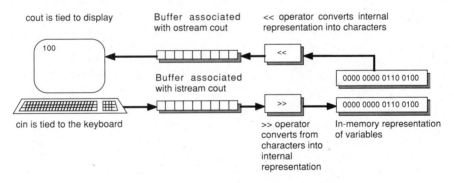

Fig. 5.1. Buffered I/O with streams `cin` and `cout`.

When you see the `<<` and `>>` operators in use, you will realize their appropriateness. For example, consider the following program that prints some variables to the `cout` stream, which is usually connected to standard output:

```
#include <iostream.h>

main()
{
    int    count = 2;
    double result = 5.4;
    char   *id = "Trying out iostream: ";

    cout << id;
    cout << "count = " << count << '\n';
    cout << "result = " << result << '\n';
}
```

When you run this program, it prints the following:

```
Trying out iostream: count = 2
result = 5.4
```

You can make three observations from this example:

- The << operator is a good choice to represent the output operation, because it points in the direction of data movement that, in this case, is toward the cout stream.

- You can concatenate multiple << operators in a single line, all feeding the same stream.

- You use the same syntax to print all the basic data types on a stream. The << operator automatically converts the internal representation of the variable into a textual representation. Contrast this with the need to use different format strings for printing different data types using printf.

Accepting input from the standard input is also equally easy. Here is a small example that combines both input and output:

```
#include <iostream.h>

main()
{
    int    count;
    float  price;
    char   *prompt =
            "Enter count (int) and unit price (float): ";

// Display the prompt string and flush
// to force it to be displayed
    cout << prompt << flush;
```

```
    // Read from standard input
      cin >> count >> price;

    // Display total cost
      cout << count << " at " << price << " will cost: ";
      cout << (price * count) << endl;
}
```

When you run the program and enter the input shown in boldface, the program interacts as follows:

```
Enter count (int) and unit price (float): 5 2.5
5 at 2.5 will cost: 12.5
```

Ignoring, for the moment, items that you do not recognize, notice how easy it is to read values into variables from the cin stream: you simply send the data from cin to the variables using the >> operator. Like the << operator, you can also concatenate multiple >> operators. The >> operator automatically converts the strings into the internal representations of the variables according to their types. The simple syntax of input from cin is in sharp contrast with ANSI C's rather complicated scanf function, which serves the same purpose but needs proper format strings and addresses of variables as arguments.

Manipulators

Among the new items in the last example, you may have noticed the identifiers flush in the first cout statement and endl in the last one. These are special functions known as *manipulators*, which are written in such a way that by placing a manipulator in the chain of << operators, you can alter the state of the stream. The flush manipulator forces cout to display its output without waiting for its buffer to get filled up—the buffer is flushed. The endl manipulator sends a newline to the stream and also flushes the buffer.

Table 5.1 summarizes some of the manipulators available in the iostream package. The manipulators that take arguments are declared in the file <iomanip.h>; the rest are in <iostream.h>.

Table 5.1. C++ iostream Manipulators.

Manipulator	Sample Usage	Effect
dec	cout << dec << intvar; cin >> dec >> intvar;	Converts integers into decimal digits. Similar to the %d format in C.

continues

Table 5.1. continued

Manipulator	Sample Usage	Effect
hex	`cout << hex << intvar;` `cin >> hex >> intvar;`	Hexadecimal conversion as in ANSI C's %x format.
oct	`cout << oct << intvar;` `cin >> oct >> intvar;`	Octal conversion (%o format in C).
ws	`cin >> ws;`	Discards whitespace characters in the input stream.
endl	`cout << endl;`	Sends newline to `ostream` and flushes buffer.
ends	`cout << ends;`	Inserts null character into a string.
flush	`cout << flush;`	Flushes `ostream`'s buffer.

resetiosflags(long)	`cout << resetiosflags`
	`   (ios::dec);`
	`cin >> resetiosflags`
	`   (ios::hex);`
		Resets the format bits specified by the long integer argument.

setbase(int)	`cout << setbase(10);` `cin >> setbase(8);`	Sets base of conversion to integer argument (must be 0, 8, 10, or 16). Zero sets base to the default.
setfill(int)	`cout << setfill('.');` `cin >> setfill(' ');`	Sets the fill character used to pad fields (width comes from `setw`).

setiosflags(long)	`cout << setiosflags`
	`   (ios::dec);`
	`cin >> setiosflags`
	`   (ios::hex);`
		Sets the format bits specified by the long integer argument.

setprecision(int)	`cout << setprecision(6);` `cin >> setprecision(15);`	Sets the precision of floating-point conversions to the specified number of digits.
setw(int)	`cout << setw(6) << var;` `cin >> setw(24) >> buf;`	Sets the width of a field to the specified number of characters.

Formatted I/O

You can use the manipulators for some simple formatted I/O. *Formatting* refers to the process of converting to and from the internal binary representation of a variable and its character string representation. For example, if a 16-bit integer variable holds the bit pattern 0000 0000 0110 0100, its character string representation in the decimal number system is 100 and 64 in hexadecimal. If the base of conversion is octal, the representation will be 144. You can display all three forms on separate lines using the following output statements:

```
#include <iostream.h>

int i = 100;  // Integer initialized to 100 (decimal)

cout << dec << i << endl;  // Displays 100
cout << hex << i << endl;  // Displays 64
cout << oct << i << endl;  // Displays 144
```

This produces the following output:

```
100
64
144
```

What if you want to use a fixed field width of six characters to display each value? You can do this by using the setw manipulators as follows:

```
#include <iostream.h>
#include <iomanip.h>

int i = 100;  // Integer initialized to 100 (decimal)

// Set field widths to 6
cout << setw(6) << dec << i << endl;
cout << setw(6) << hex << i << endl;
cout << setw(6) << oct << i << endl;
```

This changes the output to the following:

```
100
  64
144
```

Here each variable is displayed in a six-character field aligned at the right and padded with blanks at the left. You can change both the padding and the alignment. To change the padding character, you can use the setfill manipulator. For example, just before the cout statements just shown, insert the following line:

```
cout << setfill('.');
```

With that line in place, the output changes to this:

```
...100
....64
...144
```

The spaces to the left are now padded with dots, (which are the fill characters specified by the previous call to the setfill manipulator.)

The default alignment of fixed-width output fields is to pad on the left, resulting in right-justified output. The justification information is stored in a bit pattern called the *format bits* in a class named ios, which forms the basis of all stream classes (see the later discussion and Figure 5.2). You can set or reset specific bits by using the setiosflags and resetiosflags manipulators, respectively. Following is a sample use of these manipulators:

```cpp
#include <iostream.h>
#include <iomanip.h>

int i = 100;  // Integer initialized to 100 (decimal)

cout << setfill('.');

// Left-justified labels followed by right-justified values...

cout << setiosflags(ios::left);
cout << setw(20) << "Decimal";
cout << resetiosflags(ios::left);
cout << setw(6) << dec << i << endl;

cout << setiosflags(ios::left);
cout << setw(20) << "Hexadecimal";
cout << resetiosflags(ios::left);
cout << setw(6) << hex << i << endl;

cout << setiosflags(ios::left);
cout << setw(20) << "Octal";
cout << resetiosflags(ios::left);
cout << setw(6) << oct << i << endl;
```

This example generates the following output:

```
Decimal................100
Hexadecimal............64
Octal.................144
```

This output amply illustrates how the `setiosflags` and `resetiosflags` manipulators work and how they should be used. All you need to know are the names of the enumerated list of formatting flags so that you can use them as arguments to the `setiosflags` and `resetiosflags` manipulators. Table 5.2 lists the format bit flags and their meaning.

To use any of the format flags shown in Table 5.2, insert the manipulator `setiosflags` with the name of the flag as the argument. Use `resetiosflags` with the same argument to revert to the format state before you use the `setiosflags` manipulator.

Table 5.2. Names of Format Flags in `iostream`.

Name of Flag	Meaning When Flag Is Set
`ios::skipws`	Skips whitespace on input.
`ios::left`	Left justifies output within the specified width of the field.
`ios::right`	Right justifies output.
`ios::scientific`	Uses scientific notation for floating-point numbers (such as $-1.23e+02$).
`ios::fixed`	Uses decimal notation for floating-point numbers (such as -123.45).
`ios::dec`	Uses decimal notation for integers.
`ios::hex`	Uses hexadecimal notation for integers.
`ios::oct`	Uses octal notation for integers.
`ios::uppercase`	Uses uppercase letters in output (such as F4 in hexadecimal, $1.23E+02$).
`ios::showbase`	Indicates the base of the number system in the output (a 0x prefix for hexadecimal and a 0 prefix for octal).
`ios::showpoint`	Includes a decimal point for floating-point output (for example, $-123.$).
`ios::showpos`	Shows a positive sign when displaying positive values.

> The notation `ios::left` uses the scope resolution operator `::` to identify `left` as a member of the class `ios`. The names of the format flags are specified with an `ios::` prefix because they are defined in the `ios` class.

Floating-Point Formats

You can control the floating-point format by three flags: `scientific`, `fixed`, `showpoint`, and the `setprecision` manipulator. To illustrate how these affect floating-point formatting, consider the following code, which displays a floating-point value:

```
cout << "123.4567 in default format = ";
cout << 123.4567 << endl;

cout << "123.4567 in 2-digit precision = ";
cout << setprecision(2) << 123.4567 << endl;

// Set the precision back to default
cout << setprecision(0);
cout << "123.4567 in scientific notation = ";
cout << setiosflags(ios::scientific) << 123.4567 << endl;
```

This code displays:

```
123.4567 in default format = 123.4567
123.4567 in 2-digit precision = 123.46
123.4567 in scientific notation = 1.234567e+02
```

The first line displays the value in the fixed format, which is the default. The next line sets the precision to 2—that means you want at most two digits after the decimal point. The floating-point number is rounded and printed. The last line shows the same number in the scientific notation. If you set the `ios::uppercase` flag, the e in the exponent would appear in uppercase.

Overloading <<

Suppose you have defined a class for complex numbers, and you want to use the << operator to display objects of your class. In other words, you want to write code like this:

```
complex z(1.1, 1.2);
// . . .
cout << z;
```

You can do this easily by overloading the << operator. To redefine this operator, you have to define the function `operator<<` for your class. Because the << operator will be used with an `ostream` object on the left and a complex class object on the right, the prototype for the `operator<<` function is this:

```
ostream& operator<<(ostream& s, const complex& x);
```

where the arguments are passed by reference for efficiency, and the const prefix in the second argument says that you do not want the operator to alter the complex number. When you learn more about references, you will see that the operator<< function must return a reference to the stream—this is the key to being able to concatenate the << operators. To illustrate an actual overloading of the << operator, the following sample program uses an abbreviated definition of a complex class and goes through the steps necessary to define and use the << operator:

```cpp
#include <iostream.h>

class complex              // A simple class for complex numbers
{
    float real, imag;
public:
    complex() { real = imag = 0.0;}
    complex(float a, float b) { real = a; imag = b;}
    void print(ostream& s) const;
};

// Need this function so that operator<< can do its job
// by calling this one
void complex::print(ostream& s) const
{
    s << real << " + " << imag;
}

// Overload the operator << for use with complex class

ostream& operator<<(ostream &s, const complex& z)
{
    z.print(s);
    return s;
}

// Test the overloaded << operator . . .

main()
{
    complex a(1.5, 2.1);
    cout << " a = " << a << endl;
}
```

When compiled, linked, and run, this program produces the expected output:

```
a = 1.5 + 2.1
```

The key points are the following:

- First define a member function that prints the class members the way you want.

- Define the operator<< function with a reference to an ostream and a reference to your class as its first and second arguments, respectively. The function's return type should be ostream&. In the body of the function, call your class member function to do the printing and return the first argument, which happens to be the reference to the stream.

- Now you can use the << operator to print objects of your class on a stream.

The iostream *Class Hierarchy*

Now that you know how to use the iostream library for simple I/O, step back and look at Figure 5.2, which graphically illustrates the hierarchy of classes in a typical implementation of the iostream library. As shown in that figure, the streambuf class provides the buffer used by the streams.

All the stream classes are derived from the base class ios, which stores the state of the stream and handles errors. The ios class has an associated streambuf object that acts as the buffer for the stream. The istream and ostream classes, derived from ios, are meant for input and output, respectively. The iostream class uses multiple inheritance to acquire the capabilities of both istream and ostream classes and therefore supports both input and output. The classes istream_withassign, ostream_withassign, and iostream_withassign are derived from istream, ostream, and iostream, respectively, by adding the definition of the assignment operator (=) so that you can redirect I/O by assigning one stream to another.

The predefined streams cout, cerr, and clog are of class ostream_withassign, whereas cin is an instance of istream_withassign class.

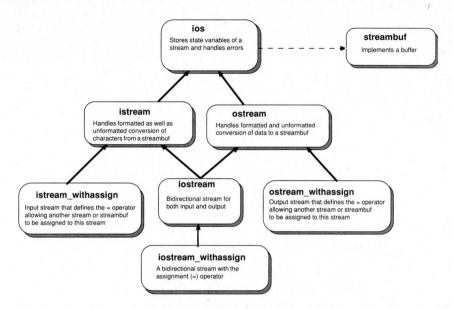

Fig. 5.2. Classes in the C++ `iostream` library.

The classes declared in `<iostream.h>` use inheritance to organize the classes in the library. The iostream classes illustrate an interesting consequence of multiple inheritance. In C++, an instance of a derived class contains a copy of all members of its base class. Thus, a class like `iostream` that inherits from both `istream` and `ostream`—each with the same base class, `ios`—can end up with two copies of the members of `ios`. C++ helps you avoid this when you declare `istream` and `ostream` with `ios` as a *virtual base class*, like so:

```
class istream : virtual public ios { /* ... */ };
class ostream : virtual public ios { /* ... */ };
```

Chapters 8 and 9 give further details about virtual base classes.

File I/O

In ANSI C, file I/O is handled by functions such as fopen to open a file, fclose to close it, and fscanf and fprintf to read from and write to a file. In the iostream package, the classes meant for file I/O are defined in the header file <fstream.h>. Thus, for file I/O, you have to use the following:

```
#include <fstream.h>
```

There are three classes of interest in <fstream.h>: The ifstream class is meant for input, ofstream for output, and the fstream supports both input and output. This section explains how to use the file I/O facilities in <fstream.h>.

Simple File I/O

The simplest way to open a file for I/O is to create an instance of the ifstream or ofstream class, as follows:

```
#include <fstream.h>     // Define classes ifstream and ofstream

// Open file named "infile" for input operations only and
// connect it to the istream "ins" ifstream ins("infile");

// Open file named "outfile" for output operations only and
// connect it to the ostream "outs" ofstream outs("outfile");

// . . .
```

As you can see, you can open a file and connect it to a stream when you create the stream. There are two distinct streams for input and output—ifstream for input and ofstream for output. The ANSI C equivalent of connecting a file to an ifstream is to call fopen with the "r" mode. On the other hand, using ofstream in C++ is similar to calling fopen with the "w" mode in ANSI C.

Before using the stream connected to a file, you should check whether the stream was successfully created. The logical NOT operator ! is overloaded for the stream classes so that you can check a stream using a test like this:

```
// Open stream
   ifstream ins("infile");

// Check whether stream has been opened successfully . . .
   if(!ins)
     {
        cerr << "Cannot open: infile\n";
        exit(1);
     }
```

You do not have to attach an `ifstream` or `ofstream` to any file at the time of creation. You can first create the stream and then open the file later using the open member function of the stream, like this:

```
   ifstream ins;
//...
   ins.open("infile");
// Check whether file opened successfully . . .
   if(!ins)  // Open failed . . .
// . . .
```

You can disconnect the file from the stream by closing it. To do this call the stream's `close` member function:

```
// Close file
   ins.close();
```

This does not destroy the stream, so you can reconnect the stream to another file by calling open again.

Controlling the Stream Operating Modes

When you open a stream by simply providing the name of a file to the stream's constructor, you are taking advantage of C++'s allowance for default argument values. When you call

```
   ifstream ins("infile");
```

the constructor that gets invoked is declared as follows:

```
ifstream(const char *, int = ios::in, int = filebuf::openprot);
```

The last two integer-valued arguments are used with the default values. The second argument to the constructor indicates the mode in which the stream operates. For ifstream, the default is ios::in, which means the file is opened for reading. For an ofstream object, the default mode is ios::out, implying that the file is opened for writing.

What if you want to open a file for output, but you want to append it to an existing file instead of destroying its current contents? You can do this by specifying an operating mode of ios::app. Like the format flags shown in Table 5.2, the stream operating modes are also defined in the ios class—hence the ios:: prefix for the names. Table 5.3 summarizes these modes.

Table 5.3. Stream Operating Modes.

Mode Name	Operation
ios::app	Appends data to the file.
ios::ate	When first opened, positions file at end-of-file (ate stands for *at end*).
ios::in	Opens file for reading.
ios::nocreate	Fails to open file if it does not already exist.
ios::noreplace	If file exists, open for output fails unless ios::app or ios::ate is set.
ios::out	Opens file for writing.
ios::trunc	Truncates file if it already exists.

Note that you can specify more than one mode for a file—simply use a bitwise OR of the required modes. For example, to open a file for output and position it at the end, you would use the modes ios::out and ios::ate as follows:

```
ofstream outs("outfile", ios::out [svb] ios::ate);
```

An Example: Copying Files

As an example of file I/O in C++, consider a utility program that copies one file to another. Assume that the utility is named filecopy and that when you type the following command:

```
filecopy in.fil out.fil
```

filecopy copies the contents of the file named in.fil to a second file named out.fil. Implementing such a program is straightforward: You open the two files, one for input, the other for output, and as you read characters from the input file, write each character to the output file. Listing 5.1 shows a sample implementation of the filecopy utility program.

Listing 5.1. `filecopy`—A utility program that copies one file to another.

```
//------------------------------------------------------------
// File: filecopy.cpp
//
// Copy contents of one file to another.
//------------------------------------------------------------

#include <stdlib.h>
#include <fstream.h>

main(int argc, char **argv)
{
// Check whether there are enough arguments
    if(argc < 3)
    {
        cerr << "Usage: filecopy infile outfile\n";
        exit(0);
    }

// Open the input file and connect it to stream "ins"
    ifstream ins(argv[1]);
    if(!ins)
    {
        cerr << "Cannot open: " << argv[1];
        exit(1);
    }

// Open the output file and connect it to stream "outs"
    ofstream outs(argv[2]);
    if(!outs)
    {
        cerr << "Cannot open: " << argv[2];
        exit(1);
    }

// Read from "ins" and write to "outs"
    char c;
    while(ins.get(c)&& outs) outs.put(c);
}
```

There is another way to implement the last while loop that actually copies between the files. You can read a line at a time and write it out. To read a line, use the same get function but with the address of a buffer and the buffer's size as arguments:

```
const bufsize = 128;
char buf[bufsize];
// . . .
ins.get(buf, bufsize);
```

This call to get will extract from the input stream into the specified buffer, up to
bufsize-1 characters or until a newline character is encountered. Then get places
a terminating null character in the buffer. By default, the get function stops at the
newline character, but you can specify another delimiter as a third argument to the
get function. Note that this call to get is similar to the fgets function in C except
that unlike fgets, get does not copy the newline character into the buffer. Nor does
get skip over the newline character. Therefore, to read lines repeatedly from a file,
you have to extract the newline separately after each line is read. Here is an example
that does this:

```
#include <string.h>      // For prototype of "strlen"
#include <fstream.h>
// . . .
// Assume that streams "ins" and "outs" are already set up
// as shown in Listing 5.1



// Read lines from "ins" and write to "outs"

    const bufsize = 256;
    char buf[bufsize];
    char c;

    while(ins.get(buf, bufsize) && outs)
    {
// Write out buffer using the "write" function
        outs.write(buf, strlen(buf));

// Read leftover newline character and write that out also
        ins.get(c);
        outs.put(c);
    }
```

You can use this as the replacement for the last while loop of Listing 5.1. The actual
writing of the buffer to the output file is done by the write function of the output
stream. As shown, this function simply copies the specified number of characters
from the buffer to the output stream.

Positioning in a File

Many times you have to read files containing binary data that have a specific internal structure. For instance, there may be a 128-byte header followed by blocks of data. Information extracted from the header might tell you that the data you need is at a specific location inside the file. To read this data, you have to be able to position the stream properly before reading from it. In ANSI C, you can use functions such as fseek and ftell for positioning streams. The iostream library also enables you to reposition streams and, as expected, classes provide member functions that accomplish it.

You can position a stream in the iostream library by calling the member functions seekg or seekp of that stream. Because the same stream may be used for both input and output, the stream classes have the concept of a *get position* and a *put position* that respectively indicate the location from which the next read or write will occur. You set the *get position* using seekg, whereas seekp alters the *put position*. For example, to position the stream at the 513th byte in the input stream ins, you can use seekg as follows:

```
ins.seekg(512);     // Next get will start at 513th byte
```

Relative Reference

On the other hand, you can also specify the position relative to some reference point such as the end of the file. For example, to move 8 bytes backward from the end of the stream, use the following:

```
ins.seekg(-8, ios::end);
```

There are three reference points identified by constants defined in the ios class: ios::beg is the beginning of the stream, ios::end is the end, and ios::cur represents the current position.

Getting the Current Position

You can also retrieve the current get or put position in a file. The tellg function returns the current location in an input stream, and tellp returns the corresponding item for an output stream. Both functions return a variable of type streampos. You can save the returned value and use it with seekg or seekp to return to the old location in a file:

```
      streampos saved_pos = ins.tellg();
// Other operations on stream . . .
//  . . .
// Get back to old location
      seekg(saved_pos);
```

Detecting Errors in File I/O

The `iostream` library provides a number of functions for checking the status of a stream. The `fail` function tells you whether something has gone wrong. Thus, you can check for problems by calling `fail` for the stream as follows:

```
      ifstream ins("infile");
      if(ins.fail())
      {
// Stream creation has failed; take appropriate action
//  . . .
      }
```

In fact, the logical NOT operator ! has been overloaded to call `fail` for a stream so that the `if` test can be written more simply as:

```
      if(!ins)
      {
// Handle error . . .
      }
```

Detecting the End-of-File

When reading from or writing to a file, you will want to know whether the end-of-file is reached. The `eof` function returns `true` if the stream is at the end-of-file. Once a stream has reached the end-of-file, it does not perform any I/O even if you attempt an I/O after moving the stream away from the end by using `seekg` or `seekp`. This is because the stream's internal state remembers the encounter with the end-of-file. You have to call `clear` to reset the state before any further I/O can take place. Thus, sometimes `eof` and `clear` are used as follows:

```
// "ins" is an istream. If the stream reached eof, clear the
// state before attempting to read from the stream
      if(ins.eof()) ins.clear();
// Reposition stream and read again . . .
      ins.seekg(-16, ios::cur); // Move back 16 bytes
      ins.get(buf, 8);          // Read 8 bytes into buffer
```

Good and Bad Conditions

Two other member functions, good and bad, indicate the general condition of a stream. As the names imply, good returns true (a nonzero value) if no error has occurred on the stream, and bad returns true if an invalid I/O has been attempted or if the stream has an irrecoverable failure. You can use good and bad in tests such as this:

```
    if(ins.bad())
    {
// Invalid operation . . .
    }

    if(ins.good())
    {
// Everything ok. Continue using stream . . .
    }
```

String I/O

When your application uses a windowing system for I/O, you cannot readily use the streams cin and cout for I/O. With most windowing systems, you can display a string (a null-terminated array of characters) in a window by calling a designated function from the windowing system's library. This is easy to do with plain strings, but how would you display the value of a variable? What you need is a way to send the formatted output to a string that you can then display by using the windowing system's text output functions. In ANSI C, you can use the sprintf function to prepare a formatted string. Similarly, you can use sscanf to extract variables from a string. The C++ iostream package also includes these capabilities in the form of the classes istrstream and ostrstream for reading from and writing to a string, respectively. These classes are declared in the file <strstream.h>.

> The file name strstream.h is too long for MS-DOS systems, because MS-DOS limits file names to eight characters and a three-character extension. Thus, in C++ compilers for MS-DOS systems such as Borland International's Turbo C++, this file is named strstrea.h. However, you can continue using #include <strstream.h> in the source files, because MS-DOS conveniently truncates long file names to eight characters, and the correct file (strstrea.h) gets included.

Writing to a String

A common use of string I/O is to prepare write-formatted output to a string. You need an instance of an `ostrstream` class for this purpose. Typically, you would have a buffer of fixed size in which to place the formatted output. To set up an `ostrstream` object connected to such a buffer, you can use the following code:

```
#include <strstream.h>  // Define the ostrstream class
// . . .
    const buflen = 128;
    char buf[buflen];

// Set up an ostrstream connected to this buffer
    ostrstream s(buf, sizeof(buf));
```

This sets up an output stream connected to a buffer and assumes a stream operating mode of `ios::out`. As with file I/O, you can specify another mode such as `ios::app` to append to an existing string. Sending output to this stream is as easy as writing to `cout`. Here is an example:

```
#include <strstream.h>

main()
{
    const buflen = 128;
    char buf[buflen];
    int   i = 100;
    float x = 3.1415;
// Open an output stream and connect to the buffer
    ostrstream s(buf, buflen);

// Write to the stream
    s << "i = " << i << " x = " << x << ends;

// Display the string on cout
    cout << buf << endl;
}
```

The program displays the following:

```
i = 100 x = 3.1415
```

Although here the program simply displays the buffer by sending it to `cout`, in practice you prepare the output in a buffer because you need it for use by a function that cannot handle formatting.

Reading from a String

Another use of string I/O is to convert characters from a string into internal representations of variables. The istrstream class is meant for reading from buffers. For example, suppose a string holds an integer and a floating-point number. You can extract the variables using the >> operator just as you would from cin. The following program illustrates the use of an istrstream class:

```
#include <strstream.h>

main()
{
    const buflen = 128;
    char  buf[buflen] = "120    6.432";  // A sample buffer
    int   i;
    float x;

// Open an input stream and connect to the buffer
    istrstream s(buf, buflen);

// Read from the stream
    s >> i >> x;

// Display the result on cout
    cout << "i = " << i << " x = " << x << endl;
}
```

The program displays this:

```
i = 120 x = 6.432
```

Conversion from a string to variables is necessary when you read data from a text file into your program.

Summary

Although you can continue to use the ANSI C I/O routines—the printf and scanf family—in C++ programs, there is a better alternative. The iostream I/O library included in AT&T C++ release 2.0 provides a cleaner, object-based mechanism for I/O. Like ANSI C's stdin, stdout, and stderr, the iostream package comes with the following predefined streams: cin; cout; cerr; and clog, which is a buffered version of cerr.

The stream classes use a simple syntax for I/O: The << and >> operators are used for output and input, respectively. The iostream library includes built-in support for I/O operations involving the basic data types such as int, char, float, and double. Additionally, you can overload the << and >> operators to handle I/O for your own classes. This enables you to use a consistent style for all I/O in your program.

The iostream package supports opening and closing files and performing I/O operations with files. The classes declared in <fstream.h> implement the file I/O capabilities similar to those provided by the C functions fopen, fclose, fscanf, and fprintf. Additionally, the I/O package includes several classes, declared in the header file <strstream.h>, that can read from and write to arrays of characters just like C's sscanf and sprintf.

Using the iostream classes is easy, provided you know what classes are available and how to call their public member functions. Although you can learn some of this by browsing through the header files, to make proper use of the member functions you need the documentation for the class. This chapter provides a reasonable amount of information about the iostream classes so that you can begin using them for I/O in your C++ programs.

Apart from the I/O capabilities, the iostream package is also a good example of how C++'s support for OOP can be exploited in a class library. The classes in the library make extensive use of inheritance, including multiple inheritance and the virtual base class mechanism. Chapter 9 covers the details of these features of the C++ language.

## Chapter 6

Building Objects with Classes

Starting with this chapter, you will learn the details of C++'s syntax and see how its constructs support OOP. Instead of going through a litany of seemingly unrelated features, Chapters 6 through 9 explain the syntax of most C++ features in light of some well-defined need that arises when you use object-oriented techniques in your programs. Small examples illustrate the need for a feature and show how a particular construct fulfills the need. This chapter focuses on the `class` and `struct` constructs that you use to define new types of objects. It also provides general guidelines for implementing and using classes.

Classes as Objects

Before you manipulate objects, you need a way to create them. Defining an object involves describing a new data type together with the functions that can manipulate that type. How do you represent a new data type? Clearly, you have to declare the new data type in terms of some existing types. For instance, you can express a `Point` in a two-dimensional plane by an x-y coordinate pair. If each coordinate is represented by an integer type such as `int`, then you can declare a `Point` as a structure:

```
struct Point          // Declare a Point structure
{
    int x, y;
};

struct Point ul, lr;  // Define two Points
```

These are facilities that are already existing in C. If you prefer calling the new type `Point` (without the `struct` prefix), you can do so with the `typedef` facility:

```
typedef struct Point  // Declare a Point type
{
```

```
     int x, y;
} Point;

Point ul, lr;            // Define two Points
```

With this code you use `Point` as the name of a type; however, this is far from being a new data type. For example, you may want to define the addition (+) operator for `Point`. This is not possible with C's `struct`, because C permits you to group data items together into a single entity, but it does not provide any way to declare the functions and operators inside the structure. Thus, it is not a complete data type with well-defined operations. Of course, you can write functions that manipulate `Point` structures, but you do not get any support from the compiler to help associate these functions closely with `Points`.

User-Defined Data Types

To support the definition of a full-fledged data type, all C++ had to do was extend the syntax of `struct` by permitting you to include functions and operators as members of a struct. C++ also made the structure tag or name—the symbol following the `struct`—a stand-alone name, meaning that you can use that name without the `struct` prefix. With these extensions to C's `struct`, C++ enables you to declare and use a `Point` type as follows:

```
struct Point      // Declare a Point type
{
    int x, y;

// Define operations on Point
    void operator+(const Point& p) const
    {
        return Point(x+p.x, y+p.y);
    }
// ...
};

Point ul, lr;    // Define two Points
```

For now, ignore the definition of the operator +; it will be covered in Chapter 7. Note how you can place function definitions inside a `struct` and how the name of a struct serves as a data type.

As an example of another user-defined type, suppose you want to create a `String` data type that provides the functionality of C's null-terminated strings but that uses an object-oriented approach. What you essentially want is to have a pointer to an array of characters and be able to store C-style null-terminated strings in them. Because the length of the string is needed often, you decide to store it as a member as well. Finally, suppose you plan to use the strings to store lines of text that are being edited. Because the number of characters in each line can fluctuate as characters are added or removed, you decide to allocate a slightly larger array than is necessary. To manage the string's storage properly, you also need to store the size of the allocated array. Allowing for the moment a lone function that returns the length of the string, you end up with a preliminary definition of the String as follows:

```
#include <stddef.h>    // For size_t type

struct String
{
    size_t length(void);
// Other member functions...

    char    *p_c;      // Pointer to allocated space
    size_t _length;    // Current length of string
    size_t _maxlen;    // Number of bytes allocated
};
```

This looks clean enough, but there is a problem. By default, all members of the structure are accessible to any function that wants to use them. You do not want this accessibility, because that goes against one of the basic principles of *data abstraction*. This principle advocates that you define an abstract data type (a user-defined type) but hide the internal details of the new type. In particular, for the String objects you would want to hide such details as the way you have decided to implement the string's internal storage. If programs come to rely on these details, you cannot change the implementation in the future, even if a change will clearly make the manipulation of the String type more efficient.

Controlling Access to Class Members

For complete support of data abstraction, you need control over who can access what is in a structure. C++ does introduce a new keyword, class, which you can use exactly like struct. Unlike a struct, however, the members of a class are *not* accessible to any outside functions. In other words, a struct is wide open, but a class is totally hidden. Because neither of these is a good solution, C++ adds three new keywords to help specify access: private, public, and protected. You can explicitly mark sections of a class or a struct as private, public, and protected as follows:

```
#include <stddef.h>    // For size_t type

class String           // Declare the String class
{
public:
    size_t length(void);
// Other publicly accessible member functions...

protected:
// Members accessible to derived classes only
// . . .

private:
// Members accessible to other members of this class

    char    *p_c;      // Pointer to allocated space
    size_t _length;    // Current length of string
    size_t _maxlen;    // Number of bytes allocated
};
```

The `public` section lists the members that are accessible to any function in the program. Only member functions of the class can access the `private` section. When you read about inheritance in Chapter 8, you will learn why the `protected` section is needed. For now, remember that the members in the `protected` section are accessible to classes that are derived from this one. Figure 6.1 illustrates how the access-control keywords work.

Note that you can have multiple `public`, `private`, and `protected` sections in a class. Each section label determines the access level of the members listed between that label and the next label or the closing right brace that marks the end of the class declaration. If you do not provide any label at the beginning of a class, the compiler considers as `private` all members up to the next access control label. On the other hand, everything before the first access specifier is `public` in a `struct`.

Public Functions Can Return Private Values

The `public` section of a class usually declares all the member functions of the class that can be invoked from anywhere in the program. You can think of these functions as the interface to the outside world.

To provide the value of a `private` variable to the outside world, you can write a `public` member function. A good example is the `length` member function of the rudimentary `String` class. The private variable `_length` holds the current length of the `String`. If you were working with a `struct`-based implementation of `String` without the `private` keyword, you would be tempted to access the length as follows:

```
    String this_line;
//  . . .
    if(this_line._length > 0)  // This refers to length of string
//  . . .
```

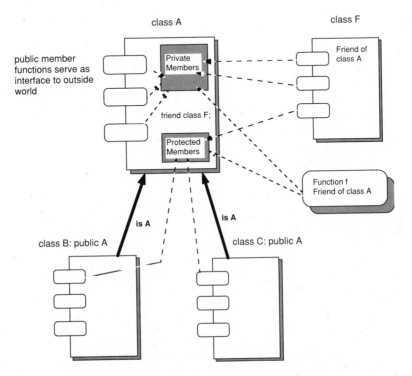

Fig. 6.1. Access control in C++ classes.

However, the principle of information hiding, enforced by the `private` keyword, prevents you from doing this. You can solve the problem by writing a `length` function that returns `_length`. In this case, any function can refer to the length of a string as follows:

```
    if(this_line.length() > 0)  // This refers to length of string
```

This simple example illustrates what you will encounter in all class-based designs: Public member functions provide access to private variables of the class. This insulates the users of the class from any changes to its internal variables.

Member Functions

Member functions are the functions that are designed to implement the operations allowed on the data type represented by a class. To declare a member function, place its prototype in the body of the `class` or `struct`. You do not have to define the function inside the class; the definition can be outside the class or even in a separate file.

Inline Member Functions

In fact, defining a function inside the body of a class has a special consequence. Such definitions are considered to be *inline*, and the entire body of an inline function is repeated whenever that function is called. Thus, if you have an inline function in a class and you call that function often, you can end up using a large amount of memory for the program. The advantage of inline functions is that you avoid the overhead of a function call to execute the body of the function.

Thus, you should make a function inline only if the overhead of calling the function is a large proportion of the time needed to execute the body of the function. When you have a simple function, such as `length` in the `String` class, you can safely define the entire function inside the body of the class, thereby making it inline:

```
class String
{
public:
    size_t length(void) { return _length; }
// . . .

private:
// . . .
    size_t _length;
};
```

You do not have to define a function inside a class to make it inline. C++ provides the `inline` keyword that, when placed in front of a function's definition, makes it inline. Note, however, that you can use an inline function only in the file in which it is defined. This is because the compiler needs the entire definition of an inline function so that it can insert the body of the function wherever the function is called. Thus, you should place the definitions of inline functions in the same header file that declares a class to ensure that every program that uses the class can also use its inline functions.

Inline functions are like preprocessor macros without the pitfalls of macros. For example, the following macro:

```
#define  square(x)  x*x
```

gives you a wrong answer when it is used to evaluate an expression such as square(a+b), because it doesn't use parentheses around the macro's argument. However, if you define square as an inline function:

```
inline double square(x) { return x*x; }
```

you can safely use square(a+b) to evaluate the square of a+b, because inline functions work just like any C++ function.

Typical Public Member Functions

The public member functions of a class are important because they are the outside world's gateway to a class. For a class to be useful, it must include a complete set of public member functions. A minimal set should include the following categories of functions:

Class management functions: This is a standard set of functions that perform chores such as creating an instance of the class (*constructor*), destroying it (*destructor*), creating an instance and initializing it by copying from another instance (*copy constructor*), assigning one instance to another (operator= *function*), and converting an instance to some other type (*type conversion operator*). These functions have a standard declaration syntax. You will encounter these functions in this and the following chapter.

Class implementation functions: These functions implement the *behavior* of the data type represented by the class. They are the workhorse of the class. For a String class, these functions might include operator+ for concatenating strings and comparison operators such as operator==, operator>, and operator<. Chapter 7 explains how such functions are defined.

Class access functions: These functions return information about the internal variables of a class. The outside world can access the object's internal state through these functions. The length function in the String class is a good example of this type of member function.

Class utility functions: These member functions, often declared to be private, are used internally within the class for miscellaneous tasks such as error-handling.

const Member Functions

If a member function does not alter any data in the class, you should declare that member function to be a const function. For instance, the length function of the String class simply returns the value of a member variable. It is definitely a const function, because it does not change any data of the String class. You can declare it as such by appending a const to the usual function prototype, like so:

```
size_t length(void) const;
```

This informs the compiler that the length function is not supposed to alter any variable in the class. The compiler will generate an error message if the definition of the length function includes any code that inadvertently assigns a value to any variable in the String class.

Implementing Classes

The difficult part of writing object-oriented programs is deciding which classes or abstract data types you need to solve your problem. Once you know the classes, their inheritance hierarchy, and their desired behavior, implementing the classes is straightforward. The following sections offer some general guidelines.

Header Files: Describing the Interface to a Class

When you implement a class, think of the class as a provider of some service that other classes or functions need. In other words, the class is a server that acts on the requests of its clients. This is the idea behind the client-server architecture, and it works well when you are implementing classes in object-oriented programs. The clients of a class make requests by calling the member functions of that class. The interface to the class refers to the information that a client must have in order to use the facilities of a class. At a minimum, the client has to know the following:

- The names of the public member functions of the class

- The prototypes of the member functions

- The purpose of each member function

Ideally, if you want to use a class, you would want a textual description of the class and how its facilities are meant to be used. In the absence of this information, you may have to manage with the header file that declares the class.

The header file describes the interface to a class. In fact, it shows you everything except the functions that are defined in another file, but your program can access only those members that appear in the public section. Because the public section interface to the class is important to its clients, you should place these declarations at the very beginning of a class. These can be followed by the protected section. The private members can come last, because these members are visible only to the member functions of that class.

Assuming a reasonable assortment of public member functions, a String class might have a header file str.h as shown in Listing 6.1.

Listing 6.1 str.h—Header file for the String class.

```
//------------------------------------------------------------
//  File: str.h
//
//  Declare a "String" data type.
//
//  Note: Couldn't use String.h as name because we include
//        ANSI C's string.h, and some systems (such as MS-DOS)
//        do not differentiate between uppercase and lowercase
//        letters in file names
//------------------------------------------------------------

#if !defined(__STR_H)  // Make sure file is included only once
#define __STR_H

// Include any other required header files . . .
// Note: The header files from the ANSI C library must enclose
//        all function declarations inside a block like this:
//            extern "C"
//            {
//                . . .
//            }
//        Make sure your C compiler does this

#include <stddef.h>     // For "size_t" type
#include <iostream.h>   // For stream I/O
#include <string.h>     // For ANSI C string library

typedef int Boolean;    // For return type of operators

class String
{
public:
// Constructors with a variety of arguments
```

```
    String();
    String(size_t len);
    String(const char *str);
    String(const String &s);

// Destructor
    ~String();

// Overloaded operators
    Boolean operator==(const String &s) const;
    Boolean operator<(const String &s) const;
    Boolean operator>(const String &s) const;
    Boolean operator<=(const String &s) const;
    Boolean operator>=(const String &s) const;
    Boolean operator!=(const String &s) const;

// Assignment operator
    String& operator=(const String& s);

// Type conversion operator
    operator const char*() const;

// Access operator
    char& operator[](int index);

// The + operator concatenates strings
    friend String operator+(const String& s1, const String& s2);

// Function giving access to internal variable
    size_t length(void) const;

// Function to print a String
    void print(ostream& os) const;

private:
// Internal data members of this class

    char   *p_c;     // Pointer to allocated space
    size_t _length;  // Current length of string
    size_t _maxlen;  // Number of bytes allocated
};

// Stream I/O operators for String class

#include <iostream.h>
```

```
ostream& operator<<(ostream& os, String& s);
istream& operator>>(istream& is, String& s);


//---------------------------------------------------------------
//     I N L I N E     F U N C T I O N S
//---------------------------------------------------------------
// l e n g t h
// Return the length of the String

inline size_t String::length(void) const
{
    return _length;
}
//---------------------------------------------------------------
// ~ S t r i n g
// Destroy a String

inline String::~String()
{
    delete p_c;
}
//---------------------------------------------------------------
// o p e r a t o r   c o n s t   c h a r   *
// Convert from String to char pointer

inline String::operator const char*() const
{
    return p_c;
}
//---------------------------------------------------------------
// o p e r a t o r = =
// String equality operator. Returns nonzero if strings are
// equal

inline Boolean String::operator==(const String &s) const
{
// Use ANSI C's strcmp function to compare the strings
// Remember strcmp returns 0 if the strings match, but this
// function has to return non-zero (true) for a match
    return(strcmp(s.p_c, p_c) == 0);
}


#endif
```

Notice the use of the `#if !defined` directive to ensure that the header file is included only once in any file.

It is also good practice to make your header file complete by including all other header files that are required by your class. For example, the `String` class uses the `size_t` type, which is defined in `<stddef.h>`. Instead of making the users of the `String` class include `<stddef.h>` whenever they use the class, you should include that file in the header file for the `String` class. That way, all that a user of the `String` class has to remember is to include `str.h`, the header file that defines the interface to the `String` class.

The file suffix or extension—the characters following the period in a file's name—used for header files and other source files, varies among C++ compilers. In UNIX systems, C++ source files generally use the `.C` extension, whereas C files use the `.c` extension. In UNIX, header files end with `.h` for both C and C++ languages. Under MS-DOS, this is not possible because MS-DOS does not distinguish between lowercase and uppercase letters in file names. C++ compilers under MS-DOS use either `.cpp` or `.cxx` as the extension for C++ files. Header files often mirror this convention and use `.hpp` or `.hxx` as extensions instead of plain `.h`. This book uses `.h` for header files and `.cpp` for C++ source files. By the way, in case you are wondering, the pp in `.cpp` and `.hpp` come from plus-plus, the last two characters in *C++*. The xx in `.cxx` and `.hxx` were picked because if you rotate the plus sign (+) by just the right amount, it looks like an x.

Separate Implementation from Interface

The clients of a class do not need the definition of the member functions of a class, provided they are adequately documented. Therefore, you can place the actual definitions of the member functions in a separate file. For a class like `String`, you would define the interface to the class in the file `str.h`, whereas the member functions are implemented in a second file, such as `str.cpp`. The general layout of `str.cpp` might be like this:

```
//------------------------------------------------------------
//  File: str.cpp
//
//  Implement the member functions of the "String" class.

#include "str.h"    // For declaration of String class
```

```
// Other header files, if needed . . .
// Header files needed by String class should be included
// in str.h

const chunk_size = 8;   // Allocation unit for Strings

//-------------------------------------------------------------
// S t r i n g
// Create a String object and initializes it from a
// from a null-terminated C string

String::String(const char *s)
{
    _length = strlen(s);
    _maxlen = chunk_size * (_length / chunk_size + 1);
    p_c = new char[_maxlen];
    strcpy(p_c, s);
}
//-------------------------------------------------------------
// p r i n t
// Output the String on a specified output stream

void String::print(ostream& os) const
{
    os << p_c;
}
//-------------------------------------------------------------
// o p e r a t o r < <
// Stream insertion operator for String class

ostream& operator<<(ostream& os, String& s)
{
    s.print(os);
    return os;
}
//-------------------------------------------------------------
// Definitions of other member functions . . .
// . . .
//-------------------------------------------------------------
```

When you define a member function outside the body of a class, you have to associate each function with the class by explicitly using the scope resolution operator (::). For the String class, you have to use a String:: prefix with each member function, as shown in the example. The implementation of the other parts of the String class is covered in Chapter 7, and the str.cpp file is shown in its entirety in Listing 8.2.

Using Classes

A well-designed C++ class behaves like one of the basic data types such as `int`, `char`, or `double`, except that a class is likely to allow different types of operations than those allowed for the basic types. This is because the operations defined for a class include all of its public member functions, which can be as diverse as the functionality of a class warrants. Like the basic data types, to use a class in a program, you have to follow these steps:

1. Define one or more instances of the class. These are the objects of object-oriented programming. Just as you would write:

    ```
    double x, y, z;  // doubles named x, y, z
    ```

    to create three instances of `double` variables, you can create three `String` objects with this code:

    ```
    String s1, s2, s3; // Strings named s1, s2, s3
    ```

    For a class that provides all required interface functions, you should be able to create and initialize instances in a variety of ways:

    ```
    String s1 = "String 1";
    String s2("Testing.1..2...3");
    String s3 = s1;
    ```

    In each of these cases, the compiler calls the appropriate constructor and creates the `String`.

2. Call the member functions of the objects and use the available operators to manipulate the objects. For `String` objects, you might write code such as this:

    ```
    #include "str.h"

    main()
    {
        String title("Object-Oriented Programming in C++");

        cout << "title = " << title << endl;

        String first_name("Naba"), last_name("Barkakati");
        String full_name = first_name + " " + last_name;

        cout << "full_name = " << full_name << endl;

        cout << "Enter some text (end with a return):";
        String response;
    ```

```
        cin >> response;
        cout << "You typed: " << response << endl;
    }
```

If you use this program with the full implementation of the String class shown in Listing 8.2, the following is the result when you run this program (user input is in boldface):

```
title = Object-Oriented Programming in C++
full_name = Naba Barkakati
Enter some text (end with a return):This is a test.
You typed: This is a test.
```

Creating Objects on the Fly

There are two ways of creating instances of classes:

- To define the objects just as you define int or double variables

- To create the objects dynamically as needed

When you create objects through definition, the compiler can reserve storage for the objects during compilation. To dynamically create objects, you need a way to get a chunk of memory for the object. In C, you can dynamically create variables or arrays by calling the functions such as malloc or calloc from the C library.

Although you can often create objects by defining instances of classes, dynamic allocation of objects is more interesting because this approach enables you to use as much memory as is available in a system.

Allocating Objects on the Free Store

You may have encountered the term *heap* in reference to dynamic memory allocation in C. The *heap* is the pool of memory from which standard C functions such as malloc and calloc parcel out memory. C++ books and manuals refer to the heap using the term *free store*. In C++, you get the functionality of malloc and calloc by using the new operator, which allocates enough memory to hold all members of a class or a struct.

In C, if you were to define a structure such as Opcode:

```
struct Opcode
{
    char    *name;
    void    (*action)(void);
};
```

you would allocate space for an instance of this structure as follows:

```
struct Opcode *p_code;
p_code = (struct Opcode *) malloc(sizeof(struct Opcode));
```

In C++, the equivalent code to create a new Opcode reduces to this:

```
Opcode *p_code;
p_code = new Opcode;
```

In addition to the cleaner syntax, the new operator provides another advantage. If the Opcode structure has a constructor that takes no arguments, the new operator automatically calls that constructor to initialize the newly created instance of Opcode.

In fact, you have the option of specifying other initial values for an object allocated by new. For example, you can write:

```
String *file_name = new String("cpphelp.doc");
int    *first_byte = new int(128);
```

to allocate and initialize a String and an int object. The String is initialized to "cpphelp.doc", whereas the int is set to 128. The String is initialized by calling the String(const char*) constructor of the String class.

Destroying Objects on the Free Store

In C, when you no longer need memory that you had previously allocated in the heap, you would call the free function to release the memory. In C++, the delete operator serves the same purpose as C's free. Like free, the delete operator expects a pointer to an object as its operand. Thus, if p_code is the pointer to an instance of Opcode created by the new operator, you can destroy it by the statement:

```
delete p_code;  // Frees storage pointed to by p_code
```

In addition to freeing up storage used by the object, if that object's class has a destructor defined, delete calls it to ensure a proper clean-up.

Arrays of Objects on the Free Store

One use of new is to allocate an array of objects. The syntax for this is very much like the way you define arrays. For example, you could define an array of String objects by writing:

```
String edit_buf[128];
```

To create the same array on the free store, you would use this:

```
String *edit_buf = new String[128];
```

You can use the array of Strings as you would any other array. The first String is edit_buf[0], the second one is edit_buf[1], and so on.

There is a special syntax for deallocating the array of objects on free store. You have to specify the size of the array when deallocating it by using the delete operator as follows:

```
delete[128] edit_buf;
```

This ensures that the destructor of the String class is called for each element of the array. Each String object maintains an internal pointer to a character array that is allocated by the constructor and freed by the destructor. Thus, a call to the destructor of each String in the array takes care of properly deallocating the internal char arrays used by the String objects.

Handling Errors in Memory Allocation

If you allocate many objects dynamically, chances are that sooner or later the free space will be exhausted and the new operator will fail. In ANSI C, when malloc or calloc fails, the function returns a NULL pointer (a pointer set to zero). C++ gives you a way to intercept allocation errors. When the new operator fails, it tests a function pointer named _new_handler. If this pointer is zero, new returns a zero just as malloc and calloc do. However, if _new_handler is nonzero, new calls the function whose address is in _new_handler. In other words, you can handle all memory allocation errors in a central function by setting _new_handler to the address of your error-handling function. The advantage of handling errors this way is that you no longer have to test each use of the new operator for a return value of zero.

You can install an error-handler for new in one of two ways:

- The function pointer _new_handler pointer is defined in the header file <new.h> as follows:

  ```
  void (*_new_handler)();
  ```

  Thus, you can simply include <new.h> and directly set the _new_handler pointer as follows:

  ```
  #include <new.h>
  // . . .
  void my_new_handler();  // Our own error-handler
  _new_handler = my_new_handler;
  ```

- The second method is to use the set_new_handler function to install your error-handling function as follows:

  ```
  #include <new.h>
  set_new_handler(my_new_handler);
  ```

Calling Member Functions

In C++, object-oriented programs are built by creating instances of classes (the objects) as necessary. The program does its work by calling the member functions of the objects. The syntax for calling the member functions is similar to the syntax used to call any other function, except that you have to use the . and -> operators to identify the member function within the object. For example, to use the `length` function of a `String` object named s1, you use the . operator to specify the function:

```
String s1;
size_t len;
len = s1.length();
```

Apart from the use of the . operator to identify the function, the calling syntax is like other function calls. As with any function, you have to know the member function's return type as well as the number and type of arguments that it takes. For dynamically allocated objects, use the -> operator as illustrated here:

```
String *p_s = new String("Hello, World!");
size_t len;
len = p_s->length();
```

Using static Member Variables

When you define member variables for a class, each instance of the class gets its own unique copy of the member variables. However, sometimes you want a single variable for all instances of a class. C++ makes use of the `static` keyword to introduce this type of member variable. Here the `static` member variables appear in the context of a rather useful class.

Most C programmers at some time have debugged their program by inserting calls to `printf` or `fprintf` and printing out messages as well as values of variables of interest. These messages can help you pinpoint where a program fails. Often programmers enclose these calls to `fprintf` in an `#if` directive like this:

```
#if defined(DEBUG)
            fprintf(stderr, "Loop ended. Index = %d\n", i);
#endif
```

so that such messages are printed only when the preprocessor macro DEBUG is defined. In C++, you can use a similar strategy for debugging, but instead of inserting calls to `fprintf`, you can get the work done by a Debug class. The class is designed so that whenever an instance of the Debug class is created, it prints a message, properly indented to make it easier to follow the sequence of function calls. The Debug class also provides a member function called `print` that can be used just like `printf`. Listing 6.2 shows the header file `debug.h`, which declares the interface to the class and defines the inline functions.

Listing 6.2. debug.h—Interface to the Debug class.

```
//------------------------------------------------------------
//  File: debug.h
//
//  A class for debugging C++ programs.
//
//------------------------------------------------------------
#if !defined(__DEBUG_H)
#define __DEBUG_H

#include <stdio.h>
#include <stdarg.h>

class Debug
{
public:
    Debug(const char *label = " ");
    ~Debug();
    void print(const char *format, ...);
private:
    unsigned int indent();
    void draw_separator();

    static unsigned int debug_level;
    static unsigned int debug_on;
    static unsigned int indent_by;
    static unsigned int line_size;
    enum {off = 0, on = 1};
};

//------------------------------------------------------------
//        I N L I N E   F U N C T I O N S
//------------------------------------------------------------
// ~ D e b u g
// Destructor for the Debug class

inline Debug::~Debug()
{
    debug_level—;
    draw_separator();
}

#endif
```

At the end of the body of the Debug class, you will notice a number of member variables that are declared with the `static` keyword. These variables are known as `static` *member variables* and the idea is that there will be exactly one copy of these variables for the Debug class.

To see the need for such `static` member variables, consider the `debug_level` member variable which keeps track of how many instances of Debug class have been created thus far. As you can see from Listing 6.3, this information is used to appropriately indent the messages printed by the `print` member function. Clearly, you cannot use `debug_level` to keep a count of the instances of the Debug class if each instance has its own copy of the `debug_level` variable. The solution is to have what you might call a *class-wide global* variable. This is what happens when you use the `static` keyword in front of a member variable.

Listing 6.3. `debug.cpp`—Implementation of the `Debug` class.

```
//------------------------------------------------------------
//   File: debug.cpp
//
//   Implementation of the "Debug" class.
//------------------------------------------------------------
#include "debug.h"

//------------------------------------------------------------
// D e b u g
// Constructor for Debug class

Debug::Debug(const char *label)
{
    if(debug_on)
    {
        int i;
        draw_separator();
        (void) indent();
        fprintf(stderr, "%s\n", label);
    }
    debug_level++;
}
//------------------------------------------------------------
// p r i n t
// Use ANSI C's vfprintf function to print debug message

void Debug::print(const char *format, ...)
{
    if(debug_on)
```

```
        {
            (void) indent();
            va_list argp;
            va_start(argp, format);
            vfprintf(stderr, format, argp);
        }
    }
    //----------------------------------------------------------
    // i n d e n t
    // Indent line according to debug_level; return the
    // number of spaces indented

    unsigned int Debug::indent()
    {
        int i;
        unsigned int num_spaces = debug_level*indent_by;
        for(i = 0; i < num_spaces; i++)
            fputc(' ', stderr);
        return(num_spaces);
    }
    //----------------------------------------------------------
    // d r a w _ s e p a r a t o r
    // Draw a separator using dashes (-) to identify debug levels

    void Debug::draw_separator()
    {
        if(debug_on)
        {
            unsigned int i;
            for(i = indent(); i < line_size; i++)
                            fputc('-', stderr);
            fputc('\n', stderr);
        }
    }
    //----------------------------------------------------------
```

Initializing static *Member Variables*

Listing 6.4 shows a test program that illustrates how the Debug class of Listings 6.2 and 6.3 might be used. At the beginning of this program, you can see the syntax used to refer to the static member variables of the Debug class. To refer to the static member variable of a class, you have to use as prefix the name of the class (not the name of the instance) followed by the scope resolution operator (::). Thus, you can set the debug_level member of the Debug class to zero by writing the following:

```
// Initialize static member "debug_level" of the Debug class
unsigned int Debug::debug_level = 0;
```

Note that except for the Debug:: prefix, this looks like the definition of any other variable in the program.

If you examine Listing 6.3, you will notice that inside the member functions, you can access the static member variables such as debug_level in the same way as you would access any other member variable of the class. Thus, you need the scope resolution prefix (Debug::) for the static member variables only when referring to them outside the scope of the class.

Listing 6.4. dbgtst.cpp—Program to test the Debug class.

```
//-----------------------------------------------------------
//   File: dbgtst.cpp
//
//   Test the "Debug" class.
//-----------------------------------------------------------
#include "debug.h"

// Initialize the debug_level to 0 and debug_on to "on"
unsigned int Debug::debug_level = 0;
unsigned int Debug::debug_on = Debug::on;

// Set number of characters per line to 55
unsigned int Debug::line_size = 55;

// Indent by four spaces for each level
unsigned int Debug::indent_by = 4;
//-----------------------------------------------------------
// f a c t o r i a l
// Recursive function that evaluates factorial

unsigned long factorial(int n)
{
    Debug dbg("factorial");
    dbg.print("argument = %d\n", n);
    if(n == 1) return 1;
    else return n*factorial(n-1);
}
//-----------------------------------------------------------
// m a i n
// Main function to test "Debug" class
```

```
main()
{
    Debug dbg("main");
    unsigned long n = factorial(4);
    dbg.print("result = %ld\n", n);
}
```

To show the effect of `debug_level`, the sample program defines and calls a `factorial` function, which is a recursive function that evaluates the factorial of its integer argument. The `factorial` function creates an instance of the Debug class on each entry. The Debug class increases the indentation as the `debug_level` increases and draws dashed lines to show the increase as well as decrease in `debug_level`. Thus, you expect to see an indented list of calls to `factorial` in the output of this program. Indeed, when you run the program built by compiling and linking the files shown in Listings 6.3 and 6.4, it displays the following output:

```
- - - - - - - - - - - - - - - - - - - - - - - - - - - - - - - - - - - - - - - -
main
    - - - - - - - - - - - - - - - - - - - - - - - - - - - - - - - - - - - - - -
    factorial
        argument = 4
        - - - - - - - - - - - - - - - - - - - - - - - - - - - - - - - - - - - -
        factorial
            argument = 3
            - - - - - - - - - - - - - - - - - - - - - - - - - - - - - - - - - -
            factorial
                argument = 2
                - - - - - - - - - - - - - - - - - - - - - - - - - - - - - - - -
                factorial
                    argument = 1
                    - - - - - - - - - - - - - - - - - - - - - - - - - - - - - -
                - - - - - - - - - - - - - - - - - - - - - - - - - - - - - - - -
            - - - - - - - - - - - - - - - - - - - - - - - - - - - - - - - - - -
        - - - - - - - - - - - - - - - - - - - - - - - - - - - - - - - - - - - -
    result = 24
    - - - - - - - - - - - - - - - - - - - - - - - - - - - - - - - - - - - - - -
```

Here the indentation of the dashed lines clearly shows the sequence of function calls and returns.

> Declare a member variable `static` if you want a single copy of the variable for all instances of a class. You can count the number of instances of a class by incrementing a static member variable in the constructor of the class.

Static Member Functions

Like static member variables, your C++ programs can also use static member functions. In C programs, programmers often define static functions to confine the visibility of a function to a specific file. By using the `static` keyword, you can have more than one function with the same name in different files. C++ goes one step further and enables you to use functions that are `static` within a class. You can invoke such functions without creating any instance of the class. All you have to do is use the scope resolution operator with the name of the class. As an example, suppose you want a static member function of the Debug class that sets the `debug_on` variable. You can declare such a function inside the body of the class as follows:

```
class Debug
{
public:
// . . .
static void set_debug(int on_off);    // Static member function
// . . .
private:
// . . .
}
```

The function is defined just like any other member functions (notice that you do not need the `static` keyword in the definition):

```
void Debug::set_debug(int on_off)
{
    if(on_off) debug_on = on;
    else       debug_on = off;
}
```

Once defined, you can call this function just like an ordinary function but with a `Debug::` prefix as follows:

```
// Turn debugging off
    Debug::set_debug(0);
// . . .
// Turn debugging on
    Debug::set_debug(1);
```

Notice that you do not need an instance of the Debug class to call the `set_debug` function. The scope resolution prefix (`Debug::`) is necessary to indicate which `set_debug` function you are calling. After all, another class may have also defined a static member function named `set_debug`.

Using Pointers to Class Members

Because of encapsulation of data and functions in a class, C++ includes the notion of a *pointer to a class member* in addition to ordinary pointers to class and functions. The pointer to a class member is actually the offset of the member from the beginning of a particular instance of that class. In other words, a pointer to a class member is a relative address, whereas regular pointers denote the absolute address of an object. The syntax for declaring a pointer to a class member is X::*, where X is the name of the class. Thus, if you declare a class as follows:

```
class Sample
{
public:
    short step;              // Member variable
    void set_step(short s);  // Member function
//  . . .
private:
};
```

you can define and initialize a pointer to a short member variable of the Sample class like this:

```
short Sample::*p_s;   // Pointer to short in class Sample
p_s = &Sample::step;  // Initialize to member "step"
```

Notice that to define and even initialize the pointer, you do not need an instance of the Sample class. Contrast this with the way you would initialize a regular pointer to a short variable. With the regular pointer you would have to define a short variable before you can assign its address to the pointer.

With pointers to class members, you need a concrete instance of the class only when using the pointers. Thus, you have to define an instance of the Sample class before you can use the pointer p_s. A typical use of p_s might be to assign a new value to the class member through the pointer:

```
Sample s1;
s1.*p_s = 5;
```

Note that the syntax for dereferencing the pointer is of the form x.*p, where x is an instance of the class and p is a pointer to a class member. If, instead of a class instance, you had a pointer to an instance of a Sample class, the syntax for using p_s changes to this:

```
Sample s1;
Sample *p_sample1 = &s1;
p_sample->*p_s = 5;
```

Pointer to Member Function

The syntax for declaring a pointer to a member function of the class is similar to the syntax used for declaring pointers to ordinary functions. The only difference is that you have to use the class name together with the scope resolution operator (::). Here is an example that defines a pointer to a member function of the class Sample. The definition says that the member function to which p_func points will return nothing but requires a short as argument:

```
void (Sample::*p_func)(short) = Sample::set_step;
```

The sample definition also initializes the pointer p_func to the address of the function set_step of class Sample. You can call the function through the pointer like this:

```
Sample s1;
(s1.*p_func)(2);   // Call function through pointer
```

The following is another small program that shows how pointers to member functions are used:

```
//-----------------------------------------------------------
// Illustrate use of pointer to member function of a class.

#include <iostream.h>

class CommandSet
{
public:
    void help(){cout << "Help!" << endl;}
    void nohelp(){cout << "No Help!" << endl;}
private:
// . . .
};

// Initialize pointer to member function "f_help"

void (CommandSet::*f_help)() = CommandSet::help;

main()
{
    CommandSet set1;

// Invoke a member function through the "f_help" pointer
    (set1.*f_help)();
```

```
    // Redefine the "f_help" pointer and call function again
        f_help = CommandSet::nohelp;
        (set1.*f_help)();
}
```

The example makes two calls to the function via the pointer. In between calls, it changes the value of the pointer. When run, the program displays two messages as follows:

```
Help!
No Help!
```

Pointers to Static Members

Static members of a class are not covered by the syntax used for defining and using pointers to other members of a class. A pointer to a static member is treated just like a regular pointer. For example, if you declare the class in this way:

```
class Clock
{
public:
// . . .
      static double ticks_per_sec;
private:
// . . .
};
```

you can define a pointer to its static member variable as follows:

```
double *p_tick = &Clock::ticks_per_sec;
```

The variable p_tick is just a regular pointer to double, which has been initialized to the static member variable ticks_per_sec of the Clock class. The only point to note is that you have to use the class name with the scope resolution operator to identify the static variable with whose address you are initializing the pointer p_ticks. You would use the pointer p_ticks just like an ordinary pointer to double. For instance, the following statement sets the static variable ticks_per_sec of the Clock class to 18.2:

```
*p_tick = 18.2; // Set 'ticks_per_sec' through pointer
```

Summary

C++ extends the syntax of C's struct and introduces the class construct. These enhancements allow the creation of user-defined data types that you can use just like the built-in types such as int, char, and double. In the terminology of object-oriented programming, the class and struct mechanisms support *data abstraction*, which is one of the basic requirements for creating objects. The class declaration indicates how the object should behave, whereas instances of the class are the objects being manipulated by the program.

A C++ class can include both data and functions as members. The data members represent the internal state of an object of that class; the functions define the behavior of the object. By grouping the members into sections labeled public, private, and protected, you can control which members are accessible to the functions outside the class. The data members are usually made private, and all interactions with the class are through a set of public member functions. To implement a class, you have to declare the class and define all of its member functions. A good strategy for modular implementation is to declare the class in a header file and define the member functions in a separate implementation file.

Once a class is defined, you can create and use objects of that class just as you use built-in data types such as int, char, and double. You can either define the objects like any other variable or create them dynamically by calling the new and delete operators, which are analogous to the C library's malloc and free functions.

## Chapter 7

Defining Operations on Objects

Chapter 6 described how you can use the class and struct constructs to encapsulate data with functions to define a new data type complete with its own operators. That chapter explains the general strategy for implementing and using a class. The implementation should include two components: a header file with the declaration of the class and a source file with the actual definition of the member functions of the class. This chapter describes how to define the member functions and the operators for a class. Although the concept of creating objects using class is straightforward, many small details become important when you are implementing classes in C++. For example, you need to know when to pass arguments by reference and how to ensure that objects are initialized properly. This chapter addresses these questions.

Arguments and Return Values

In C++, you manipulate objects using member functions and operators defined for the class of which the object is an instance. As a C programmer, you know that functions accept one or more arguments and return a value. C employs the *pass-by-value* mechanism for providing a function with its arguments. In pass-by-value, functions receive their argument in a special area of memory called the *stack*, which is a last-in, first-out (LIFO) data structure. Before calling a function, the calling program copies each argument's value onto the stack and passes control to the function. The function retrieves the arguments from the stack and uses them in the body of the function. If necessary, the function can return a single value to the calling program. The net effect of this mechanism of passing arguments is that the function never accesses the actual storage locations of the arguments that its caller provides. Instead, it always works with a local copy of the arguments. On return from the function, the local copies of the arguments are discarded from the stack.

This *pass-by-value* approach is a good choice for argument passing, because it guarantees that a function never alters its arguments. However, as you will see next, pass-by-value is not always good when you have to pass objects around.

Pointers and References

Although a function that receives its arguments by value cannot alter the arguments, what if an argument is the address of a variable—in other words, a *pointer* to the variable? In this case, the function can clearly alter the value of the variable through that pointer. For example, suppose you want to swap the contents of two integer variables. One way to do this is to write a function that accepts pointers to the two int variables, like this:

```
void swap_int(int *p_a, int *p_b)
{
    int temp;
    temp = *p_a;
    *p_a = *p_b;
    *p_b = temp;
}
```

You can use this function to swap integer variables as follows:

```
int x = 2, y = 3;

swap_int(&x, &y);   /* Now x = 3 and y = 2 */
```

Although you can continue to use this type of function in C++ programs, C++ introduces the concept of a reference, which makes it much easier to write this type of function. A *reference* is an alternate name for an object, and you can use it just as you would use the object itself. You can think of a reference as the address of an item except that unlike a pointer, a reference is not a real variable— a reference is initialized when it is defined, and you cannot modify its value later on. The syntax of a reference mimics that of a pointer except that a reference needs an ampersand (&) where the pointer declaration has an asterisk (*). Thus,

```
int *p_i;  // An uninitialized pointer to integer
```

defines an int pointer, whereas the following is a reference to an int variable named i:

```
int &r_i = i;  // Reference to i (an int variable)
```

As a practical example of the use of reference, here is the swap_int function with arguments passed by reference:

```
void swap_int(int &a, int &b)
{
    int temp;
    temp = a;
    a = b;
    b = temp;
}
```

Compare this version of the function with the one that uses pointers. You can see that the version that uses references looks cleaner. You no longer have to dereference pointers in each expression. It is also simpler to use the new version of the function, because you do not have to provide as arguments the address of the integers being swapped. Instead, you call the function as if the arguments were being passed by value:

```
void swap_int(int&, int&);   // Prototype of function

int x = 2, y = 3;

swap_int(x, y);              // Now x = 3 and y = 2
```

The compiler knows from the function's prototype that it has to pass references to the variables x and y.

As you can see from the examples in this section, you can think of a reference as a pointer with a constant value that the C++ compiler automatically dereferences whenever you use it. In other words, given the following:

```
int i;            // An integer variable
int &r_i = i;     // A reference to "i"
int *p_i = &i;    // A pointer to "i"
```

you can think of r_i as being equivalent to p_i, except that wherever you use the expression r_i, the compiler substitutes *p_i for it. Because the value of a reference cannot change from its initial assignment, the C++ compiler does not have to allocate storage for a reference. All it has to do is to implement the semantics of each reference.

Passing by Value Versus Passing by Reference

From the example of swapping integers, you might surmise that references are good for writing functions that need to alter the values of its arguments. Although this is certainly one of the uses of passing arguments by reference, there is another important reason for providing the reference mechanism in C++.

Consider what happens when an object is passed to a function by value. To implement the pass-by-value semantics, the compiler has to copy the object onto the stack before the function is called. For large class objects, copying involves a penalty in space and time. You can avoid these overheads of copying by using a reference to the object as the argument instead of using the object itself. If the function does not modify an argument, you can indicate this by using the const qualifier for that reference argument. Thus, passing argument by reference enhances the efficiency of object-based programming in C++.

Returning a Reference

Just as passing arguments by reference prevents unnecessary copying to the stack, you can return an object by reference to avoid copying the returned object. Check what happens when you return an object by value. Suppose you return a String object from a function add_strings that returns the concatenation of two strings:

```
String add_strings(const String& s1, const String& s2)
{
// In function's body
    String s;
// Append s1 and s2 to s
// . . .
    return s;
}
```

In this case, the return statement has to copy the String s to an area of memory provided by the calling program. To do so properly, the return statement will call a special constructor, the *copy constructor*, which can create and initialize a new instance of an object from an existing one. After creating the copy, return calls the destructor of the String class to destroy String s before returning to the calling program. This is a good example of the work done behind the scenes by the C++ compiler. You probably did not realize that so much extra work was going on in an innocuous return statement.

The example you have just seen illustrates what happens when a function returns an object. Although returning by reference would save the time spent in copying the object, you cannot return a reference to String s, because s is a temporary object that exists only within the function add_strings and is destroyed when the function returns. Thus, you have to be careful what you return by reference. Because a reference is like a pointer, you cannot return a reference to anything that is temporary.

By qualifying an argument to a function by the const keyword, you can inform the C++ compiler that the function should not modify the argument. The compiler will generate an error message if the function inadvertently tries to alter that argument. The const qualifier is significant only for arguments that are pointers or that are passed by reference. This is because changes made by a function to arguments passed by value cannot be seen in the calling program.

A common use of returning by reference is in an access function—a function that gives access to an internal element of an existing object. For example, suppose you want to write a member function named char_at_pos for the String class that gives access to the character at a specified location in an instance of String. In this case, you can safely return a reference to the character at the specified location. Thus, you might write the char_at_pos function as follows:

```
//-------------------------------------------------------------
// c h a r _ a t _ p o s
// Access a character in a String

char& String::char_at_pos(int index)
{
// Check whether index goes beyond allocated length.
// Return last element, if it does
    if(index > _maxlen-1) return p_c[_maxlen-1];
    else   return p_c[index];
}
```

Here is a typical use of the function:

```
    String s1 = "Test";
// . . .

// Print the second character of String s1
    cout << "3rd char = " << s1.char_at_pos(2) << endl;

// Change the first character of s1
    s1.char_at_pos(0) = 'B';   // Now s1 = "Best"
```

You expect the first use of the char_at_pos function to get the character at a specific position in the string, but you may not have realized that you can even set a character to a new value. The second use of char_at_pos is possible only because the function returns a reference to a char. A reference being exactly like the variable itself, you can assign a new value to the returned reference.

If you already know C++, you will realize that a better solution for accessing a character in String would be to overload the [ ] operator. This is indeed true, and a little later in this chapter you will see how to define such operators for a class.

Guidelines for Using References

There are rules of thumb that you can follow when deciding where to use references. You should pass arguments to a function via reference when

- You want the function to modify the arguments.

- The function is not going to modify the arguments, but you want to avoid copying the objects to the stack. In this case, use the const qualifier to indicate that the argument being passed by reference will not be altered by the function.

As for return values, you should return a reference to an object whenever you want to use that return value as the left-hand side of an assignment. Of course, you should return a reference to an object only when the object is guaranteed to persist after the function returns.

Creating and Destroying Objects

Although basic data types such as int and float are simply a chunk of memory that holds a single value, a user-defined class can have many more components, some of which may require additional work during creation besides setting aside a number of bytes of storage. For instance, the String class internally stores a pointer to an array of characters that holds the null-terminated string. For proper functioning, a newly created String object has to set this pointer to a properly allocated array of chars and, quite possibly, initialize that array to a specific string. After all, if you are going to treat String like any other type of variable, you have to be able to handle statements such as these:

```
String this_os = "UNIX";
String new_os = this_os;
```

For proper handling of this type of initialization, C++ allows each class to have a special function called the *constructor*, which has the same name as the class and which does not have any return type. Thus, the constructor for the String class is a function named String. Of course, as with other functions, you can have more than one constructor, each with a unique list of arguments and each meant for a specific type of initialization.

A constructor for a class like String will allocate extra memory for the null-terminated string. This means that there must be a way to release this memory when the String is no longer needed. C++ handles this need through a *destructor*, which is a function with the same name as the class but with a tilde (~) as prefix. Thus, the destructor of the String class is named ~String. Destructors do not take any argument. Therefore, you cannot overload a destructor.

Constructors and Destructors for the String Class

In Chapter 6 you saw a brief description and the declaration of a String class that represents a text string data type, complete with its own operators and string manipulation functions. Based on the general description of the String class in Chapter 6, an instance of a String is shown in Figure 7.1. The idea is to hold a pointer to an array of bytes that will hold a null-terminated array of characters, which is the standard way of representing strings in C and C++. The variables _maxlen and _length denote the size of the allocated array and the length of the string stored in the array, respectively. To allow for insertion of characters into the String, the size of the char array is rounded up to the next higher multiple of a specified chunk of bytes. For example, if the chunk is 8 bytes, the allocated size of array to hold a 10-character string will be 16 bytes—the nearest multiple of 8 that exceeds 10. This idea is useful if you plan to use the String objects in a text editor, for instance, where you will have to allow for insertion of characters into a String.

Listing 6.1 shows the header file str.h, which declares the String class. To refresh your memory, here is a skeleton declaration of the String class showing the private members, the constructors, and the destructor:

```
class String
{
public:
// Constructors with a variety of arguments
    String();
    String(size_t len);
    String(const char *str);
    String(const String &s);

// Destructor
    ~String();

// . . .

private:
// Internal data members of this class
```

```
char   *p_c;      // Pointer to allocated space
size_t _length;   // Current length of string
size_t _maxlen;   // Number of bytes allocated

};
```

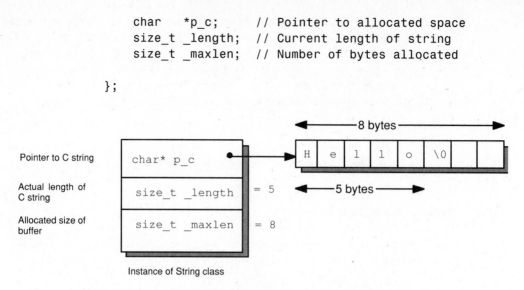

Fig. 7.1. An instance of the `String` class.

Which Constructor Is Called?

If a class defines constructors, the C++ compiler calls an appropriate constructor to initialize each instance of a class. The way you define the class instances controls the constructor that gets called. The constructor with no arguments is called when you define an instance but do not specify any initial value. For other cases, the type of initial value determines the constructor that the C++ compiler calls.

You can define and initialize a class instance in three ways:

- Use the C-style syntax as illustrated by the following example for an instance of the `String` class:

  ```
  String operating_system = "MS-DOS";
  ```

- Use a function call syntax such as this:

  ```
  String operating_system("MS-DOS");
  ```

- Use the `new` operator to allocate on the free store:

  ```
  String *lines = new String[25];
  ```

In the first two cases, the C++ compiler calls the `String(const char*)` constructor because you are initializing the `String` object with a null-terminated character array. Thus, the compiler calls the constructor, which takes as an argument the type of value that you are using to initialize the class instance. In the last case, the compiler calls the constructor that takes no arguments—and it calls this constructor for each of the 25 String objects being created.

Because the String class defines a constructor that accepts a string length as argument, the following is an initialization that might look strange to C programmers but that is appropriate to use with the String class:

```
String eight_blanks = 8;  // A string with eight blanks
```

Based on the description of the String(size_t) constructor, as you will see shortly, this statement creates a String initialized with eight blank spaces.

Default Constructor

The *default constructor* is a constructor that takes no arguments. For the String class, you can define the default constructor as a function that allocates a single chunk of bytes and initializes it to a zero-length string:

```
//------------------------------------------------------------
// S t r i n g
// Creates a String and stores a zero-length string in it

String::String()
{
    _maxlen = chunk_size;    // const chunk_size = 8;
    p_c = new char[_maxlen];
    _length = 0;
    p_c[0] = '\0';
}
```

In lieu of a constructor with no arguments, the upcoming ANSI standard for C++ plans to allow the compiler to use as the default constructor any constructor that has default values specified for all of its arguments. For a Point class that represents a point in the *x-y* plane, such a default constructor might be as follows:

```
Point::Point(int x = 0, int y = 0)
{
// Copy x and y coordinates into internal variables of Point
}
```

The default constructor is called whenever you define an instance of the class without providing any explicit initial value. Thus, if you were to write:

```
String s1;  // s1 is initialized by calling default constructor
```

the String s1 will be initialized by calling String::String(), which is the default constructor of the String class.

There is another case in which the default constructor plays an important role. When you allocate an array of class instances, the C++ compiler automatically calls the default constructor for each element of the array. Thus, if you were to write this:

```
String edit_buf[24];   // Create an array of 24 Strings
```

the default constructor of String will be called to initialize each element of the array edit_buf.

> If you define constructors for a class, you should always define a *default constructor* as well. When you define an array of instances of that class, the C++ compiler initializes each instance in the array by calling the default constructor, which is a constructor that requires no arguments.

Defining Other String Constructors

The String class has a few other constructors besides the default one. One of them takes a number of bytes as argument and creates a blank string with that many bytes. Following is the definition of that constructor:

```
//------------------------------------------------------------
// S t r i n g
// This version creates a blank string of size "len"

String::String(size_t len)
{
    _length = len;
// NOTE: const chunk_size = 8;
    _maxlen = chunk_size*(_length / chunk_size + 1);
    p_c = new char[_maxlen];
    int i;
    for(i = 0; i < len; i++) p_c[i] = ' ';
    p_c[i] = '\0';
}
```

First the constructor computes _maxlen, the number of bytes to allocate. Then it uses the new operator to allocate the array of chars and initialize the array to a null-terminated string containing the specified number of space characters.

Another useful constructor for the String class is one that accepts a null-terminated character array and creates a String from it. You might define this constructor as follows:

```
//-----------------------------------------------------------
// S t r i n g
// Creates a String object and initializes it from a
// null-terminated C string

String::String(const char *s)
{
    _length = strlen(s);
// NOTE: const chunk_size = 8;
    _maxlen = chunk_size*(_length / chunk_size + 1);
    p_c = new char[_maxlen];
    strcpy(p_c, s);
}
```

String Destructor

The destructor's job is to reverse anything that was done in the constructor. Usually, this means releasing memory that was allocated by the constructor when it created the object. For the `String` class, the constructor allocates the array that holds the null-terminated string. The pointer to this array is stored in the private member variable p_c. Thus, the destructor ~`String` should free up the memory allocated for the character array:

```
//-----------------------------------------------------------
// ~ S t r i n g
// Destroy a String

String::~String()
{
    delete p_c;
}
```

Copy Constructor

Another special type of constructor is the copy constructor that is capable of creating a new object as a replica of an existing one. To understand why a copy constructor is necessary, consider the following example. Suppose you decide to pass a `String` object by value to a function append_space that, presumably, adds a space at the end of the string. Thus, the function is declared and used as follows:

```
void append_space(String s);   // Expect argument by value
String s1 = "Result is";
append_space(s1);                // A sample call
```

To implement the call to append_space, the C++ compiler has to make a copy of the String s1 on the stack. As shown in Figure 7.1, the body of a String object contains a pointer to the actual null-terminated string. The constructor of the String class takes care of allocating and initializing this memory.

To make a copy of String s1 on the stack, the compiler will, by default, copy each member of String s1 to the stack. But this results in the situation shown in Figure 7.2. Both the copy and the original String point to the same null-terminated string because the character pointers are identical.

First instance of String class

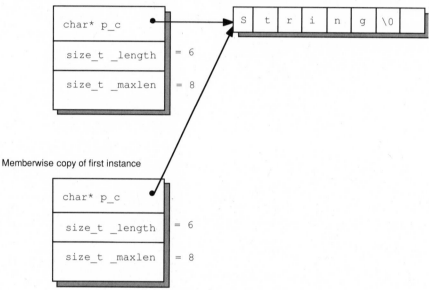

Memberwise copy of first instance

Fig. 7.2. Memberwise copy of one String to another.

To create a complete copy, you have to define a constructor for String that takes a String reference as the argument—in other words, a constructor that can create a copy of a String. For the String class, you might implement this *copy constructor* as follows:

```
#include "str.h"    // Header file that declares the String class

//-----------------------------------------------------------
// S t r i n g   ( c o n s t   S t r i n g & )
// Create a new String as a copy of another String
// This is called the "copy constructor"
```

```
String::String(const String &s)
{
    _length = s._length;
    _maxlen = s._maxlen;
    p_c = new char[_maxlen];
    strcpy(p_c, s.p_c);
}
```

Notice that the copy constructor allocates room for the null-terminated string and copies into it the C string from the String that was passed to it as an argument. When the copy constructor is used, you get a complete copy of the String as shown in Figure 7.3.

First instance of String class

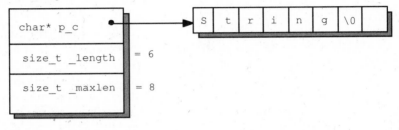

Copy of first instance created by
the copy constructor

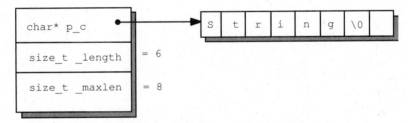

Fig. 7.3. Copying with the copy constructor.

The copy constructor also comes into play when you write:

```
String s1 = "Hello!";
String s2 = s1;
```

In this case, the C++ compiler has to initialize s2 with the value of another String s1. To do this, the compiler looks for a copy constructor for the String class. Note that the copy constructor for String is declared as follows:

```
String(const String&);
```

Because of the form of the declaration, books and manuals on C++ often refer to this as the X(const X&) constructor, where X denotes any class.

When To Provide a Copy Constructor

If your class does not include any pointers that have to be initialized properly, you do not have to provide a copy constructor. The C++ compiler will use a default copy constructor that performs a memberwise copy of one class instance to another. You must provide a copy constructor only for classes with a pointer variable, like the String class. If you do not, the result of copying will be as shown for the String objects in Figure 7.2. Both copies will hold pointers to a single array of characters.

Even if you can live with the memberwise copy, you will run into another problem because of the destructor. If a String object created by a memberwise copy operation is no longer needed, the String destructor will be called. The destructor will free the storage whose address is in the character pointer of that String. This leaves the remaining copy of String with a *dangling* pointer—a pointer that does not point to any valid block of memory. When that remaining copy of String has to be destroyed, the delete operator will be called with the address of memory that has already been freed. Worse yet, if that memory has been allocated to some other object, the destructor will inadvertently free memory belonging to some other object. To avoid such problems, you should always provide a copy constructor for any class that includes dynamically allocated members.

Provide a copy constructor of the form X::X(const X&) for any class that allocates memory in its constructor. The copy constructor ensures that instances of that class are copied correctly.

Member Initializer List

How do you initialize a class that contains an instance of another class? Suppose you decide to implement a Line class that contains two instances of the Point class, each representing an end-point of the line. In this case, your class declaration might look like this:

```
class Point
{
public:
```

```
        Point(double _x=0.0, double _y=0.0)
        {
            x = _x;
            y = _y;
        }
        Point(const Point& p) { x = p.x, y = p.y;}

    private:
        double x,y;      // Coordinates of point
    };

    class Line
    {
    public:
        Line(const Point& b, Point& e) : p1(b), p2 {}
    // . . .
    private:
        Point p1, p2;  // End-points of line
    };
```

Notice the curious way of defining the constructor for the Line class. The constructor takes two Point references as arguments. All it needs to do is copy the points to the internal Points p1 and p2. Of course the obvious way is to write this:

```
    Line::Line(const Point& b, Point& e)
    {
        p1 = b;
        p2 = e;
    }
```

This initialization would work, but it first sets up points p1 and p2 using the default constructor of the Point class and then performs a memberwise copy of b to p1 and e to p2. A more efficient approach is to initialize p1 and p2 with the copy constructor, but by the time you are inside the constructor of Line, the Point instances p1 and p2 are already constructed. C++ solves this problem by allowing the *member initializer list*, which is a list of member variable initializations of the form

```
    variable_name(value)
```

separated by commas. Here variable_name refers to a member variable of the class, and the value within parentheses denotes the value with which that variable is initialized. The member initializer list appears between the function's argument list and its body and is guaranteed to be processed *before* the statements in the function's body are executed.

Initializer List Versus Assignment

For another example of a member initializer list, consider a class Name, which has two String members as follows:

```
class Name
{
public:
    Name(const char *first, const char *last);
// Other public member functions . . .
private:
    String first_name;
    String last_name;
};
```

How would you define the constructor for this class? Most C programmers would define it as follows:

```
Name::Name(const char *first, const char *last)
{
    first_name = first;
    last_name = last;
}
```

Although this looks straightforward, there is a lot of behind-the-scenes work done in initializing the first_name and last_name members in the Name class. To be specific, the compiler takes the following steps:

1. It calls the default constructor of the String class to create the Strings first_name and last_name. Note that the default constructor allocates some space for a character array.

2. The compiler creates two temporary String objects from the character arrays first and last.

3. The compiler calls the copy constructor of the String class to initialize first_name and last_name with the temporary Strings of previous step. The copy constructor also allocates storage for the character array.

4. Finally, the compiler destroys the temporary Strings created in Step 2.

Consider what would happen if you were to rewrite the Name constructor using a member initializer list. The definition changes to this:

```
Name::Name(const char *first, const char *last)
            : first_name(first), last_name(last) {}
```

Now the compiler can construct an instance of Name in a single step by simply processing the initializer list:

1. The compiler calls the `String(const char*)` constructor of the `String` class to create the `String` `first_name` out of `first` and the `String` `last_name` out of `last`.

In this case, storage for character arrays is allocated only once for each `String`, and there are no unnecessary temporary objects. Thus, for reasons of efficiency, you should use initializer lists to initialize member variables. Note that you can use the initializer list syntax for built-in types such as `int`, `double`, and `char*` as well.

Initialization of `const` Member Variables and References

Even if you were to ignore the efficiency of initializer lists, on some occasions you must use member initializers to create an instance of a class. This occurs when the class in question has one of the following:

- A `const` member variable

- A reference member variable

Both of these member variables, according to the rules of C++, must be initialized when they are defined. In other words, these member variables must have a constant value as soon as the class instance is created. The following fictitious class illustrates how to do this:

```
class SampleClass
{
public:
// Constructor uses member initializer list
    SampleClass(int id) : obj_id(id), r_i(i) {}
// . . .
private:
    const int obj_id;
    int        i;
    int&       r_i;
};
```

Notice that the integer argument to the constructor is used to initialize the `const` variable `obj_id`, and the `int` reference `r_i` is set to another integer variable within the class.

Use *member initializer lists* to efficiently initialize class members that are instances of other classes. You must use member initializers to initialize nonstatic `const` and reference members of a class.

Exploiting the Side Effects of Constructor and Destructor

You know that whenever an instance of a class is created, the C++ compiler automatically calls the constructor of that class. If the class instance is an automatic variable, the destructor is called when the instance goes out of scope and has to be destroyed. This means that you can have classes that do all their work in the constructors and destructors. There is nothing wrong with using classes only for the side effects of their constructors and destructors. In fact, sometimes they can lead to an elegant solution to a problem.

As an example, consider the problem of estimating the time taken to execute a block of code. Typically, you would get the time at the start of the computation and then perform the computations a large number of times so that the elapsed time can be measured accurately. The ANSI C library includes functions such as time to get the current time and clock to get the clock ticks elapsed since the program started running. Of these, time has an accuracy of seconds, and clock is somewhat more accurate—each *clock tick* is approximately 55 milliseconds on MS-DOS systems.

A Timer Class

To do the timing in a C++ program, write a Timer class whose constructor calls clock to get the current clock ticks. In the destructor, call clock again and compute the difference of the starting and ending clock ticks. Report the elapsed time in seconds between construction and destruction of an instance of Timer. You can convert clock ticks to seconds by using the preprocessor macro CLOCKS_PER_SEC, which gives the number of clock ticks per second. This macro and the prototype of the clock function appear in the ANSI C header file time.h. Listing 7.1 shows the header file timer.h, which is a typical implementation of the Timer class.

Listing 7.1. timer.h—Implementation of a Timer class.

```
//------------------------------------------------------------
//  File:  timer.h
//
//  Implement a timer that works solely through its
//  constructor and destructor. Use the "clock" function
//  of the ANSI standard C library. The "clock" function
//  returns the number of clock ticks used by the current
//  process. The preprocessor macro CLOCKS_PER_SEC tells
//  how to convert clock ticks to seconds.
//------------------------------------------------------------
#if !defined(__TIMER_H)
#define __TIMER_H
```

```
#include <time.h>      // For definition of the clock_t type
                       // and the CLOCKS_PER_SEC macro

#include <iostream.h> // For output to "cerr" stream

class Timer
{
public:
    Timer() { start = clock();}  // Constructor

    ~Timer()  // Destructor (compute and display elapsed time)
    {
        clock_t stop = clock();
        cerr << "Elapsed time = ";
        cerr << (stop - start)/CLOCKS_PER_SEC;
        cerr << " seconds" << endl;
    }
private:
    clock_t start;     // Store starting clock tick count
};

#endif
```

Using the Timer Class

Listing 7.2 shows the C++ program timertst.cpp, which uses the Timer class to estimate the time taken to execute a set of computations. In Listing 7.2, the function compute does all the work. It defines an instance of Timer. That starts the clock ticking, so to speak. Then the function repeatedly executes the computations in a loop. When the loop ends and the function returns, the Timer object is destroyed. The C++ compiler automatically calls the destructor of the Timer class and the destructor prints out the elapsed time.

Listing 7.2. timertst.cpp—Sample use of the Timer class.

```
//----------------------------------------------------------
//  File: timertst.cpp
//
//  Use the Timer class to time a function.
//----------------------------------------------------------
#include "timer.h"
```

```
//--------------------------------------------------------------
//   c o m p u t e
//   A function that performs some computations

static void compute(unsigned long count)
{
    unsigned long i;
    double a, b, c, d;
    Timer t;                          // Create Timer to time function
    for(i = 0; i < count; i++)
    {
        a = (double)(i-1);
        b = (double)(i+1);
        c = (double)(i+i);
        d = a*b - c;
    }
}
//--------------------------------------------------------------
//  m a i n
//  Main function that times the "compute" function

main()
{
    unsigned long count;
    cout << "How many times? ";
    cin >> count;
    compute(count);
}
```

When you compile the file `timertst.cpp`, the compiler is likely to give a warning about the variable d in the function compute, because that variable is assigned a value but never used. Ignore this warning and build the program. When you run the program, here is a typical output on a 6-MHz IBM PC-AT with an Intel 80287 floating-point coprocessor (user's input is in boldface):

```
How many times? 10000
Elapsed time = 3.406593 seconds
```

The same program running on a 33-MHz Intel 80386-based PC-AT compatible MS-DOS system without a floating-point coprocessor gives the following result:

```
How many times? 10000
Elapsed time = 2.032967 seconds
```

These answers should be accurate to 0.055 second because CLOCKS_PER_SEC is 18.2 on these systems and that translates to 1/18.2 or 0.055 second per clock tick.

As you can see from this example, you can have perfectly useful classes whose instances are used only for the side effects of their construction and destruction.

Defining Functions and Operators

You have seen how to construct and destroy class instances. This section covers the topic of defining functions and operators for a class. The member functions and operators model the behavior of a class. They define how you use the objects represented by a class. The functions are defined like any other functions, except that you have to indicate the association of a function with a class by using the scope resolution operator (::). You have already seen the definition of several constructors for the String class. The following sections present a few other functions for the String class and describe how to define operators for a class.

The this *Pointer*

Before you see how member functions and operators are defined, you need to know about the this keyword. First, here is an observation about the member variables and member functions of a class. Although there is a unique copy of member variables for each instance of a class, all instances share a single set of member functions. Yet none of the member functions that you have seen thus far have any way of indicating the class instance whose member variables are being used in the function. Take, for instance, the length function of the String class. If you write this:

```
String s1 ("Hello"), s2("Hi");
len1 = s1.length();  // len1 = 5
len2 = s2.length();  // len2 = 2
```

each call to length returns a unique answer, yet the length function is defined as follows:

```
inline size_t String::length(void) const
{
    return _length;
}
```

where _length is a member variable of the String class. How did the function know how to return the correct length for each string? The answer is in this.

this *Points to Instance of Class*

The C++ compiler alters each member function in a class by making two changes:

- It passes an additional argument named this, which is a pointer to the specific object for which the function is being invoked. Thus, the call s1.length() will include an argument this set to the address of the String instance s1.

- It adds the this-> prefix to all member variables and functions. Thus, the _length variable in the length function becomes this->_length, which refers to the copy of _length in the class instance whose address is in this.

Typically, you do not have to use this explicitly in a member function, but you can refer to this if there is a need. For example, if you have to return the object to the calling program, you can do so with the following statement:

```
return *this;
```

You can return a *reference* to the object with the same statement. As you will see in the following sections, you have to return references when defining certain operators such as the assignment operator (=).

If you are still wondering about the this keyword and its use, you may want to revisit the example of object-oriented programming in C that appears in Chapter 1. That example showed that the C functions implementing the OOP techniques need a pointer to the object as an argument. The requirement remains in C++, but the syntax of writing member functions is made more palatable to programmers by the behind-the-scenes handling of the pointer to the object through the this keyword.

Operators as Functions

Defining operators for a class is easy once you know how the application of an operator is translated to a function call. For a unary operator such as &, when you write the following:

```
&X
```

where X is an instance of some class, the C++ compiler applies the operator by calling this function:

```
X.operator&()
```

The compiler automatically passes a pointer to the class instance to the function. For binary operators such as +, an expression such as this:

```
X + Y
```

where X and Y are class instances, the compiler calls the function:

```
X.operator+(Y)
```

As you can see, the C++ compiler reduces the application of operators to function calls. Thus, you can overload an operator by defining a function whose name begins with the keyword operator followed by the symbolic notation of that operator.

Arguments to Operator Functions

Like all member functions, operator functions receive a pointer to the class instance in the hidden argument named this. Because this argument is implicit, unary operator functions are defined with no arguments at all. Binary operator functions that are members of the class take a single argument, which is the right-hand side of the operator expression.

However, you can define an operator function as a friend instead of as a member function of the class. As you will see next, there are times when you need to define friend operator functions. When declared as a friend, the operator function requires all arguments explicitly. Thus, to declare operator+ as a friend function of class X, you would write the following:

```
friend X operator+(X&, X&);  // Assume X is a class
```

and thereafter, to evaluate the expression x1 + x2 for two instances of class X, the C++ compiler will call the function operator+(x1, x2).

Every member function of a class implicitly receives a pointer to the current instance of the class in a pointer named this. Inside the body of a member function, you can use this to refer to the address of the class instance upon which the function is to operate. Thus, if a function has to return the instance or a reference to it, you can write the following:

```
return *this;
```

However, you do not have to explicitly use the this pointer in the member functions. The C++ compiler will automatically use the pointer behind the scenes during the process in which members of that instance of the class are accessed.

Operators That You Can Overload

Table 7.1 lists the C++ operators that you are allowed to overload. As you can see, you can overload almost all predefined operators in C++. The only ones that you may not overload are the following:

Member access operator	x.y
Dereferencing pointer to member	x.*y
Scope resolution operator	x::y
Conditional operator	x?y:z

Note that you can only overload the predefined operators and cannot introduce any new operator notations. For example, FORTRAN uses ** to denote exponentiation. In FORTRAN, X**Y means X raised to the power Y. However, even with operator overloading, you cannot define a similar ** operator in C++, because C++ lacks a predefined ** operator.

Table 7.1. C++ Operators That You Can Overload.

Type	Name	Notation	Comments
Unary	Preincrement	++x	Use operator++()
	Postincrement	x++	Use operator++()
	Predecrement	--x	Use operator--()
	Postdecrement	x--	Use operator--()
	Address of	&x	
	Indirection	*x	
	Plus	+x	Define as operator+()
	Minus	-x	Define as operator-()
	Bitwise NOT	~x	
	Logical NOT	!x	
	Type cast	(type)x	Define as operator type()
Arithmetic	Multiply	x*y	
	Divide	x/y	
	Remainder	x%y	
	Add	x+y	Define as operator+(y) or as friend operator+(x,y)
	Subtract	x-y	Define as operator-(y) or as friend operator-(x,y)
Shift	Left shift	x<<y	
	Right shift	x>>y	
Relational	Greater than	x>y	
	Greater than or equal	x>=y	
	Less than	x<y	

Type	Name	Notation	Comments
	Less than or equal	`x<=y`	
	Equal to	`x==y`	
	Not equal to	`x!=y`	
Bitwise	Bitwise AND	`x&y`	
	Bitwise exclusive OR	`x^y`	
	Bitwise OR	`x¦y`	
Logical	Logical AND	`x&&y`	
	Logical OR	`x¦¦y`	
Assignment	Assignment	`x=y`	
	Multiply assign	`x *= y`	
	Divide assign	`x /= y`	
	Remainder assign	`x %= y`	
	Add assign	`x += y`	
	Subtract assign	`x -= y`	
	Left shift assign	`x <<= y`	
	Right shift assign	`x >>= y`	
	Bitwise AND assign	`x &= y`	
	Bitwise XOR assign	`x ^= y`	
	Bitwise OR assign	`x ¦= y`	
Data Access	Subscript	`x[y]`	
	Member selection	`x->y`	
	Dereference member pointer	`x->*y`	
Function call	Function call	`x(y)`	
Comma	Comma	`x,y`	
Storage	new	`x *p=new x`	
	delete	`delete p`	

Operator Precedence Remains Unchanged

Although C++ enables you to redefine the meaning of most of the built-in operator symbols for a class, you cannot change the precedence rules that dictate the order in which operators are evaluated. C++ operators have the same precedence as those of their ANSI C counterparts as shown in Table 4.5. Even if, for some class, you were to define operators + and * to have entirely different meanings from addition and multiplication, in an expression such as this:

```
a + b*c     // a, b, c are some class instances
```

the C++ compiler will still invoke the operator* function to evaluate b*c before calling operator+.

Defining operator+ *for the* String *Class*

As an example of operator overloading, consider the + operator—the binary version—for the String class. A good interpretation of this operator for the String class would be to concatenate two String objects. In other words, a typical use of the + operator for String might be this:

```
String s1("This "), s2("and that"), s3;
s3 = s1+s2;  // Now s3 should contain "This and that"
```

You can get this functionality by defining the following function as a member of the String class:

```
//-----------------------------------------------------------
// o p e r a t o r +
// Member function to concatenate two String objects

String String::operator+(const String& s)
{
    size_t len = _length + s._length;
    char *t = new char[len+1];
    strcpy(t, p_c);
    strcat(t, s.p_c);
    return String(t);
}
```

Because this version of the operator+ is a member function of the String class, it takes only one argument—a reference to the String on the right-hand side of the + operator. The function returns a new String object that is a concatenation of the two Strings that are being added.

Although the member function operator+ works well when adding Strings, it cannot handle another type of use for the operator. Because a String is meant to model a dynamic array of characters, it is natural to allow the use of the operator in expressions such as this:

```
String s1 = "World!";
String s2 = "Hello," + s1; // s2 should be "Hello, World!"
```

In this case, the C++ compiler will interpret the right-hand side of the expression as the following:

```
"Hello".operator+(s1)
```

This is an error, because `"Hello"` is not an instance of a class and therefore has no member `operator+` function that can be applied to `"Hello"`. You might think that a solution would be to convert `"Hello"` to a `String` and then apply the `operator+` function of the `String` class. But, this does not happen because the C++ compiler does not automatically convert the left-hand operand of any member operator functions. However, if you were to define a nonmember `friend operator+` function in the `String` class:

```
friend String operator+(const String& s1, const String& s2)
```

the compiler would convert the expression `"Hello"` + s1 to the following function call:

```
operator+(String("Hello"), s1)
```

which automatically converts the left-hand side of the + operator to a `String`. The definition of the `friend operator+` function is similar to the member function, except that it takes two `String` arguments, and the body of the function has to refer to each argument explicitly. Following is a definition of the function:

```
//-----------------------------------------------------------
// o p e r a t o r +
// Nonmember function that concatenates two String objects
// (Declare as "friend" in String class)

String operator+(const String& s1, const String& s2)
{
    size_t len = s1._length + s2._length;
    char *t = new char[len+1];
    strcpy(t, s1.p_c);
    strcat(t, s2.p_c);
    String s3(t);
    return (s3);
}
```

Also note that the `friend` version of `operator+` function does not require the `String::` scope resolution prefix, because it is not a member function of the `String` class.

Testing Strings for Equality

Another interesting operator is the == operator. A good use of this operator with the String class is to compare two String instances for equality. Because the String class internally maintains a C string, the easiest way to implement this operator is to call the strcmp function from the C library, as shown in the following:

```
#include "str.h"  // Include <string.h>
// . . .


//-----------------------------------------------------------
// o p e r a t o r = =
// String equality operator; return nonzero if strings are
// equal

inline Boolean String::operator==(const String &s) const
{
// Use ANSI C's strcmp function to compare the strings.
// Remember that strcmp returns 0 if the strings match, but
// this function has to return nonzero (true) for a match
    return(strcmp(s.p_c, p_c) == 0);
}
```

You can similarly define other relational operators, such as operator!=, operator>, and operator<.

Accessing and Altering Individual Characters in a **String**

Earlier in this chapter, you encountered a function char_at_pos that returned a reference to a character at a specific position in the character array inside an instance of a String. A better way to provide the functionality of the char_at_pos function is to overload the [ ] operator for the String class. Knowing the implementation of the char_at_pos function, you can define the operator[ ] function as follows:

```
//-----------------------------------------------------------
// o p e r a t o r [ ]
// Access a character in a String

char& String::operator[](int index)
{
// Check whether index goes beyond allocated length.
// If it does, return last element
```

```
            if(index > _maxlen-1) return p_c[_maxlen-1];
            else  return p_c[index];
    }
```

With the [ ] operator defined in this way, you can use it in statements such as this:

```
String s = "hello";
char c = s[4];       // c = 'o', the fifth character of "hello"
s[0] = 'H';          // Now String s contains "Hello"
```

Type Conversion Operator

The String class is an abstraction of a character string and suitable for use in places where C-style null-terminated strings are required. Suppose you want to allow String instances to be used in calls to the C library's string manipulation functions—the ones defined in the header file <string.h>. An example might be an expression such as this:

```
#include <string.h>
// . . .
String command;
// . . .
if(strcmp(command, "quit") == 0) exit(0);
```

Because the strcmp function is declared to accept two const char* arguments, the C++ compiler will successfully make this call, provided it can convert the String command into a const char*. You can help the C++ compiler to do this conversion by defining a *type conversion operator* of the following form:

```
String::operator const char*()
```

Of course, for the String class, all you have to do is return the private char pointer member p_c. Because this function is so simple, you may even want to define it as inline like this:

```
//---------------------------------------------------------
// o p e r a t o r   c o n s t   c h a r   *
// Convert from String to char pointer

inline String::operator const char*() const
{
    return p_c;
}
```

Once this conversion operator is defined, calls to functions such as strcmp will work even with a String as argument.

Assignment Operator for **String** *Class*

The assignment operator, =, is similar to the copy constructor, except that the copy constructor works with an uninitialized copy of an object, and the assignment operator copies an object to another that is already initialized. Thus, for a String object, the assignment operator has to get rid of the existing character array and set up a new one with the new value. A typical implementation of this operator function looks like this:

```
//-----------------------------------------------------------
// o p e r a t o r =
// Assign one String object to another

String& String::operator=(const String& s)
{
// Do nothing if left- and right-hand sides are the same
    if(this != &s)
    {
        _length = s._length;
        _maxlen = s._maxlen;
        delete p_c;
        p_c = new char[_maxlen];
        strcpy(p_c, s.p_c);
    }
    return *this;
}
```

If you compare this function with the copy constructor, you will find the two to be very similar. One crucial difference is the if statement at the beginning of the operator+ function. This test ensures that the assignment operator works properly even when the left- and right-hand sides of the assignment operator are identical. When this happens, the variables p_c and s.p_c refer to the same pointer. Thus, you cannot indiscriminately delete p_c and expect strcpy(p_c, s.p_c) to work. The correctness of the assignment operation is ensured by simply comparing the this keyword with the operator's right-hand side, which is the argument of the opera- tor= function.

Why **operator=** *Returns a Reference*

You may have noticed that the operator= function for the String class returns a String& and may have wondered why this is so. The reason is to allow assignments such as this:

```
String s1, s2, s3;
s1 = s2 = s3 = "None";
```

where the second statement initializes all three strings to the same value. This statement is possible only because the operator= function of the String class returns a reference to a String object and thereby can be the left-hand side of further assignments.

In C++, assignment and initialization are often denoted by very similar statements. Consider the following definitions of String objects:

```
String s1 = "This is initialization";
String s2;
s2 = "This is assignment"
```

This defines two Strings s1 and s2. String s1 is initialized by calling the String(const char*) constructor, and s2 is initially constructed by the default constructor String(). The third statement assigns a value to String s2.

Thus, the definition of a class instance followed by an equal sign indicates *initialization*, whereas a previously defined class instance name appearing on the left-hand side of an equal sign denotes *assignment*.

Overloading the Input and Output Operators

In Chapter 5, you saw the iostream class, which defines the >> and << operators for input and output, respectively. As defined in the header file <iostream.h>, these operators work with all predefined types such as int, long, double, and char*. When you define your own classes such as the String class, you might want to overload the definitions of the << and >> operators so that they work with your classes. For example, once you overload the >> operator, you can read characters from an input stream into a String by writing this:

```
String user_input;
cin >> user_input;   // Accept user's input
```

Similarly, to display a String, you would write the following:

```
String greetings = "Hello, World!";
cout << greetings << endl;
```

Input Operator

The stream extraction operator, >>, is easy to implement. The following version assumes a maximum string length of 256 characters including the null byte and uses the get function of the input stream to read in the characters into an internal array. Then it creates a new String object from that character array and returns the String.

```
//--------------------------------------------------------------
//  o p e r a t o r > >
// Stream extraction operator for String class

istream& operator>>(istream& is, String& s)
{
    const bufsize = 256;
    char buf[bufsize];

    if(is.get(buf, bufsize)) s = String(buf);
    return is;
}
```

Output Operator

To overload the output operator, <<, you need a public member function for the class that can handle the actual output. For the String class, you can define a print function that performs the output as follows:

```
#include "str.h"    // This includes <iostream.h>
// . . .
//--------------------------------------------------------------
//  p r i n t
// Output the String on a specified output stream

void String::print(ostream& os) const
{
    os << p_c;
}
```

Once the print function is defined, you can overload the << operator for a String argument as follows:

```
//--------------------------------------------------------------
//  o p e r a t o r < <
// Stream insertion operator for String class

ostream& operator<<(ostream& os, String& s)
```

```
{
    s.print(os);
    return os;
}
```

As you can see, this operator function does its work by calling the member function named `print` from the `String` class. Note that the `ostream` class declares `operator<<` as a `friend` function.

Overloading Operators `new` *and* `delete`

You have already seen how to overload quite a few operators for a specific class. The dynamic storage allocation operators `new` and `delete` are two more interesting operators that you can overload. You might overload operator `new` to use another method for allocating storage. For instance, it is inefficient to allocate many small objects on the free store using the default operator `new`. One way to improve the efficiency is to obtain a large chunk of memory and use that as the pool of memory from which an overloaded version of operator `new` doles out storage for the objects.

Like other operators, overriding `new` and `delete` for any class involves defining the functions `operator new` and `operator delete`.

Some Rules for `new` and `delete`

You have to follow some rules when overriding `new` and `delete`:

- The first argument of `operator new` must be of type `size_t` (as defined in the ANSI C header file `<stddef.h>`) and it must return a `void*`. Thus, a prototype for `operator new` would be:

  ```
  void* operator new(size_t numbytes);
  ```

- The first argument to `operator delete` must be of type `void*`, and it must not return a value. You can also have a second argument of type `size_t`. Thus, a typical prototype for operator delete is the following:

  ```
  void operator(void *p);
  ```

Another interesting point is that whenever you define the functions `operator new` and `operator delete` for a class, the C++ compiler automatically treats them as `static` member functions of that class. This is true even if you do not explicitly declare them `static`. Note that the C++ compiler has to call `new` before the constructor and `delete` after the destructor. In other words, the compiler must be able to call these operators even when no instance of the class exists. To make this possible, the compiler treats `operator new` and `operator delete` as `static`.

The Placement Syntax for `operator new`

There is an intriguing way of using the `new` operator to initialize objects in preallocated memory. This is done with the placement syntax of the `new` operator. The following example shows how you might initialize in-place a buffer with instances of a fictitious `my_widget` class:

```
//------------------------------------------------------------
//  Illustrate placement syntax of operator "new".

#include <iostream.h>
#include <stddef.h>

class my_widget
{
public:
    my_widget(int x, int y) : _x(x), _y(y){}

// Define default new operator
// NOTE: This simply calls global copy of "operator new"
    void* operator new(size_t sz) { return ::operator
new(sz);}

// Define "new" invoked with placement syntax
    void* operator new(size_t sz, void* p)
    {
        return (my_widget*)p;
    }

// Another member function
    int& getx(){ return _x;}

private:
    int _x, _y;
};

//------------------------------------------------------------
// Test program

main()
{
    char buf[10*sizeof(my_widget)];
    int i=1;
```

```
    // Initialize chunks of buf with instances of "my_widget"
        for(char *b=buf; b < buf+10*sizeof(my_widget);
            b += sizeof(my_widget), i++)
        {
            (void) new(b) my_widget(i, i);  // Placement syntax
        }

    // See whether it worked . . .
        my_widget* widget = (my_widget*) buf;

        for(i=0; i<10; i++)
            cout << widget[i].getx() << " ";

        cout << endl;
}
```

When run, this sample program generates the following output:

```
1 2 3 4 5 6 7 8 9 10
```

which is what you would expect because of the way the instances of my_widget are initialized.

This approach of placing a new object in a predefined area of memory is not without purpose. Some environments such as Microsoft Windows and Apple Macintosh have their own memory management schemes that good programs are supposed to follow. If you happen to use C++ to write application programs for such environments, you can get a block of memory by calling an environment-specific function and use the placement syntax of operator new to initialize instances of objects in that block of memory.

Using friend Classes

Sometimes the data hiding rules of C++ classes can be too restrictive. If, for reasons of efficiency, you want a class A to have access to all members of class B, you can do so by embedding the following statement in the declaration of class B:

```
class A;
class B
{
    friend A;  // A can access all members of this class
// . . .
};
```

To see how friend classes are used, consider the following example.

File as an Array

Suppose you want to treat a file as an array of characters. To be specific, you want to create a `File` class and then use it as follows:

```
File f("sample.dat");   // Open a file
char c = f[10];          // Get byte at index 10
f[128] = ']';            // Store ']' into a byte in the file
```

This tells you that you need a `File` constructor that takes a file's name as an argument. In the constructor, you have to open the file and remember the `FILE` pointer, assuming that you use the standard C file I/O functions to the actual I/O operations with the file. Additionally, you have to overload `operator[]` to read from as well as write to the file. With the `File` class alone, it is difficult to define this operator. You can, however, do this elegantly by using a helper class that I call `FileLoc`.

The idea is to define `operator[]` for the `File` class so that applying the operator to a `File` implies creation of a `FileLoc` object—as the name implies, this object keeps track of position within the file. The `FileLoc` object positions the stream and defines appropriate operators to read from and write to the disk file. The `File` class and `FileLoc` classes are declared as friends of each other so that the I/O operations can be as efficient as possible.

Listing 7.3 shows the actual declarations of the classes as well as a small test program.

Listing 7.3. `farray.cpp`—Illustration of classes that treat a disk file as an array of characters.

```
//-----------------------------------------------------------
//   File: farray.cpp
//
//   Treat a file as an array of bytes.
//-----------------------------------------------------------

#include <stdio.h>
#include <iostream.h>


//-----------------------------------------------------------
// Declare the "FileLoc" class—the helper of File class

class File;

class FileLoc
{
public:
    friend File;
```

```
        void operator=(char c);
        void operator=(const char* str);
        operator const char();

    private:
        File* p_file;
        fpos_t file_loc;
        FileLoc(File& f, fpos_t loc): p_file(&f),
file_loc(loc){}
    };
//-----------------------------------------------------------
// Now declare the "File" class

class File
{
public:
    friend FileLoc;

// Constructor open file for read and write operations
    File(const char* name)
    {
        fp = fopen(name, "r+");   // Open for read and write
    }

// Destructor closes file
    ~File() { fclose(fp);}

// operator[] positions file and creates an instance of
FileLoc
    FileLoc operator[](fpos_t loc)
    {
        fseek(fp, loc, SEEK_SET);
        return FileLoc(*this,loc);
    }

private:
    FILE* fp;   // ANSI C stream pointer
};
//-----------------------------------------------------------
//      M e m b e r   F u n c t i o n s
//-----------------------------------------------------------
// o p e r a t o r = ( c h a r )
// Handle assignments of the form:
//      f[n] = c, where f[n] is a FileLoc and c is a char
// by storing the character in the file
```

```
                void FileLoc::operator=(char c)
                {
                    if(p_file->fp != NULL)
                    {
                        putc(c, p_file->fp);
                    }
                }
                //------------------------------------------------
                // o p e r a t o r = ( c h a r * )
                // Handle assignments of the form:
                //      f[n]="string", where f[n] is a FileLoc object
                // This stores the string into the file

                void FileLoc::operator=(const char* str)
                {
                    if(p_file->fp != NULL)
                    {
                        fputs(str, p_file->fp);
                    }
                }
                //------------------------------------------------
                // o p e r a t o r   c o n s t   c h a r ( )
                // Handle assignments of the form:
                //      c = f[n], where f[n] is a FileLoc and c is a char
                // This reads a character from the file.

                FileLoc::operator const char()
                {
                    if(p_file->fp != NULL)
                    {
                        return getc(p_file->fp);
                    }
                    return EOF;
                }
                //------------------------------------------------
                // m a i n
                // A program to test the File and FileLoc classes
                // Before you run program, create a file "test.dat"
                // with the following line:
                //
                //      Testing: File and FileLoc classes

                main()
                {
```

```
        File f("test.dat");
        int i;
        char c;
        cout << "First 14 bytes = " << endl;
        for(i=0; i<14; i++)
        {
            c = f[i];
            cout << c;
        }
        cout << endl;

// Change first 7 bytes to ' ' (blank space)
        for(i=0; i<7; i++) f[i] = ' ';

// Display the first 14 characters again
        cout << "Now the first 14 bytes = " << endl;
        for(i=0; i<14; i++)
        {
            c = f[i];
            cout << c;
        }
        cout << endl;

// Store a string in the file
        f[0] = "Creating";

        cout << "After string insert: the first 25 bytes = " <<
endl;
        for(i=0; i<25; i++)
        {
            c = f[i];
            cout << c;
        }
        cout << endl;
}
```

If you prepare a file named test.dat with the following line:

```
Testing: File and FileLoc classes.
```

and run the program shown in Listing 7.3, you should see the following output:

```
First 14 bytes =
Testing: File
Now the first 14 bytes =
        : File
```

```
After string insert: the first 25 bytes =
Creating File and FileLoc
```

Here is what happens. When you write the following:

```
char c = f[i];  // f is a File, i an integer
```

the expression f[i] results in a FileLoc object, which positions the file to the character at location i. The C++ compiler then applies FileLoc::operator const char() to this FileLoc object. As you can see from the definition of FileLoc::operator const char(), this results in reading a character from the file.

On the other hand, when you write the following:

```
f[i] = c;  // f is a File, i is an integer, c, a char
```

the expression f[i] again creates a FileLoc object, which positions the file to the position i. Next, to write the character to the file, the C++ compiler invokes the function FileLoc::operator=(char). This operator is overloaded for a string argument as well, so that an entire string can be written to a file.

This is a good example of using a friend class as an intermediary when implementing a desired syntax of usage for a class. Here the sole purpose of the FileLoc class is to allow convenient use of the File class so that you can not only view a disk file as an array of characters but you can even use the array-access syntax to read from and write to a file.

Summary

The class construct forms the basis of object-oriented programming in C++. The member functions of a class control how the class may be used. For a class to be as easy to use as the built-in data types, you have to define a complete assortment of member functions for each class. Important among them are the constructors which the C++ compiler calls to initialize a newly created instance of a class. At a minimum, you should provide the default constructor, which takes no arguments, and the copy constructor, which initializes a new instance of a class from an existing instance. When initializing a class that includes instances of other classes as members, you should use member initializer list syntax to initialize these class instances. The initializer list is the only way to initialize constant member variables.

To make classes easy to use, C++ enables you to redefine most operators so that they can be used with instances of a class to perform meaningful operations. For example, for a String class, the + operator can be defined so that it concatenates two Strings. The process of overloading operators involves defining functions whose names begin with the operator keyword followed by the symbol used for the operator.

Although C++ supports strict data hiding, you can use the `friend` keyword to declare one class or a function as a `friend` of another class. A `friend` can access all members of a class—`public` as well as `private` and `protected`. An example illustrates how you can use a `friend` class to implement a convenient syntax of usage for a class that permits you to treat a file as an array of bytes.

## Chapter 8

Using Inheritance in C++

Chapters 6 and 7 focus on data abstraction, which is only one ingredient, albeit an important one, of object-oriented programming. The other two components of OOP are inheritance and polymorphism. Data abstraction helps you define a new data type, but you need inheritance to exploit the common features of related data types or to extend the functionality provided by one or more existing classes. Inheritance is what enables you to categorize circles, rectangles, and triangles as different types of shapes and to share everything that shapes have in common. Through inheritance you can express the differences among related classes as you share the functions and member variables that implement the common features.

Inheritance also helps you to reuse existing code from one or more classes by simply deriving a new class from them. Additionally, you can use inheritance to extend an existing class by adding new members to it. This chapter explains how to use inheritance in C++ classes.

Derived Classes

Suppose you have a C++ class that implements a specific data type, and you need another data type that is similar to the first but has some additional member variables or functions. Instead of creating the new data type from scratch, OOP techniques suggest that you inherit from the existing type and add the necessary additional capabilities to the inherited type. In C++, you can do this by deriving the new class from the existing class. You can add additional capabilities to the derived class by

- defining new member variables.

- defining new member functions.

- overriding the definition of inherited member functions.

Inheritance Can Represent the Is a Relationship

One common use of inheritance is to express the *is a* relationship among various types of objects. The geometric shapes of Chapter 2 are based on this idea. Because a circle *is a* shape and a rectangle *is a* shape, you say that the `circle_shape` and `rectangle_shape` classes inherit from the `shape` class. In some object-oriented languages such as Smalltalk, `circle_shape` would be called a *subclass* of `shape`, which, in turn, would be the *superclass* of `circle_shape`. In C++, you would say that the `circle_shape` and `rectangle_shape` classes are derived from the `shape` class which is their *base class*. Figure 8.1 illustrates this concept graphically. As the figure shows, you might further specialize the `rectangle_shape` class by deriving a `rounded_rectangle_shape` class from it that represents rectangles with rounded corners.

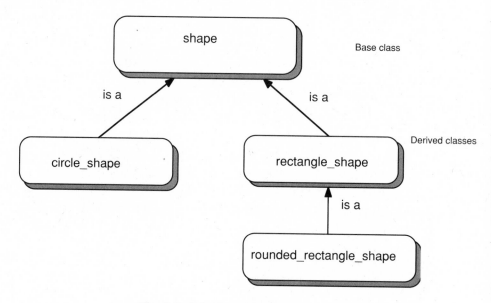

Fig. 8.1. Inheritance in C++.

As you can see, a base class can have more than one derived class, and a derived class can serve as the base class for others. Thus, you end up with a tree-structured hierarchy of classes, in which the classes near the bottom—the leaves—are more specialized versions of the classes at the top.

Inheritance Can Extend a Class

In addition to the view of inheritance as a mechanism for implementing the *is a* relationship among types of objects, you can also use inheritance to extend the functionality provided by one or more classes. Suppose you have a class named single_link that maintains a pointer to another instance of the same class. The plan is to use the single_link objects in a linked list. You might declare the single_link as follows:

```
class single_link
{
public:
    single_link(): _next(0) {}

    single_link(single_link& sl) : _next(sl._next) {}

// Other member functions . . .

protected:
    single_link* _next;  // Link to next "single_link"
};
```

Later on, you might want a doubly linked list for which you would need a double_link class whose instances are capable of holding two pointers—one to the next instance and the other to the previous one. Instead of defining from scratch, you can create the double_link class by simply deriving it from single_link and adding a new member variable like this:

```
// Include declaration of "single_link" class here

class double_link: public single_link
{
public:
    double_link() : single_link(), _previous(0){}

// Other member functions . . .

protected:
    single_link* _previous;  // Add another "link"
};
```

As you will learn soon, making the _next data item in the single_link class protected will allow derived classes such as double_link to directly access the _next pointer. This can improve the speed with which a program can manipulate the items in linked lists that use these classes. Later on in this chapter, you will see an example that uses these *link* classes to construct linked list data structures.

Syntax of a Derived Class

The class construct of C++ already includes the syntax necessary to indicate that a class is derived from another. For a base class, you would declare the class just like a struct, like this:

```
class shape
{
public:
// . . .
};
```

For a derived class, you have to list the name of its base class as follows:

```
class circle_shape: public shape   // Circle is derived from shape
{
public:
// . . .
private:
    double x_center, y_center;
    double radius;
};
```

Access to the Base Class

The public keyword preceding the name of the base class indicates how circle_shape is derived from shape. In this case, circle_shape is publicly derived from shape or, in other words, shape is a public base class of circle_shape. This means that all public and protected members of shape will also be public and protected members of circle_shape.

You can also specify a private keyword in front of the base class name. In this case, all public and protected members of the base class become private members of the derived class. As illustrated in Figure 8.2, the net effect is that if rectangle_shape were privately derived from the shape class, the rounded_rectangle_shape class derived from rectangle_shape could no longer access the public and protected members of shape. In effect, a privately derived class blocks any further access to members of its base class.

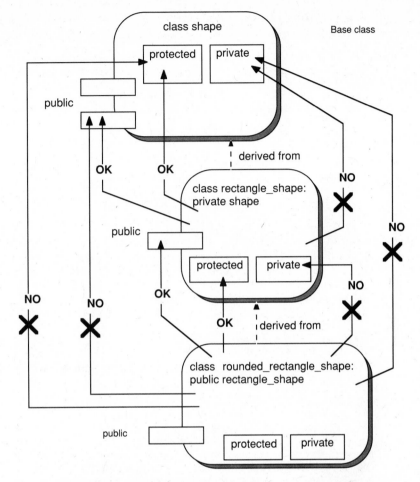

Fig. 8.2. Controlling access to the members of base class.

Note that when you use the `class` keyword to define object types, the default derivation is `private`. In other words, if you forget the access specifier and write this:

```
class rectangle_shape: shape
{
// rectangle_shape is privately derived from shape
// . . .
};
```

you end up with a private derivation of shape. On the other hand, with the `struct` keyword, all derivations are, by default, `public`. Thus, the following declares a `rectangle_shape` class with a `public` base class named `shape`:

```
struct rectangle_shape: shape
{
// rectangle_shape is publicly derived from shape
// . . .
};
```

Using Inheritance to Build a Substring Class

Chapters 6 and 7 use a `String` class as an example. Suppose you want to create a new class called `Substring` that, as the name implies, you use to access a part of a `String` object. Specifically, the following code should be possible:

```
String path_name(32); // 32-character string, set to all blanks
path_name(0,4) = "/bin"; // Replace substring with "/bin"
```

One way to make this work is to overload the `operator()` for the `String` class so that it returns a `Substring`. The C string `"/bin"` is then copied into the substring. The net result of this code should be to set the first four characters of `String` `path_name` to `"/bin"`.

Deriving Substring from String

Because a `Substring` is a `String`, a good way to define `Substring` is to derive it from `String`. Another benefit of deriving it from the `String` class is that all operations defined for the `String` class will be immediately available for the `Substring` class. A `Substring` is a full-fledged `String`, but it holds a reference to the `String` from which it was derived. This is necessary so that the original `String` can be altered through a statement like this:

```
String path_name(32);
path_name(0,4) = "/bin";
```

Here, the expression `path_name(0,4)` should create a `Substring`, and the function `Substring::operator=(const char*)` should replace four characters starting at the first character of `path_name` with the `string` `/bin`.

Listing 8.1 shows a revised `str.h` header file, which declares both the `String` and `Substring` classes. Before defining the `Substring` class, you should change the `private` members of `String` to `protected` so that `Substring` objects can access the internal variables of the `Strings`.

Initializing the Base Class

As you can see from Listing 8.1, declaring the Substring class is straightforward. One important point is the way you initialize a base class from the constructor of the derived class. In Chapter 7 you saw how member initializer lists are used to initialize static members and member classes—class instances that appear as a member of another class. You can use the same technique to initialize the base class in the constructor of a derived class. As an example, consider the following Substring constructor:

```
// Substring constructor
    Substring(String& s, const char *cs, size_t pos, size_t len)
    :
        String(cs, len), s_original(s), _pos(pos) { }
```

This creates a Substring by copying len characters starting at position pos of the specified String. As you can see, the body of this constructor is empty. All initializations are done through the initializer list, which invokes an appropriate String constructor and initializes the members of the newly created Substring.

**Listing 8.1. Revised `str.h` file with declaration of `String` and
`Substring` classes.**

```
//----------------------------------------------------------------
//  File: str.h
//
//  Declare a "String" class and a "Substring" class derived
//  from the "String" class.
//----------------------------------------------------------------
#if !defined(__STR_H)    // Make sure file is included only once
#define __STR_H

// Include other required header files . . .
// The ANSI C headers work because they are already enclosed
// in an extern "C"{...}
// Make sure your compiler does this

#include <stddef.h>      // For "size_t" type
#include <iostream.h>    // For stream I/O
#include <string.h>      // For ANSI C string library

typedef int Boolean;     // For return type of operators
```

```cpp
class Substring;

class String
{
public:
// Constructors with a variety of arguments
    String();
    String(size_t len);
    String(const char *str);
    String(const char *str, size_t len);
    String(const String &s);

// Destructor
    ~String() { delete p_c;}

// Overloaded operators
    Boolean operator==(const String& s) const
    {
        return(strcmp(s.p_c, p_c) == 0);
    }

// Assignment operator
    String& operator=(const String& s);

// Type conversion operator
    operator const char*() const { return p_c;}

// Access operator
    char& operator[](int index);

// Replace a portion of a string with another
// Used to insert or delete parts of a string
    String& replace(size_t pos, size_t len, const char* s);

//---------------------------------------------------------------
// o p e r a t o r ( )
// Overload the function call operator to return a Substring

    Substring operator()(size_t pos, size_t len);

// The + operator concatenates strings
    friend String operator+(const String& s1, const String& s2);

    // Function giving access to internal variable
        size_t length(void) const { return _length;}
```

```
// Function to print a String
    void print(ostream& os) const;

protected:    // So that derived classes can access this data

    char    *p_c;      // Pointer to allocated space
    size_t _length;  // Current length of string
    size_t _maxlen;  // Number of bytes allocated

};

// Stream I/O for String class

ostream& operator<<(ostream& os, String& s);
istream& operator>>(istream& is, String& s);

//------------------------------------------------------------
// Declare the "Substring" class

class Substring: public String
{
public:
    friend String;   // Give the String class access to this one

// Substring operators . . .
    String& operator=(const char* str)
    {
        return s_original.replace(_pos, _length, str);
    }
    String& operator=(Substring& s)
    {
        return s_original.replace(_pos, _length, s.p_c);
    }

private:
    String& s_original;  // Reference to original String
    size_t  _pos;        // Position of Substring in String

// Substring constructor
    Substring(String& s, const char *cs, size_t pos, size_t len)
    :
        String(cs, len), s_original(s), _pos(pos) { }
```

```
// Substring copy constructor

    Substring(const Substring& s) : String(s),
        s_original(s.s_original), _pos(s._pos) { }

};


#endif
```

Modifying the Original String Through a Substring

As mentioned earlier, one reason for introducing the Substring class is to use it in statements such as the following, which modifies a portion of a String through an intermediate Substring created by the String::operator():

```
    String hello = "Hello . . . . . .";
    hello(5,3) = " there";   // Now hello = "Hello there . . ."
```

To make this work, you have to define Substring::operator=(const char*) and have a way of replacing a number of characters in a String. To this end, we added a String::replace function, shown toward the end of Listing 8.2, which shows the file str.cpp, an implementation of the String class. With the String::replace function in place, you can implement the operator= function for the Substring class by simply calling String::replace as follows:

```
    String& operator=(const char* str)
    {
    // Invoke the original String's "replace" function
        return s_original.replace(_pos, _length, str);
    }
```

The `String::operator()`

Substrings are created through the operator() function of the String class. This operator is invoked with two size_t arguments, the first denoting the starting position of the substring, and the second, the substring's length. Once you have defined a constructor for the Substring class that can create a Substring out of a String, you can define the String::operator() as follows:

```
Substring String::operator()(size_t pos, size_t len)
{
    return Substring(*this, &(p_c[pos]), pos, len);
}
```

This function simply returns a new Substring by calling the Substring constructor.

Listing 8.2. `str.cpp`—Implementation of the `String` class.

```
//------------------------------------------------------------
//  File: str.cpp
//
//  Implement the member functions of the "String" class.

#include "str.h"     // For declaration of String class

const chunk_size = 8;

//------------------------------------------------------------
// S t r i n g
// Create a String object and initialize it from a
// null-terminated C string

String::String(const char *s)
{
    _length = strlen(s);
    _maxlen = chunk_size*(_length / chunk_size + 1);
    p_c = new char[_maxlen];
    strcpy(p_c, s);
}
//------------------------------------------------------------
// S t r i n g
// Create a String object and initialize it using a
// specified number of characters from a null-terminated
// C string

String::String(const char *s, size_t len)
{
    _length = len;
    _maxlen = chunk_size*(_length / chunk_size + 1);
    p_c = new char[_maxlen];
    p_c[len] = '\0';
    strncpy(p_c, s, len);
}
```

```
//-------------------------------------------------------------
// S t r i n g
// Create a String and store a zero-length string in it

String::String()
{
    _maxlen = chunk_size;
    p_c = new char[_maxlen];
    _length = 0;
    p_c[0] = '\0';
}
//-------------------------------------------------------------
// S t r i n g
// This version creates a blank string of size "len"

String::String(size_t len)
{
    _length = len;
    _maxlen = chunk_size*(_length / chunk_size + 1);
    p_c = new char[_maxlen];
    int i;
    for(i = 0; i < len; i++) p_c[i] = ' ';
    p_c[i] = '\0';
}
//-------------------------------------------------------------
// S t r i n g
// Create a new String as a copy of another String
// This is often called the "copy constructor"

String::String(const String &s)
{
    _length = s._length;
    _maxlen = s._maxlen;
    p_c = new char[_maxlen];
    strcpy(p_c, s.p_c);
}
//-------------------------------------------------------------
// o p e r a t o r +
// Concatenate two String objects

String operator+(const String& s1, const String& s2)
{
    size_t len = s1._length + s2._length;
    char *t = new char[len+1];
```

```
        strcpy(t, s1.p_c);
        strcat(t, s2.p_c);
        String s3(t);
        return (s3);
}
//-------------------------------------------------------------
// o p e r a t o r =
// Assign one String object to another

String& String::operator=(const String& s)
{
    if(this != &s)
    {
        _length = s._length;
        _maxlen = s._maxlen;
        delete p_c;
        p_c = new char[_maxlen];
        strcpy(p_c, s.p_c);
    }
    return *this;
}
//-------------------------------------------------------------
// p r i n t
// Output the String on a specified output stream

void String::print(ostream& os) const
{
    os << p_c;
}
//-------------------------------------------------------------
// o p e r a t o r < <
// Stream insertion operator for String class

ostream& operator<<(ostream& os, String& s)
{
    s.print(os);
    return os;
}
//-------------------------------------------------------------
// o p e r a t o r > >
// Stream extraction operator for String class

istream& operator>>(istream& is, String& s)
{
```

```
        const bufsize = 256;
        char buf[bufsize];

        if(is.get(buf, bufsize)) s = String(buf);
        return is;
}
//-----------------------------------------------------------------
// o p e r a t o r [ ]
// Access a character in a String

char& String::operator[](int index)
{
// Check whether index goes beyond allocated length
// Return last element, if it does
        if(index > _maxlen-1) return p_c[_maxlen-1];
        else  return p_c[index];
}
//-----------------------------------------------------------------
// r e p l a c e
// Replace a portion of a string with another C string

String& String::replace(size_t pos, size_t len, const char* s)
{
        size_t new_len = strlen(s);

// Check whether there is enough room
        if(_length + new_len - len < _maxlen)
        {
// Move bytes around using ANSI C function "memmove"
            memmove(&(p_c[pos+new_len]), &(p_c[pos+len]),
                    _length-pos-len);
            memmove(&(p_c[pos]), s, new_len);
        }
        else
        {
// Have to reallocate string
            _maxlen = chunk_size * ((_length+new_len-len) /
                                            chunk_size + 1);

            char *t = new char[_maxlen];
// Copy strings over . . .
            memmove(t, p_c, pos);
            memmove(&(t[pos]), s, new_len);
            memmove(&(t[new_len+pos]),
                    &(p_c[pos+len]), _length-pos-len);
```

```
            delete p_c;
            p_c = t;
        }
// Adjust the length of the String
    _length += new_len - len;

// Terminate the new C string
    p_c[_length] = '\0';

    return *this;
}
//------------------------------------------------------------
// o p e r a t o r ( )
// Overload the function call operator to return a Substring

Substring String::operator()(size_t pos, size_t len)
{
    return Substring(*this, &(p_c[pos]), pos, len);
}
```

Testing the Substring Class

The following is a small program that tries out the Substring class through operator() applied to a String variable named hello:

```
// Test Substring class
#include "str.h"

main()
{
    String hello = "Hello......";
    cout << "Before: " << hello << endl;

    hello(5,3) = " there";
    cout << "After: " << hello << endl;

    hello(11,1) = " C++ Programmer";
    cout << "After another 'replace': " << hello << endl;
}
```

You will have to compile this program as well as the str.cpp file shown in Listing 8.2 and link them together to create the executable. When run, the program generates the following output:

```
Before: Hello......
After: Hello there...
After another 'replace': Hello there C++ Programmer..
```

Other Issues for Derived Classes

Now that you have seen a how the `Substring` class is created by deriving from `String`, you should be aware of a few more details about derived classes that were not illustrated by the `Substring` class. This discussion briefly covers these issues.

Overriding Inherited Member Functions

Presumably your reason for declaring a derived class is to model a new type of object in terms of one or more existing types or to extend the functionality of an existing class. Usually, this means that you will be adding new member variables and member functions to complete the functionality of the derived class. Adding new members is straightforward. Simply place in the definition of the derived class any new member you want to add.

Apart from adding new members, you also can redefine member functions that already appear in a base class. You can do so to improve efficiency or to alter the functionality of an existing function. Whatever the reason, you can redefine member functions of the base class freely *provided* you keep in mind the following rule:

> *An overloaded member function in the derived class hides all inherited member functions of the same name.*

This means that if a base class provides one or more versions of a member function, overloading that function in a derived class will hide all inherited versions of the function. An example will make this clear.

Suppose the `String` class defines two versions of a member function called `insert`, one to insert a single character at a specific position and the other to insert a C string. The functions might be declared as follows:

```
class String
{
public:
// . . .
    void insert(size_t pos, char c);
    void insert(size_t pos, char* str);

protected:
// . . .
}
```

After deriving the Substring class from String, you get the bright idea to add another version of the insert function, this one to insert the formatted representation of a float variable into a Substring. With this in mind, you declare the new insert function as follows:

```
class Substring: public String
{
public:
// . . .
    void insert(size_t pos, float x);
private:
// . . .
};
```

The rule for overriding member functions of the base class says that the function Substring::insert hides the functions String::insert. In other words, once you define the new insert function for Substring, you lose access to the insert function that the Substring class inherits from the String class. Keep this in mind when you overload inherited member functions in a derived class.

Order of Initialization of Classes Under Single Inheritance

Another important detail that is worth knowing is the order in which the C++ compiler initializes the base classes of a derived class. When the C++ compiler initializes an instance of a derived class, it has to initialize all the base classes first. If you are working with a hierarchy of classes, it helps to know how C++ initializes the base classes so that you can track down problems that may be caused by improper initialization of a class instance. For single inheritance, the C++ compiler uses the following basic rule during initialization:

1. Initialize the base class, if any.

2. Within the base class, initialize the member variables in the order in which they are declared in the class.

The only catch is that the compiler applies these rules recursively. Also, note that the order in the initializer list does not affect the order in which member variables of a class are initialized. The best way to see the order of initialization is to run a simple example. The following example has a class hierarchy where class C is derived from B and B, in turn, is derived from A. Another class named Data is a member of A and B. The following is a sample implementation of the classes:

```
// Illustrate order of initialization.
#include <iostream.h>
```

```
class Data
{
public:
    Data(int x = 0): _x(x)
    { cout << "Data::Data(" << x << ") ";}
private:
    int _x;
};

class A
{
    Data d1;
public:
    A(int x): d1(x-1) { cout << "A::A(" << x << ") ";}
};

class B: public A
{
    Data d2;
public:
    B(int x): d2(x-1), A(x-2)
    { cout << "B::B(" << x << ") ";}
};

class C: public B
{
public:
    C(int x): B(x-1) { cout << "C::C(" << x << ") ";}
};

main()
{
    C(5);
}
```

When run, this program generates the following output:

```
Data::Data(1) A::A(2) Data::Data(3) B::B(4) C::C(5)
```

If you trace through the program's code, you will see that the C++ compiler first initializes the Data member of class A, followed by class A itself. Then it initializes the Data member of class B, then class B, and finally, class C. Note that all the base classes are initialized before the derived classes.

As you will see in the following discussions, the order of initialization is more complicated when you use multiple inheritance.

Multiple Inheritance

The examples thus far show a derived class with a single base class. This is known as *single inheritance*. C++ also supports the notion of *multiple inheritance*, which enables you to derive a class from several base classes. Support for multiple inheritance was introduced in C++ Release 2.0 to allow implementation of classes that need to share the data and function members of several classes at once. As you will see here, multiple inheritance is often employed to reuse code from several base classes. Of course, you can also use multiple inheritance when you feel that a particular class truly manifests the characteristics of more than one class of objects. For instance, suppose you have two classes: CollectorsItem and Cars. Perhaps the CollectorsItem class has member functions that can estimate the value of an object based on its age and rarity. You might decide to define a new class, AntiqueCars, that inherits from both Cars and CollectorsItem. In C++, you can do so by deriving AntiqueCars from two base classes in the following manner:

```
class Cars;
class CollectorsItem;

class AntiqueCars: public Cars, public CollectorsItem
{
// . . .
};
```

Now the AntiqueCars class can use all public members of both Cars and CollectorsItem classes. Of course, if need be, the AntiqueCars class can also add new member functions and variables. Additionally, the member functions of AntiqueCars can access all protected members of its base classes.

iostream *Uses for Multiple Inheritance*

The iostream class library, included with AT&T C++ Release 2.0, uses multiple inheritance. As elaborated in Chapter 5 and illustrated in Figure 5.2, the iostream library has the istream class for input; the ostream class for output; and a bidirectional iostream class, which is derived from both istream and ostream. Thus, multiple inheritance allows the iostream class to support both input and output operations on a stream.

Virtual Base Class

One problem with inheriting from multiple base classes is that you may end up with more than one instance of a base class. For the sake of concreteness, consider the following hierarchy of classes:

```cpp
// Illustrate the need for "virtual base class"

#include <iostream.h>

class device
{
public:
    device()
    { cout << "device: constructor" << endl;}
};

class comm_device: public device
{
public:
    comm_device()
    { cout << "comm_device: constructor" << endl;}
};

class graphics_device: public device
{
public:
    graphics_device()
    { cout << "graphics_device: constructor" << endl;}
};

class graphics_terminal: public comm_device,
                         public graphics_device
{
public:
    graphics_terminal()
    { cout << "graphics_terminal: constructor" << endl;}
};

main()
{
    graphics_terminal gt;
}
```

Here the device class models a generic UNIX-style device with functions to open and close the device and control it. The comm_device class models a communication device—it adds functions to set the communications parameters. The graphics_device class models a device capable of drawing graphics. Finally, the graphics_terminal class is derived from both comm_device and graphics_device classes. Notice what happens when an instance of the graphics_terminal class is created. The program prints the following:

```
device: constructor
comm_device: constructor
device: constructor
graphics_device: constructor
graphics_terminal: constructor
```

Notice that the constructor for the device base class is called twice, because it appears twice in the inheritance hierarchy—once as base class of comm_device and another time as base class of graphics_device.

Because the graphics_terminal class models a physical device, you would not want two instances of the device base class in every instance of graphics_terminal. What you need is a way to create a graphics_terminal class that inherits from both comm_device and graphics_device, but has only one instance of the device class. You can accomplish this with the virtual base class. Simply add the virtual keyword wherever the class name device appears in the inheritance list of a class. Thus, the new class definitions appear as follows:

```cpp
// Illustrate how "virtual base class" works

#include <iostream.h>

class device
{
public:
    device()
    { cout << "device: constructor" << endl;}
};

class comm_device: public virtual device
{
public:
    comm_device()
    { cout << "comm_device: constructor" << endl;}
};

class graphics_device: public virtual device
{
public:
```

```
        graphics_device()
        { cout << "graphics_device: constructor" << endl;}
};

class graphics_terminal: public comm_device,
                         public graphics_device
{
public:
    graphics_terminal()
    { cout << "graphics_terminal: constructor" << endl;}
};

main()
{
    graphics_terminal gt;
}
```

With this version of the test program, you get the following output:

```
device: constructor
comm_device: constructor
graphics_device: constructor
graphics_terminal: constructor
```

Notice that now the device class is constructed only once.

Restrictions on Virtual Base Classes

The virtual base class mechanism fills an important need, but you must be aware of the following restrictions when you use virtual base classes:

- You cannot initialize a virtual base class via an initializer list. For an example, look at the constructor of the Substring class in Listing 8.1. There the String class is initialized through the initializer list. You cannot do the same with a virtual base class. This implies that a class that you plan to use as a virtual base class should have a default constructor, which is a constructor that takes no arguments.

- You cannot cast a pointer to a virtual base class to a pointer to any class that derived from it. Thus, in the example, you cannot cast a device* pointer to a graphics_terminal* pointer.

Order of Initialization of Classes Under Multiple Inheritance

The exact rules for initializing classes in the presence of multiple inheritance are rather complicated. Roughly speaking, the C++ compiler uses the following order of initialization:

1. All virtual base classes are initialized first. Of course, the constructor of each virtual base class is called exactly once.

2. Nonvirtual base classes are initialized in the order in which they appear in a class declaration.

3. Member variables are initialized next, again in the order in which they appear in the class declaration.

The C++ compiler applies these rules recursively, just as it does under single inheritance. For further details on this topic, consult *The Annotated C++ Reference Manual* by Margaret Ellis and Bjarne Stroustrup.

Using Inheritance

You can use inheritance to create specialized versions of a general-purpose class. Suppose you have a class named `plain_window`, which gives you a rectangular area of screen wherein you can display text and graphics output. Typical members of such as class might include foreground and background colors, font used for text display, and a member function that refreshes the contents of the window.

Given the `plain_window` class, you can create a window that displays a text *label* in a window—let us call it a `static_text_window`, by simply deriving it from the `plain_window` class and by adding a new member variable to store the text for the label. Furthermore, you can derive from `static_text_window` a `pushbutton_window` that displays a label but, unlike a `static_text_window`, performs some action when a user selects the pushbutton with a pointing device such as a mouse. Figure 8.3 illustrates the inheritance hierarchy of these window classes. This is an example of specializing classes through inheritance.

On the other hand, you can use inheritance to extend the functionality of a class. In other words, instead of specializing, you can use inheritance for even broader functionality than before. This should not come as a surprise, because you can view the `class` construct in two ways:

- As a means for defining new data types

- As a module for packaging data and functions

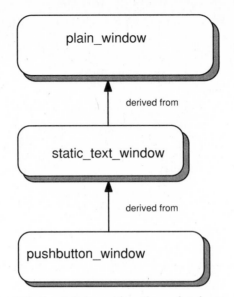

Fig. 8.3. Specializing a class through inheritance.

When you use class to define a data type, inheritance is useful for creating more specialized types. When you think of a class as a means for packaging functions, you can use inheritance to add new functions, thus extending the capabilities of the module.

Linked Lists

Basic data structures such as linked lists, queues, stacks, and trees are popular targets for implementation as abstract data types, because they lend themselves well to the object oriented style. Inheritance is often useful for defining such classes. A linked list, for instance, can be the basis of several types of data structures including queues, stacks, and trees. Let us start with an example of a singly linked list and see how inheritance can be used to create such a data structure.

Figure 8.4 shows a representation of a singly linked list of elements. As you can see, the list consists of a number of data items, each capable of holding a pointer to another such item. In the singly linked list, each item points to the next one on the list so that you can start at the beginning of the list and reach every element in the list by following these pointers. In addition to these items, the list needs a pointer to the first element so that you know where to start looking for data stored in the list. Sometimes you may also want to maintain a pointer to what you might call the "current element," the element being accessed at that time. Another item of interest is the number of elements in the list.

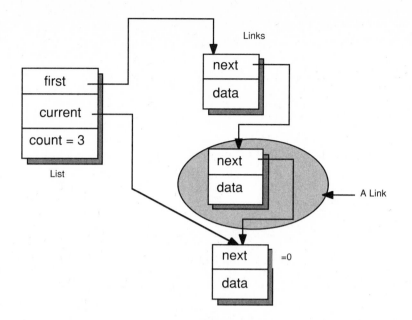

Fig. 8.4. A singly linked list.

The Link and the List

As shown in Figure 8.4, one of the basic objects in a linked list is the *link*—an object with some data and a pointer to another link. The other object is the *list*, which holds information about the linked list such as a pointer to the first item and the number of items. Having identified the basic objects, you can proceed to declare the C++ classes for them.

Making a Generic List

Before we declare the classes for the linked list, let us digress a bit to consider an important issue. The reason you define data structures such as linked lists is to use them to store objects. What you really want is a linked list that can hold any type of object. If you could define a parameterized class with a parameter denoting the data type stored in each link, you could easily create linked lists capable of holding different data types by substituting an appropriate type for the parameter. As explained in Chapter 16, the `template` keyword of C++ will be used to provide such a facility, but right now C++ does not support parameterized classes.

All is not lost however, because you can simulate generic lists through inheritance. The idea is to create a list capable of holding links of a class named `single_link`, for instance. A `single_link` object does not have any data other than a pointer to the next `single_link` object. Later on, if you want a singly linked list of `String` objects, you can create a new type—let us call it `slink_string`—that inherits from both `single_link` and `String`. Then objects of the `slink_string` class should be able to reside in the singly linked list you had designed to hold `single_link` objects. Figure 8.5 illustrates the idea, and the following discussions illustrate how this works. The major drawback of this approach is that you cannot have a list of built-in data types such as `int`, `char`, and `double`, because they are not defined as classes and you therefore cannot create derived classes from these types.

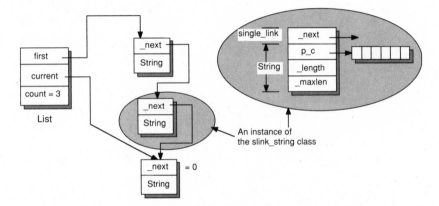

Fig. 8.5. A singly linked list capable of holding `String` objects.

The `single_link` Class

Listing 8.3 shows the header file `slink.h`, which declares the `single_link` class. The class has only one `protected` data member named `_next`, which is a pointer to the next `single_link` object. Thus, instances of `single_link` class can be strung together through their `_next` pointers.

Apart from the constructors, the `single_link` class also provides the next member function, which returns its `_next` pointer and the `set_next` function to set the `_next` pointer to a new value.

The class also includes two virtual functions: `clone` and `destroy`. The purpose of these functions is to ensure that you can correctly create and destroy instances of a class that is derived from `single_link`. The `clone` function makes a duplicate copy of an object, whereas `destroy` properly deletes objects derived from `single_link`. As you will learn in Chapter 9, these functions are declared to be pure virtual, that is what the =0 assignment following the function's declaration does. The side effect of this declaration is that you cannot create instances of the single_link class until you have derived another class from it and defined the functions clone and destroy.

Listing 8.3. slink.h—Declares the single_link class.

```
//-------------------------------------------------
//  File: slink.h
//
//  Declare a "single link" class.

#if !defined (__SLINK_H)
#define __SLINK_H

class single_link
{
public:
    single_link(): _next(0) {}
    single_link(single_link* next) : _next(next) {}
    single_link(single_link& sl) : _next(sl._next) {}

    single_link* next() { return _next; }

    void set_next(single_link *next) { _next = next;}

    virtual single_link* clone() = 0;
    virtual void destroy() = 0;

protected:
    single_link* _next;
};

#endif
```

The singly_linked_list Class

Now that you have the links defined, you can proceed to the list itself. Listing 8.4 shows the header file sllist.h, which declares the singly_linked_list class. Listing 8.5 has the actual implementation of some of the member functions. As expected, the singly_linked_list class provides member functions to traverse the list and to insert and remove elements from the list.

Listing 8.4. sllist.h—Declares the singly_linked_list class.

```cpp
//---------------------------------------------------------------
//  File: sllist.h
//
//  Declare a "singly linked list" class.

#if !defined (__SLLIST_H)
#define __SLLIST_H

#include "slink.h"

class singly_linked_list
{
public:
// Constructors
    singly_linked_list() : _first(0), _current(0), _count(0){}

    singly_linked_list(single_link& sl)
    {
        _first = sl.clone();
        _count = 1;
      _current = _first;
    }

// Destructor
    ~singly_linked_list();

// Member-access functions . . .
    single_link* current() { return _current;}

    single_link* first()
    {
        _current = _first;
        return _current;
    }

    single_link* next()
    {
        single_link* t = _current->next();
        if(t != 0) _current = t;
        return t;
    }

    unsigned count(){ return _count;}
```

```
// List insertion and deletion
    void insert(single_link& sl);
    void remove();

protected:
    single_link *_first;
    single_link *_current;
    unsigned    _count;
};

#endif
```

The `insert` function in Listing 8.5 shows how the virtual function `clone` is used. Suppose you are inserting a `slink_string` object into the list. Remember that the `slink_string` class is derived from `String` and `single_link`. The `insert` function requires as argument a reference to a `single_link` object. C++ permits you to call `insert` with a reference to an instance of any class derived from `single_link`. When you call `insert` with a `slink_string` reference, `insert` calls the `clone` function through the reference to the `slink_string` object. Because `clone` is a virtual function, this invokes the `clone` function of the `slink_string` class, which, as you will see shortly, returns a pointer to a copy of that instance of `slink_string`. Thus, you can get a proper copy of an object by using this mechanism. Chapter 9 provides further details about virtual functions.

The `remove` function uses the virtual function `destroy` in a similar manner to properly delete an item from the linked list.

**Listing 8.5. `sllist.cpp`—Member functions of the
singly_linked_list class.**

```
//-------------------------------------------------------------
//  File: sllist.cpp
//
//  Implement a singly linked list.

#include "sllist.h"

//-------------------------------------------------------------
// ~ s i n g l y _ l i n k e d _ l i s t
// Destructor for the list

singly_linked_list::~singly_linked_list()
{
    int          i;
    single_link *p_sl = _first, *t;
    if(_count > 0)
    {
```

```
            for(i = 0; i < _count; i++)
            {
                t = p_sl->next();
                p_sl->destroy();
                p_sl = t;
            }
        }
}
//-------------------------------------------------------------
// i n s e r t
// Insert a new item into the list

void singly_linked_list::insert(single_link& sl)
{
// Clone the element passed to the function and
// hook it up in the linked list
    single_link *t = sl.clone();
    if(_current != 0)
    {
        t->set_next(_current->next());
        _current->set_next(t);
    }
    else
    {
        _first = t;
    }

// Make this one the current item in the list
    _current = t;

// Increment of count of elements on the list
    _count++;
}
//-------------------------------------------------------------
// r e m o v e
// Remove the current element from the list

void singly_linked_list::remove()
{
// Locate element that points to current
    single_link *p_sl;
    int          i;

    if(_current == 0) return;
```

```
        for(i = 0, p_sl = _first;
            p_sl->next() != _current && i < _count;
            i++, p_sl = p_sl->next()) ;

        if(i != _count)
        {
            p_sl->set_next(_current->next());
            _current->destroy();
            _current = p_sl;
            _count—;
        }
    }
```

A Linkable String Class

You have already seen the String class in Listings 8.1 and 8.2. If you want to store String objects in a singly_linked_list, you have to create a new type of String, which might be called a *linkable* String. To do this, simply use multiple inheritance to derive from String as well as from single_link. Listings 8.6 and 8.7 show this new class. Its name here is slink_string, because these are String objects onto which we have added a single_link.

Notice how the clone and destroy functions are defined in Listing 8.6. The clone function simply creates a "clone" of the current slink_string and returns a pointer to the new copy. The destroy function calls the delete operator for the current slink_string. These functions ensure that objects stored in the singly linked list are properly initialized and destroyed.

Listing 8.6. slstr.h—Declaration of the slink_string class.

```
//-----------------------------------------------------------
//  File: slstr.h
//
//  Declare a singly linkable string class.

#if !defined(__SLSTR_H)
#define __SLSTR_H

#include "str.h"      // String class
#include "slink.h"    // single_link class
```

```
class slink_string: public single_link, public String
{
public:
    slink_string(const char *s): String(s), single_link(0){}

    slink_string(const slink_string& s) :
        String(s.p_c), single_link(s._next) {}

    slink_string(const String& s):
        String(s), single_link() {}

    slink_string& operator=(slink_string& s);

    void destroy() { delete this;}

    single_link* clone()
    {
        slink_string* t = new slink_string(*this);
        return t;
    }

};

#endif
```

Listing 8.7. `slstr.cpp`—Implementation of the assignment operator for the `slink_string` class.

```
//--------------------------------------------------------------
//  File: slstr.cpp
//
//  Implement a singly linkable string class.

#include "slstr.h"

//--------------------------------------------------------------
// o p e r a t o r =
// Assign one "slink_string" to another

slink_string& slink_string::operator=(slink_string& s)
{
    if(this != &s)
    {
```

```
            _next = s._next;
            _length = s._length;
            _maxlen = s._maxlen;
            delete p_c;
            p_c = new char[_maxlen];
            strcpy(p_c, s.p_c);
        }
        return *this;
    }
```

A String List Iterator Class

Now you have all the machinery to create a linked list of String objects, but there is still one problem. Specifically, the singly_linked_list class maintains a list of single_link objects. It does not know anything about slink_string objects. The question is how you traverse the list and process the slink_string objects in the list. You could use the first, current, and next member functions of the singly_linked_list class to traverse the list, but these return pointers to single_link objects. To treat them as pointers to slink_string objects, you have to use an explicit cast. Instead of getting into details like this, it is best to create a helper class—what is commonly known as an *iterator class* that gives you access to the linked list of String objects. The class is called an iterator because it enables you to iterate or loop over the list.

Listing 8.8 shows the header file slsiter.h, which implements the sllist_iterator class. This class acts as an iterator for the linked list of Strings. The sllist_iterator class is quite simple. It holds a reference to the list over which it iterates, and it provides the same interface to the list as does singly_linked_list, but the member functions of the sllist_iterator class always return pointers to slink_string objects instead of pointers to single_link objects.

**Listing 8.8. slsiter.h—An iterator for a singly linked list
of String objects.**

```
//----------------------------------------------------------
//  File: slsiter.h
//
//  Iterator for singly linked list of strings.

#if !defined(__SLSITER_H)
#define __SLSITER_H

#include "slstr.h"
#include "sllist.h"
```

```
class sllist_iterator
{
public:
    sllist_iterator(singly_linked_list& sl): sllist(sl){}

    slink_string* current()
    {
        return (slink_string*) sllist.current();
    }

    slink_string* next()
    {
        return (slink_string*) sllist.next();
    }

    slink_string* first()
    {
        return (slink_string*)sllist.first();
    }

private:
    singly_linked_list& sllist;
};

#endif
```

Trying Out a Singly Linked List of `Strings`

With all the machinery in place for working with singly linked lists of `slink_string` objects, all that remains is to try using one. Listing 8.9 shows a sample program that does this. It creates a linked list of `slink_string` objects and an iterator for the list. Then it inserts several `slink_string` objects into the list and displays what the list contains. Notice that you can display `slink_string` objects using the `<<` operator, because this operator is defined for the `String` class and the `slink_string` is derived from `String`. Finally, the program removes an item from the list and again displays the contents of the list.

Listing 8.9. `tstsls.cpp`—A test of a singly linked list of `Strings`.

```
//-------------------------------------------------------------
//  File: tstsls.cpp
//
//  Test linked list of strings.
```

```
#include "slsiter.h"
//-----------------------------------------------------------
// m a i n
// Program that exercises a singly linked list of Strings
main()
{
// Create a String with a single link
    slink_string s1("One");

// Create a singly linked list with s1 as first element
    singly_linked_list strlist(s1);

// Create an iterator for this linked list
    sllist_iterator si(strlist);

// Insert another copy of s1 into the list
    strlist.insert(s1);

// Change the string value of s1 and insert it again
    s1 = "Two";
    strlist.insert(s1);
    strlist.insert(s1);
    s1 = "Three";
    strlist.insert(s1);

// Display what the list contains
    cout << "------------------------------------" << endl;
    cout << "List contains:" << endl;
    slink_string* x;
    for(x = si.first(); x != 0; x = si.next())
        cout << *x << endl;

// Remove the current element from the list
// At this point, current element is the last element
    strlist.remove();

// Display the final contents of the linked list
    cout << "------------------------------------" << endl;
    cout << "Now list contains:" << endl;
    for(x = si.first(); x != 0; x = si.next())
        cout << *x << endl;
}
```

To build this program, you will have to compile and link the files from Listings 8.2, 8.5, 8.7, and 8.9. When run, the program displays the following output:

```
- - - - - - - - - - - - - - - - - - - - - - - - - - - - - - - - - - - - - - - - - - - - - -
List contains:
One
One
Two
Two
Three
- - - - - - - - - - - - - - - - - - - - - - - - - - - - - - - - - - - - - - - - - - - - - -
Now list contains:
One
One
Two
Two
```

A Doubly Linked List

Now that you have seen a singly linked list, let us see whether we can extend this design to create a doubly linked list. This data type is important, because it can be used as the basis of other, higher-level data structures such as queues and stacks. As shown in Figure 8.6, a doubly linked list is like a singly linked list except that each link can point to the previous as well as the next link on the list. The list also has a pointer to the last element, because now you can go backward as well as forward on the list.

A `double_link` Class

You can create a class with two links by deriving from a class with a single link. Listing 8.10 shows the header file `dlink.h` which declares the double_link class, derived from the `single_link` class. This will become the basis of a doubly linked list.

Notice that the virtual functions `clone` and `destroy` are still declared as pure virtual. This means that the `double_link` is still an abstract class whose only purpose is to provide two links to some other data class so that the instances of the newly derived class can reside in a doubly linked list.

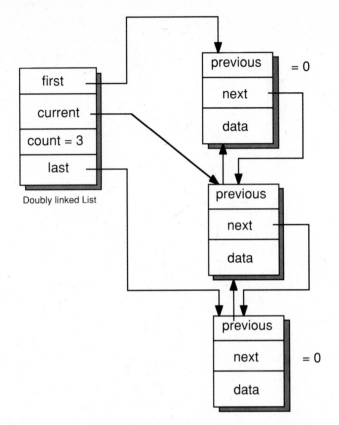

Fig. 8.6. A doubly linked list.

Listing 8.10. `dlink.h`—Program to declare the `double_link` class.

```
//------------------------------------------------------------
//  File: dlink.h
//
//  Declare a "double link" class.

#if !defined (__DLINK_H)
#define __DLINK_H
```

```
#include "slink.h"

class double_link: public single_link
{
public:
    double_link(): single_link(0),_previous(0) {}
    double_link(double_link& dl) : single_link(dl._next),
        _previous(dl._previous) {}
    double_link(single_link* prev, single_link* next) :
        single_link(next), _previous(prev) {}

    single_link* previous() { return _previous; }

    void set_previous(single_link *previous)
    {
        _previous = previous;
    }

    virtual single_link* clone() = 0;
    virtual void destroy() = 0;

protected:
    single_link* _previous;
};

#endif
```

The doubly_linked_list Class

You can also exploit the existing singly_linked_list class (see Listings 8.4 and 8.5) when you define the doubly_linked_list class. As shown in Listings 8.11 and 8.12, you can derive the doubly_linked_list from the singly_linked_list.

The doubly_linked_list class provides the insert_last and remove_first functions for insertion and removal of elements from the list. The insertion is at the front of the list, whereas the remove_last function always returns the last item in the list. We include only these two functions because we plan to use the doubly_linked_list as a queue. To use it as a stack, you have to provide another insertion function—insert_first—because a stack inserts at the top and removes from the top.

Listing 8.11. dllist.h—Declaration of the `doubly_linked_list` class.

```cpp
//------------------------------------------------------------
//  File: dllist.h
//
//  Declare a "doubly linked list" class.

#if !defined (__DLLIST_H)
#define __DLLIST_H

#include "dlink.h"
#include "sllist.h"

class doubly_linked_list: public singly_linked_list
{
public:
// Constructor
    doubly_linked_list(double_link& dl) : singly_linked_list(dl)
    {
        _last = (double_link*)_current;
    }

    single_link* previous()
    {
        double_link* cur = (double_link*)_current;
        single_link* t = cur->previous();
        if(t != 0) _current = t;
        return t;
    }

    double_link* last() { return _last; }

// New list insertion and deletion functions
    void insert_last(double_link& sl);
    double_link* remove_first();

protected:
    double_link *_last;
};

#endif
```

If you examine the `remove_last` function in Listing 8.12, you will note that the function "unhooks" the last element from the list and returns a pointer to that element to the calling program. Because every item in the list is created on the free store, you somehow have to destroy them when they are no longer needed. The idea is that there will be a queue class that provides the final interface to the programmer. The queue class will call `remove_last` to get an item, copy that item into a programmer-supplied variable, and then get rid of the item by calling its `destroy` function. The `get` function of the `string_queue` class defined in Listing 8.15 illustrates how this is done.

Listing 8.12. `dllist.cpp`—Implementation of the `doubly_linked_list` class.

```
//------------------------------------------------------------
//  File: dllist.cpp
//
//  Implement "insert_last" and "remove_first" functions for a
//  doubly linked list.

#include "dllist.h"

//------------------------------------------------------------
// i n s e r t _ l a s t
// Insert a new item at the end of the list

void doubly_linked_list::insert_last(double_link& dl)
{
// Clone the element passed to the function and
// hook it up in the linked list
    double_link *t = (double_link*)dl.clone();

    if(_last != 0)
    {
        _last->set_next(t);
        t->set_previous(_last);
        t->set_next(0);
    }
    else
    {
        _first = t;
        _current = t;
    }

// Make this one the last element in the list
    _last = t;
```

```
    // Increment of count of elements on the list
        _count++;
    }
    //-------------------------------------------------------------
    // r e m o v e _ f i r s t
    // Remove the element from the beginning of the list

    double_link* doubly_linked_list::remove_first()
    {
        if(_count == 0) return 0;

        double_link* cp = (double_link*)_first;
        if(_current == _first) _current = _first->next();
        _first = _first->next();

        double_link* t = (double_link*)_first;
        if(t != 0) t->set_previous(0);

        if(_last == cp) _last = 0;
        _count-;

        return cp;
    }
```

A Doubly Linkable String

To show a real use of the `doubly_linked_list` class, you need a data item that can be stored in the list. Like the `slink_string` class of Listings 8.6 and 8.7, you can create a `dlink_string` class that is derived from String and `double_link`. Instances of this class will be a String object with two links—`_previous` and `_next`—that come from the `double_link` class. Listings 8.13 and 8.14 show the files `dlstr.h` and `dlstr.cpp`, which implement the `dlink_string` class.

Listing 8.13. `dlstr.h`—Declares the `dlink_string` class.

```
//-------------------------------------------------------------
//  File: dlstr.h
//
//  Declare a doubly linkable string class.

#if !defined(__DLSTR_H)
#define __DLSTR_H
```

```
#include "str.h"        // String class
#include "dlink.h"      // double_link class

class dlink_string: public double_link, public String
{
public:
    dlink_string() : String(), double_link(0,0) {}
    dlink_string(const char *s): String(s), double_link(0,0){}

    dlink_string(const dlink_string& s) :
        String(s.p_c), double_link(s._previous, s._next) {}

    dlink_string(const String& s):
        String(s), double_link() {}

    dlink_string& operator=(dlink_string& s);

    void destroy() { delete this;}

    single_link* clone()
    {
        dlink_string* t = new dlink_string(*this);
        return t;
    }
};

#endif
```

Listing 8.14. `dlstr.cpp`—Implementation of the assignment operator for the `dlink_string` class.

```
//-----------------------------------------------------------
//  File: dlstr.cpp
//
//   Implement member function of the doubly linked string
class.

    #include "dlstr.h"

//-----------------------------------------------------------
// o p e r a t o r =
// Assign one "dlink_string" to another
```

```
dlink_string& dlink_string::operator=(dlink_string& s)
{
    if(this != &s)
    {
        _next = s._next;
        _previous = s._previous;
        _length = s._length;
        _maxlen = s._maxlen;
        delete p_c;
        p_c = new char[_maxlen];
        strcpy(p_c, s.p_c);
    }
    return *this;
}
```

A Queue of String Objects

In place of the iterator class that was used for the singly linked list, this time we create a class that maintains a queue of dlink_string objects. This class, named string_queue, is defined in the file squeue.h, which appears in Listing 8.15. The string_queue enables you to create a queue—actually a doubly_linked_list for which string_queue provides a queue-like interface. The get and put functions, respectively, permit you to store dlink_string objects in the queue and retrieve them.

You can think of string_queue as a class that knows how to use a doubly_linked_list class and that provides a first-in, first-out (FIFO) interface that is appropriate for a queue. It inserts objects at the end of the list and returns items from the front. You could similarly construct a stack class that provides a last-in, first-out (LIFO) interface to the doubly_linked_list class.

In this case, the queue is dynamically growing one, but you could easily limit the size of the queue with some added code.

Listing 8.15. squeue.h—Definition of the string_queue class.

```
//-----------------------------------------------------------
//  File: squeue.h
//
//  Interface for a queue of doubly linkable String objects.

#if !defined(__SQUEUE_H)
#define __SQUEUE_H
```

```cpp
#include "dlstr.h"
#include "dllist.h"

class string_queue
{
public:
    string_queue(dlink_string& ds)
    {
        my_queue = new doubly_linked_list(ds);
        created_here = 1;
    }

    string_queue(doubly_linked_list& q) :
        my_queue(&q), created_here(0) {}

    ~string_queue() { if(created_here) delete my_queue;}

    int get(dlink_string& dl)
    {
        dlink_string *p;
        p = (dlink_string*)my_queue->remove_first();

        if(p)
        {
// Copy the item and then destroy it
            dl = *p;
            p->destroy();
            return 1;
        }
        else
            return 0;
    }

    void put(dlink_string& dl)
    {
        my_queue->insert_last(dl);
    }

private:
    doubly_linked_list* my_queue;
    int                 created_here;
};


#endif
```

Testing the Queue

Listing 8.16 shows a small program that tests the queue of dlink_string objects defined by the string_queue class. The program first creates a queue and inserts three dlink_string objects into it. Then it retrieves the items one by one and displays them. Because the dlink_string objects are also of type String, the << operator can be used with the dlink_string objects.

The program generates the following output:

```
- - - - - - - - - - - - - - - - - - - - - - - - - - - - - - - - - - - - - - - - - - - - - - - - -
Queue contains:
One
Two
Three
```

Listing 8.16. Sample program to exercise the string_queue class.

```
//--------------------------------------------------------------
//  File: tstsq.cpp
//
//  Test queue of strings.

#include "squeue.h"
//--------------------------------------------------------------
// m a i n
// Program that exercises a queue of Strings

main()
{
// Create a String with a double link
    dlink_string ds1("One");

// Create a queue with ds1 as first element
    string_queue strq(ds1);

    ds1 = "Two";
    strq.put(ds1);

    ds1 = "Three";
    strq.put(ds1);

  // Get entries from the queue and display them
```

```
            cout << "Queue contains:" << endl;
            cout << "---------------" << endl;

            while(strq.get(ds1))
            {
                cout << ds1 << endl;
            }
        }
```

Summary

The first major component of OOP—data abstraction—enables you to introduce new data types from which you can create instances of objects. The second component, inheritance, saves you effort by enabling you to define new specialized data types in terms of existing ones or to extend the functionality of an existing type. C++'s class construct handles both of these needs: It encapsulates data and functions, and you can derive a class from one or more *base classes*. A derived class inherits all public and protected members of its base classes. Furthermore, you can differentiate the derived class from its base classes by one of the following:

- Adding new member variables

- Adding new member functions

- Overriding the definition of functions inherited from the base classes

When the class construct is used to define an abstract data type, inheritance helps you create specialized subtypes. On the other hand, when a class is simply a module that encapsulates some data and functions, inheritance can be used to extend the capabilities offered by the module. When you define functions in a derived class, be aware that any overloaded function will hide all inherited versions of the same name.

C++ supports single as well as multiple inheritance. In single inheritance, each derived class has exactly one base class; in multiple inheritance, you derive a class from more than one base class. You can use multiple inheritance to simulate generic classes such as linked lists and queues. This works by making the data structures capable of storing links, for instance, and then creating a linkable data type by inheriting from the link class as well as from your data type. Examples in this chapter illustrate this type of use of multiple inheritance.

Another interesting feature of inheritance is that a pointer to an instance of the base class can hold the address of any of its derived class instances. As you will see in Chapter 9, this feature enables you to exploit polymorphism in C++ programs.

Virtual Functions and Polymorphism

This chapter focuses on polymorphism, the last of the three basic components of OOP: data abstraction, inheritance, and polymorphism. (Chapters 7 and 8, respectively, cover data abstraction and inheritance.) Polymorphic functions can work with many different argument types. C++ supports this kind of polymorphism through function overloading. The other type of polymorphism simplifies the syntax of performing the same operation with a hierarchy of classes. This is what enables you to use the same function name, such as draw, to draw all types of shape objects, be they circle_shapes, rectangle_shapes, or triangle_shapes. Thus, you can use polymorphism to keep the interface to the classes clean, because you do not have to define unique function names for similar operations on each derived class. This type of polymorphism goes hand in hand with inheritance and *late binding* or *dynamic binding*. This chapter explains the terminology and describes how the virtual keyword supports polymorphism.

Dynamic Binding

The term *binding* refers to the connection between a function call and the actual code executed as a result of the call. This section explains how binding is determined and how it affects the style of code you write.

Static Binding

Like any new concept, the best way to explain the concept of binding is through an example. Suppose you want to process a one-character command and you have defined a number of functions that perform the tasks requested by the various commands. Using a `switch` statement, you might handle the commands as follows:

```
#include <ctype.h>
#include <iostream.h>
// . . .
static void quit(), newparams() showparams();
char ch;
// . . .
// Respond to user command
// Assume 'ch' holds the command character

    int code = toupper(ch);
    switch (code)
    {
        case 'Q': quit();
        case 'P': newparams();
                  break;
        case '?': showparams();
                  break;
        default:  cout << "Unknown command:" << ch << endl;
    }
```

Of course, in this case the function invoked in response to each command is known at compile-time, because each function is being explicitly called by name. This is called *static binding*, because the compiler can figure out the function to be called before the program is ever run.

Function Call Through a Pointer

Now consider an alternate implementation of this command—processing code. Start with a table of commands that can be implemented as an array of structures. Each structure holds a command character and a pointer to the function to be called when the user types that character. The processing loop simply compares the input command character with the entries in the table and, if a matching entry is found, calls the function whose pointer appears in that slot of the table. Here is a sample implementation of this scheme:

```
#include <ctype.h>
#include <iostream.h>

// Command-processing functions . . .
static void quit(), newparams(), showparams();

struct command
```

```
{
    char cmdchar;      // Each command is a character
    void (*action)();  // Function called to process command
};

command cmdtable[] =   // This is the table of commands
{
    'Q',  quit,
    'q',  quit,
    'P',  newparams,
    'p',  newparams,
    '?',  showparams
};

// Number commands in the command table
int cmdcount = sizeof(cmdtable) / sizeof(command);

char ch;
int  i;

// . . .
// Sample command-processing loop:
// Assume character 'ch' holds input character
// Search the command table for matching command

    for(i = 0; i < cmdcount; i++)
    {
        if(cmdtable[i].cmdchar == ch)
        {
// Found command . . . call the corresponding function
            (*cmdtable[i].action)();
            break;
        }
    }

    if(i == cmdcount)
        cout << "Unknown command: " << ch << endl;
```

Notice that this version of the command-processing loop differs from the previous one in two respects:

- The switch statement is no longer needed.

- A function call via a pointer is used to invoke the function that performs the task requested by each command. The content of the pointer determines the actual function that gets called.

Dynamic binding is so named because the actual function called at run-time depends on the contents of the function pointer, which, in turn, depends on the character in the `char` variable `ch`. It is also known as *late binding*, because the connection between the function call and the actual code executed by the call is determined late—during the execution of the program and not when the program is compiled.

Incidentally, the lack of a `switch` statement is a characteristic feature of dynamic binding. By using the indirection afforded by the function pointer, you are able to forego the tests required in a `switch` statement. Instead, a different function can be called simply by altering the content of the function pointer.

C++ compilers usually implement dynamic binding through the use of function pointers. Of course, like most other features of C++, this happens behind the scene. All that you need to do is use the `virtual` keyword.

Virtual Functions

Most of the examples you have seen thus far include classes with one or more `virtual` member functions. Consider, for instance, the geometric shape classes introduced in Chapter 2. Recall that the `shape` class is the base class from which we derived several other classes such as `rectangle_shape`, `circle_shape`, and `triangle_shape`. For a sample implementation, we wanted each shape to be able to compute its area and draw itself. In this case, the `shape` class declares the following virtual functions:

```
class shape
{
public:
    virtual double compute_area(void) const;
    virtual void draw(void) const;

// Other member functions that define an interface to all
// types of geometric shapes
};
```

Here, the `virtual` keyword preceding a function signals the C++ compiler that should the function be defined in a derived class, the compiler may have to call it indirectly through a pointer. You need to qualify member function of a class with the `virtual` keyword only when there is a possibility that other classes may be derived from this one.

The `shape` class is an example of an *abstract base class*—a class that embodies a standard interface to a group of classes but that does not provide a concrete implementation for any of the member functions. A common use of virtual functions is in defining such abstract base classes.

Pure Virtual Functions

One problem in defining a base class with virtual functions is that you may not be able to provide appropriate implementation for all of the functions. For example, you cannot define a draw or a compute_area function for a generic shape. Programmers often solve this problem by providing a dummy function that prints an error message. For the compute_area function of the shape class, you might write the following:

```
virtual void draw()
{
    cerr << "Derived class must implement!" << endl;
}
```

In this case, if you forget to implement draw in a derived class such as circle_shape and the program calls draw for a circle_chape, it prints an error message. This is not so bad, but the situation could be worse, for example, if you had decided to call exit after printing the error message. A better way to handle this lack of implementation is to let the C++ compiler detect an unimplemented instance of a virtual class. That way, the error can be caught before it is too late.

C++ includes the notion of *pure virtual functions* that you can use to indicate that certain member functions of an abstract base class are not implemented. For example, in the shape class you can make draw and compute_area pure virtual functions as follows:

```
class shape
{
public:
// Make these "pure virtual functions"
    virtual double compute_area(void) const = 0;
    virtual void draw(void) const = 0;

// Other member functions
};
```

Pure virtual functions are virtual functions that the base class cannot implement. You can indicate a pure virtual function by adding the =0 initializer following the declaration of the function. You gain two error-checking capabilities from pure virtual functions:

- The C++ compiler does not allow creation of instances of a class containing pure virtual functions. Thus, if you write:

  ```
  shape s1;
  ```

  the compiler will flag this as an error. This is good, because you do not want anyone to create instances of an abstract base class anyway.

- The compiler checks to make sure that the pure virtual functions of a base class are implemented by one of its derived classes. If an immediate derived class cannot provide an implementation, it can simply pass the problem on to one of its derived classes by also declaring it as a pure virtual function.

Concrete Implementation of virtual Functions

An abstract base class uses the virtual keyword to qualify the member functions that constitute the interface to all the classes derived from that class. Each specific derived class must define its own concrete versions of the functions that have been declared virtual in the base class. Thus, if you derive the circle_shape and rectangle_shape classes from the shape class, you have to define the member functions compute_area and draw in each class. For instance, the definitions for the circle_shape class might be like this:

```
class circle_shape: public shape
{
public:
    virtual double compute_area(void) const;
    virtual void draw(void) const;
// . . .
private:
    double xc, yc;  // Coordinates of center
    double radius;  // Radius of circle
};

// Implementation of "compute_area" function
circle_shape::compute_area(void) const
{
    return (M_PI * radius * radius); // Include <math.h> for
M_PI
}

// Implementation of "draw" function
circle_shape::draw(void) const
{
// . . .
}
```

When you declare the draw and compute_area functions in the derived class, you can optionally add the virtual keyword to emphasize that these are indeed virtual functions. The function definitions do not need the virtual keyword.

Dynamic Binding Through virtual Functions

You do not have to do anything special to use virtual functions—treat them like any other member function of a class. As an example, consider the following calls to the virtual functions draw and compute_area:

```
circle_shape    c1;
rectangle_shape r1;
double area = c1.compute_area(); // Compute area of circle
r1.draw();                       // Draw a rectangle
```

When used in this manner, the virtual functions are like any other member functions. In this case, the C++ compiler can determine that you want to call the compute_area function of the circle_shape class and the draw function of the rectangle_shape class. In fact, the compiler will make direct calls to these functions, and the function calls will be bound to specific code at link time—a case of static binding.

The interesting case occurs when you make the function calls through a pointer to a shape, as in the following:

```
shape*   s[10];  // Pointers to 10 shape objects
int      i, numshapes=10;
// . . . create shapes and store pointers in array "s"
// Draw the shapes
    for(i = 0; i < numshapes; i++) shape[i]->draw();
```

Because the individual entries in the array of shape pointers can point to any type of shape derived from the shape class, the C++ compiler cannot determine which specific implementation of the draw function to call. This is where dynamic binding and the virtual keyword play their part.

In C++, you can use a reference or a pointer to any derived class in place of a reference or a pointer to the base class without an explicit type cast. Thus, if circle_shape and rectangle_shape are both derived from the shape class, you can call a function that requires a pointer to shape with a pointer to a circle_shape or a rectangle_shape. The opposite is not true: You cannot use a reference or a pointer to the base class in place of a reference or a pointer to an instance of a derived class.

Virtual Function Call Mechanism

As explained in previous sections, an indirect function call—a function call through a pointer—provides dynamic binding. C++ compilers use this idea when calling virtual functions. The `virtual` keyword is a signal to the compiler that the member function qualified by the keyword may have to be called through a pointer. In a typical C++ compiler, the compiler will construct an array of virtual function pointers for each class. This array goes by the name of *virtual table* or *vtable* for short. Each instance of the class has a pointer to its class-wide virtual table. Figure 9.1 illustrates the situation for the `circle_shape` class. Given this arrangement, the C++ compiler can achieve dynamic binding by transforming a call to a virtual function into an indirect call through a pointer in the class virtual table. For example, if the virtual table were laid out as shown in Figure 9.1, the compiler can implement the following call:

```
circle_shape *c1 = new circle_shape(100.,100.,50.);
c1->draw();
```

by generating code for the following:

```
(*(c1->vtable[1]))(c1);   // c1 is "this"
```

where the second entry in the virtual table holds the pointer to the `draw` function of the `circle_shape` class. The pointer to the object is passed as first argument of the function just as it is done implicitly for every member function of a class. This is the `this` pointer that a member function can use to refer to the current instance of the class.

As a C++ programmer, you need not know how the compiler takes care of calling the right virtual function, but you may find the knowledge helpful in understanding why a C++ program behaves the way it does. Also, C++ compilers are not required to implement the virtual function call mechanism exactly as illustrated in Figure 9.1. However, most C++ compilers do follow the same techniques, partly because these ideas are outlined in *The Annotated C++ Reference Manual* by Margaret Ellis and Bjarne Stroustrup and also because their book is the basis of the ongoing standardization of C++ by the ANSI X3J16 committee.

If you are curious, consult their book for further information on how various features of C++ can be implemented. For instance, with multiple inheritance, implementing virtual function calls is somewhat more complicated. You can find the details for this case in Chapter 10 of *The Annotated C++ Reference Manual*.

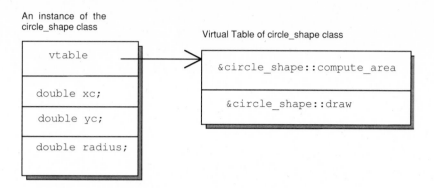

Fig. 9.1. Virtual function implementation under single inheritance.

Suppressing Virtual Function Calls

The virtual call mechanism is very useful for implementing polymorphism, but there may be occasions when you want to call the function from the base class instead of the one from the derived class. For example, suppose you have a base class called `BaseWindow` with a virtual function called `event_handler`, which presumably processes events in a user interface. You are happy with the function, but you want a derived class called `SpecialWindow` whose `event_handler` augments the processing done in the event-handling function of its base class. In the `event_handler` of the `SpecialWindow` class, you want to catch a special type of event and process it there. For all other types of events, you want to call the `event_handler` of the `BaseWindow` class. You can do this as follows:

```
class BaseWindow
{
public:
    virtual void event_handler(int event_id);
// Other members . . .
};

class SpecialWindow: public BaseWindow
{
```

```
public:
    void event_handler(int event_id)
    {
        if(event_id == SPECIAL_EVENT)
        {
// process special event . . .
        }
        else
        {
// Call BaseWindow's event_handler
            BaseWindow::event_handler(event_id);
        }
    }

// Other members . . .
};
```

Notice that you can suppress the virtual call mechanism by explicitly qualifying a function with its class name. In this example, you can call the `event_handler` of the `BaseWindow` class by explicitly qualifying the function name with the `BaseWindow::` prefix.

Using Polymorphism

As you have seen from the examples in this chapter and in Chapter 2, polymorphism eliminates the `switch` statement and, in general, simplifies the interface to a hierarchy of classes. The geometric shapes of Chapter 1 and 2 provide a good example of the use of polymorphism. Suppose you have a collection of shape objects in some storage structure—maybe an array or a linked list. The array simply stores pointers to shape objects. These pointers could point to any type of shape as long they are derived from the shape class. When operating on these shapes, you can simply loop through the array and invoke the appropriate member function via the pointer to the instance. Of course, for this to work the member functions must have been declared as `virtual` in the shape class, which happens to be the base class for all geometric shapes.

As you might gather from the examples, to use polymorphism in C++, you have to do the following:

1. Create a class hierarchy with the important operations defined by member functions that are declared `virtual` in the base class. If the base class is such that you cannot provide implementations for these func-

tions, you can declare them to be pure `virtual`. The `draw` function of the shape class is an example:

```
virtual void draw() const = 0;
```

2. Provide concrete implementations of the virtual classes in the derived classes. Each derived class can have its own version of the functions. For example, the implementation of the `draw` function will vary from one shape to another.

3. Manipulate instances of these classes through a reference or a pointer. This is what causes the C++ compiler to use dynamic binding and call the functions using the virtual function mechanism described earlier.

The last item—invoking member functions through a pointer—is the essence of polymorphic use in C++. This is because you get dynamic binding only when `virtual` member functions are invoked through a pointer to a class instance and you need dynamic binding for polymorphism.

Implications of Polymorphic Use of Classes

Because polymorphic use of class instances require you to manipulate objects through pointers or references, you should be aware of certain problems that you can encounter when programming this way. Some of the pitfalls are briefly discussed here.

Virtual Destructors

When you manipulate objects through pointers, you often tend to create them dynamically through the `new` operator and later on destroy them by using the `delete` operator. A typical situation might be as shown in the following example:

```
// Illustrate why "virtual destructor" is needed.

#include <iostream.h>

class Base
{
public:
    Base() { cout << "Base: constructor" << endl; }

// The destructor should be "virtual"
    ~Base() { cout << "Base: destructor" << endl; }
};
```

```
class Derived: public Base
{
public:
    Derived() { cout << "Derived: constructor" << endl; }
    ~Derived() { cout << "Derived: destructor" << endl; }
};

main()
{
    Base* p_base = new Derived;

// Use the object . . .

// Now delete the object
    delete p_base;
}
```

This is a case where the main function creates a copy of a derived class by using the new operator and later destroys that instance using delete. When you compile and run this program, here is what it displays:

```
Base: constructor
Derived: constructor
Base: destructor
```

The first two lines indicate the order in which the class constructors are called: the constructor for the base class followed by that for the derived class. This is in keeping with the order of initialization explained in Chapter 8. The third line of output, however, seems odd. Why isn't there a call to the destructor of the derived class?

The reason is that when you call the constructor, you used the derived class name with the new operator and, therefore, the C++ compiler correctly created the right type of object. You saved the pointer in a variable, p_base, which is declared to be a pointer to the base class. Subsequently, when you write

```
delete p_base;
```

the compiler cannot tell that you are destroying a derived class instance.

Because delete does its job by calling the destructor for the class, you can solve the problem by declaring the destructor of the base class virtual. That way the destructor will be invoked through the virtual function table and the correct destructor will get called. Indeed, if you use the following for the base class destructor:

```
virtual ~Base() { cout << "Base: destructor" << endl; }
```

and rerun the program, you will get the correct output, as follows:

```
Base: constructor
Derived: constructor
Derived: destructor
Base: destructor
```

Notice that the order of calls to the destructors is the reverse of the order in which the constructors were called. Thus, the virtual destructor ensures that the object is properly destroyed.

How do you decide whether to declare a destructor virtual? If a class has any virtual functions, then chances are that instances of classes derived from this one will be manipulated through pointers to get polymorphic behavior. In this case, you should declare a virtual destructor for the class.

Calling Virtual Functions in a Base Class Constructor

Another pitfall of using virtual functions is that there are certain times when they do not work as expected. One place where calling a virtual function may produce undesired results is in the constructor of a base class. You can see the problem from the following sample program:

```cpp
// Illustrate what happens when a virtual function
// is called from the constructor of a base class.

#include <iostream.h>

class Base
{
public:
    Base()
    {
        cout << "Base: constructor. Calling clone()" << endl;
        clone();
    }
    virtual void clone()
    {
        cout << "Base::clone() called" << endl;
    }
};

class Derived: public Base
{
```

```
public:
    Derived()
    {
        cout << "Derived: constructor" << endl;
    }

    void clone()
    {
        cout << "Derived::clone() called" << endl;
    }
};

main()
{
    Derived x;
    Base *p = &x;

// Call "clone" through pointer to class instance
    cout << "Calling 'clone' through instance pointer";
    cout << endl;
    p->clone();
}
```

When you run this program, you get the following output:

```
Base: constructor. Calling clone()
Base::clone() called
Derived: constructor
Calling 'clone' through instance pointer
Derived::clone() called
```

Let us go through the output and see what happened. When you create an instance of the derived class, as expected, the C++ compiler first calls the constructor of the base class. At this point, the derived class instance is only partially initialized. Therefore, when the compiler encounters the call to the virtual function clone, it cannot bind that call to the version of clone for the derived class. Instead, the compiler calls the version of clone from the base class.

The last two lines of output show that once the object is created, you can correctly invoke the clone function for the derived class instance through a base class pointer, as is common in polymorphic use of virtual functions.

The bottom line is that if you call a virtual function in a class constructor, the compiler will invoke the base class's version of the function, not the version defined for the derived class.

Summary

The three features of object-oriented programming—data abstraction, inheritance, and polymorphism—go hand in hand. For realistic object-oriented programs, you have to use all of these concepts in tandem. The data and functions are encapsulated into an object by a class or a struct. Inheritance helps you to implement the *is a* relationship among objects—as in, *a circle is a shape*. Finally, polymorphism enables you to use the same functional interface such as member functions named draw and compute_area to work with all kinds of shapes.

Several features of C++ work in concert to support polymorphism:

- You can use a pointer to a derived class anywhere a pointer to the base class is expected. The same rule applies to references.

- If a base class declares a member function with the virtual keyword, the compiler places the function in the class-wide virtual function table and uses the base class's implementation of the function as a default, which will be used *only if* a derived class does not define the function.

- If a derived class redefines a virtual function and you call that function through a pointer to the class instance, the compiler invokes the function through the pointer stored in the virtual table, thereby invoking the version of the function from the derived class. This is known as *dynamic binding*.

Dynamic binding makes polymorphism possible. With polymorphism, you can control a particular behavior of a whole group of objects by calling the same member function. The draw function of shape classes provide a good illustration of polymorphic usage.

When you use virtual functions in C++, you have to watch out for some pitfalls. For example, if you call a virtual function from the constructor of a class, the compiler will call the version from itself or one of the bases, but not from a version defined by derived classes. Also, for correct destruction of objects, you may have to declare the destructor of the base class to be virtual.

Using C Libraries in C++ Programs

The first two parts of the book, comprising Chapters 1 through 9, explain the terminology of object-oriented programming and introduce the C++ programming language. Chapters 6 through 9, in particular, focus on the features of C++ that support data abstraction, inheritance, and polymorphism—the concepts that form the basis of object-oriented programming.

This part of the book, Chapters 10 through 12, covers the topics of building and using C++ class libraries. Because there are no standard C++ libraries yet, the standard C libraries remain an important source of functionality for C++ programmers. Therefore, Chapter 10 describes how you can use C libraries, the standard one as well as your own, in C++ programs. The chapter also provides a summary description of the functions in the ANSI standard C library and shows some examples of using these functions in C++ programs. Chapter 11 goes on to the topic of building C++ class libraries and presents some strategies for designing such libraries. The last chapter of this part, Chapter 12, summarizes the capabilities of two off-the-shelf commercial class libraries and discusses how you can supplement your own classes with these commercial offerings.

Linkage Between C and C++

Suppose you have a library of functions—functions that have been compiled into object code and stored in the library object code form. When you call a function from such a library in your program, the compiler will mark the name of the function as an unresolved symbol in the object code of your program. To create an executable program, you have to use a linker and make sure that the linker searches the right library for the code of that function. If the linker finds the function's object code in the library, it will combine that code with your program's object code to create an executable file. To use C functions in C++ programs, you must be able to complete this process of linking. As you will see in this section, you can do this by using the linkage specifier syntax of C++.

Type-Safe Linkage

The key to linking C++ programs with C functions lies in understanding how C++ resolves the names of functions. As you know, C++ lets you overload a function name, whereby you can declare the same function with different sets of arguments. To help the linker, the C++ compiler uses an encoding scheme that creates a unique name for each overloaded function. The general idea of the encoding algorithm is to combine the following components:

- The name of the function
- The name of the class in which the function is defined
- The list of argument types accepted by the function

to generate a unique signature for each function. You do not have to know the exact details of the encoding algorithm, because it differs from one compiler to another. But knowing that a unique signature is generated for each function in a class should help you understand how the linker can figure out which of the many different versions of a function to call.

Effect of Function Name Encoding

How does function name encoding affect C++ programs? To see one benefit of name encoding, consider the following C program:

```
//  Illustrate effect of wrong argument type.

#include <stdio.h>

void print(unsigned short x)
{
    printf("x = %u", x);
}

void main(void)
{
    short x = -1;
    print(x);
}
```

The print function expects an unsigned short integer argument, but main calls print with a signed short integer argument. You can see the result of this type mismatch from the output of the program:

```
x = 65535
```

Even though print was called with a -1, the printed value is 65535. The explanation for this result is as follows. This program was run on a system that uses a 16-bit representation for short integers. The bit representation of the value -1 happens to be 0xffff (all 16 bits are 1), which when treated as an unsigned quantity, results in the value 65535.

In C++, you can avoid problems like this by defining overloaded functions: one version of print for unsigned short type and another for plain short. With this modification, the C++ version of the C program looks like this:

```c
//  C++ version avoids problem by overloading function.

#include <stdio.h>

void print(unsigned short x)
{
    printf("x = %u", x);
}

void print(short x)
{
    printf("x = %d", x);
}

void main(void)
{
    short x = -1;
    print(x);
}
```

When you run this C++ program, you get the following output:

```
x = -1
```

This time, the result is correct because the C++ compiler uses function name encoding to generate a call to the version of print that takes a signed short argument. This ability of C++ to distinguish between overloaded functions based on argument types, is known as *type-safe linkage*, because you cannot inadvertently call a function with incorrect types of arguments.

C Linkage Directive

Now that you know that C++ encodes all function names, you can see the main problem in calling C functions from C++ programs. Suppose a C++ program calls the C function `strlen` to get the length of a null-terminated string of characters:

```
// C++ program

#include <stddef.h>              // For definition of "size_t"

size_t strlen(const char* s); // Prototype of "strlen"

// . . .
char str[] = "Hello";
size_t length = strlen(str);
```

When you compile and link the program containing this C++ code with the C library, the linker will inform you that the function named `strlen` is unresolved, even though you are linking with the C library that contains the code for `strlen`. This happens because the C++ compiler uses the function prototype `strlen(const char*)` to create a name that is very different from plain `strlen`, the name under which the C library stores the object code of the `strlen` function.

To successfully link C object code with C++ programs, you need some mechanism to inhibit the C++ compiler from encoding the names of C functions. The linkage directive of C++ provides this escape mechanism. For instance, you can successfully link the C++ program that uses `strlen`, provided you qualify `strlen` as a C function by declaring it as follows:

```
// Specify "C" linkage for the strlen function

extern "C" size_t strlen(const char* s);
```

Other Forms of Linkage Directive

To declare a number of functions with the `"C"` linkage, you can use the compound form of the linkage directive:

```
// Compound form of linkage directive

extern "C"
{
    int printf(const char* format, ...);
    void exit(int status);
```

```
/* Other functions . . . */
}
```

Typically such linkage directives appear in header files because that is where the functions are declared.

Sharing Header Files Between C and C++ Programs

Because of the close ties between C++ and C, you will often find the need to use C functions in C++ programs. This means that in your C++ programs, you have to declare the C functions with an extern "C" linkage. You can do this easily with the compound form of the linkage directive, but that leaves the declarations unacceptable to the C compiler, because the extern "C" directive is not a standard C construct. You can solve this problem by using a conditional compilation directive of the C preprocessor as follows:

```
/* Header file shared between C and C++ */

#ifdef __cplusplus
extern "C" {      /* If it's C++, use linkage directive */
#endif

/* Declare C functions here */
void clearerr(FILE *f);
FILE* fopen(const char* name, const char* mode);
int fclose(FILE* f);

/* . . . */

#ifdef __cplusplus
}
#endif
```

The __cplusplus macro is predefined in every C++ compiler. Compilers that can handle C as well as C++ programs define this symbol as they compile C++ programs. Usually, such compilers provide header files that use the #ifdef __cplusplus construct to declare the C library functions with extern "C" linkage so that all you have to do is include the header file in your C++ program. All the programs in this book assume that the standard C header files such as <stdio.h> are designed to work with C++ programs.

If you are using C header files that have not been conditioned to work with C++ compilers and you cannot alter the C header files, you can still specify the extern "C" linkage by surrounding the #include directive within braces as follows:

```
extern "C"
{
#include <stdio.h>
}
```

If you have to do this, the best approach is to create a new header file with the an `extern "C"` wrapper around the `#include` directive as just shown. That way, you avoid cluttering the C++ programs with linkage directives that rightfully belong in header files so that all source files that use the C functions can do so with a consistent linkage directive.

Restrictions on Linkage Directive

You can specify the linkage directive for exactly one instance of an overloaded function. Suppose you have declared the `sqrt` function for the `complex` and `binary_coded_decimal` classes as follows:

```
class complex;
class binary_coded_decimal;

extern complex  sqrt(complex&);
extern binary_coded_decimal sqrt(binary_coded_decimal&);
```

In addition to these, you can also use the standard C `sqrt` function, provided you declare it as follows:

```
extern "C" double sqrt(double);
```

In this case, you have two instances of `sqrt` for C++ classes and one from the C library. What you cannot have is more than one version of `sqrt` defined in C.

Another restriction on linkage specifications is that you cannot place them within a local scope—all linkage specifications must appear in the file scope. In particular, the C++ compiler flags the following as an error:

```
// This is an error: cannot have linkage specification in a
// function's scope

main()
{
extern "C" size_t strlen(const char*); // Flagged as error
// . . .

}
```

You can fix this error by moving the linkage specification to file scope as follows:

```
// This is the right place for linkage specifications, in
// file scope (outside the body of functions)

extern "C" size_t strlen(const char*);

main()
{
// . . .

}
```

Linkage to Other Languages

Although so far you have seen only the extern "C" linkage directive, the appearance of C within quotation marks should give you a clue that this linkage mechanism may be intended to link C++ programs with functions written in other languages as well. Indeed, the linkage specification mechanism is intended for this purpose, but C++ compilers are required to support only two linkages: "C" and "C++". You have seen examples of the first, and the second is the default linkage for all C++ programs.

Using the ANSI Standard C Library

By now you know how to use C functions in C++ programs. If your C compiler's standard header files have been designed to work with a C++ compiler, you can use the C functions by simply including the appropriate header files in your C++ program. If you are a C programmer, you also know that C relies on its library to provide capabilities such as I/O, memory management, and mathematical functions. Every C program of any significance uses functions such as printf, scanf, and gets that are declared in the header file <stdio.h>. In addition to the I/O functions, the standard C library has many more functions such as those for string manipulation and functions that return date and time in various formats. The following sections summarize the capabilities of the ANSI C library and show their use in sample C++ programs.

Overall Capabilities of the ANSI C Library

From the overview of ANSI standard C in Chapter 4, you know that the standard defines not only the C programming language but also the contents of the library. Even the header files and the prototypes of the functions are specified by the standard. Because most C compilers are beginning to conform to the ANSI standard for C, the standard C library is a good place to look for functions that may be useful in your C++ programs.

The ANSI standard specifies over 140 functions for the C library, but a number of these functions are for handling international character sets and are not yet available in most C compilers. Table 10.1 lists most of the functions in the standard C library grouped according to capability. The following discussions further explore each category of functions and how each might be used in C++ programs.

Table 10.1. Capabilities of the Standard C Library.

Category of Function	Comma-Separated List of Function Names
Standard I/O	clearerr, fclose, feof, ferror, fflush, fgetc, fgetpos, fgets, fopen, fprintf, fputc, fputs, fread, freopen, fscanf, fseek, fsetpos, ftell, fwrite, getc, getchar, gets, printf, putc, putchar, puts, remove, rename, rewind, scanf, setbuf, setvbuf, sprintf, sscanf, tmpfile, tmpnam, ungetc, vfprintf, vprintf, vsprintf
Process control	abort, assert, atexit, exit, getenv, localeconv, longjmp, perror, raise, setjmp, setlocale, signal, system
Memory allocation	calloc, free, malloc, realloc
Variable-length argument list	va_start, va_arg, va_end
Data conversions	atof, atoi, atol, strtod, strtol, strtoul
Mathematical functions	abs, acos, asin, atan, atan2, ceil, cos, cosh, div, exp, fabs, floor, fmod, frexp, labs, ldexp, ldiv, log, log10, modf, pow, rand, sin, sinh, sqrt, srand, tan, tanh

Category of Function	Comma-Separated List of Function Names
Character classification	`isalnum, isalpha, iscntrl, isdigit, isgraph, islower, isprint, ispunct, isspace, isupper, isxdigit, tolower, toupper`
String and buffer manipulation	`memchr, memcmp, memcpy, memmove, memset, strcat, strchr, strcmp, strcoll, strcpy, strcspn, strerror, strlen, strncat, strncmp, strncpy, strpbrk, strrchr, strspn, strstr, strtok`
Search and sort	`bsearch, qsort`
Time and date	`asctime, clock, ctime, difftime, gmtime, localtime, mktime, strftime, time`

Standard I/O Functions

The standard I/O functions, declared in the header file <`stdio.h`>, include functions such as `printf` and `scanf` that are some of the most commonly used functions in the C library. Almost all C programs use one or more of these functions. You can continue to use these functions in C++. However, as explained in Chapter 5, most C++ compilers include the `iostream` class library, which provides a cleaner object-based mechanism for I/O in C++ programs.

Process Control Functions

This broad category of the standard C library includes the signal-handling functions that take care of error conditions and utility functions that terminate a process, communicate with the operating system, and set up numeric and currency formats depending on the locale for which your program is customized. These functions are declared in the following header files:

- <`locale.h`> declares `localeconv` and `setlocale`.
- <`signal.h`> declares `raise` and `signal`.
- <`setjmp.h`> declares `longjmp` and `setjmp`.

- `<stdlib.h>` declares `abort`, `atexit`, `exit`, `getenv`, `perror`, and `system`.

- `<assert.h>` declares `assert`.

Here is a summary of these functions and how they may be used.

Environment Variables

The term *process* refers to an executing program. Whenever you run a program, you create a process. The *environment* of a process includes the information necessary to execute the process. The exact interpretation of the environment differs from one operating system to another. In UNIX and MS-DOS, the environment consists of an array of null-terminated strings, with each string defining a symbol of the form:

```
VARIABLE=value
```

where the symbol appearing on the left-hand side of the equality is an environment variable. In a UNIX system, you can see the environment variables using one of the commands `printenv` and `env`. Under MS-DOS, type SET at the DOS prompt to see a list of environment variables.

Environment variables are used to pass information to processes. For example, under UNIX, the full-screen editor `vi` uses the TERM environment variable to determine the type of terminal on which the text is being displayed. You, the user, indicate the terminal type in the TERM environment variable, and the `vi` editor picks up this setting by looking up the value of TERM. Your programs can exploit environment variables as well. For instance, in UNIX systems, the TZ environment variable indicates your time zone. If you need it, you can get the value of this environment variable by calling the `getenv` function which is one of the utility routines defined in the header file `<stdlib.h>`.

Exception Handling Using `setjmp` and `longjmp`

In C, you can use the pair of functions `setjmp` and `longjmp` to handle exceptional conditions. You can save the *state* or the *context* of the process by calling `setjmp` and, later on, call `longjmp` with the saved context to revert to a previous point in your program. The context of a process refers to the information needed to reconstruct exactly the way the process is at a particular point in its flow of execution. ANSI C requires a compiler to define an array data type named `jmp_buf` that can hold the information needed to restore a calling environment. This data type is defined in the header file `<setjmp.h>`. To understand the mechanics of `setjmp` and `longjmp`, look at the following C code:

```
/*------------------------------------------------------------*/
/*   Illustrate use of "setjmp" and "longjmp" to
 *   handle exceptions.
 */

#include <setjmp.h>
jmp_buf last_context;

void process_commands(void);
/*------------------------------------------------------------*/
void main(void)
{
/* Establish a context to which you can return */
    if (setjmp(last_context) == 0)
    {
        process_commands();
    }
    else
    {
/* This part executed when longjmp is called.
 * Place code for handling error here . . .
 */

    }
}
/*------------------------------------------------------------*/
void process_commands(void)
{
    int error_flag;
/* . . . */
/* In case of error, return to last context */
    if(error_flag) longjmp(last_context, 1);
}
```

The setjmp function saves the current context in the variable last_context and returns a 0. In this case, the if statement in main is satisfied and process_commands is called. Assume that the integer error_flag is set to 1 when any error occurs in the process_commands function. Then, you can handle the error by testing this flag and by calling the longjmp function with two arguments, of which the first one is the jmp_buf array that contains the context to which you want to return. When the calling environment reverts to this saved state, and longjmp returns, it will be exactly like returning from the call to setjmp that originally saved the buffer last_context. The second argument to longjmp specifies the value to be returned by the function. It should be nonzero so that the `if` statement in `main` branches to the `else` clause when the return is induced by a `longjmp`.

Thus, you can use the combination of `setjmp` and `longjmp` to jump unconditionally from one C function to another without using the conventional `return` statement. Essentially, `setjmp` marks the destination of the jump, and `longjmp` acts as a nonlocal `goto` that executes the jump.

It is tempting to use `setjmp` and `longjmp` to handle exceptions in C++, but the calls to constructors and destructors create some problems. All objects initialized up to the point of the error must be destroyed before you call `longjmp` to jump to an error-handling section of the program. This can be done only if you keep track of all objects created in your program. Still, at least one major C++ class library,[3] the *NIH Class Library*, uses `setjmp` and `longjmp` to handle exceptions. However, you may not have to devise your own exception handling scheme using `setjmp` and `longjmp`, because the ANSI standard for C++ is expected to include a well-defined method for handling exceptions in C++ programs. Chapter 16 has further details on this topic.

Customizing Programs to a Locale

The term *locale* refers to the locality—a geographic region—for which certain aspects of your program can be customized. ANSI C groups the locale-dependent aspects of a C program into six categories and defines macros to identify them. Table 10.2 summarizes the locale categories defined in the header file <locale.h>. You can use the `setlocale` function to selectively set each category shown in Table 10.2 to conform to a selected locale. The locale named "C" indicates the minimal environment for C programs. Most compilers support only the locale named "C", but future C compilers may support other locale names as well.

You can obtain the numeric and currency formatting style for the current locale by calling the function `localeconv`, which returns a pointer to a statically allocated `lconv` structure. You will find the `lconv` structure declared in the header file <locale.h>. This structure includes formatting information, such as the decimal point character and the currency symbol for the current locale.

Table 10.2. Locale Categories in ANSI Standard C.

Locale Category	Parts of Program Affected
LC_ALL	The entire program's locale-specific parts (all categories shown in this table)
LC_COLLATE	Behavior of the functions `strcoll` and `strxfrm` that uses the collating sequence of the character set

Locale Category	Parts of Program Affected
LC_CTYPE	Behavior of the character classification functions
LC_MONETARY	Monetary formatting information returned by the localeconv function
LC_NUMERIC	Decimal point character for the formatted output functions (for example, printf) and the data conversion functions, and the nonmonetary formatting information returned by the localeconv function
LC_TIME	Behavior of the strftime function that formats time

You can use the locale mechanism to ensure that the output generated by your application conforms to the standard representation of monetary and numeric information as practiced in the locality where the program is being used. For instance, you may use localeconv to get formatting information in a C++ class designed to represent currency. Unfortunately, though, most C compilers still support only the "C" locale that does not include any information on formatting monetary information.

Executing Operating System Commands

Yet another useful function in this category is system, which enables you to pass a command to the command processor of the environment where your C or C++ program is running. The system function accepts the command in a null-terminated string and returns to your program after the command has been executed. You can even test if a command-processor such as the UNIX shell is running by calling system with a null pointer as argument and testing for a nonzero return value. The following is a small C++ program that uses system to display a list of environment variables in an MS-DOS environment:

```
// Demonstrate the use of "system" in a C++ program.
// Assumes an MS-DOS environment.

#include <iostream.h>
#include <stdlib.h>

main()
{
    if(system(NULL))
    {
```

```
            cout << "Command Processor available" << endl;
            cout << "Current environment variables are:" <<
    endl;
            system("SET");
        }
        else
            cout << "Sorry, no command processor!" << endl;
    }
```

Similarly, on a UNIX system, you can execute the `ls` command with the following call:

```
/* Execute the "ls" command */
system("ls");
```

Memory Allocation

One advantage that C enjoys over older languages such as FORTRAN is its ability to manage memory at run-time. In FORTRAN, there is no provision for requesting memory at run-time. All data items and arrays must be declared in the program. You have to guess the maximum size of an array beforehand, and there is no way to exceed the maximum without recompiling the program. This is inefficient, because you often define large arrays but use only a small portion of each.

In C, you can request blocks of memory at run-time and release the blocks when your program no longer needs them. This allows your application to exploit all available memory in the system. Like most other capabilities in C, this capability comes in the form of four standard functions—`calloc`, `malloc`, `realloc`, and `free`—which are defined in the header file `<stdlib.h>`. Of these, `calloc` and `malloc` allocate memory, `realloc` adjusts the size of a previously allocated block, and `free` releases memory.

C++ not only retains C's ability to allocate memory at run-time but also makes it a part of the language by providing two built-in operators, `new` and `delete`, to handle allocation and deallocation of objects. Of course, many C++ compilers define `new` and `delete` in terms of `malloc` and `free`, respectively. If you need to overload the `new` and `delete` operators for one of your C++ classes, you can use `malloc` and `free` to define the overloaded versions of the operators.

Variable-Length Argument Lists

When writing C programs, you have used functions such as `printf` and `scanf`, which can take a variable number of arguments. In fact, their prototypes use an ellipsis in the argument list to reflect this:

```
        int printf(const char *format_string,...);
        int scanf(const char *format_string,...);
```

ANSI standard C includes the va_start, va_arg, and va_end macros, which are defined in the header file <stdarg.h> and which allow you to write functions capable of accepting a variable number of arguments. The only requirement of such functions is that they must accept at least one required argument. You can use these macros in C++ programs as well. As an example, consider a menu_widget class whose constructor accepts a variable number of strings and creates a menu with those strings as labels. Here is a skeleton C++ program that illustrates how you can use the ANSI standard approach to handle a variable number of arguments in a class member function:

```
//-------------------------------------------------------------
//  Demonstrate the use of variable-length argument lists.

#include <iostream.h>
#include <stdarg.h>

#define MENU_BAR   1
#define PULL_DOWN  2

typedef char *P_CHAR;

class menu_widget
{
public:
    menu_widget(int style, ...);
// . . .
private:
// . . .
};

//-------------------------------------------------------------
// NOTE: The following function does not use its first argument.
//       By declaring the argument type without a name, we stop
//       the C++ compiler from warning that the argument is
//       not used. You can use this trick whenever a function
//       does not use one or more of its arguments

menu_widget::menu_widget(int, ...)
{
// Get the first optional parameter using "va_start"
    va_list  argp;        // Used to access arguments
    va_start(argp, style);
```

```
// Get items one by one
    char    *item_text;
    int     count = 0;

    cout << "----------------------------------" << endl;
    while((item_text = va_arg(argp, P_CHAR)) != NULL)
    {
        cout << "Item " << count << " = " << item_text << endl;
        count++;
    }
}
//----------------------------------------------------------------
// Test the use of variable-length argument lists

main()
{
    menu_widget m1(MENU_BAR, "File", "Edit", "Utilities", NULL);
    menu_widget m2(PULL_DOWN, "Open", "Close", "New", "Save",
                              "Save As . . .", "Quit", NULL);
// . . .
}
```

If you run this program, you get the following output, showing that the menu_widget constructor is indeed processing a variable number of arguments:

```
----------------------------------
Item 0 = File
Item 1 = Edit
Item 2 = Utilities
----------------------------------
Item 0 = Open
Item 1 = Close
Item 2 = New
Item 3 = Save
Item 4 = Save As . . .
Item 5 = Quit
```

Data Conversions

The functions in this category—atof, atoi, atol, strtod, strtol, and strtoul—are for converting character strings into internal representations of variables. They are declared in the header file <stdlib.h>.

The conversion routines are ideal for converting command-line arguments from their string representation into the internal format. For example, in a small calculator program, you might want to process an input line of the following form:

```
eval 12.43 + 17.52
```

where `eval` is the name of the program that accepts a command line of the form `<value1> <operator> <value2>` and prints out the result of the operation. In this example, the program should print `29.95` as the answer. When implementing this program, you can use the `atof` function to convert the second and the fourth command-line argument (the first argument is always the name of the program) to `double` variables. The code for the addition operator might be written like this:

```cpp
#include <stdlib.h>
#include <iostream.h>

main(int argc, char **argv)
{
    double op1, op2, result;

    op1 = atof(argv[1]);
    op2 = atof(argv[3]);

    switch(argv[2][0])
    {
// . . .
        case '+':
            result = op1 + op2;
// . . .
    }
    cout << result << endl;
}
```

This example assumes a decimal calculator. If you want a hexadecimal calculator so that all input and output is in hexadecimal, you can use the `strtoul` function to convert the input arguments to unsigned long integers. This is a typical use of the data conversion functions.

Mathematical Functions

C and C++ both support basic floating-point data types `float` and `double` and permit you to write arithmetic expressions using these data types. Additionally, the standard C library also includes a set of mathematical functions that you use to evaluate common functions such as the *sine* and the *cosine*. Here is a short overview of these functions, most of which are declared in the header file `<math.h>`.

Basic Functions

The trigonometric functions `cos`, `sin`, `tan`, `acos`, `asin`, `atan`, and `atan2` perform calculations such as evaluating the cosine, sine, or tangent of any angle in radians as well as compute their respective inverses. These functions are useful for transforming from rectangular to polar coordinates, which graphics programs often do. Other commonly used mathematical functions include the following:

- `sqrt` computes square roots.

- The `log` and `log10` return the logarithm, natural and to the base 10 respectively, of an argument.

- Exponentials can be computed by calling `exp`. For example, you would call `exp(1.75)` to evaluate $e^{1.75}$.

- The `fabs` function returns the absolute value of a floating-point value.

- The `ceil` function returns the nearest integer larger than a given floating-point number.

- `floor` returns the nearest integer smaller than its floating-point argument.

Integer Arithmetic

There are four functions, declared in `<stdlib.h>`, that handle arithmetic using integer arguments. The functions `abs` and `labs` return the absolute value of an integer and a long integer, respectively. The `div` function divides one integer by another and returns the integer quotient and an integer remainder. The `ldiv` function operates similarly but with long integer arguments.

Generating Random Numbers

If you need to generate random numbers for uses such as a random screen pattern, a game, or a statistical analysis problem, the ANSI C library includes a function named `rand` that generates a random positive integer in the range 0 to RAND_MAX, which is a constant defined in `<stdlib.h>`. The `rand` function generates the random numbers by using a well-defined algorithm. Therefore, given the same starting number, `rand` always generates the same sequence of random numbers. In other words, instead of being truly random, the sequence generated by `rand` is a *pseudo-random* sequence. If the algorithm used to generate the random numbers is good, the sequence will not repeat itself too soon and all numbers between 0 and RAND_MAX will appear with equal probability. ANSI C provides a function named `srand` to set the starting point (the *seed*) of the random sequence.

Sometimes you need to pick a random sequence of random numbers. For example, you wouldn't want a card game to deal the same hands each time. ANSI C does not provide a routine to generate a random seed, but you can use the value returned by the time function as the argument to srand to set a new random seed for rand.

Character Classification

The C header file <ctype.h> contains several functions that are useful for classifying and converting characters. The behavior of these functions is affected by the LC_CTYPE category of the current locale. Table 10.3 summarizes the ANSI C functions that you can use to classify and convert characters. The functions are useful when your programs parse strings. For instance, you can use the isspace function to locate a valid whitespace character in a string.

Table 10.3. Summary of ANSI C's Character Classification Functions.

Name	Description
isalnum	Returns nonzero if character is alphanumeric.
isalpha	Returns nonzero if character is alphabetic.
iscntrl	Returns nonzero if character belongs to the set of control characters.
isdigit	Returns nonzero if character is a numerical digit.
isgraph	Returns nonzero if character is printable (excluding the space character).
islower	Returns nonzero if character is lowercase.
isprint	Returns nonzero if character is printable (includes space).
ispunct	Returns nonzero if character belongs to the set of punctuation characters.
isspace	Returns nonzero if character belongs to the set of *whitespace* characters, which include space, formfeed, newline, carriage-return, horizontal tab, and vertical tab.
isupper	Returns nonzero if character is uppercase.
isxdigit	Returns nonzero if character is a hexadecimal digit.
tolower	Converts a character to lowercase only if that character is an uppercase letter.
toupper	Converts a character to uppercase only if that character is a lowercase letter.

String and Buffer Manipulation

You have already encountered some of ANSI C's string manipulation functions in the `String` class shown in Chapters 7 and 8. These functions, declared in `<string.h>`, are primarily for comparing two strings or buffers, copying one string or a buffer into another, and searching for the occurrence of a character in a string.

> A *buffer* is a contiguous block of memory, whereas a *string* refers to an array of characters. By convention, a string in C is marked by a null character—a byte with all zero bits. Because of this, C strings are known as *null-terminated strings*.

Strings in C and C++

Neither C nor C++ has any built-in data type for strings. Instead, strings are treated as an array of characters with a null character marking the end of the string. You can declare strings just as you would declare any other array objects:

```
char line[81], filename[]=".mwmrc";
```

Here, `line` will be a string with room for 81 characters, but because of the terminating null character, `line` can hold at most 80 characters. The second string, `filename`, is declared without a size, but the initial value of the string provides enough information about the size. The compiler will reserve enough storage for the string and the terminating null character. As shown in Figure 10.1, the `filename` string will require 7 bytes of storage.

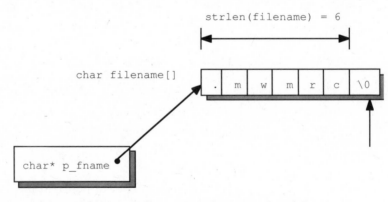

Fig. 10.1. Null-terminated string in C and C++.

Because a string is an array of characters, you can also access a string through a char* pointer. For example, to access the filename string using a pointer named p_fname, you would write the following:

```
char  filename[] = ".mwmrc";
char *p_fname = filename;
```

Once the pointer p_fname is initialized, you can use it to access the filename string in the same manner as you would through the array named filename. Of course, as shown in Figure 10.1, the pointer p_fname requires some additional storage space. You can also declare and initialize a char* pointer to a string in a single statement. For example, you would write

```
char *p_str = "Some string";
```

to initialize the character pointer p_str to the string constant Some string. What you actually have is p_str initialized to the address of the first character of the string Some string.

Length of a String

The length of a C string is the number of characters in the string up to but not including the terminating null character. For example, the string filename in Figure 10.1 is 6 bytes long, although 7 bytes are needed to store the string. You can use the strlen function to get the length of a C string.

Comparing Strings and Buffers

There are five functions in this category for comparing strings or buffers: memcmp, strcmp, strncmp, strcoll, strxfrm. Each function takes two arguments and returns a zero when the arguments match perfectly. The functions return a negative value if the first argument is less than the second. On the other hand, they return a positive value if the first argument is greater than the second, which for strings means that the first argument will appear after the second one in a dictionary of words in that character set.

The strcmp function is for case-sensitive comparison of two strings. The memcmp and strncmp functions behave like strcmp, but they compare a specified number of characters from the beginning of each string.

The strcoll function is meant for comparing strings using a collating sequence determined by the LC_COLLATE category of the locale. The strxfrm function is a utility routine that transforms a string into a new form such that if strcmp were used to compare two transformed strings, the result would be identical to that returned by strcoll applied to the original strings.

Concatenating and Copying Strings

The `memcpy`, `memmove`, `strcat`, `strcpy`, `strncat`, and `strncpy` functions are for concatenating and copying strings and buffers. Each of these functions accepts two arguments. In all cases, the second argument is the source and the first one, the destination. When copying or concatenating strings, you must ensure that there is enough room in the destination string to hold the source string. You can do this either by declaring an array of characters with enough room or by allocating memory at run-time.

The `memcpy` and `memmove` functions are for copying one buffer into another. Of these two, the `memmove` function is guaranteed to work properly when the source and destination buffers overlap.

The `strcat` function appends the second string argument to the first one and produces a null-terminated string as the result. The `strncat` function is similar to `strcat`, but it copies only a specified number of characters from the second string to the first.

The `strcpy` function copies the second string argument onto the first one. Whereas `strcpy` copies the entire string, `strncpy` will copy only a specified number of characters. When using `strncpy`, you have to watch out for cases in which the characters being copied do not include a null character, because `strncpy` does not automatically append a null character to the destination string.

Search and Sort

The standard C library also includes two very useful functions: `qsort` for sorting an array of objects and `bsearch` for searching for an object in a sorted array. These sort and search functions are suitable for in-memory operations wherein the entire array fits into memory.

Using `qsort` and `bsearch`

Figure 10.2 shows a typical scenario for sorting. You have an array of pointers to `String` objects (see Chapter 8 for the `String` class), each of which contains a C string. You want to sort the array by rearranging the pointers so that the C strings appear in ascending order. Figure 10.2 shows the original array of pointers and the array after sorting. Notice that sorting has rearranged the pointers, but the `String` objects have stayed put. This results in faster sorting, because the pointers are usually much smaller than the objects being sorted. Thus, it is faster to shuffle the pointers rather than copy the objects around. However, you pay the price in memory usage, because the pointers require extra storage space.

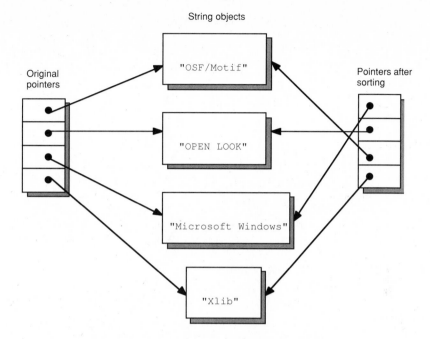

Fig. 10.2. Sorting an array of String objects.

The qsort and bsearch functions are declared in <stdlib.h> as follows:

```
void *bsearch(const void *key, const void *base, size_t num,
          size_t width,
          int (*compare)(const void *elem1, const void *elem2));

void qsort(const void *base, size_t num, size_t width,
          int (*compare)(const void *elem1, const void *elem2));
```

As you can see from the prototype, the qsort function expects as argument the starting address of the array, the number of elements in it, the size (in bytes) of each element, and a pointer to a function that performs the comparison of any two elements in the array. The bsearch function additionally requires a pointer to the value being sought, and it also requires the array being searched to be already sorted in ascending order.

The key to using qsort and bsearch is to provide an appropriate comparison function, which is the last argument to either function. This function will receive as argument pointers to the two elements being compared. It must return one of the following integer values:

- A positive value if the first element is greater than the second one

- A zero if the two elements are equal

- A negative value if the first element is less than the second one

The meaning of *less than*, *greater than*, and *equal* is up to you. When sorting `String` objects, for example, you would compare the C string field of the two objects and return a value based on the lexicographic ordering of the strings.

Sorting an Array of `String` Objects

As an example of using `qsort`, consider the problem of sorting an array of `String` objects. To be more precise, we first define a `StringArray` class that holds an array of pointers to instances of the `String` class. As shown in Listing 10.1, the `StringArray` class provides member functions to add new `String` objects to the array, display the current contents of the array, and sort the array. Note that the file `str.h`, which declares the `String` class, appears in Listing 8.1.

For this discussion, the interesting part of `StringArray` is the `sort` function. This function performs the sorting by calling `qsort` from the ANSI C library. The final argument to `qsort`, the `compare` function, is the crucial component in making this scheme work. For the `StringArray` class, you can implement the `compare` function as a class static function that performs the comparison by calling `strcmp` from the ANSI C library. You can use `String` objects as arguments to `strcmp` because the `String` class provides a type conversion operator that allows the C++ compiler to convert the `String` type to `const char*` type.

Listing 10.1. `strarray.h`—Implementation of the `StringArray` class.

```
//------------------------------------------------------------
//  File: strarray.h

//  Implement an array of String objects.
//
// NOTE: The "sort" function sorts the contents of the
//       array by calling the "qsort" function from the
//       standard C library

#if !defined(__STRARRY_H)
#define __STRARRAY_H

#include <stdlib.h>
#include "str.h"
```

```cpp
const size_t default_capacity = 16;

typedef String* StringPtr;

class StringArray
{
public:
// Constructor
    StringArray() : _count(0), _capacity(default_capacity)
    {
        _strp = new StringPtr[default_capacity];
    }

// Destructor
    ~StringArray();

    void add(const char* s)
    {
// If there is no more room, you should expand the capacity
// by allocating more space. Here, we simply return
        if(_count == _capacity) return;
        _strp[_count] = new String(s);
        _count++;
    }

// Function to be used with "qsort"
    static int compare(const void* s1, const void* s2)
    {
        return strcmp(**(String**)s1, **(String**)s2);
    }

// The "sort" function simply calls "qsort"
    void sort()
    {
        qsort(_strp, _count, sizeof(String*),
            StringArray::compare);
    }

    void show();

private:
    String** _strp;
    size_t   _count;
    size_t   _capacity;
```

```
    };

    //-----------------------------------------------------------
    // ~ S t r i n g A r r a y
    // Destructor for the StringArray class

    StringArray::~StringArray()
    {
        int i;
        for(i = 0; i < _count; i++)
            delete _strp[i];
        delete _strp;
    }
    //-----------------------------------------------------------
    // s h o w
    // Display the contents of the array

    void StringArray::show()
    {
        cout << "Contents of String array:" << endl;
        cout << "-------------------------" << endl;
        int i;
        for(i = 0; i<_count; i++)
        {
            cout << *_strp[i] << endl;
        }
    }

    #endif
```

Listing 10.2 shows a sample program that tests the sorting operation of the StringArray class. The program sets up an instance of the `StringArray` class, adds some `String` objects to it, and sorts the array. Finally, it displays the contents after sorting the array.

Listing 10.2. Sample program to illustrate sorting.

```
    //-----------------------------------------------------------
    //  Sample program to create an array of String objects,
    //  add some Strings, and sort the array.

    #include "strarray.h"
```

```
main()
{
    StringArray sa;
// Add some strings to the array
    sa.add("OSF/Motif");
    sa.add("OPEN LOOK");
    sa.add("Microsoft Windows");
    sa.add("Xlib");
// Sort the array
    sa.sort();
// Display contents
    sa.show();
}
```

When you run this program, it displays the following as the contents of the sorted array:

```
Contents of String array:
-------------------------
Microsoft Windows
OPEN LOOK
OSF/Motif
Xlib
```

As you can see, the array is sorted in ascending order. You can reverse the order of sorting by placing a minus sign in front of the `strcmp` function call in the body of the `compare` function of the `StringArray` class.

Time and Date

The ANSI C library includes a set of functions for obtaining, displaying, and manipulating date and time information. These functions are declared in the header file `<time.h>`. Figure 10.3 is a pictorial representation of the different formats of date and time in ANSI C and the functions that enable you to convert from one format to another. At the heart of these functions lies the `time` function, which returns a value of type `time_t`, which is defined in the header file `<time.h>`. This `time_t` value represents the calendar time in encoded form (often called *binary time*), and you can convert it to a `tm` structure by the functions `gmtime` and `localtime`. The `gmtime` function accept a binary time and sets the fields in a `tm` structure to correspond to Greenwich Mean Time (GMT) or Universal Time Coordinated (UTC) as this standard time reference is nowadays called. The `localtime` function sets the fields of the `tm` structure to the local time. The `mktime` function converts time back from a `tm` structure to a value of type `time_t`.

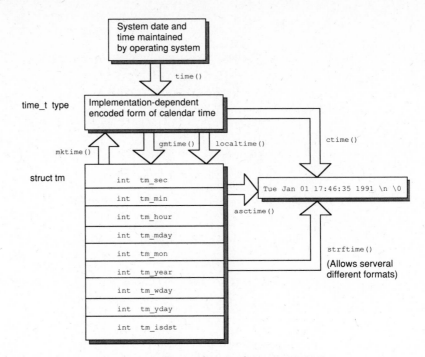

Fig. 10.3. Different forms of time in ANSI C.

Printing Date and Time

The asctime function converts the value in a tm structure to a null-terminated C string that you can print. The ctime function converts the output of time directly to a string. Thus, you can print the current time from a C++ program as follows:

```
#include <iostream.h>
#include <time.h>

main()
{
    time_t tnow;
// Get the current time in binary form
    time(&tnow);
// Convert the time to a string and print it
    cout << "Current time = " << ctime(&tnow) << endl;
}
```

The following is sample output from this program:

```
Current time = Mon Dec 31 00:18:50 1990
```

A DateTime class

As a more concrete example of using the time-manipulation functions in C++, here is a DateTime class that represents data and time information. As shown in Listing 10.3, the DateTime class maintains the calendar time in binary format. Its default constructor calls the time function to get the current time. The other interesting member of this class is the addition operator, which advances the date by a specified number of days.

The addition operator makes use of the mktime function to accomplish this task. The mktime function converts calendar time from a tm structure into a time_t format. Before making this conversion, mktime also adjusts all members of the tm structure to reasonable values. As you can see from the definition of the operator+ function in Listing 10.3, you can exploit this feature of mktime to advance the DateTime values by a number of days.

The DateTime class also overloads the << operator so that you can use << to print DateTime variables on an output stream. This overloading is done with the help of the print member function of the DateTime class, which prints on an ostream. The print function, in turn, calls ctime from the standard C library. Note that the ctime function converts a binary time into a formatted C string.

Listing 10.3. datetime.h—Definition of the DateTime class for manipulating calendar time.

```
//-----------------------------------------------------------
//  File: datetime.h
//
//  A date and time class.

#if !defined(__DATETIME_H)
#define __DATETIME_H

#include <time.h>       // ANSI standard "Time" functions
#include <iostream.h>  // For stream I/O

class DateTime
{
public:
    DateTime() { time(&_bintime); }
    DateTime(time_t t) : _bintime(t) { }

    friend DateTime operator+(DateTime d, int n)
    {
        struct tm *ltime = localtime(&d._bintime);
        ltime->tm_mday += n;
```

```
            time_t t = mktime(ltime);
            return DateTime(t);
        }

        friend DateTime operator+(int n, DateTime d)
        {
            return d+n;
        }

        DateTime operator+=(int n)
        {
            struct tm *ltime = localtime(&_bintime);
            ltime->tm_mday += n;
            _bintime = mktime(ltime);
            return *this;
        }

        void print(ostream& os) { os << ctime(&_bintime);}

    private:
        time_t      _bintime;
    };

    // Stream output operator for DateTime class

    ostream& operator<<(ostream& os, DateTime& d)
    {
        d.print(os);
        return os;
    }

    #endif
```

The DateTime class is far from being complete. It is meant to serve as an example that illustrates how to use ANSI C's time-manipulation functions in a C++ class. However, you can still use the class as-is for some useful work. Listing 10.4 shows a small program that displays the current date and time and also illustrates the use of the addition operators.

Listing 10.4. Sample program to test the `DateTime` class.

```
//-----------------------------------------------------------
//   Test the DateTime class.

#include "datetime.h"
```

```
main()
{
    DateTime d1;
    cout << "Current date and time = " << d1 << endl;

// Advance by 45 days
    d1 += 45;
    cout << "45 days later, it will be = " << d1 << endl;

// Try addition operator . . . (add another 5 days)
    cout << "50 days later, it will be = ";
    cout << d1+5 << endl;
}
```

Sample output from this program looks like this:

```
Current date and time = Tue Jan 01 17:46:35 1991

45 days later, it will be = Fri Feb 15 17:46:35 1991

50 days later, it will be = Wed Feb 20 17:46:35 1991
```

Note that there is an extra linefeed after each line because the `ctime` function (which the print member function of `DateTime` class calls) formats the binary time into a string with a newline character at the end. This feature of `ctime` and the explicit use of the `endl` manipulator are responsible for the extra blank lines. If you want to format the time into a string without an extra newline character, you can do so by calling the ANSI C `strftime` function, which is specifically meant for formatting time information.

Compiler-Specific Libraries

Although the standard C library is a good source of portable functions, you should also examine your C++ compiler's offering of nonstandard libraries. In particular, C++ compilers for MS-DOS systems, such as those from Borland International and Zortech, include many additional functions in their libraries. The most notable among these functions are the ones for accessing the services of the MS-DOS operating system and those for graphics output. If you are developing a program specifically for the MS-DOS environment and you do not mind being tied to a specific compiler's library, you should consider making full use of the compiler-specific functions. These functions are as easy to use as the standard C functions. In all likelihood, the header files are already conditioned to work with the C++ compiler.

All you have to do is include the header file and call the function. You do need to know the overall capabilities of the additional functions. You can usually find this information from the documentation that comes with the C++ compiler. Another possible source of information may be a book[2] that specifically covers your C++ compiler's library.

Summary

Like C, C++ is built around a sparse core with all major functions relegated to support libraries. The core of the language provides a small set of built-in data types, constructs such as `class` and `struct` to define new types, operators to build expressions, and control structures to manage the flow of execution of the program. You have to rely on libraries for everything from I/O to string manipulations. Because C++ is still evolving rapidly, it does not yet have a standard library like ANSI C's. Typical C++ compilers include the `complex` class for complex arithmetic and the `iostream` library for I/O. You can, however, use the functions from the standard C library in your C++ programs. To link C++ programs with C libraries, you have to enclose the declaration of the C functions and data inside an `extern "C" { ... }` linkage specifier. Many C++ compilers already provide C header files in which all declarations are enclosed in an `extern "C" { ... }` block. With such header files, using C functions is as easy as including the header files in a C++ program and making the function calls.

The standard C library includes a large assortment of functions that you are guaranteed to find in all standard-conforming C compilers. Because C++ does not have any standard library yet, the ANSI C library is a good place to look for functions that may be useful in your C++ classes. This chapter provides a summary description of the ANSI C library and shows you how to use these capabilities in C++ programs and in C++ classes.

Further Reading

If you need a reference guide for ANSI standard C and the standard C library, you will find the second edition of Kernighan and Ritchie's book[1] handy. This book provides summary descriptions of all standard C functions. If you are using Borland International's Turbo C++ compiler, you will find *The Waite Group's Turbo C++ Bible*[2] a useful source of detailed information on the huge library—with over 460 functions—that comes standard with Turbo C++. That book includes a tutorial on each category of functions and provides sample programs for each function in the library.

The exception-handling mechanism used in the *NIH Class Library* is described in Chapter 14 of the recent book[3] by Keith Gorlen, Sanford Orlow, and Perry Plexico.

1. Brian W. Kernighan and Dennis M. Ritchie, The C Programming Language, Second Edition (Englewood Cliffs, N.J.: Prentice-Hall, 1988), 284 pages.

2. Nabajyoti Barkakati, *The Waite Group's Turbo C++ Bible* (Carmel, Ind.: Howard W. Sams, 1990), 1098 pages.

3. Keith E. Gorlen, Sanford M. Orlow, and Perry S. Plexico, *Data Abstractions and Object-Oriented Programming in C++* (Chichester, West Sussex, England: John Wiley & Sons, 1990), 424 pages.

## Chapter 11

Building Class Libraries in C++

In Chapter 10, you saw how to use existing C libraries in C++ programs. This chapter looks at the problem of designing, organizing, and building C++ classes that can provide specific functionality for use in C++ programs. When designing a class library, you have to decide the inheritance hierarchy of the classes, the way one class uses the facilities of others, and the kind of operations that the classes will support. This chapter covers these issues.

Organizing C++ Classes

If there were a standard class library for C++, it would be easy to decide how to organize C++ classes. You would model your classes after the standard ones. Unfortunately, C++ does not have any standard classes yet. The `iostream` class library, which is part of AT&T's C++ 2.0 and which is described in Chapter 5, may be the only standard class library that you can currently expect to find. Of course, the `iostream` class library is only for I/O. You need much more than the `iostream` classes to develop complete applications in C++. Additionally, even if there were many more standard classes for C++, you would still have to write new classes that were customized for your particular application. The point is that, sooner or later, you would face the task of organizing a library of classes that will form the basis of your application.

Organization of C++ classes refers to their inheritance hierarchy as well as how one class might use the facilities of another. First let us consider the question of inheritance hierarchy.

Inheritance Hierarchy Under Single Inheritance

Before AT&T C++ Release 2.0, a class could inherit from at most one base class. As shown in Figures 11.1 and 11.2, there are two distinct ways to organize the inheritance tree of classes under single inheritance:

- A single class hierarchy in which all classes in the library are derived from a single root class. The Smalltalk-80 programming language provides a class hierarchy of this type. Therefore, this organization of C++ classes is known as the *Smalltalk model* or a *single-tree model*. Here, the term *root class* refers to a base class that is not derived from any other class.

- Multiple disjoint class hierarchies with more than one root class. This has been referred to as the *forest model*, because there are multiple trees of class hierarchies in the library.

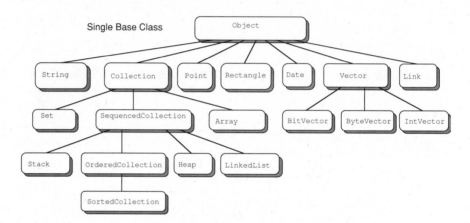

Fig. 11.1. Typical single-tree organization C++ classes patterned after Smalltalk-80.

Single Class Hierarchy

As Figure 11.1 shows, a library that uses a single class hierarchy starts with a base class, usually named Object, which declares a host of virtual functions that apply to all other classes in the library. These virtual functions are for standard operations, such as copying, printing, storing, retrieving, and comparing objects. Each derived class defines concrete versions of these functions, thus providing a standard interface to the library. Several prominent C++ class libraries, including the *NIH Class Library* by Keith Gorlen, use this model of organization. Proponents of the single class hierarchy point out the following benefits of this approach:

- By defining a single root class, you can ensure that all classes provide the same standard set of public interface functions. This enhances the consistency and compatibility among classes.

- With this organization, it is easier to provide capabilities such as *persistence*, which is the ability to store collections of objects in a disk file and retrieve them later. This is a consequence of having a single base class from which all classes are guaranteed to inherit. The single class hierarchy also makes it easy to provide a standard exception-handling mechanism. Once again, you can achieve this by placing the exception-handling code in the `Object` class.

- Because every class in the library is an `Object`, it is easy to define polymorphic data structures. For example, the following array of pointers:

```
Object *ArrayOfObjPtr[16];
```

can hold pointers to instances of any class in the library. This makes it easy to define data structures such as linked lists and stacks capable of holding instances of any class in the library.

Looking at the other side of the coin, many programmers find the following disadvantages with a monolithic class hierarchy:

- The compiler cannot provide strict type-checking, because many objects in the library are of type `Object*`, which can point to an instance of any class in the library. Such pointers to the base class are routinely used in polymorphic container classes that are capable of storing instances of any class in the library.

- The root base class, `Object`, typically includes a large number of virtual functions representing the union of all the virtual functions implemented by the derived classes. This makes it burdensome to create a derived class, because you have to provide the definition of all the virtual functions, even though many may not have any relevance to that derived class.

- Although having a single root `Object` class makes it easy to create a container class capable of storing any other object from the library, you cannot use these containers to store standard C data types such as `float`, `int`, and `char`. To store these types in a container, you have to write your own classes that mimic the built-in types of C. For example, you might define `Float` and `Integer` classes that model C's `float` and `int` data types, respectively.

- Because of the large monolithic class hierarchy, compiling a single program may require processing a large number of header files. This can be a problem on MS-DOS systems that typically have a limited amount of memory.

Multiple Class Hierarchies

In contrast to the monolithic, single class hierarchy of the Smalltalk-80 library, a C++ class library based on the forest model includes multiple class trees, with each tree providing a well-defined functionality. For instance, Figure 11.2 shows a number of class hierarchies in a C++ class library that provides the objects needed to build window-based user interfaces. Different types of windows are grouped together in the class hierarchy, with the Window class as the root. Each window has a rectangle represented by the Rectangle class, which, in turn, uses the Point class to represent the corners of a window. The Event class models user inputs that can come from one of the devices shown in the class hierarchy whose root is the Device class. The stand-alone String class represents text strings that might appear in windows. You can model the physical display by a class hierarchy with a generic Display as the base class. From this generic display, you can further specialize to text or graphics displays. You might categorize text displays into either ANSI-standard terminals or IBM PC-compatible displays. Graphics displays may be based on one of the following: the X Window System, Borland International's Borland Graphics Interface (BGI), or Zortech's Flash Graphics (FG) package.

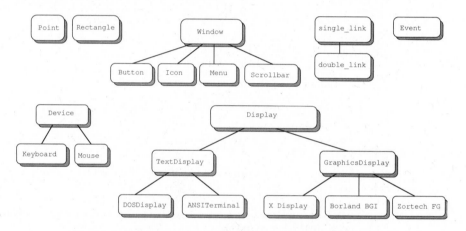

Fig. 11.2. A forest of C++ classes for building user interfaces.

Here are the main advantages of the forest model of class libraries:

1. Each class hierarchy is small enough so that you can understand and use the classes easily.

2. Virtual functions declared in each root class are relevant to that class tree.

Therefore, it is not difficult to implement the derived classes in each hierarchy.

On the other hand, the lack of an overall structure implies that you cannot have the elegant container classes of the Smalltalk model. Thus, the primary disadvantages of the forest model are these:

- Because there is no common base class, it is difficult to design container classes such as linked lists, stacks, and queues that can store any type of object. You have to devise your own schemes for creating such data structures.

- Anything that requires a library-wide discipline becomes difficult to implement. For example, exception handling and persistence are harder to support under the forest model than under a single-tree model.

Effects of Multiple Inheritance

The introduction of multiple inheritance in AT&T C++ Release 2.0 changed the implications of organizing C++ class libraries according to one of the models just described. Because multiple inheritance allows a derived class to inherit from more than one base class, now you can combine and customize the capabilities of classes in unique ways. A good example is the singly linked list of `String` objects illustrated in Chapter 8. There, the linked list is constructed by linking instances of a new class named `slink_string`, which is defined from the `String` class and the `single_link` class as follows:

```
class slink_string: public single_link, public String
{
// . . .
};
```

The `single_link` class is capable of holding a pointer to another instance of `single_link`. Here, multiple inheritance allows you to combine the capabilities of two classes into a single class. Following are some ways of applying multiple inheritance to extend the capabilities of C++ class libraries:

- You can derive a class from two or more classes in a library. You can do this even if the class library follows a single-tree model of inheritance hierarchy. For example, the NIH Class Library includes a `Link` class and a `String` class. You can combine these two classes with multiple inheritance to define a `String` with a `Link`, just as we did to define the `slink_string` in Chapter 8.

- Even with a multiple-class hierarchy, you can add a standard capability such as persistence by defining a new base class and deriving other classes from it. You have to do extra work to create a whole new set of derived classes that incorporates the capability defined in the new base class, but at least you can add the new capability with multiple inheritance. With single inheritance, you lack the opportunity to combine the behavior of two or more classes packaged in a library.

Client-Server Relationship Among Classes

In addition to the inheritance relationship among classes, a class may also use the facilities of another class. This is referred to as the *client-server relationship* among classes, because the client class calls the member functions of the server class to use its capabilities. In C++, the client class needs an instance of the server class to call the member functions of the server. The client class can get this instance in one of the following ways:

- One of the member functions of the client class receives an instance of the server class as an argument.

- A member function of the client class calls a function that returns an instance of the server class.

- An instance of the server class is available as a global variable.

- The client class incorporates an instance of the server class as a member variable.

- A member variable of the client class is a pointer to an instance of the server class.

Of these, the last two cases are of interest because they constitute the most common ways of expressing a client-server relationship between two classes. This approach of using a class by incorporating an instance or a pointer to an instance has been referred to as *composition*. The following sections briefly describe and contrast these two approaches of composition.

Class Instance as a Member

In Chapter 2, Listing 2.4 shows the declaration of several classes meant to represent geometric shapes such as triangles and rectangles. There is an abstract shape class from which all geometric shapes are derived. In particular, the `rectangle_shape` class is declared as follows:

```
class shape
{
public:
    virtual double compute_area(void) const = 0;
    virtual void draw(void) const{ } = 0;
};

// Define the "rectangle" class

class rectangle_shape: public shape
```

```
{
private:
    double x1, y1;   // Coordinates of opposite corners
    double x2, y2;
public:
    rectangle_shape(double x1, double y1, double x2, double y2);
    double compute_area(void) const;
    void draw(void) const;
};
```

A better way to define the `rectangle_shape` class is to make use of the notion of a point in a plane. For instance, you can first define a `Point` class as follows:

```
//------------------------------------------------------------
//  File: point.h
//
//  Define a point in two-dimensional plane.

#if !defined(__POINT_H)
#define __POINT_H

#include <math.h>

typedef double Coord;

class Point
{
public:
    Point() : _x(0), _y(0) {}
    Point(Coord x, Coord y) : _x(x), _y(y) {}
    Point(const Point& p) : _x(p._x), _y(p._y) {}

    Point& operator=(const Point& p)
    {
        _x = p._x;
        _y = p._y;
        return *this;
    }

    Point operator-(const Point& p) const
    {
        return Point(_x-p._x, _y-p._y);
    }
```

```
        Coord xdistance() const { return fabs(_x);}
        Coord ydistance() const { return fabs(_y);}
    private:
        Coord _x, _y;
    };

    #endif
```

Because a rectangle is uniquely defined by any two opposite corners, you can implement the rectangle_shape class using two instances of the Point class as follows:

```
//-------------------------------------------------------------
// File: rect.h
//
// C++ header file with definitions of a rectangle shape.


#if !defined(__RECT_H)
#define __RECT_H

#include <stdio.h>
#include <math.h>

#include "point.h"  // For definition of the Point class

class shape
{
public:
    virtual double compute_area(void) const = 0;
    virtual void draw(void) const = 0;
};

// Define the "rectangle" class

class rectangle_shape: public shape
{
public:
    rectangle_shape(Point& c1, Point& c2) : _c1(c1), _c2(c2){}

    double compute_area(void) const
    {
        Point p = _c1 - _c2;
        return p.xdistance() * p.ydistance();
    }
```

```
        void draw(void) const { } // Not defined

    private:
        Point _c1, _c2;  // Opposite corners of rectangle
    };

    #endif  // #if !defined(__RECT_H)
```

The two Points, _c1 and _c2, denote two opposite corners of the rectangle. Following is a sample program that uses the rectangle_shape class:

```
#include <iostream.h>
#include "rect.h"

int main(void)
{
    Point p1(10,10), p2(30,40);
    rectangle_shape r(p1,p2);

    cout << "Area of rectangle = " << r.compute_area();
    cout << endl;

    return 0;
}
```

When you run the program, it displays the expected output:

```
Area of rectangle = 600
```

This is an example of the rectangle_shape class making use of the Point class. Member functions of the rectangle_shape class access the member functions of the Point class through the Point instances _c1 and _c2.

Pointer to Class Instance as a Member

An alternative to incorporating Point instances in the rectangle_shape class is to define pointers to the Point class as members of rectangle_shape. With proper care, this approach enables you to declare the rectangle_shape class without including the definition of the Point class. For instance, you can rewrite the declaration of the rectangle_shape class as follows:

```
//-----------------------------------------------------------
//  File: rect_p.h
//
//  C++ header file with definitions of rectangle_shape class.
//  This version uses pointers to Point class.
```

```
#if !defined(__RECT_P_H)
#define __RECT_P_H

#include <stdio.h>
#include <math.h>

class Point;

class shape
{
public:
    virtual double compute_area(void) const = 0;
    virtual void draw(void) const = 0;
};

// Define the "rectangle" class

class rectangle_shape: public shape
{
public:
    rectangle_shape() : _p1(0), _p2(0) {}
    rectangle_shape(const Point& p1, const Point& p2);
    rectangle_shape(const rectangle_shape& r);
    ~rectangle_shape();

    void operator=(const rectangle_shape& r);

    double compute_area(void) const;

    void draw(void) const { } // Not defined

private:
    Point *_p1, *_p2;    // Pointers to Points
};

#endif  // #if !defined(__RECT_P_H)
```

Notice that this declaration of the rectangle_shape class does not include the complete declaration of the Point class. This effectively hides the specification of the Point class from the users of the rectangle_shape class. The trick is not to invoke any member functions of the Point class within the declaration of the rectangle_shape class.

You can place the actual definition of the member functions of rectangle_shape in another file. There, you would have to include the declaration of the Point class. For example, the definition of the member functions of the revised rectangle_shape class follows:

```cpp
#include "rect_p.h"
#include "point.h"

double rectangle_shape::compute_area(void) const
{
    Point p = *_p1 - *_p2;
    return p.xdistance() * p.ydistance();
}

rectangle_shape::rectangle_shape(const Point& p1, const Point& p2)
{
    _p1 = new Point(p1);
    _p2 = new Point(p2);
}

rectangle_shape::rectangle_shape(const rectangle_shape& r)
{
    _p1 = new Point(*r._p1);
    _p2 = new Point(*r._p2);
}

void rectangle_shape::operator=(const rectangle_shape& r)
{
    if(this != &r)
    {
        if(_p1 != 0) delete _p1;
        if(_p2 != 0) delete _p2;
        _p1 = new Point(*r._p1);
        _p2 = new Point(*r._p2);
    }
}

rectangle_shape::~rectangle_shape()
{
        delete _p1;
        delete _p2;
}
```

Although the `rectangle_shape` is now implemented differently, you can use it just like the previous version. For example, to create a rectangle with corners at (30, 20) and (130, 60), you would write:

```
Point p1(30,20), p2(130,60); // Define the corner points
rectangle_shape r1(p1,p2);   // Create a rectangle
```

You may have noticed that this version of the `rectangle_shape` class is much more complicated than the previous one that uses instances of `Point` class as member variables. The reasons for this are the following:

- The C++ compiler automatically creates and destroys class instances that are member variables of another class. The compiler also takes care of the copy and assignment operations for such class member instances.

- On the other hand, when you use pointers to class instances, you are responsible for creating and destroying these class instances. You also have to define the copy constructor and the assignment operator so that these operations work correctly. That is why the revised version of `rectangle_shape` class requires several additional member functions, including a destructor, a copy constructor, and an assignment operator.

Despite the additional work associated with managing pointers to class instances, they are necessary when you want to use polymorphism. Chapter 9 explains why this is so.

Public Interface to C++ Classes

The term *public interface* refers to the public member functions through which you access the capabilities of a class. The public interface to the classes in a library is as important as the relationships among the classes. Just as there is no standard C++ class library, there is also no standard interface to C++ classes. However, if you are designing a class library, it is good practice to provide a minimal set of member functions. Some member functions are needed to ensure proper operations, others to provide a standard interface to the library. This section briefly describes some of the functions that should be in each class's interface.

Default and Copy Constructors

Each class in the library should have a default constructor that is a constructor that takes no argument. The default constructor should initialize any data members that the class contains. For example, here is the default constructor for the `rectangle_shape` class:

```
class rectangle_shape : public shape
{
public:
    rectangle_shape() : _p1(0), _p2(0) {}
// . . .
private:
    Point *_p1, *_p2;
};
```

This constructor sets the data members _p1 and _p2 to zero.

The default constructor is important because it is called when you are allocating arrays of class instances or when a class instance is defined without any initial value. Thus, the rectangle_shape::rectangle_shape() constructor is called to initialize the rectangle_shape objects in the following:

```
rectangle_shape rects[16];
rectangle_shape r;
```

Each class should also include a copy constructor of the form X(const X&) where X is the name of the class. The copy constructor is called in the following cases:

- Whenever an object is initialized with another of the same type, such as

    ```
    rectangle_shape r2 = r;// where r is a rectangle_shape
    ```

- When an object is passed by value to a function

- When an object is returned by value from a function

As explained in Chapter 7, the copy constructor must be included for classes that contain members that are pointers. The reason is that if you do not define a copy constructor for a class, the C++ compiler defines one that uses memberwise copy. When a class has pointers as members, a memberwise copy will cause pointers in two objects to point to identical areas of the free store.

Copying Objects

Often, you need to make a copy of an object. For instance, Chapter 8 shows how to create a linked list capable of holding String objects. A new class, slink_string, is created there by multiply deriving from single_link and String classes. This slink_string class has links that enable its instances to reside in a singly_linked_list. To insert elements into the list, you must be able to create a copy of the object. In the slink_string class, this is done by the virtual member function called clone (see Listings 8.3 and 8.7). In the terminology of other C++ libraries such as the NIH Class Library, the clone function is equivalent to what is known as the deepCopy function. This is because clone makes a complete copy of a slink_string object, including a copy of the character string allocated by the String class. For a class X, you can define the clone function as follows:

```
X* X::clone() { return new X(*this); }
```

As long as all classes define appropriate copy constructors, the clone function will make a duplicate copy of the object on the free store and return a pointer to the copy. When you use functions such as clone that return a pointer to a dynamically created object, you have to remember to destroy the object by using the delete operator. Once again, this will delete the object, provided that appropriate destructors are defined for all classes with member variables that are pointers.

Destructors

Defining a destructor is important for classes that include pointers as member variables. The destructor should reverse the effects of the constructor. Thus, if the constructor allocates memory by calling new, the destructor should deallocate the memory by using the delete operator. As explained in Chapter 9, if the class contains any virtual member functions, you should declare the destructor to be virtual.

Assignment Operator

You should define the assignment operator for each class, because derived classes do not inherit the assignment operator from the base class. Also, if you do not define the assignment operator, the C++ compiler provides a default one that simply copies each member of one class instance to the corresponding member of another. If a class has member variables that are pointers to other class instances, such memberwise copying will result in multiple pointers pointing to a single area of the free store. When you define the assignment operator, remember the following:

- Handle the special case where an object is assigned to itself.

- Return a reference to the target of the assignment so that statements of the type x=y=z; work properly.

For an example, see the definition of the String::operator= function in Listing 8.2.

Input and Output Functions

Each class should also define two functions for I/O:

- An output function that prints a formatted text representation of each member of an object on an output stream.

- An input function that can read from an input stream the representation generated by the output function and reconstruct the object.

These functions enable you to define the << and >> operators so that they can accept as arguments instances of any class in the library. For example, you might use the names `print_out` and `read_in` for the output and input functions, respectively. Each of these functions should take a single argument—the reference to the stream on which the I/O operation occurs. Then, for a class X, you would define the output operator << as follows:

```
#include <iostream.h>
// . . .
ostream& operator<<(ostream& os, const X& x)
{
    x.print_out(os);
    return os;
}
```

Summary

Organizing a C++ class library involves deciding the inheritance hierarchy of the classes, how one class uses the facilities of other classes, and what public member functions each class supports. There are two trends in picking an inheritance hierarchy for the classes in a library: the single-tree model, in which all classes are ultimately derived from a single base class; and the forest model, in which there are multiple disjoint hierarchies of classes. The single-tree model of inheritance hierarchy is patterned after the basic classes of the Smalltalk-80 programming language, which does not support multiple inheritance as does C++. With multiple inheritance, you can mix and match classes from one or more class hierarchies and create custom classes.

Inheritance is not the only relationship among classes—a class may also incorporate instances of other classes as member variables. Whereas inheritance models the *is a* relationship among classes, inclusion of class instances captures the *has a* relationship. The inclusion takes the form of a member variable that is either a class instance or a pointer to a class instance. Defining a class instance as a member variable is simpler than maintaining a pointer to an instance, but the pointer is necessary to exploit polymorphism.

In addition to these relationships among the classes, each class in the library should present a consistent set of member functions so that there is a standard public interface to the library. This makes the library easy to use.

Further Reading

The article by Vaughn Vernon[1] briefly describes the pros and cons of the tree and the forest model of class inheritance hierarchies. He mentions having heard the term *forest of classes* used by Doug Lea[2] to describe the GNU C++ class library.

You will find a detailed description of the NIH Class Library in the recent book[3] by that library's authors. That book also tells you how to get a copy of the NIH Class Library.

The short tutorial articles[4,5] by Ted Goldstein describe the use of derivation and composition as techniques for defining new types of objects. Derivation involves inheritance, whereas composition refers to the inclusion of one class in another.

1. Vaughn Vernon, "The Forest for the Trees," *Programmer's Journal* 7.5 (September/October 1989), pp. 39–42.

2. Douglas Lea, "libg++, The GNU C++ Library," *Usenix Proceedings*, C++ Workshop, 1988.

3. Keith Gorlen, Sanford Orlow, and Perry Plexico, *Data Abstraction and Object-Oriented Programming in C++*, (West Sussex PO19 1UD, England, John Wiley & Sons Limited, 1990), 425 pages.

4. Ted Goldstein, "The Object-Oriented Programmer, Part 1: Derivation," *The C++ Report* 1, Number 1 (January 1989), pp. 4–6.

5. Ted Goldstein, "The Object-Oriented Programmer, Part 2: Composition," *The C++ Report* 1, Number 5 (May 1989), pp. 4–6.

## Chapter 12

Using Commercial Class Libraries

Developing an application in C++ can be easy provided you can get most of the functionality of the program from existing C++ classes. Recent reports[1] on large-scale C++ programming efforts indicate that programmers embarking on a large-scale project typically start off by designing and developing a library of classes. Then they build the final software products using these classes. Clearly, software development time can be reduced if an off-the-shelf class library meets the needs of a software project, and the library is easy for project programmers to use. This is where commercially available class libraries can be useful.

As C++ gains popularity as a programming language, commercial offerings of C++ class libraries are beginning to appear in increasing numbers. You will find these libraries advertised in many popular computer magazines. Each of these class libraries is geared toward a specific functionality. Some of the popular categories of commercially available C++ class libraries include the following:

- C++ classes for building user interfaces: text-based ones for MS-DOS as well as classes for graphical user interfaces with Microsoft Windows and the X Window System

- Classes for handling arrays

- Classes for implementing numerical methods such as least square estimation, optimization, and statistical methods

- Classes modeled after the Smalltalk-80 library, which includes general-purpose containers, linked lists, hash tables, stacks, queues, dynamic arrays, and strings

This chapter briefly describes two commercially available C++ class libraries, M++ and C++/Views. Note that you can get the full source code for each of these libraries.

> An *array* is an indexed collection of objects of identical type. The dimension of an array refers to the number of indexes used to access an element of the array. A *vector* is a one-dimensional array; a *matrix* is a two-dimensional array.
>
> The term *M×N matrix* implies that the first index of the matrix has M values and the second one has N values. An M×N matrix has M rows and N columns. Therefore, a 1×N matrix is called a *row vector* with N elements, whereas a M×1 vector is an M-element *column vector*.

M++

Dyad Software Corporation's *M++* class library provides a set of classes to support convenient handling of arrays in C++ programs. The M++ library essentially adds an array type corresponding to each built-in type (such as `char`, `int`, `double`, or `float`) as well as the `complex` type. In addition to the array classes, M++ also includes a number of memory-handling classes that you can use for memory management even if you do not use the array classes. The following sections briefly describe the M++ class library.

Matrix-Vector Operations with M++

To illustrate the ease of use of the array types supported by the M++ classes, consider the task of adding a three-element vector to each column of a 3×3 matrix of double variables. More specifically, here is what you have to do:

Given the 3×3 matrix A and the 3×1 column vector b:

$$
A = \begin{matrix} a^{11} & a^{12} & a^{13} \\ a^{21} & a^{22} & a^{23} \\ a^{31} & a^{32} & a^{33} \end{matrix} \qquad b = \begin{matrix} b^1 \\ b^2 \\ b^3 \end{matrix}
$$

compute:

$$
B = \begin{matrix} a^{11}+b^1 & a^{12}+b^1 & a^{13}+b^1 \\ a^{21}+b^2 & a^{22}+b^2 & a^{23}+b^2 \\ a^{31}+b^3 & a^{32}+b^3 & a^{33}+b^3 \end{matrix}
$$

Here is how you might do this job in "plain" C++:

```
#include <iostream.h>

main()
{
// Define and initialize the 3x3 matrix A
    double A[3][3] = { 0.0, 0.0, 0.0,
                       0.0, 0.0, 0.0,
                       0.0, 0.0, 0.0};

// Define and initialize vector b
    double b[3] = { 1.0, 2.0, 3.0};

// Define matrix B where the result will be stored
    double B[3][3];
    int i, j;

// Add vector b to each column of matrix A
// and store result in matrix B
    for(i = 0; i < 3; i++)
        for(j = 0; j < 3; j++)
            B[i][j] = A[i][j] + b[i];

// Print the result . . .
    for(i = 0; i < 3; i++)
    {
        for(j = 0; j < 3; j++)
          cout << B[i][j]) << " ";
        cout << endl;
    }
}
```

When you execute this code, it displays the expected result in matrix B:

```
1 1 1
2 2 2
3 3 3
```

M++ gives you a much simpler way to operate on arrays. By using the doubleArray class from M++, you can add a vector to every column of a matrix with the following program:

```
#include <darray.h>  // So that we can use the doubleArray class

main()
{
```

```
   // Define the necessary arrays
   doubleArray A(3,3), B, b = "{{1.0}, {2.0}, {3.0}}";

// Add vector b to matrix A. Store result in B and display
// the result
   B = A + b;
   B.print();
}
```

The first statement defines a 3×3 matrix named A whose elements are initialized to zero, an array B of unspecified dimensions (it will be a single element by default), a 3×1 column vector b initialized to

```
1.0
2.0
3.0
```

The result of applying the operator + on A and b is to produce a 3×3 matrix by adding the vector b to each column of A. The assignment of this matrix to B automatically resizes B to a 3×3 matrix and copies the result into B. Finally, when the `print` member function is called, it displays the matrix.

Clearly, the `doubleArray` class with its overloaded + operator and `print` function makes the job of adding a vector to each column of a matrix much simpler than that in plain C++ where you have to keep track of the array sizes and indices. Even with this simple example, you can see the benefits of having array types that take care of the details of operations on arrays:

- With an array class, you do not have to write loops and take care of indexing through the array. The array class can hide these details from you.

- Arrays are dynamically resized without any extra programming effort. In the example, the array B is initially a 1×1 array, but it is resized to a 3×3 matrix when a 3×3 matrix is assigned to it.

Importance of Documentation

Although it is easy to use the classes from the M++ library, you do have to know how each class behaves and what an operator does when applied to an instance of a class. For instance, in the example, the `vector` b is initialized as follows:

```
doubleArray b = "{{1.0}, {2.0}, {3.0}}";
```

Without reading the documentation of the M++ library, you would not know that the character string on the right-hand side specifies the initial value of the array b. Each inner pair of curly braces ({ }) represents one row of b. In this case, b is a three-element column vector and, consequently, it has three rows. Without the inner pairs of curly braces, M++ will treat b as a three-element row vector. The assertion is that you have to be aware of the functionality of each class before you can use classes effectively.

Classes in M++

Figure 12.1 shows the hierarchy of classes in the M++ library. The array types are implemented by the classes in the tree that have the abstract base class Array as the root. As summarized in Table 12.1, there is an array type for each built-in type in C++. Additionally, M++ also includes a complexArray class for arrays of complex type. The complex class is defined by most C++ compilers in the header file complex.h. M++, however, provides its own complex.h header file and the documentation suggests that you use their definition of the complex class.

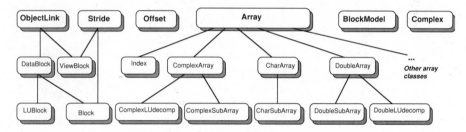

Fig. 12.1. Class hierarchy in the M++ library.

Table 12.1. Array Types in M++.

Class Name	Array of Type	Header File to Include
charArray	char	charray.h
ucharArray	unsigned char	ucarray.h
intArray	int	iarray.h
unsignedArray	unsigned int	uarray.h
longArray	long	larray.h
ulongArray	unsigned long	ularray.h
floatArray	float	farray.h
doubleArray	double	darray.h
complexArray	complex	carray.h

Because dynamic arrays require memory allocation and deallocation, M++ also includes its own memory-handling classes. In Figure 12.1, the classes meant for memory handling appear in a distinct hierarchy with the classes `ObjectLink` and `Stride` as the roots. There are also some helper classes, such as `BlockModel` and `Offset`, that are used internally by the array classes.

Using the Array Classes

The M++ array classes have a common set of public interface functions through which you can create, destroy, and otherwise manipulate the arrays. This discussion summarizes these member functions using the `doubleArray` class as an example. You can use the other array types similarly.

Creating Arrays

You can create and initialize an array in one of several ways:

- Define the array with specific dimensions. For example, to create a zero-filled 3×3 matrix named `transform`, you would write:

  ```
  doubleArray transform(3,3); // A 3×3 matrix
  ```

  By default, M++ supports arrays of up to four dimensions. You can alter the source code to support arrays of higher dimensions.

- Define the array without any dimension:

  ```
  doubleArray result; // Result is 1×1
  ```

  The array named `result` will be a single double variable, initialized to zero.

- Define an array from existing data:

  ```
  double i3[3][3] = {{1, 0, 0},{0, 1, 0},{0, 0, 1}};
  doubleArray xfrm(&i3[0][0], 3, 3);
  ```

  In this case, you are creating the `doubleArray` xfrm from the existing matrix, i3. You have to provide the address of the first element of the data and the desired dimensions of the array.

- Define an array in terms of an existing one using the copy constructor:

  ```
  doubleArray new_xfrm = xfrm;
  ```

  As you know by now, this creates new_xfrm by invoking the constructor:

  ```
  doubleArray(const doubleArray&)
  ```

with xfrm as the argument. Note that the copy constructor of an M++ array class does not create a unique copy of the array. Therefore, the new_xfrm array uses the same storage as xfrm. To get a unique copy, use the assignment operator as follows:

```
doubleArray new_xfrm;
new_xfrm = xfrm; // xfrm is an existing array
```

The doubleArray class in the M++ library enables you to define multidimensional arrays of double variables.

Filling Arrays

When working with vectors and matrices, you often have to fill a vector or a matrix with a specific sequence of numbers. M++ enables you to fill an array in one of four ways:

- Call the fill member function to set each element of an array to a constant value. For example, you can set all elements of matrix A to 1 as follows:

```
doubleArray A(3,3);
A.fill(1);
```

- Use seqAdd to fill the array with a sequence of numbers. You have to provide the starting value and the increment. For example, to set a 3×3 matrix to

```
1    7    13
3    9    15
5    11   17
```

you would write

```
doubleArray A(3,3);
A.seqAdd(1,2); // seqAdd(start, increment)
```

- Fill an array with random numbers. Call randUniform to fill the array with uniform random numbers between zero and one. Use randNormal for random numbers with a Gaussian probability density function (also known as *normal* random numbers).

- For matrices, you can use the identity function to create a square matrix (a matrix with the same number of elements in each column and row) with ones along the diagonal and zeros everywhere else. For example, to create a 3×3 identity matrix, write

```
doubleArray i3;
i3.ident(3);  // i3 is now a 3×3 identity matrix
```

If you define an array without initializing it, M++ fills the array with zeros.

Array Indexing

In the M++ array classes, the `operator()` is overloaded to act as array index operator. If you have a `doubleArray` A defined as follows:

```
doubleArray A(3,3);
```

in keeping with C++'s convention of starting array indexes at zero, `A(0,0)` and `A(2,2)` refer to the first and last element of A, respectively. However, as you will see next, you can change things so that the indexes do not have to start at zero.

In C++, the index for an array starts at zero. If you were to define the arrays:

```
double x[10], Y[3][3];
```

the first elements of these arrays would be `x[0]` and `Y[0][0]`. Unfortunately, many numerical algorithms originated in FORTRAN, where an array index starts at one. To make it easy to implement such algorithms, with M++ you can alter the starting index (the *base* index) of an array by calling the `setBase` member function to set the base index of the array. For instance, for the 3×3 matrix A, if you use the expression `A(1,1)` to access its first element, you can do so as follows:

```
      doubleArray A(3,3), b(3);
      A.setBase(1);
      b.setBase(1);
 // Now A(1,1) refers to first element of A and
 //      b(1) refers to the first element of b
```

In addition to making provisions for a base index other than zero, M++ includes an `Index` class with which you access elements of an array in an arbitrary manner. For example, if you want to access every other element in a vector, you can do so with an instance of the `Index` class:

```
doubleArray x(10);
x.seqAdd(0,1);  // Fill array with sequence 0,1,2,3, . . .
Index i(0,5,2); // Create indexes: 0 2 4 6 8
cout << x(i);
```

This code prints:
```
0
2
4
6
8
```

showing that, indeed, the `Index` i causes the expression `x(i)` to access every other element of x. You can also use instances of the `Index` class with two-dimensional arrays. An example illustrates what you access in this case:

```
doubleArray A(3,3);
A.seqAdd(0,1);        // A is  0  3  6
                      //       1  4  7
                      //       2  5  8
Index j(0,2,2);       // Index set: 0 2
cout << A(j,j);
```

What you get as output is the following:

```
0 6
2 8
```

which happen to be

```
A(0,0) A(0,2)
A(2,0) A(2,2)
```

Thus, if you were to write `A(i,j)` for two `Index` objects, `i` and `j`, you will access the elements obtained by a loop that can be expressed as the following pseudocode:

> *for every integer* m *in the* Index *object* i
> {
>   *for every integer* n *in the* Index *object* j
>   *access element* A(m,n)
> }

Finally, if you were to index a multidimensional M++ array with an empty index, the array is converted into a vector by laying out the columns one after another. For example, given the A matrix of the previous example, if you write

```
doubleArray vecA;
vecA = A();
vecA.print();
```

you will get as output

```
0
1
2
3
4
5
6
7
8
```

which is a vector with the columns of matrix A laid out one after another.

Operators

You have already seen an example of using the + operator for adding arrays. Another operator that you have seen in action is operator(), which is used for indexing into an array. Additionally, the array classes in M++ define most of the arithmetic and logical operators with their usual meanings. Unary operators apply to each element of an array. For binary operators, such as +, the two arrays must be *conformable*, which means that the corresponding dimensions of the arrays must match or one of the nonmatching dimensions must be a one. Following are some examples to illustrate this rule:

```
doubleArray A(3,3), b(3), c(1,3), X(3,2), Z(1,1,4), R;
R = A + b;  // Allowed, first dimensions match,
            // missing dimension assumed to be one
R = A + c;  // Allowed
R = A + X;  // Illegal: Second dimension does not match
R = A + Z;  // Allowed. R will be a 3×3×4 array
```

Array I/O

The M++ library overloads the C++ stream insertion and extraction operators << and >> to work with the array objects. You have already seen the << operator used in examples to display an array. You can use the >> operator to read in an array. For instance, given the following program:

```
#include <iostream.h>
#include <darray.h>

main()
{
    doubleArray A;
    cin >> A;
    A.print();
}
```

if you type in this line:

```
{{1,2,3},{4,5,6}}
```

the program prints the following as the A matrix:

```
1 2 3
4 5 6
```

Apart from overriding the << and >> operators, the M++ array classes also include the following I/O functions for storing and retrieving binary as well as ASCII representations of the data in an array:

- readASCII and writeASCII to perform file read and write operations of the ASCII representation of the array's data. For example, you can store the contents of matrix A in a file named A.mat as follows:

```
doubleArray A(5,5);
A.seqAdd(0,1);
A.writeASCII("A.mat"); // Save data to a file
// . . .
A.readASCII("A.mat");  // Read data from a file
```

- readBin and writeBin to perform file write operations of the binary representation of the array's data. These functions are used just like readASCII and writeASCII.

Overloaded Mathematical Functions

M++ conveniently defines the following mathematical functions to operate on each element of an array:

abs	ceil	log10
acos	cos	pow
acosh	cosh	sin
asin	exp	sinh
asinh	fabs	sqrt
atan	floor	tan
atanh	fmod	tanh
atan2	log	

For example, you can use the sin function of the doubleArray class to evaluate the sine of each element of an array of angles as follows:

```
// Create a vector of angles
    doubleArray angle(10);

// Fill the vector with the sequence: 0, 10, 20, . . .
    angle.seqAdd(0,10);

// Convert to radians (M_PI should be defined in <math.h>)
    doubleArray radians  = angle * M_PI/180.;

// Evaluate the sine function for each element of array
    doubleArray result = sin(radians);
```

Other Numerical Methods

In addition to overloading the mathematical functions for array types, the M++ library includes member functions in the array classes for the following numerical methods:

- The `inverse` function computes the inverse of a square matrix.

- The `product` function performs matrix multiplication.

- The `regress` function solves linear regression problems.

- The `solve` function simultaneously solves a system of linear equations.

- There are also a number of statistical functions such as `mean`, `stdDev`, and `variance` for computing the mean, standard deviation, and variance, respectively.

The following discussions briefly describe the first two of these numerical methods. The M++ library's documentation has the details on the other numerical methods.

Solving Linear Equations

Many scientific and engineering problems require the solution of a set of linear equations. For the sake of concreteness, consider a simple example: you want to find the point in a plane where two nonparallel lines intersect. To put the problem in a form suitable for matrix-vector operations, let the (x_1, x_2) denote the coordinates of a point in the plane. A line in the plane can be represented by an equation of the form $a\ x_1 + b\ x_2 = c$. Let the two lines be given by

$$x_1 + x_2 = 2$$
$$2x_1 - 3x_2 = 0$$

You can write this in matrix-vector notation as

$$A\ x = b$$

where A is a 2×2 matrix and x and b are 2×1 column vectors:

$$A = \begin{matrix} 1 & 1 \\ 2 & -3 \end{matrix} \qquad x = \begin{matrix} x_1 \\ x_2 \end{matrix} \qquad b = \begin{matrix} 2 \\ 0 \end{matrix}$$

The problem is to solve for the vector x, given the matrix A and the vector b. If you express A, x, and b as instances of the `doubleArray` class from M++, you can solve this problem by calling the `solve` function as follows:

```
#include <darray.h>

main()
{
    doubleArray A = "{{1, 1}, {2, -3}}", b = "{{2},{0}}", x;

// Solve the equation A x = b
    x = b.solve(A);
    x.print();
}
```

In this case, the resulting x vector is

```
1.2
0.8
```

which means that the lines intersect at the point whose coordinates are (1.2, 0.8).

Linear Regression

Often a problem can be expressed as a system of linear equations, but there are more equations than the number of unknown variables. Such systems of equations are called *overdetermined*, because the equations impose more conditions on the unknown variables than can be met. The array classes in M++ library include a numerical method known as *linear regression* that can be used to solve overdetermined systems of equations.

A specific example of such an overdetermined system of linear equations occurs when you try to determine the trend in a set of data. Take, for instance, the Dow Jones Industrial Average (DJIA) for a period of five days:

Day	Dow Jones Average
0	2475
1	2480
2	2510
3	2625
4	2640

You want to find a line that best fits this data so that you can extrapolate into the near future using the trend indicated by this data. You can model the line representing the trend by the equation

```
Coefficient * Day + ZeroOffset = DJIA
```

where the unknown parameters are `Coefficient` and `ZeroOffset`. From the given daily Dow Jones Average, you can write the following equations for the unknown parameters:

```
Coefficient * 0  +  ZeroOffset  = 2475
Coefficient * 1  +  ZeroOffset  = 2480
Coefficient * 2  +  ZeroOffset  = 2510
Coefficient * 3  +  ZeroOffset  = 2625
Coefficient * 4  +  ZeroOffset  = 2640
```

In terms of matrix-vector product, these equations can be written as

```
A x = DJIA
```

where A is a 5×2 matrix, DJIA is a 5×1 column vector, and x is 2×1 column vector:

```
      0  1                 2475    x =      Coefficient
A =   1  1      DJIA =     2480             ZeroOffset
      2  1                 2510
      3  1                 2625
      4  1                 2640
```

The problem is to solve for x, given the matrix A and the vector DJIA. Notice that A is no longer a square matrix, so you cannot use the `solve` function. The array classes of the M++ library provide the `regress` function for solving this type of problem. Here is how you might determine the unknown parameters in this case:

```cpp
#include <darray.h>
#include <iostream.h>

enum {Coefficient, ZeroOffset};

main()
{
    doubleArray A = "{{0,1},{1,1},{2,1},{3,1},{4,1}}",
        DJIA = "{{2475},{2480},{2510},{2625},{2640}}", x;

// Solve the linear regression problem
    x = DJIA.regress(A);
    cout << "x =" << endl;
    x.print();

// Compute values on the line for six days—the value for
// the sixth day can be used as a "predicted" value
    doubleArray days(6), DJIA_est;
    days.seqAdd(0,1);  // Set up days 0, 1, 2, 3, 4, 5
```

```
// Use the equation for the line
    DJIA_est = x(Coefficient) * days + x(ZeroOffset);
    cout << "DJIA Estimates = " << endl;
    DJIA_est.print();
}
```

When executed, this program prints the following:

```
x =
47.5
2451


DJIA Estimates =
2451
2498.5
2546
2593.5
2641
2688.5
```

This indicates that the unknown parameters `Coefficient` and `ZeroOffset` are 47.5 and 2451, respectively. This means that the first day's Dow Jones Average should have been 2451 according to the linear trend and that the average goes up by 47.5 points every day. The estimated values of the Dow Jones Average indicate that if the current trend continues, the average on the sixth day is expected to be 2688.5.

Using the Memory-Management Classes

M++'s memory-management classes (Figure 12.1) are used by the array classes to manage their internal memory requirements. Dynamic arrays (arrays that change size) tend to require many memory allocations and deallocations. If a program does too many allocations and deallocations, you can have two problems:

- The free store becomes fragmented by many small chunks allocated throughout the free store. *Fragmentation* refers to the problem of having the available memory broken up into many smaller chunks instead of a single contiguous block. Fragmentation can cause memory allocations to fail because a single block of the requested size may not be available even though there are many smaller blocks throughout the free store.

- The time spent in allocating and deallocating memory can become a significant percentage of the total execution time of the program.

The reason for using the memory-management classes is to reduce fragmentation and to minimize calls to memory allocation functions. The idea is to allocate a large block of memory once and use it for new arrays until the block is exhausted.

The classes Model and ObjectLink are the keys to using the memory-management facilities of M++. For example, suppose you have a class Point and you plan to create arrays of Point. To use the memory management facilities offered by M++, you have to create a new class that inherits from ObjectLink and define an instance of Model that specifies the memory-management model you want to use. The ObjectLink class provides overloaded operators, new and delete, that are aware of the memory-handling techniques supported by M++. To learn more about the memory-management facilities of the M++ class library, you should consult the *M++ Class Library Reference Manual*.

C++/Views for Microsoft Windows

The C++/Views library from CNS, Inc. includes over 60 C++ classes meant for modeling data structures and developing complete applications for the Microsoft Windows environment. The design of the library is such that it insulates your program from the underlying windowing system. You can think of the C++/Views library as a layer between your program's code and the windowing system. Your program uses classes from the C++/Views library while the member functions of those classes interact with Microsoft Windows.

The result of this isolation from the windowing system is the following. Suppose you have built an application using C++/Views for Microsoft Windows. At a later date, if a version of C++/Views becomes available for the X Window System (X), for instance, you should be able to move your existing application to the X environment with minimal effort. In fact, CNS, Inc., the developer of C++/Views, indicates that versions of C++/Views for the X Window System, OS/2 Presentation Manager, and the Apple Macintosh will be available in the near future.

The following discussions briefly describe the capabilities of the C++/Views class library. Although C++/Views reduces the complexity of programming in a graphical windowing system such as Microsoft Windows, C++/Views is complicated enough that a complete coverage is beyond the scope of this book. You can find a more detailed coverage in the *C++/Views for Microsoft Windows User Guide*.

Hardware and Software Requirements

To use C++/Views for Microsoft Windows, you will need the following:

- An Intel 80286- or 80386-based computer running MS-DOS version 3.0 or later and the Microsoft Windows environment.

- Microsoft Windows Software Development Kit (SDK) available from Microsoft Corporation.

- A C++ compiler compatible with the header files and libraries of the Microsoft Windows SDK. The Zortech C++ Compiler V2.1 and Borland C++ 2.0 work with C++/Views for Microsoft Windows.

- A Microsoft Windows-compatible linker such as the linker (LINK.EXE) that comes with Microsoft C version 5.1 (or later).

Model-View-Controller Architecture

C++/Views provides a complete framework for developing applications with graphical user interfaces. It uses Smalltalk-80's Model-View-Controller (MVC) architecture for the classes. As illustrated in Figure 12.2, the C++/Views MVC architecture separates an application into three layers:

1. *Model* refers to the *application layer* where all application-dependent objects reside. For example, in a drawing program, this is the layer that maintains the graphics objects.

2. *View* is the *presentation layer* that presents the application's data to the user. This layer extracts information from the Model and displays the information in windows. In a drawing program, this layer would get the list of graphics objects from the Model and render them in a window. Of course, in an object-oriented program, the View would draw the objects by "sending a draw message" to each of the objects stored in the Model.

3. *Controller* is the *interaction layer* that provides the interface between the input devices (such as keyboard and mouse) and the View and Model layers. In C++/Views, the Controller layer is completely encapsulated in a class named `Notifier`. In fact, the C++/Views library creates a single, global instance of this class, named `notifier`. Programmers can handle all user-interactions in a C++/Views-based application by calling `notifier.start()`.

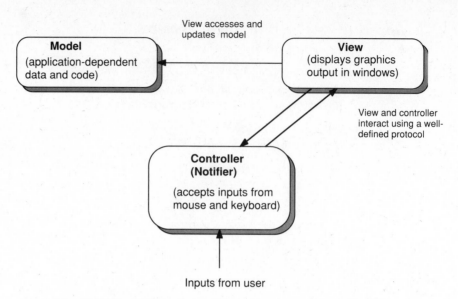

Fig. 12.2. Model-View-Controller architecture of C++/Views.

C++/Views Class Hierarchy

Figure 12.3 gives an overview of the C++/Views class hierarchy. Because there are over 60 classes in the library, Figure 12.3 does not show each individual class. Instead, it shows the major branches of the class tree. As Figure 12.3 shows, all except 2 of the C++/Views classes are organized in a single-tree inheritance hierarchy patterned after the Smalltalk-80 class library. The exceptions are

- The `Notifier` class that implements the controller layer of the MVC architecture.

- A class named `Class` that provides class identity. You can use the `defineClass` macro to create an instance of `Class` for each class you define. Here is an example. Given a generic `Object*` pointer to the instance of a class, you can test whether the instance is of type `Circle`, for example, with a statement like this:

```
Object *p_obj;
// Test if pointer points to an instance of "Circle"
if(p_obj->isA(CircleCls))
{
// Yes. p_obj is pointing to a Circle object
}
```

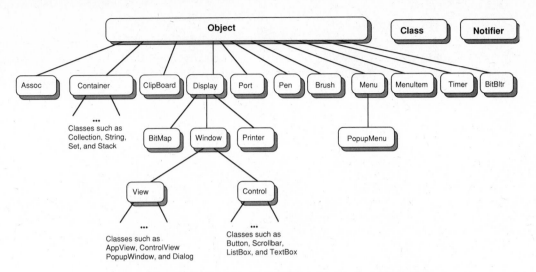

Fig. 12.3. An overview of C++/Views class hierarchy.

The rest of the class tree, rooted at the `Object` class, provides three broad categories of classes:

1. *General-Purpose Data Storage*: This category includes general-purpose container classes that can store instances of any class in the library. Specific examples include `String` for storing C strings; `Container` and `Collection` classes; and `Stack`, `Set`, and `Dictionary` classes.

2. *Windows, Menus, and Dialogs*: This group of classes is used to implement the view layer. Most of these classes inherit from `Window`, which, in turn, is derived from `Display`. The classes in this category include `AppView`, `PopupWindow`, `Button`, `ScrollBar`, `ListBox`, and `TextBox`.

3. *Graphics Output*: These classes are used to draw graphics and text in windows. Output to a bitmap or a printer is also supported. This category includes classes such as `Bitmap`, `Printer`, `Port`, `Pen`, and `Brush`.

Additionally, there are several specialty classes, such as `Timer` for timing services and `BitBltr` for transferring pixels between displayable objects.

An Application in C++/Views

A simple example is the best way to understand the basic capabilities of C++/Views. To keep things simple, we will create an application using C++/Views that runs under Microsoft Windows and displays `Hello, World!` in a window. Even with the C++/Views library, you have to attend to many details when writing a Microsoft Windows application. This discussion will describe the steps.

The main Function

Because of the MVC architecture, the `main` function of every C++/Views-based application is almost the same. Listing 12.1 shows the file `hello.cpp`, which implements the `main` function for our sample application. Here are the steps you should follow:

1. Create a model of the application. For this application, the model is a class named `HelloModel`, defined in the header file `hellomdl.h` (see Listing 12.2).

2. Create a view and store a pointer to the model in the view. In this case, the view class is named `HelloView` and it is declared in the file `hellovw.h` (Listing 12.3). You will see later that the `HelloView` class is derived from the `AppView` class of the C++/Views library.

3. Call the `show` function of the view to display the window.

4. Call `notifier.start()` to start interaction with the user.

The `CTWindow` variable must be a string that holds a unique name to be used to meet certain requirements of Microsoft Windows. An easy way to meet this requirement is to set it to the preprocessor macro `__FILE__`, which standard C defines to be the name of the source file and, therefore, is guaranteed to be unique for each program.

Listing 12.1. `hello.cpp`—The main function of the application.

```
//------------------------------------------------------------
//   File: hello.cpp
//
//   A C++/Views application.

#include "hellovw.h"
#include "hellomdl.h"

char *CTWindow = __FILE__; // Class name for this application

main()
{
    HelloModel *m = new HelloModel();
    HelloView *v = new HelloView(m);
    v->show();
    notifier.start();        // Start accepting input from user
      m->free();
    }
```

The Model Class

An application's model is supposed to store data unique to the application. In this case, the application is simple enough that we could have displayed the Hello, World! string directly from the view class. We have, however, chosen to create a model class to illustrate how realistic applications are built. This application's model, the HelloModel class (Listing 12.2), contains the string to be displayed in the window. The string is stored in an instance of a String class (defined in the header file str.h) that is created by the constructor of the HelloModel class. A member function named get_string returns a pointer to this String instance. The view class uses this function to access the string.

Listing 12.2. hellomdl.h—Definition of the HelloModel class.

```
//-------------------------------------------------------------------
//  File: hellomdl.h
//
//  The "model" for the "hello" application. In this case,
//  the model simply stores a string to be displayed in a window.

#if !defined(__HELLOMDL_H)
#define __HELLOMDL_H

#include "object.h"
#include "str.h"

class HelloModel : public Object
{
public:
    HelloModel()
    { p_str = new String("Hello, World!");}

    ~HelloModel() { delete p_str;}

    String* get_string() { return p_str;}

    boolean free() { delete this; return TRUE;}
private:
    String *p_str;
};

#endif
```

The View Class

The HelloView class is declared in the file hellovw.h (Listing 12.3) and implemented in hellovw.cpp (Listing 12.4). This class is responsible for displaying in a window the message stored in the HelloModel class. HelloView is derived from the AppView class, which is designed to serve as the view layer of an application. The view class uses the model class through a pointer to the model that it stores. Additionally, HelloView creates an instance of a Port that is needed for drawing in the window.

The most important function of the view class is called paint. The C++/Views notifier calls a view's paint function whenever that view's window needs repainting. Because our application is supposed to display a string in its window, the code for displaying the string is embedded in the paint function (see Listing 12.4). In that paint function, we get the String from the model by calling the get_string function of the HelloModel class as follows:

```
boolean HelloView::paint()
{
// Retrieve the String from the model
    String* p_string = ((HelloModel*)model)->get_string();

// Display string . . .
}
```

The model variable is of type Object*. Therefore, we use a typecast before invoking get_string through the pointer.

The actual rendering of the string is done by calling member functions of the Port class. Before drawing in a port, you have to call its open function; after finishing the drawing, you have to call its close function. In this case, the drawing commands are as follows:

```
// Draw in the port (open the port, draw in it, then close it)
    port->open();
    port->wrtText(p_string, xpos, h/2);  // Text output function
    port->close();
```

Here xpos is the x-coordinate of the location in the window where the string output starts and h denotes the height of the window. You can get the size (width and height) of the window by calling the sizeOfImage function like this:

```
// Get window size
    int w, h;
    sizeOfImage(&w, &h);
```

The location where the first character of the string is drawn can be computed from the window's width, w, and the font width:

```
// Get font size: fw = width, fh = height
    int fw, fh;
    fontSize(&fw, &fh);

// Compute x-position of first character of string
    int xpos = (w - p_string->size() * fw) / 2;
    if(xpos < 0) xpos = 0;
```

If you want to draw other graphics in the window, you can make calls to other member functions of the Port class. The documentation of C++/Views library has detailed information on this and other classes.

Listing 12.3. `hellovw.h`—Declaration of the `HelloView` class.

```
//------------------------------------------------------------
//  File: hellovw.h
//
//  Header file for the "View" layer of the application.
#if !defined(__HELLOVW_H)
#define __HELLOVW_H

// Include necessary header files
#include "appview.h"
#include "notifier.h"
#include "port.h"

class HelloView : public AppView
{
public:
    HelloView() { init_view();}

    HelloView(id a_model);

    ~HelloView();

    void init_view();

    boolean paint();   // Called by notifier whenever window's
                       // contents need to be redrawn
    boolean free();

private:
    Port *port;        // For drawing
};
#endif
```

Listing 12.4. `hellovw.cpp`—Implementation of the `HelloView` class.

```cpp
//------------------------------------------------------------
// File: hellovw.cpp
//
// The "View" layer for the "hello" application.
//------------------------------------------------------------
#include "hellovw.h"
#include "hellomdl.h"


//------------------------------------------------------------
// i n i t _ v i e w
// Initialize this view (create a port where we can draw)

void HelloView::init_view()
{
    port = new Port(this);
    setTitle("Hello");
}
//------------------------------------------------------------
// H e l l o V i e w
// Constructor for HelloView class

HelloView::HelloView(id a_model)
{
    model = a_model;
    init_view();
}
//------------------------------------------------------------
// ~ H e l l o V i e w
// Destructor for HelloView class (destroy the port)

HelloView::~HelloView()
{
    if(port) port->free();
}
//------------------------------------------------------------
// p a i n t
// Draw contents of window

boolean HelloView::paint()
{
// Display the message
    String* p_string = ((HelloModel*)model)->get_string();
```

```
// Get window size
    int w, h;
    sizeOfImage(&w, &h);

// Get font size
    int fw, fh;
    fontSize(&fw, &fh);

// Display string roughly at the center of window
    int xpos = (w - p_string->size() * fw) / 2;
    if(xpos < 0) xpos = 0;

// Draw in the port (open the port, draw in it, then close it)
    port->open();
    port->wrtText(p_string, xpos, h/2);
    port->close();

    return TRUE;
}
//--------------------------------------------------------------
// f r e e
// Destroy this instance of the View

boolean HelloView::free()
{
    delete this;
    return TRUE;
}
```

Building the Application

Once you have the header files and source files ready, you have to compile and link them to create a Microsoft Windows application. You can use the make utility that comes with most C++ compilers. The input to the make utility is called a *makefile*. For Zortech C++ Version 2.1, the makefile hello.mak is shown in Listing 12.5. We will not go into the details of the makefile's format. The compiler's documentation describes this in detail. Given the makefile of Listing 12.5, you can build the file HELLO.EXE with the following command:

```
make -fhello.mak
```

where make refers to the make utility that comes with Zortech C++ 2.1.

You need two more files to complete the process specified in the makefile:

- HELLO.DEF (Listing 12.6): This file is known as the *module definition* file and is needed to build Microsoft Windows applications.

- HELLO.LNK (Listing 12.7): This file contains inputs for the Microsoft's LINK.EXE linker.

Listing 12.5. hello.mak—The make file for building HELLO.EXE.

```
CFLAGS = -a -p -u -W -c -ml -g -br -DARCHIVER -DZORTECH \
-DMSDOS -DMS_WINDOWS -DFAR_OBJECT

OBJECTS = hello.obj hellovw.obj

CC = ztc

hello.exe:        hello.obj $(OBJECTS)
        link    @hello.lnk
        rc      hello.exe

.cpp.obj:
        $(CC) $(CFLAGS) $*

hellovw.obj:    hellovw.cpp hellovw.h

hello.obj:      hello.cpp
```

Listing 12.6. HELLO.DEF—Module definition file for HELLO.EXE.

```
NAME            Hello
DESCRIPTION     'Hello, World! in C++/Views'
EXETYPE         WINDOWS
STUB            'WINSTUB.EXE'
CODE            MOVEABLE
DATA            FIXED MULTIPLE
HEAPSIZE        22000
STACKSIZE       8192
EXPORTS         CTalkWndProc
```

Listing 12.7. HELLO.LNK—Linker input to build HELLO.EXE.

```
hello+hellovw+
/align:16/pac:8192
hello.exe
hello.map
cppview+llibcew+libw /NOD /NOE
hello.def
```

Testing HELLO.EXE

Once you have successfully compiled and linked the sample application, HELLO.EXE, you can run it under Microsoft Windows by typing the following command at the DOS prompt:

```
win hello
```

Figure 12.4 shows the output from the program. If you resize the window, the Hello, World! should appear centered in the window.

Fig. 12.4. Hello, World! from C++/Views-based HELLO.EXE.

Managing the Complexity

As you have seen, even with C++/Views classes, building a Microsoft Windows application requires attention to many details. For instance, we had to write seven files of which four dealt with code needed by the application. The C++/Views product includes a utility called *C++/Views Browser*, patterned after a utility of the same name in the Smalltalk-80 environment, that helps you manage the complexity by taking care of many details for you. The Browser is a Microsoft Windows application that lets you traverse the class hierarchy and browse (read) header files and source code through a graphical interface. A complete description of the Browser is beyond the scope of this book, but you should be aware that there are tools available to help users harness the complexity wrought by a large collection of classes in a library.

Summary

You can reduce the time needed to develop C++ programs by using commercially available class libraries provided

- the library includes classes that match your need

- the public interface to the classes is well-documented

This chapter briefly describes two C++ class libraries (you can get the source code for both libraries):

- M++ from Dyad Software Corporation, meant for manipulating arrays

- C++/Views from CNS, Inc. for developing Microsoft Windows applications

Several examples illustrate the usefulness of such class libraries.

Further Reading

Chapter 3 of a recent compendium[1] on object-oriented programming describes one company's experience in developing software products using C++.

For more information on M++ and C++/Views, you should contact the publishers[2,3] of these class libraries. If you already own any of these products, you will find detailed information on their usage in the product documentation.

New C++ class libraries are emerging at a steady rate. You will find the latest offerings advertised in computer magazines such as *Computer Language* and *Dr. Dobb's Journal*.

1. Raghunath Raghavan, "Building Interactive Graphical Applications Using C++" in *Applications of Object-Oriented Programming*, Lewis J. Pinson and Richard S. Wiener, eds. (Reading, Mass.: Addison-Wesley, 1990), pp. 66–100.

2. *M++ Class Library*, Dyad Software Corporation, 16950 151st Ave. S.E., Renton, WA 98058.

3. *C++/Views for Microsoft Windows*, CNS, Inc., 1250 Park Rd., Chanhassen, MN 55317.

## Part Four

Developing Applications in C++

Building MS-DOS Applications in C++

The first three parts of the book cover the terminology of object-oriented programming, the syntax of the C++ programming language and its relationship to ANSI standard C, and the use of C and C++ libraries in C++ programs. This part shows how to build complete applications in C++. The examples are realistic enough to show the essential features of most full-fledged applications: a user-interface and some computational modules that accomplish the tasks the application is supposed to do. The examples are grouped according to the operating environment for which they are designed. Chapter 13 starts off with an example for the MS-DOS environment. Chapter 14 presents an example for Microsoft Windows, and Chapter 15 covers application development with the X Window System under UNIX. Chapter 16, the last chapter of Part IV, describes some proposed additions to C++ that are in the offing.

A Forms Package

To illustrate the use of C++ in a realistic DOS application, consider the task of writing a Forms package that users run to create and fill up forms, and save the filled-up forms in a file for later retrieval. For the DOS version, you can keep the screen display simple so that you can focus on creating the C++ classes necessary for representing a form in memory and devising a scheme for storing forms in a file. That way, Chapter 14 can tackle the task of creating a Microsoft Windows-based user interface for this forms package while the examples reuse the classes developed in this chapter.

Figure 13.1 shows a partially filled form as it appears to the user of the Forms software. In this case, the form is an invoice, but the software should be able to create and display any form. As you can see, the form has a number of fields. The user fills in the form by moving the cursor to a field and typing information. To start the process of designing the Forms software, you need a description of what the Forms software is supposed to do. You can start with the following requirements:

- The Forms software lets the user open a form, fill it, and save the form in a disk file. The software should support the notions of a blank form and a filled-in form.

- There should be a way to define blank forms and to store a "pile" of blank forms in a file and retrieve them, one at a time, using a name or a number as a keyword.

- The storage scheme should be reasonably efficient. In particular, the software should maintain only one blank form, but allow many instances of the filled-in data for a form.

These requirements are admittedly rather broad, but they are good enough as a starting point. You can start the design from this, and as you refine the design, the requirements (at least your interpretation of the requirements) will become clearer. The rest of this chapter will develop and implement the C++ classes that form the basis of the Forms package.

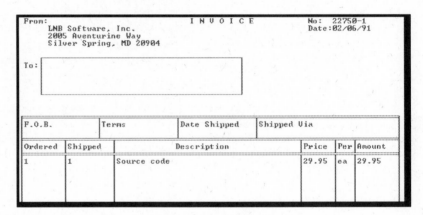

Fig. 13.1. A sample form.

Storage and Retrieval of Forms

Because storage and retrieval of forms is a major requirement of the software, you can start building the Forms package by looking at a possible solution to the problem of storing a form in a file and retrieving it later. For efficient storage, you can save the "blank form" in one file and the fields' data in a separate file. That way, there will be a single copy of the blank form but multiple sets of data to fill up the form. The two files are called

- The *definitions file*

- The *data file*

The *definitions file* has to store the definitions of multiple blank forms; a *data file* can have filled-in data for many different forms. To help locate an individual form's definition and data, you can store an index at the end of each file. Figure 13.2 shows the layout of these files.

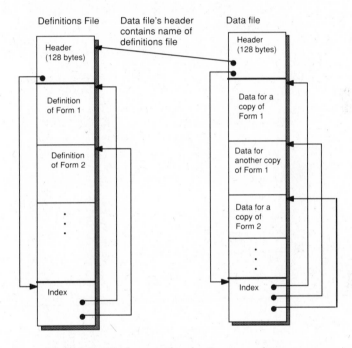

Fig. 13.2. File formats for the Forms package.

To simplify matters, both files have similar layouts—this simplifies the code that reads and interprets the header and the index. Each file starts with a header of fixed size, followed by the "data" for a number of form. The header contains the starting location of the index in the file—it is at the end of the file. The index, in turn, holds "pointers" to the starting locations of each form's data. In case of the *definitions file*, the data describes the layout of the form while the entries in the *data file* represent the data entered by the user.

Everything, except the header, is of variable size. Also, the data is stored in a textual form, so that you can inspect the files with any text editor.

File Header

You can encapsulate the reading and writing of headers in a C++ class. The class named `FileHeader`, declared in the header file `filehdr.h` (Listing 13.1), shows one possible implementation of the class. The data members of the class represent the essential information in the header:

1. A signature string (`_signature`) and a version number (`_version`) to help identify the version of the Forms software that created the form.

2. A `_filetype` string that can take two values, interpreted as follows:

   If it is FDEF, the file contains definitions of forms (*definitions file*).

   If it is FDAT, the file is a *data file* with filled-in data from users.

3. A `_filename` string. For a *definitions file*, this is simply the name of the file itself. However, in a *data file*, this is interpreted as the name of the file containing the definitions of the forms whose filled-in data is in that file. This is a mechanism you use to get to a form's definition, given its filled-in data.

4. A count of the number of entries (`_entries`) in the file.

5. A `streampos` variable indicating the starting location of the index in the file.

6. Two static `String` members—`form_definition` and `form_data`—used to test the `_filetype` field.

Note that the classes in this and subsequent chapters use the `String` class, which appears in Chapter 8 (see `str.h` in Listing 8.1 and `str.cpp` in Listing 8.2). This is a good example of packaging a class once and using it everywhere just like a built-in C++ data type.

Listing 13.1. `filehdr.h`—Declaration of the `FileHeader` class that models the file's header.

```
//-------------------------------------------------------------
//  File: filehdr.h
//
//  Declare the FileHeader class.

#if !defined(__FILEHDR_H)
#define __FILEHDR_H
```

```
#include <fstream.h>
#include "str.h"

class FileHeader
{
public:
    FileHeader(ifstream& ifs) { read(ifs);}
    FileHeader();

// Get and set location of index in the file
    streampos indexloc() { return _indexloc;}
    void indexloc(streampos pos) { _indexloc = pos;}

    unsigned short entries() { return _entries;}
    void entries(unsigned short num) { _entries = num;}

    unsigned short version() { return _version;}
    void version(unsigned short vnum) {_version = vnum;}

    String signature() { return _signature;}
    void signature(const char* sig);

    String filename() { return _filename;}
    void filename(const char* fname);

    String filetype() { return _filetype;}
    void filetype(const char* ftype);

    void read(ifstream& ifs);
    void write(ofstream& ofs);

private:
    String          _signature;
    unsigned short _version;
    String          _filetype;
    String          _filename;
    unsigned short _entries;
    streampos       _indexloc;
    static String   form_definition;
    static String   form_data;
};

#endif
```

The header, `filehdr.h`, defines several inline member functions; the rest appear in the file `filehdr.cpp`, which appears in Listing 13.2. This file initializes the static `String` `form_definition` to FDEF and `form_data` to FDAT. These strings are used in testing the `_filetype` field in the header.

The functions `read` and `write` are the two most important member functions of the `FileHeader` class. The `read` function reads the header and interprets it; `write` writes out a new header. Both functions rely on the `iostream` package and require the caller to position the stream pointer before the call to the function. Because you implement both functions, you can ensure that the `read` function correctly extracts the information written by `write`. In particular, each `String` is written with a terminating *newline* character. After reading such a `String`, the stream pointer rests on the *newline* character. You have to read and throw away this *newline* character before you proceed to the next data item in the file. This is the reason for the extra calls to the input stream's `getc` function in the body of the `FileHeader::read` function.

Chapter 5 describes how to use the facilities of the `iostream` library.

Listing 13.2. `filehdr.cpp`—Implementation of the `FileHeader` class.

```
//-----------------------------------------------------------------
//  File: filehdr.cpp
//
// Implement the FileHeader class that reads and interprets
// the header block of a file.

#include "filehdr.h"
#include "str.h"

const HeaderSize = 128;
String FileHeader::form_definition = "FDEF";
String FileHeader::form_data = "FDAT";


//-----------------------------------------------------------------
// r e a d
// Read a header

void FileHeader::read(ifstream& ifs)
{
// As each item is read, we have to skip over the "newlines"
        char c;
```

```
        ifs >> _signature;
        ifs.get(c);
        ifs >> _version;
        ifs.get(c);
        ifs >> _filetype;
        ifs.get(c);
        ifs >> _filename;
        ifs >> _entries;
        ifs.get(c);
        ifs >> _indexloc;
        ifs.get(c);
        ifs.seekg(HeaderSize);
}
//-------------------------------------------------------------------
// w r i t e
// Write header to an output file
// Caller sets "put position" before calling this function

void FileHeader::write(ofstream& ofs)
{
// Write out a fixed number of blank spaces to the file
        String hdr(HeaderSize);
        ofs << hdr;
        streampos pos = ofs.tellp();

// Go to the beginning and write the header's information
        ofs.seekp(ios::beg);
        ofs << _signature << endl;
        ofs << _version << endl;
        ofs << _filetype << endl;
        ofs << _filename << endl;
        ofs << _entries << endl;
        ofs << _indexloc << endl;
        ofs.seekp(pos);
}
//-------------------------------------------------------------------
// Some small functions . . .

void FileHeader::signature(const char* sig)
{ _signature = sig;}

void FileHeader::filename(const char* fname)
{ _filename = fname;}
```

```
      void FileHeader::filetype(const char* ftype)
      { _filetype = ftype;}

      FileHeader::FileHeader()
      {
          _signature = "LNBFORM";
          _version = 100;
          _entries = 0;
      }
```

With this implementation of the `FileHeader` class, reading a file's header becomes as simple as writing:

```
      #include "filehdr.h"
// . . .
      ifstream ifs("invoice.def");
      FileHeader hdr(ifs);
```

This will automatically read and interpret the header. You can access the entries in the header through the member functions of the `FileHeader` class like this:

```
      cout << "Form has " << endl;
      cout << hdr.entries() << " entries" << endl;
      cout << "Index at : " << hdr.indexloc() << endl;
```

The storage and retrieval scheme relies on the premise that each component of a form—the file header, index, form definition, and its data—is capable of storing and retrieving itself. Other tasks, such as drawing the form, are accomplished using the same technique of delegating the responsibility of the job to each component in an object.

The Index

Another good candidate for a class is the index stored at the end of each file. The `FileIndex` class represents the index, which contains a number of entries. To make this index class useful, you have to ensure that each entry in the index is of a standard form so that the same index can be used in both *data file* and *definitions file*.

IndexItem Class

The IndexItem class, defined in the header file indxitem.h (Listing 13.3), shows a canonical form for each entry in the index:

1. A String named _keyword that identifies the entry.

2. A streampos variable named _loc, which indicates where the data corresponding to this entry is located in the file (streampos is defined in the header file <iostream.h>).

3. A _size field that specifies the number of bytes occupied by that entry's data.

Listing 13.3. indxitem.h—Description of the IndexItem class.

```
//------------------------------------------------------------------
//  File:  indxitem.h
//
//  Characterize entries in the file index.

#if !defined (__INDXITEM_H)
#define __INDXITEM_H

#include "dlink.h"
#include "str.h"

class FileIndex;

class IndexItem : public double_link
{
public:
    friend FileIndex;
    IndexItem(const char* kw, streampos loc, unsigned short sz) :
        _keyword(kw), _loc(loc), _size(sz) {}

    IndexItem(const IndexItem& item) : _keyword(item._keyword),
        _loc(item._loc), _size(item._size) {}

    double_link* clone() { return new IndexItem(*this);}
    virtual void destroy() { delete this;}
```

```
        void read(istream& is)
        {
            char c;
            is >> _keyword >> _loc >> _size;
            is.get;  // Skip newline
        }

        void write(ostream& os)
        {
            os << _keyword << endl;
            os << _loc << " " << _size << endl;
        }

private:
    String          _keyword;
    streampos       _loc;
    unsigned short _size;
};

#endif
```

List of `IndexItems`

Because the `FileIndex` class has to store a variable number of `IndexItem` objects, you can use a doubly linked list to store them. Chapter 8 explains an idea of creating generic linked lists by "attaching" links to a class through inheritance. For instance, to create a doubly linked list, you first create a `double_link` class that has no data except two links, `_next` and `_previous`, that will allow instances of any class derived from `double_link` to reside in a doubly linked list. Now you can exploit that idea and derive the `IndexItem` class from the `double_link` class (see Listing 13.4). Listing 13.5 shows the header file `dllist.h`, which declares the `doubly_linked_list` class that represents the generic doubly linked list. Listing 13.6 has the actual implementation of certain member functions of the class.

`IndexItem` I/O

The `IndexItem` objects have to be read from and written to files. This is done by providing `read` and `write` member functions in the `IndexItem` class. In fact, any class derived from `double_link` is required to define the `read` and `write` functions so that all objects can be saved in a stream and retrieved later. Of course, the stream can be anything from a file to a buffer in memory.

Assuming that an output stream is positioned at the location where you want to save an `IndexItem`, the `write` function can be defined as

```
void IndexItem::write(ostream& os)
{
    os << _keyword << endl;
    os << _loc << " " << _size << endl;
}
```

Then the corresponding `read` function becomes

```
void IndexItem::read(istream& is)
{
    char c;
    is >> _keyword >> _loc >> _size;
    is.get;  // Skip newline
}
```

When you write a string to a stream, be sure to write a *newline* character to mark its end. When you are reading it back, skip over the *newline* character with an extra call to the input stream's `getc` function.

Listing 13.4. dlink.h—Provide the links for building doubly linked lists.

```
//---------------------------------------------------------------
//  File: dlink.h
//
//  Provide elements for building doubly linked lists.

#if !defined(__DLINK_H)
#define __DLINK_H

#include <iostream.h>

class double_link
{
public:
    double_link(): _next(0), _previous(0) {}
    double_link(double_link& dl) : _next(dl._next),
        _previous(dl._previous) {}

    double_link* next() { return _next; }
```

```
    void next(double_link *next) { _next = next;}

    double_link* previous() { return _previous; }
    void previous(double_link *previous)
        { _previous = previous;}

    virtual double_link* clone() = 0;
    virtual void destroy() = 0;

    virtual void read(istream& is) = 0;
    virtual void write(ostream& os) = 0;

protected:
    double_link* _next;
    double_link* _previous;
};

#endif
```

Listing 13.5. dllist.h—Declaration of the doubly_linked_list class.

```
//---------------------------------------------------------------
//  File: dllist.h
//
//  Declare a doubly linked list.

#if !defined(__DLLIST_H)
#define __DLLIST_H

#include "dlink.h"

class doubly_linked_list
{
public:
// Constructors
    doubly_linked_list() : _first(0), _current(0), _last(0),
                           _count(0){}

    doubly_linked_list(double_link& dl)
    {
    _first = dl.clone();
    _count = 1;
        _current = _first;
        _last = _first;
    }
```

```
// Destructor
    ~doubly_linked_list();

// Member-access functions . . .
    double_link* current() { return _current;}
    void current(double_link* dl) { _current = dl;}

    double_link* first()
    {
        _current = _first;
        return _current;
    }

    double_link* last()
    {
        _current = _last;
        return _current;
    }

    double_link* next()
    {
        double_link* t = _current->next();
        if(t != 0) _current = t;
        return t;
    }

    double_link* previous()
    {
        double_link* cur = (double_link*)_current;
        double_link* t = cur->previous();
        if(t != 0) _current = t;
        return t;
    }

    unsigned count(){ return _count;}

// Append an item to the list
    void append(double_link& dl);

protected:
    double_link *_first;
    double_link *_current;
    double_link *_last;
        unsigned     _count;
```

```
};


#endif
```

**Listing 13.6. dllist.cpp—Member functions of the
doubly_linked_list class.**

```
//-----------------------------------------------------------
//  File: dllist.cpp

//   Implement a doubly linked list.

#include "dllist.h"

//-----------------------------------------------------------
// ~ d o u b l y _ l i n k e d _ l i s t
// Destructor for the doubly linked list

doubly_linked_list::~doubly_linked_list()
{
    int          i;
    double_link *p_dl = _first, *t;
    if(_count > 0)
    {
        for(i = 0; i < _count; i++)
        {
            t = p_dl->next();
            p_dl->destroy();
            p_dl = t;
        }
    }
}
//-----------------------------------------------------------
// a p p e n d
// Insert a new item at the end of the list

void doubly_linked_list::append(double_link& dl)
{
// Clone the element passed to the function and
// hook it up in the linked list
    double_link *t = (double_link*)dl.clone();

    if(_last != 0)
```

```
    {
        _last->next(t);
        t->previous(_last);
        t->next(0);
    }
    else
    {
        _first = t;
        _current = t;
    }

// Make this one the last element in the list
    _last = t;
// Increment of count of elements on the list
    _count++;
}
```

FileIndex Class

Notice that the member functions of the doubly_linked_list class assume that the contents of the list are objects of the double_link class. Therefore, when using a doubly_linked_list to store IndexItems, for instance, you have to cast the retrieved pointers to IndexItem* before you use them. It is best to use an intermediary class that hides these typecasts. In the Forms package, the FileIndex class serves as the intermediary that performs these chores and lets you treat the index as a doubly linked list of IndexItems. As you can see from the header file fileindx.h (Listing 13.7), the FileIndex class has a single data member: a doubly_linked_list that contains the index entries.

Listing 13.7. `fileindx.h`—Header file for the `FileIndex` class.

```
//-----------------------------------------------------------
// File: fileindx.h
//
// Declare the FileIndex class, which maintains a doubly linked
// list of IndexItems.

#if !defined(__FILEINDX_H)
#define __FILEINDX_H

#include <fstream.h>
#include "dllist.h"
```

```
#include "indxitem.h"

class FileIndex
{
public:
    FileIndex(ifstream& ifs, streampos indexloc,
            unsigned short entries)
        { read(ifs, indexloc, entries);}

    FileIndex() {}

    int locate(const char* key);
    streampos itemloc()
    {
        IndexItem* p_i = (IndexItem*)_index.current();
        return p_i->_loc;
    }
    unsigned short itemsize()
    {
        IndexItem* p_i = (IndexItem*)_index.current();
        return p_i->_size;
    }
    unsigned count() { return _index.count();}

    void add(const char* kw, streampos loc,
            unsigned short size);

    void append(IndexItem& t) { _index.append(t);}

    void read(ifstream& ifs, streampos indexloc,
            unsigned short entries);

    void write(ostream& os);

private:
    doubly_linked_list _index;
};

#endif
```

Listing 13.8 shows the file fileindx.cpp, which implements the member functions of the FileIndex class. The member functions of the FileIndex class are designed to let you view the class as a collection of index entries. Here is how you can use some of the member functions of FileIndex:

- Use read to load an index from a file. You have to provide as argument an input stream, the starting location of the index, and the number of entries in the index. This information comes from the file's header. A shortcut is to create the index with these parameters. For instance, you can read the header and create the index as follows:

```
// Open a form definitions file and read header
    ifstream ifs("invoice.def");
    FileHeader hdr(ifs);
// Load the index
    FileIndex idx(ifs, hdr.indexloc(), hdr.entries());
```

The read function loads the index by reading the components of each entry and creating an IndexItem object for each entry. These entries are stored in the doubly linked list in FileIndex by calling the append function.

- You can store an index in a stream by calling the write function. You have to position the output stream with a call to its seekp function before you call write.

- Use the locate function to find an entry with a specified keyword.

Listing 13.8. fileindx.cpp—Member functions of the FileIndex class.

```
//-------------------------------------------------------------------
// File: fileindx.cpp
//
// Implement the FileIndex class, which provides access to the
// index in "form storage" files.

#include "fileindx.h"


//-------------------------------------------------------------------
// r e a d
// Read index items from an open file

void FileIndex::read(ifstream& ifs, streampos indexloc,
                     unsigned short entries)
{
// Position stream at specified location
    ifs.seekg(indexloc);

// Read the index entries one by one
    if(entries > 0)
    {
```

```
        String kw;
        streampos loc;
        unsigned short size;

        int i;
        char c;
        for(i = 0; i < entries; i++)
        {
            ifs >> kw;
            ifs >> loc;
            ifs >> size;
            ifs.get;   // Skip newline
            IndexItem t(kw, loc, size);
            append(t);
        }
    }
}
//-------------------------------------------------------------------
// l o c a t e
// Locate an item in the index

int FileIndex::locate(const char* key)
{
    if(key == NULL) return 0;

    String kw = key;
    int found = 0;
    IndexItem* p_i;
    for(p_i = (IndexItem*)_index.first(); p_i != NULL;
        p_i = (IndexItem*)_index.next())
    {
        if(p_i->_keyword == kw)
            found = 1;
    }
    return found;
}
//-------------------------------------------------------------------
// a d d
// Add an entry to the index

void FileIndex::add(const char* kw, streampos loc,
                    unsigned short size)
```

```
{
    IndexItem t(kw, loc, size);
    append(t);
}
//------------------------------------------------------------------
// w r i t e
// Write index to a file [call ofs.seekp() before this]

void FileIndex::write(ostream& os)
{
// Write out index entries one by one
    if(_index.count() > 0)
    {
        IndexItem* p_i;
        for(p_i = (IndexItem*)_index.first(); p_i != NULL;
            p_i = (IndexItem*)_index.next())
        {
            os << p_i->_keyword << endl;
            os << p_i->_loc << " ";
            os << p_i->_size << endl;
        }
    }
}
```

Components of a Form

You can think of a form as having two major components:

- The *background*, which includes everything that you see on a blank form: the lines and grid, the graphics, and the text printed on the form.

- The *fields* where you enter information when filling up a form.

When you are storing a form in a file, both types of information—background and fields—are stored in the *definitions file*, but the actual data for the fields reside in the *data file*. The following discussions describe how you can represent the background and the fields of a form. Consult Figure 13.3 as you read the descriptions.

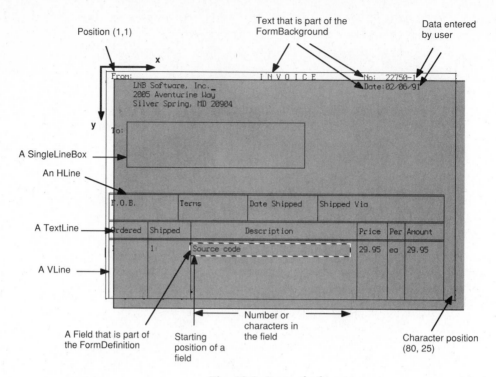

Fig. 13.3. Parts of a form.

The FormBackground *Class*

The background of a form will be made up of graphics elements: lines, boxes, and text. Assuming that there is a class named TextGraphics that provides such elements, you can create a FormBackground class to store such graphics objects in a doubly linked list. Once again, you can use the doubly_linked_list class (Listings 13.5 and 13.6) for the list. This implies that the TextGraphics class is derived from the double_link class.

Listing 13.9 and 13.10 show the files formbg.h and formbg.cpp, which define the FormBackground class. Like the FileIndex class, the FormBackground class has a doubly_linked_list named _bg, which holds all TextGraphics elements that make up the background of the form. FormBackground provides the member functions necessary to get to the TextGraphics objects maintained in the list.

Listing 13.9. formbg.h—The header file of the FormBackground class.

```c
//------------------------------------------------------------
//  File: formbg.h
//
//  Background of a form.

#if !defined(__FORMBG_H)
#define __FORMBG_H

#include "dllist.h"
#include "txtgraph.h"

class FormBackground
{
public:
    FormBackground() {}
    FormBackground(istream& is) { read(is);}

    TextGraphics* first()
        { return (TextGraphics*)_bg.first();}
    TextGraphics* last()
        { return (TextGraphics*)_bg.last();}
    TextGraphics* next()
        { return (TextGraphics*)_bg.next();}
    TextGraphics* previous()
        { return (TextGraphics*)_bg.previous();}
    TextGraphics* current()
        { return (TextGraphics*)_bg.current();}
    unsigned count() { return _bg.count();}

    void add(const char* name, istream& is);
    void add(TextGraphics& tgr) { _bg.append(tgr);}

    void read(istream& is);
    void write(ostream& os);
private:
    doubly_linked_list _bg;
};

#endif
```

Retrieving a Background from a File

An innovative aspect of the FormBackground class is the way in which its read function works. Unlike the FileIndex class, which is responsible for loading a single type of object (IndexItems), the FormBackground has to maintain TextGraphics elements that can be one of several different types. As you will see shortly, the TextGraphics class is an abstract base class from which you derive classes such as HLine (horizontal line), VLine (vertical line), SingleLineBox (box with single-line boundary), and TextLine (a line of text). You need a way to read any one of these objects from a file. The solution employed here is the following:

1. When you are storing a TextGraphics object, store an identifying string (its name) followed by the data necessary to represent that specific type of TextGraphics object (see the write function in Listing 13.10).

2. Maintain a static table of class_list objects where class_list is defined as follows:

```
struct class_list
{
    class_list(const char* s, TextGraphics& tgr) :
        name(s), obj(tgr) {}
    String        name;
    TextGraphics& obj;
};
```

The table named graphics_class_table at the beginning of Listing 13.10 is an example of such a table. This table associates a name with an instance of a class. This table also shows how to initialize a static array of class instances.

3. When you are reading the definition of a TextGraphics element from the file, read the name, locate it in the list, and append it to the list of background elements by calling the add function. This will automatically create a copy of the object and store it in the doubly linked list _bg. Next, call that object's read function so that it can initialize itself by reading from the file. To understand the process, you should study the read and add functions of the FormBackground class in Listing 13.10.

Listing 13.10. formbg.cpp—The member functions of the FormBackground class.

```
//-------------------------------------------------------------------
//  File: formbg.cpp
//
//  Implement the FormBackground class, which maintains the
```

```
//   background of the form.

#include "formbg.h"
#include "txtgraph.h"
#include "str.h"

extern HLine            HLineObj;
extern VLine            VLineObj;
extern SingleLineBox    SingleLineBoxObj;
extern DoubleLineBox    DoubleLineBoxObj;
extern TextLine         TextLineObj;

struct class_list
{
    class_list(const char* s, TextGraphics& tgr) :
        name(s), obj(tgr) {}
    String          name;
    TextGraphics& obj;
};

// Table of graphics classes that are used to draw the
// background of the form
static class_list graphics_class_list[] =
{
    class_list("HLine",          HLineObj),
    class_list("VLine",          VLineObj),
    class_list("SingleLineBox",  SingleLineBoxObj),
    class_list("DoubleLineBox",  DoubleLineBoxObj),
    class_list("TextLine",       TextLineObj)
};
static grclass_count = sizeof(graphics_class_list) /
                       sizeof(class_list);
//-----------------------------------------------------------------
// r e a d
// Read the background graphics of a form from a stream

void FormBackground::read(istream& is)
{
// How many elements to read?
    unsigned short entries;
    is >> entries;
    char c;
    is.get(c);
```

```
// Read the background elements one by one
    if(entries > 0)
    {
        const int buflen = 80;
        char bgname[buflen];
        int i;
        for(i = 0; i < entries; i++)
        {
            is.get(bgname, buflen);
            is.get(c);
            add(bgname, is);
        }
    }
}
//-------------------------------------------------------------------
// w r i t e
// Write Background to a stream [call ofs.seekp() before this]

void FormBackground::write(ostream& os)
{
// First write the total number of elements
    os << _bg.count() << endl;

// Write out Background entries one by one
    if(_bg.count() > 0)
    {
        TextGraphics* p_i;
        for(p_i = (TextGraphics*)_bg.first();
            p_i != NULL;
            p_i = (TextGraphics*)_bg.next())
        {
            os << p_i->name() << endl;
            p_i->write(os);
        }
    }
}
//-------------------------------------------------------------------
// a d d ( c o n s t   c h a r * , i s t r e a m &)
// Create the specified background element by reading
// definitions from a text buffer attached to a stream

void FormBackground::add(const char* name, istream& is)
{
// Locate specified graphics object in list of graphics classes
```

```
        int i;
        for(i = 0; i < grclass_count; i++)
        {
            if(strcmp(graphics_class_list[i].name, name) == 0)
            {
// Add this graphics object to the background and read
// in the parameters that define the graphics element
                _bg.append(graphics_class_list[i].obj);
                TextGraphics* p_i = (TextGraphics*)_bg.last();
                p_i->read(is);
            }
        }
}
```

The FormDefinition *Class*

Just as the FormBackground class maintains the background of a form, the definitions of the fields are maintained in a doubly linked list named _fields by the FormDefinition class (see Listings 13.11 and 13.12). With the FormDefinition class, you view _fields as a collection of instances of a class named Field, which models individual fields of the form.

The other data member of FormDefinition, besides _fields, is a String named _keyfield, which identifies the field whose value serves as the keyword for the index stored in the *data file*.

Listing 13.11. formdefn.h—Header file for the FormDefinition class.

```
//-------------------------------------------------------------
//  File: formdefn.h
//
//  A doubly linked list that defines the form's layout and
//  contents.

#if !defined(__FORMDEFN_H)
#define __FORMDEFN_H

#include "dllist.h"
#include "field.h"
#include "str.h"

class FormDefinition
{
```

```
public:
    FormDefinition() : _keyfield("none") {}

    FormDefinition(istream& is) { read(is);}

    Field* first()
        { return (Field*)_fields.first();}
    Field* last()
        { return (Field*)_fields.last();}
    Field* next()
        { return (Field*)_fields.next();}
    Field* previous()
        { return (Field*)_fields.previous();}
    Field* current()
        { return (Field*)_fields.current();}
    void current(Field* f) {_fields.current(f);}
    unsigned count() { return _fields.count();}

    String key_data();
    String key_field() { return _keyfield;}
    void key_field(const char* fieldname);

    Field* locate(const char* id);

    void add(Field& f) { _fields.append(f);}
    void add_data(const char* id, istream& is);
    void add_data(const char* id, String& d);
    void add_data(const char* id, const char* s);

    String data();        // Return current field's data
    void data(String& d); // Set current field's data

    void read(istream& is);
    void write(ostream& os);

    void read_data(istream& is);
    void write_data(ostream& os);
private:
    doubly_linked_list _fields;
    String             _keyfield;
};

#endif
```

Data and Definition

If you look at the member functions of FormDefinition (Listing 13.12) you notice that most functions seem to appear in two forms. For instance, there is read and read_data, and write and write_data. This differentiation is necessary because of the requirement to keep the definition of a form separate from its data. The functions with names ending in _data work with the filled-in data of the form; the functions without the suffix are meant for manipulating the definition. The implementation of the Field class, shown in Listings 13.13 and 13.14, reflect this.

Listing 13.12. `formdefn.cpp`—Member functions of the FormDefinition class.

```cpp
//--------------------------------------------------------------------
//  File: formdefn.cpp
//
//  Maintain a list of fields and their contents.

#include "formdefn.h"

//--------------------------------------------------------------------
// r e a d
// Read the field definitions from a stream

void FormDefinition::read(istream& is)
{
// How many elements to read?
    unsigned short entries;
    is >> entries;

// Skip over newline character
    char c;
    is.get;

// Read the field definitions one by one
    if(entries > 0)
    {
        int i;
        for(i = 0; i < entries; i++)
        {
            Field f(is);
            _fields.append(f);
        }
    }
```

```
// Read the name of the "key" field
    is >> _keyfield;
    is.get(c);
}
//----------------------------------------------------------------------
// w r i t e
// Write fields to a stream [call ofs.seekp() before this]
// This function writes everything except the data

void FormDefinition::write(ostream& os)
{
// First write the total number of elements
    os << count() << endl;

// Write out fields one by one
    if(_fields.count() > 0)
    {
        Field* p_f;
        for(p_f = (Field*)_fields.first();
            p_f != NULL;
            p_f = (Field*)_fields.next())
        {
            p_f->write(os);
        }
    }
// Write name of key field
    os << _keyfield << endl;
}
//----------------------------------------------------------------------
// a d d _ d a t a ( c o n s t   c h a r * , i s t r e a m &)
// Read data for a field from a stream

void FormDefinition::add_data(const char* id, istream& is)
{
    Field* p_f = locate(id);
    if(p_f != NULL)
    {
        p_f->read_data(is);
    }
}
//----------------------------------------------------------------------
// a d d _ d a t a ( c o n s t   c h a r * , S t r i n g & )
// Set the data for a field
```

```
void FormDefinition::add_data(const char* id, String& d)
{
    Field* p_f = locate(id);
    if(p_f != NULL)
        p_f->data;
}
//------------------------------------------------------------------
// a d d _ d a t a ( c o n s t   c h a r * , c o n s t   c h a r *)
// Set the data for a field

void FormDefinition::add_data(const char* id, const char* s)
{
    Field* p_f = locate(id);
    if(p_f != NULL)
        p_f->data(s);
}
//------------------------------------------------------------------
// l o c a t e ( c o n s t   c h a r * )
// Locate a specified field in the list of fields

Field* FormDefinition::locate(const char* id)
{
// Locate the field with specified id
    if(count() > 0)
    {
        Field* p_f;
        for(p_f = (Field*)_fields.first();
            p_f != NULL;
            p_f = (Field*)_fields.next())
        {
            if(strcmp(id, p_f->_id) == 0)
            {
                return p_f;
            }
        }
    }
    return NULL;
}
//------------------------------------------------------------------
// k e y _ d a t a
// Return the data in the key field

String FormDefinition::key_data()
```

```
{
    Field *p_f = locate(_keyfield);
    if(p_f != NULL)
        return p_f->data();
    else
        return String("none");
}
//--------------------------------------------------------------------
// r e a d _ d a t a
// Read the field data from a stream

void FormDefinition::read_data(istream& is)
{
// How many elements to read?
    unsigned short entries;
    is >> entries;

// Read the contents of each field one by one
// The field definitions must already exist
    if(entries > 0)
    {
        int i;
        for(i = 0; i < entries; i++)
        {
            char field_id[40], c;
            is >> field_id;
            is.get(c);
            add_data(field_id, is);
        }
    }
}
//--------------------------------------------------------------------
// w r i t e _ d a t a
// Write field data to a stream (call ofs.seekp() before this)

void FormDefinition::write_data(ostream& os)
{
// First write the total number of elements
    os << _fields.count() << endl;

// Write out fields one by one
    if(_fields.count() > 0)
    {
        Field* p_f;
        for(p_f = (Field*)_fields.first();
```

```
                    p_f != NULL;
                    p_f = (Field*)_fields.next())
        {

                    p_f->write_data(os);
        }
    }
}
//-------------------------------------------------------------------
// k e y _ f i e l d ( c o n s t   c h a r   *)
// Set the name of the "key" field. You can access the form's
// data using the value of this field as a key

void FormDefinition::key_field(const char* fieldname)
{
    _keyfield = fieldname;
}
//-------------------------------------------------------------------
// d a t a ( )
// Return current field's data

String FormDefinition::data()
{
    Field* p_f = current();
    return p_f->data();
}
//-------------------------------------------------------------------
// d a t a ( S t r i n g & )
// Set current field's data

void FormDefinition::data(String& d)
{
    Field* p_f = current();
    p_f->data;
}
```

The **Field** *Class*

Each field in the form is represented by a Field class (see Listings 13.13 and 13.14). Because the FormDefinition class maintains the Fields in a doubly linked list, the Field class has to be derived from the double_link class. This requires the Field class to define the member functions clone, destroy, read, and write (because these are pure virtual functions of the double_link class).

To keep the software simple, the Forms package assumes that each field can hold a single line of characters. Thus, you need the following data to represent a field:

- A String _id to identify the field. This is used when you are loading data into a form. The name of a field helps to locate the field into which the data goes.

- The String _data denotes the actual filled-in data for the field.

- The location of the data-entry area is given by _dxpos and _dypos. These are character locations with respect to the top left corner of the form with the positive x-axis pointing to the right and the positive y-axis pointing down.

- The _numchars variable denotes the maximum number of characters allowed in the data entry area of the field.

- The _curpos variable is provided in case you need to track the current character position within a data entry area.

Of these data members, _id, _dxpos, _dypos, and _numchars constitute the definition of the field, whereas _data represents the data used to fill the field. Therefore, the *definitions file* contains _id, _dxpos, _dypos, and _numchars; the *data file* contains _id and _data for each field. The data file has to store the identification (the "name") of each field so that you can load the data into the right field.

Listing 13.13. `field.h`—Declaration of the `Field` class.

```
//----------------------------------------------------------------
//  File: field.h
//
//  Declare the Field class.

#if !defined(__FIELD_H)
#define __FIELD_H

#include <stdlib.h>
#include <iostream.h>
#include "dlink.h"
#include "str.h"

class FormDefinition;

class Field : public double_link
   {
```

```
public:
    friend FormDefinition;

    Field() {};

    Field(istream& is) { read(is);}

    Field(const char* id, unsigned short dxpos,
          unsigned short dypos, size_t numchars) :
          _id(id), _dxpos(dxpos), _dypos(dypos),
          _numchars(numchars), _data(numchars) {}

    Field(const Field& f) : _id(f._id),
        _dxpos(f._dxpos), _dypos(f._dypos),
        _numchars(f._numchars), _data(f._data) {}

    String data() { return _data;}
    void data(String& s);
    void data(const char* d);

    String id() { return _id;}
    void id(String& s);
    void id(const char* name);

    unsigned short xpos() { return _dxpos;}
    unsigned short ypos() { return _dypos;}
    unsigned short numchars() { return _numchars;}

    void append(const char* s);
    void put(int c, int pos) { _data[pos] = c;}
    void replace(size_t pos, size_t len, const char* s)
    { _data.replace(pos, len, s);}
    unsigned short curwidth() { return _data.length();}

    double_link* clone() { return new Field(*this);}
    void destroy() { delete this;}

    void read(istream& is)
    {
        char c;
        is >> _id;
        is.get(c);
        is >> _dxpos >> _dypos >> _numchars;
        is.get(c);
```

```
        }
        void write(ostream& os)
        {
            os << _id << endl;
            os << _dxpos << " ";
            os << _dypos << " ";
            os << _numchars << endl;
        }

        void read_data(istream& is)
        {
            is >> _data;
            char c;
            is.get;
        }
        void write_data(ostream& os)
        {
            os << _id << endl;
            os << _data << endl;
        }

    private:
        String          _id;        // Field identifier
        String          _data;      // Data for this field
        unsigned short _dxpos;      // Location and size
        unsigned short _dypos;      // of data-entry
        unsigned short _numchars;   // area
        unsigned short _curpos;     // Current position in _data
    };

    #endif
```

Member Functions of the `Field` Class

The `Field` class provides `write` and `read` functions to store the definition of a field on a stream and retrieve it later. The `write_data` and `read_data` functions are analogous to `write` and `read`, but they store and retrieve the `_id` and the `_data` variables only.

A number of other member functions provide access to individual variables in the `Field` class.

Listing 13.14. `field.cpp`—Member functions of the `Field` class.

```
//-------------------------------------------------------------
// File: field.cpp
//
//   Implement the Field class.

#include "field.h"

void Field::id(const char* name) { _id = name;}

void Field::id(String& s) { _id = s;}

void Field::data(const char* d)
{
    _data = d;
    _curpos = 0;
}
void Field::data(String& s)
{
    _data = s;
    _curpos = 0;
}

void Field::append(const char* s) { _data = _data + s;}
```

Displaying a Form

So far this chapter's focus has been on the storage and in-memory representation of various elements of a form. You have seen a mention of the TextGraphics class in the description of the FormBackground class that manages the background of the form. The design of the TextGraphics class is motivated by the need to display a form. As you may have guessed, the name TextGraphics is chosen because this version of the Forms software will display on a MS-DOS PC's monitor in text mode.

As shown in Listings 13.15 and 13.17, the TextGraphics class is an abstract base class derived from the double_link class (Listings 13.5 and 13.6). This is necessary because the FormBackground class maintains TextGraphics objects in a doubly linked list. In addition to the virtual functions clone, destroy, read, and write that come from double_link, the TextGraphics class adds two more pure virtual functions:

- The draw function that should be defined by a derived class in such a way that you can draw the object on a device by calling this function with a pointer to the device (the OutputDevice class) as an argument.

- The name function returns the name of the class. This function is used in the FormBackground class when storing TextGraphics objects in a file.

TextGraphics *Class Hierarchy*

All useful graphics objects are derived from the TextGraphics abstract base class. As shown in Figure 13.4, the basic classes are

- TextLine objects, which are for displaying a line of text at a specified location.

- Line, which represents lines. This class is further specialized to the HLine and VLine classes for horizontal and vertical lines, respectively.

- Box, which is for drawing rectangles. Two classes are derived from Box: SingleLineBox and DoubleLineBox for rectangles with single-line and double-line boundaries, respectively. Internally, a box is represented in terms of the four border lines and the corners that are needed because of the assumption that the form will be displayed in a text-mode screen.

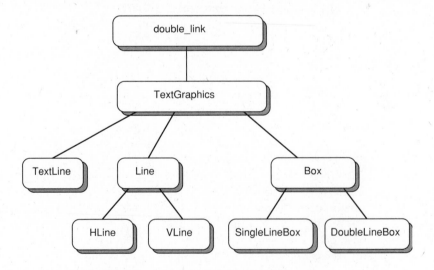

Fig. 13.4. TextGraphics class hierarchy.

Listing 13.15. `txtgraph.h`—Header file defining the graphics elements of a form's background.

```
//--------------------------------------------------------------------
//  File: txtgraph.h
//
//  Classes for text-mode graphics.

#if !defined(__TXTGRAPH_H)
#define __TXTGRAPH_H

#include <iostream.h>
#include "pcline.h"
#include "str.h"
#include "dlink.h"

class OutputDevice;
//--------------------------------------------------------------------
// T e x t G r a p h i c s

class TextGraphics : public double_link
{
public:
    virtual void draw(OutputDevice* device) = 0;
    virtual char* name() = 0;

    unsigned char drawing_char() { return _dc;}
    void drawing_char(unsigned char dc) { _dc = dc;}

    virtual double_link* clone() = 0;
    virtual void destroy(){}
    virtual void read(istream& is) = 0;
    virtual void write(ostream& os) = 0;

protected:
    unsigned char _dc;          // Drawing character
};
//--------------------------------------------------------------------
// L i n e

class Line : public TextGraphics
{
public:
```

```cpp
        Line(unsigned short x, unsigned short y, unsigned short l,
             unsigned char c) : _xpos(x), _ypos(y), _length(l)
             { _dc = c;}

        virtual void draw(OutputDevice* device) = 0;
        virtual double_link* clone() = 0;
        virtual void destroy() = 0;
        virtual char* name() = 0;

        unsigned short xpos() { return _xpos;}
        unsigned short ypos() { return _ypos;}
        unsigned short length() { return _length;}

        void read(istream& is)
        {
            char c;
            is >> _xpos >> _ypos;
            is >> _length >> _dc;
            is.get(c);
        }
        void write(ostream& os)
        {
            os << _xpos << " ";
            os << _ypos << " ";
            os << _length << " ";
            os << _dc << endl;
        }
protected:
    unsigned short _xpos;
    unsigned short _ypos;
    unsigned short _length;
};
//----------------------------------------------------------------------
// H L i n e

class HLine : public Line
{
public:
    HLine() : Line(0, 0, 0, HLINE_SL) {}
    HLine(unsigned short x, unsigned short y,
          unsigned short l, unsigned char c = HLINE_SL)
          : Line(x, y, l, c) {}
    HLine(const HLine& hl) :
        Line(hl._xpos, hl._ypos, hl._length, hl._dc) {}
```

```
        void draw(OutputDevice* device);
        double_link* clone() { return new HLine(*this);}
        void destroy() { delete this;}
        char* name() { return "HLine";}
};


class VLine : public Line
{
public:
        VLine() : Line(0, 0, 0, VLINE_SL) {}
        VLine(unsigned short x, unsigned short y,
                unsigned short l, unsigned char c = VLINE_SL) :
                Line(x, y, l, c) {}
        VLine(const VLine& vl) :
                Line(vl._xpos, vl._ypos, vl._length, vl._dc) {}

        void draw(OutputDevice* device);
        double_link* clone() { return new VLine(*this);}
        void destroy() { delete this;}
        char* name() { return "VLine";}
};
//------------------------------------------------------------------
// B o x

class Box : public TextGraphics
{
public:
        Box(unsigned short xul, unsigned short yul,
                unsigned short xlr, unsigned short ylr) :
                _topleft(xul, yul, 1),
                _topright(xlr, yul, 1),
                _botleft(xul, ylr, 1),
                _botright(xlr, ylr, 1),
                _top(xul+1, yul, xlr-xul-1),
                _bottom(xul+1, ylr, xlr-xul-1),
                _left(xul, yul+1, ylr-yul-1),
                _right(xlr, yul+1, ylr-yul-1) {}

        virtual double_link* clone() = 0;
        virtual void destroy() = 0;
        virtual char* name() = 0;
        void draw(OutputDevice* device);

        void read(istream& is);
        void write(ostream& os);
```

```
protected:
    HLine  _topleft, _topright;
    HLine  _botleft, _botright;
    HLine  _top, _bottom;
    VLine  _left, _right;
};
//-------------------------------------------------------------------
// S i n g l e L i n e B o x

class SingleLineBox : public Box
{
public:
    SingleLineBox() : Box(1, 1, 1, 1) {}
    SingleLineBox(unsigned short xul, unsigned short yul,
        unsigned short xlr, unsigned short ylr);
    double_link* clone() { return new SingleLineBox(*this);}
    void destroy() { delete this;}
    char* name() { return "SingleLineBox";}
};
//-------------------------------------------------------------------
// D o u b l e L i n e B o x

class DoubleLineBox : public Box
{
public:
    DoubleLineBox() : Box(1, 1, 1, 1) {}
    DoubleLineBox(unsigned short xul, unsigned short yul,
        unsigned short xlr, unsigned short ylr);
    double_link* clone() { return new DoubleLineBox(*this);}
    void destroy() { delete this;}
    char* name() { return "DoubleLineBox";}
};
//-------------------------------------------------------------------
// T e x t L i n e

class TextLine : public TextGraphics
{
public:
    TextLine() : _text(" "), _xpos(1), _ypos(1) {}
    TextLine(const char* s, unsigned short x, unsigned short y) :
        _text(s), _xpos(x), _ypos(y) {}

    TextLine(TextLine& tl) : _text(tl._text), _xpos(tl._xpos),
        _ypos(tl._ypos) {}
```

```
    void draw(OutputDevice* device);

    double_link* clone() { return new TextLine(*this);}
    void destroy() { delete this;}

    char* name() { return "TextLine";}

    virtual void read(istream& is)
    {
        char c;
        is >> _text;
        is >> _xpos >> _ypos;
        is.get(c);
    }
    virtual void write(ostream& os)
    {
        os << _text << endl;
        os << _xpos << " ";
        os << _ypos << endl;
    }
protected:
    String        _text;
    unsigned short _xpos;
    unsigned short _ypos;
};

#endif
```

Character-Based Graphics

In this version of the Forms software, the TextGraphics objects have to be displayed on an MS-DOS PC's text-mode screen. You can use the extended character set of the MS-DOS PCs to draw lines and boxes. Figure 13.5 shows a number of such characters useful for drawing lines and boxes. The header file pcline.h (Listing 13.16) defines symbolic names for each of these drawing character. Figure 13.5 also shows the symbolic name next to each character.

The unsigned char variable named _dc in the TextGraphics class denotes the line-drawing character to be used when drawing a TextGraphics object.

TOPLEFT_SL	┌	TOPRIGHT_SL	┐	BOTLEFT_SL	└
BOTRIGHT_SL	┘	VLINE_SL	│	HLINE_SL	─
LEFTH_SL	├	RIGHTH_SL	┤	T_SL	┬
INVT_SL	┴	CROSS_SL	┼		
TOPLEFT_DL	╔	TOPRIGHT_DL	╗	BOTLEFT_DL	╚
BOTRIGHT_DL	╝	VLINE_DL	║	HLINE_DL	═
LEFTH_DL	╠	RIGHTH_DL	╣	T_DL	╦
INVT_DL	╩	CROSS_DL	╬		
VLINE_TK	█	HLINEB_TK	▄	VLINEL_TN	▌
VLINER_TN	▐	HLINET_TK	▀	T_HDL_VSL	╥
TL_HDL_VSL	╓	TR_HDL_VSL	╖	LH_HDL_VSL	╟
RH_HDL_VSL	╢	INVT_HDL_VSL	╨	CROSS_HDL_VSL	╫

Fig. 13.5. Line drawing characters in MS-DOS PCs.

Listing 13.16. `pcline.h`—Definition of symbolic names for line drawing characters in MS-DOS PCs.

```
//------------------------------------------------------------
//   File: pcline.h
//
//   Line-drawing characters for Industry Standard
//   Architecture (ISA) PCs.

#if !defined(__PCLINE_H)
#define __PCLINE_H

/* Single-line borders */

#define TOPLEFT_SL     0xda
#define TOPRIGHT_SL    0xbf
#define BOTLEFT_SL     0xc0
#define BOTRIGHT_SL    0xd9
#define VLINE_SL       0xb3
#define HLINE_SL       0xc4
#define LEFTH_SL       0xc3
#define RIGHTH_SL      0xb4
#define T_SL           0xc2
#define INVT_SL        0xc1
#define CROSS_SL       0xc5
```

```
/* Double-line borders */

#define TOPLEFT_DL     0xc9
#define TOPRIGHT_DL    0xbb
#define BOTLEFT_DL     0xc8
#define BOTRIGHT_DL    0xbc
#define VLINE_DL       0xba
#define HLINE_DL       0xcd
#define LEFTH_DL       0xcc
#define RIGHTH_DL      0xb9
#define T_DL           0xcb
#define INVT_DL        0xca
#define CROSS_DL       0xce

/* Thick and thin solid lines */
#define VLINE_TK       0xdb
#define HLINEB_TK      0xdc
#define VLINEL_TN      0xdd
#define VLINER_TN      0xde
#define HLINET_TK      0xdf

#define T_HDL_VSL      209
#define TL_HDL_VSL     213
#define TR_HDL_VSL     184
#define LH_HDL_VSL     198
#define RH_HDL_VSL     181
#define INVT_HDL_VSL   207
#define CROSS_HDL_VSL  216

#endif
```

Listing 13.17. `txtgraph.cpp`—Implementation of the graphics objects used in a form's background.

```
//----------------------------------------------------------------
//  File: txtgraph.cpp
//
//  Implement classes for text-mode graphics drawing.

#include "txtgraph.h"
#include "outdev.h"
```

```
// Define single instances of each graphics class;
// these are used to create new copies via the "clone" function

HLine           HLineObj;
VLine           VLineObj;
SingleLineBox   SingleLineBoxObj;
DoubleLineBox   DoubleLineBoxObj;
TextLine        TextLineObj;


//----------------------------------------------------------------------
// B o x : : d r a w
// Draw a box with single-line border

void Box::draw(OutputDevice* device)
{
// Use graphics-mode functions, if possible
    if(!device->is_text())
    {
        device->draw_line(_topleft.xpos(), _topleft.ypos(),
                          _topright.xpos(), _topright.ypos());
        device->draw_line(_topright.xpos(), _topright.ypos(),
                          _botright.xpos(), _botright.ypos());
        device->draw_line(_botright.xpos(), _botright.ypos(),
                          _botleft.xpos(), _botleft.ypos());
        device->draw_line(_botleft.xpos(), _botleft.ypos(),
                          _topleft.xpos(), _topleft.ypos());
        return;
    }
// Otherwise, draw the lines and the corners using characters
    _topleft.draw(device);
    _topright.draw(device);
    _botleft.draw(device);
    _botright.draw(device);
    _top.draw(device);
    _bottom.draw(device);
    _left.draw(device);
    _right.draw(device);
}
//----------------------------------------------------------------------
// B o x : : r e a d
// Read a box's description from an input stream
void Box::read(istream& is)
{
```

```
    _topright.read(is);
    _topleft.read(is);
    _botleft.read(is);
    _botright.read(is);
    _top.read(is);
    _bottom.read(is);
    _left.read(is);
    _right.read(is);
}
//-------------------------------------------------------------------
// B o x : : w r i t e
// Write out a box's description to a output stream
void Box::write(ostream& os)
{
    _topright.write(os);
    _topleft.write(os);
    _botleft.write(os);
    _botright.write(os);
    _top.write(os);
    _bottom.write(os);
    _left.write(os);
    _right.write(os);
}
//-------------------------------------------------------------------
// S i n g l e L i n e B o x
// Construct a box with single-line border

SingleLineBox::SingleLineBox(unsigned short xul,
    unsigned short yul, unsigned short xlr, unsigned short ylr) :
    Box(xul, yul, xlr, ylr)
{
    _topleft.drawing_char(TOPLEFT_SL);
    _topright.drawing_char(TOPRIGHT_SL);
    _botleft.drawing_char(BOTLEFT_SL);
    _botright.drawing_char(BOTRIGHT_SL);
    _top.drawing_char(HLINE_SL);
    _bottom.drawing_char(HLINE_SL);
    _left.drawing_char(VLINE_SL);
    _right.drawing_char(VLINE_SL);
}
//-------------------------------------------------------------------
// D o u b l e L i n e B o x
// Construct a box with double-line border
```

```
DoubleLineBox::DoubleLineBox(unsigned short xul,
    unsigned short yul, unsigned short xlr, unsigned short ylr) :
    Box(xul, yul, xlr, ylr)
{
    _topleft.drawing_char(TOPLEFT_DL);
    _topright.drawing_char(TOPRIGHT_DL);
    _botleft.drawing_char(BOTLEFT_DL);
    _botright.drawing_char(BOTRIGHT_DL);
    _top.drawing_char(HLINE_DL);
    _bottom.drawing_char(HLINE_DL);
    _left.drawing_char(VLINE_DL);
    _right.drawing_char(VLINE_DL);
}
//-----------------------------------------------------------------
// H L i n e : : d r a w
// Draw a horizontal line

void HLine::draw(OutputDevice* device)
{
    if(device == NULL || _length == 0) return;

// If not "text mode," draw a line by calling draw_line
    if(!device->is_text())
    {
        device->draw_line(_xpos, _ypos,
                            _xpos+_length, _ypos);
        return;
    }
// Create the line by writing out the "drawing character"
// repeatedly
    char str[2];
    str[0] = _dc;
    str[1] = '\0';
    int numchar = _length;
    unsigned short x = _xpos;
    while(numchar--)
    {
        device->draw_text(str, x, _ypos);
        x++;
    }
```

```
}
//------------------------------------------------------------------
// V L i n e : : d r a w
// Draw a vertical line

void VLine::draw(OutputDevice* device)
{
    if(device == NULL || _length == 0) return;

// If not "text mode" draw a line by calling draw_line
    if(!device->is_text())
    {
        device->draw_line(_xpos, _ypos,
                            _xpos, _ypos+_length);
        return;
    }

// Create the line by writing out the "drawing character"
// repeatedly
    char str[2];
    str[0] = _dc;
    str[1] = '\0';
    int numchar = _length;
    unsigned short y = _ypos;
    while(numchar—)
    {
        device->draw_text(str, _xpos, y);
        y++;
    }
}
//------------------------------------------------------------------
// T e x t L i n e : : d r a w
// Display a line of text

void TextLine::draw(OutputDevice* device)
{
    if(device == NULL) return;
    device->draw_text(_text, _xpos, _ypos);
}
```

The OutputDevice *Class*

The draw function of the TextGraphics class requires a pointer to an OutputDevice that identifies the device where the graphics object is displayed. Like TextGraphics, OutputDevice is also an abstract base class used to model any type of device capable of displaying output. In particular, an OutputDevice can be a text-mode display, a printer, or, as you will see in Chapter 14, a window in Microsoft Windows. The graphics objects in the TextGraphics hierarchy rely on the following assumptions about the OutputDevice class:

- There is a draw_line function for drawing lines and a draw_text function for displaying text. These functions are assumed to be declared as follows:

```
void OutputDevice::draw_line(unsigned short x1,
                            unsigned short y1,
                            unsigned short x2,
                            unsigned short y2);
void OutputDevice::draw_text(const char* str,
                            unsigned short x,
                            unsigned short y);
```

- There is a function named is_text(), which returns a nonzero value if the display is text-mode.

With this information in hand, you can define the OutputDevice class as shown in the file outdev.h (Listing 13.18). For the MS-DOS version of the Forms software, you will need a TextDisplay class that represents a text-mode screen in a MS-DOS PC. We also derive a TextWindow class from TextDisplay so that we can display the form in a text-mode window. As shown in the file outdev.cpp (Listing 13.19), the actual draw_line and draw_text functions use the console I/O functions of Borland C++.

This approach isolates the device-dependent drawing functions in the OutputDevice class. The benefit is that you can easily add the code necessary to display the form on a new output device. For instance, in Chapter 14, we will display the form in the Microsoft Windows environment without changing a single line of code in the TextGraphics class (Listings 13.15 and 13.17). All we have to do is create a new type of OutputDevice class that represents a window under Microsoft Windows.

Listing 13.18. outdev.h**—Header file for classes representing output devices.**

```
//-----------------------------------------------------------------
// File: outdev.h
//
```

```
//  Classes for output (text screen, printer).

#if !defined(__OUTDEV_H)
#define __OUTDEV_H

class OutputDevice
{
public:
    virtual void draw_line(unsigned short x1, unsigned short y1,
        unsigned short x2, unsigned short y2) = 0;
    virtual void draw_text(const char* str, unsigned short x,
        unsigned short y) = 0;
    virtual unsigned is_text() = 0;
};

class TextDisplay : public OutputDevice
{
public:
    TextDisplay() : _left(1), _top(1),
        _right(80), _bottom(25) {}

    TextDisplay(unsigned short l, unsigned short t,
                unsigned short r, unsigned short b) :
        _left(l), _top(t), _right(r), _bottom(b) {}

    virtual void draw_line(unsigned short x1, unsigned short y1,
        unsigned short x2, unsigned short y2) = 0;

    virtual void draw_text(const char* str, unsigned short x,
        unsigned short y) = 0;

    unsigned is_text() { return 1;}

protected:
    unsigned short _left, _top;
    unsigned short _right, _bottom;
};

class TextWindow: public TextDisplay
{
    public:
        TextWindow() : TextDisplay(1, 1, 80, 25) {}
        TextWindow(unsigned short l, unsigned short t,
                   unsigned short r, unsigned short b) :
```

```
            TextDisplay(l, t, r, b) {}
        void draw_line(unsigned short, unsigned short,
            unsigned short, unsigned short) {}
        void draw_text(const char* str, unsigned short x,
            unsigned short y);
    };


    #endif
```

Listing 13.19. `outdev.cpp`—Implementation of classes representing output devices.

```
//-------------------------------------------------------------------
//  File: outdev.cpp
//
//  Classes for output (displaying on screen, printing,
//  and so on).
//
// NOTE: Uses text-mode output routines from library that comes
//         with Borland's C++ compiler

#include <conio.h>
#include "outdev.h"


//-------------------------------------------------------------------
// d r a w _ t e x t
// Display text in a window

void TextWindow::draw_text(const char* str, unsigned short x,
                           unsigned short y)
{
    window(_left, _top, _right, _bottom);
    gotoxy(x,y);
    cputs(str);
}
```

The Form Class

Now we have enough information to define the Form class. Listing 13.20 shows the file form.h, which declares the Form class; the file form.cpp in Listing 13.21 contains the implementation of the class. The Form class has the following private data members:

- A `String` called `_formname` that holds the name of the form whose definition and data this `Form` object holds.

- Two `FileHeaders`: `_data_filehdr` and `_defn_filehdr` that represent the headers of a *data file* and the *definitions file*, respectively.

- Two `FileIndex` objects to hold the index from the *data* and *definitions* files: `_data_index` and `_defn_index`.

- A `FormBackground` object named `_form_bg` that represents the background of the form.

- An instance of the `FormDefinition` class, `_form_defn`, that holds the fields of the form.

Member Functions of the Form Class

When you use an instance of the `Form` class, it becomes the object through which you interact with the form. Thus, the `Form` class has to provide a rich set of functions so that all parts of a `Form`, from `TextGraphics` background to `Field`, can be accessed. Following is a summary of some important `public` member functions of `Form`:

`read(const char* filename, const char* key = NULL);` opens the file specified by `filename` and reads in the data or definition identified by the string `key`. If no key is specified, the form's definition is read.

`write_defn(const char* filename);` writes the form's definition to a file with the specified name.

`write_data(const char* filename);` writes the form's data to a file with the specified name.

`add(Field& f);` adds a field to the form's definition.

`add(TextGraphics& t);` adds a graphics element to the form's background.

`add_data(const char* id, const char* data);` stores the string data as the data of the `Field` object, whose ID matches the string id.

`first_field`, `last_field`, `next_field`, `previous_field`, and `current_field` are functions for accessing `Fields` in the form's definition maintained by the `FormDefinition` object `_form_defn`.

`first_bg`, `last_bg`, `next_bg`, `previous_bg`, and `current_bg` are functions for accessing `TextGraphics` objects in the form's background maintained by the `FormBackground` object `_form_bg`.

Listing 13.20. `form.h`—Declaration of the Form class.

```
//------------------------------------------------------------------
//  File: form.h
//
//  Describe the "Form" object.

#if !defined(__FORM_H)
#define __FORM_H

#include <stdlib.h>
#include <fstream.h>
#include "str.h"
#include "filehdr.h"
#include "fileindx.h"
#include "formbg.h"
#include "formdefn.h"

class Form
{
public:
    Form() : _formname("undefined") {}

    void add(Field& f) {_form_defn.add(f);}
    void add(TextGraphics& t) {_form_bg.add(t);}

    void read(const char* filename, const char* key = NULL);

    void write_data(const char* filename);
    void write_defn(const char* filename);

    void setup_form(ifstream& ifs, const char* key = NULL);
    void setup_data(ifstream& ifs, const char* key = NULL);

    Field* first_field(){ return _form_defn.first();}
    Field* last_field(){ return _form_defn.last();}
    Field* next_field(){ return _form_defn.next();}
    Field* previous_field(){ return _form_defn.previous();}
    Field* current_field(){ return _form_defn.current();}
    void current_field(Field* f){ _form_defn.current(f);}

    TextGraphics* first_bg(){ return _form_bg.first();}
    TextGraphics* last_bg(){ return _form_bg.last();}
    TextGraphics* next_bg(){ return _form_bg.next();}
    TextGraphics* previous_bg(){ return _form_bg.previous();}
```

```
        TextGraphics* current_bg(){ return _form_bg.current();}

        String name() { return _formname;}
        void name(const char* s);

        String key_field() { return _form_defn.key_field();}
        void key_field(const char* fieldname)
        { _form_defn.key_field(fieldname);}

        void add_data(const char* id, const char* data)
        { _form_defn.add_data(id, data);}

        ~Form() {}
    private:
        String          _formname;
        FileHeader      _data_filehdr;
        FileHeader      _defn_filehdr;
        FileIndex       _data_index;
        FileIndex       _defn_index;
        FormBackground  _form_bg;
        FormDefinition  _form_defn;
    };

    #endif
```

Listing 13.21. `form.cpp`—Implementation of the `Form` class.

```
//-----------------------------------------------------------------------
//  File: form.cpp
//
//   Implement the Form class.

#include <fcntl.h>
#include <io.h>         // For Borland C++, "open" function
#include "form.h"

//-----------------------------------------------------------------------
// r e a d
// Load a form from a file

void Form::read(const char* filename, const char* key)
{
// Open an input stream on the specified file
    ifstream fs1(filename);
```

```
        if(!fs1)
        {
            cerr << "Cannot open: " << filename << endl;
            exit(1);
        }

// Read the header
        FileHeader hdr(fs1);

// Check file type
        if(hdr.filetype() == FileHeader::form_definition)
        {
            fs1.seekg(ios::beg);
            _defn_filehdr.read(fs1);
 // Set up specified form
            setup_form(fs1, key);
        }
        else
        {
            if(hdr.filetype() == FileHeader::form_data)
            {
                fs1.seekg(ios::beg);
                _data_filehdr.read(fs1);
                setup_data(fs1, key);
            }
        }
// Close any files previously opened in this function
        fs1.close();
}
//-------------------------------------------------------------------
// s e t u p _ f o r m
// Create the form (background and field definitions, not
// "filled-in" data)

void Form::setup_form(ifstream& ifs, const char* key)
{
// Save "key" as form's name
        _formname = key;

// Read index of form definitions.
        _defn_index.read(ifs, _defn_filehdr.indexloc(),
                        _defn_filehdr.entries());
        _defn_index.locate(key);
```

```
// Create a form using the selected "form definition"
    ifs.seekg(_defn_index.itemloc());

// Read in the form's background
    _form_bg.read(ifs);

// Read its field descriptions
    _form_defn.read(ifs);
}
//-------------------------------------------------------------------
// s e t u p _ d a t a
// Create a form filled with specified data

void Form::setup_data(ifstream& ifs, const char* key)
{
// First, open file containing definition of form
    ifstream fdfs(_data_filehdr.filename());
    if(!fdfs)
    {
        cerr << "Cannot open: ";
        cerr << _data_filehdr.filename() << endl;
        exit(1);
    }

// Read the header of the "definition file"
    _defn_filehdr.read(fdfs);

// Get the index and locate specified form
    _data_index.read(ifs, _data_filehdr.indexloc(),
                     _data_filehdr.entries());

    if(_data_index.locate(key))
    {
// Read the form's data
        ifs.seekg(_data_index.itemloc());

// Read the name of the form
        ifs >> _formname;
        char c;
        ifs.get(c);

// Next, set up the form (except the data)
        setup_form(fdfs, _formname);
```

```
// Load form's data
        _form_defn.read_data(ifs);
    }
    else
        setup_form(fdfs, NULL);

// Close any files previously opened in this function
    fdfs.close();
}
//----------------------------------------------------------------------
// w r i t e _ d e f n ( c o n s t   c h a r *)
// Save form definition in the specified file

void Form::write_defn(const char* filename)
{
// Try opening file for input (if it fails, file does not exist)
    ifstream ifs(filename);
    if(!ifs)
    {
// File does not exist; create a fresh file and write into it
        ofstream ofs(filename);
        if(!ofs)
        {
            cerr << "Error opening file: " << filename << endl;
            exit(1);
        }
// Set up information for file header
        _defn_filehdr.filename(filename);
        _defn_filehdr.filetype(FileHeader::form_definition);

// Write form definition as follows:
//    (1) Add this form to the index
//    (2) Write out form's background
//    (3) Write out form's definition
//    (4) Save the position of the index in the header
//    (5) Write out index
//    (6) Save header one more time and close file
        _defn_filehdr.write(ofs);
        streampos start = ofs.tellp();
        _form_bg.write(ofs);
        _form_defn.write(ofs);
        streampos end = ofs.tellp();
```

```
            FileIndex idx;
            idx.add(_formname, start, (end-start));
            _defn_filehdr.entries(idx.count());
            _defn_filehdr.indexloc(end);
            idx.write(ofs);
            ofs.seekp(ios::beg);
            _defn_filehdr.write(ofs);
            ofs.close();
      }
      else
      {
// File already exists; read file's header and check whether this
// file is of right type; if it is, append the current form
// to this file
            FileHeader hdr(ifs);
            ifs.close();
            if(hdr.filetype() == FileHeader::form_definition)
            {
                  ifstream ifs(filename);
                  FileIndex idx(ifs, hdr.indexloc(), hdr.entries());
                  ifs.close();

// If there is no form of same name, append this one to the file
                  if(!idx.locate(_formname))
                     {
// Reopen file for writing . . .
                        int fd;
                        if((fd = open(filename, O_TEXT|O_WRONLY)) == NULL)
                        {
                            cerr << "Error opening " << filename << endl;
                            exit(1);
                        }
// Attach file to an ofstream
                        ofstream ofs;
                        ofs.attach(fd);
                        if (!ofs)
                        {
                            cerr << "Error attaching to stream " << endl;
                            exit(1);
                        }
                        streampos start = hdr.indexloc();
                        ofs.seekp(start, ios::beg);
```

```
                    _form_bg.write(ofs);
                    _form_defn.write(ofs);
                    streampos end = ofs.tellp();

                            idx.add(_formname, start, (end-start));
                    hdr.entries(idx.count());
                    hdr.indexloc(end);
                    idx.write(ofs);
                    ofs.seekp(ios::beg);
                    hdr.write(ofs);
                    ofs.close();
                }
            }
        }
}
//--------------------------------------------------------------------
// w r i t e _ d a t a ( c o n s t   c h a r *)
// Save form's data in the specified file

void Form::write_data(const char* filename)
{
// Try opening file for input (if it fails, file does not exist)
    ifstream ifs(filename);
    if(!ifs)
    {
// File does not exist; create a fresh file and write into it
        ofstream ofs(filename);
        if(!ofs)
        {
            cerr << "Error opening file: " << filename << endl;
            exit(1);
        }
// Set up information for file header
// Data file should have name of "definition file" in header
        _data_filehdr.filename(_defn_filehdr.filename());
        _data_filehdr.filetype(FileHeader::form_data);

// Write form data as follows:
//    (1) Add this form to the index
//    (2) Write out form's data
//    (3) Save the position of the index in the header
//    (4) Write out index
```

```
//    (5) Save header one more time and close file
        _data_filehdr.write(ofs);
        streampos start = ofs.tellp();
        ofs << _formname << endl;
        _form_defn.write_data(ofs);
        streampos end = ofs.tellp();
        FileIndex idx;
        idx.add(_form_defn.key_data(), start, (end-start));
        _data_filehdr.entries(idx.count());
        _data_filehdr.indexloc(end);
        idx.write(ofs);
        ofs.seekp(ios::beg);
        _data_filehdr.write(ofs);
        ofs.close();
    }
    else
    {
// File already exists; read file's header and check whether this
// file is of right type. If it is, append the current form's
// data to this file.
        FileHeader hdr(ifs);
        ifs.close();
        if(hdr.filetype() == FileHeader::form_data)
        {
            ifstream ifs(filename);
            FileIndex idx(ifs, hdr.indexloc(), hdr.entries());
            ifs.close();

// If there is no form of same name, append this one to the file
            if(!idx.locate(_form_defn.key_data()))
            {
// Reopen file for writing . . .
                int fd;
                if((fd = open(filename, O_TEXT¦O_WRONLY)) == NULL)
                {
                    cerr << "Error opening " << filename << endl;
                    exit(1);
                }
// Attach file to an ofstream
                    ofstream ofs;
                    ofs.attach(fd);
                    if (!ofs)
```

```
                    {
                        cerr << "Error attaching to stream " << endl;
                        exit(1);
                    }
                    streampos start = hdr.indexloc();
                    ofs.seekp(start, ios::beg);
                    ofs << _formname << endl;
                    _form_defn.write_data(ofs);
                    streampos end = ofs.tellp();
                    idx.add(_form_defn.key_data(),
                            start, (end-start));
                    hdr.entries(idx.count());
                    hdr.indexloc(end);
                    idx.write(ofs);
                    ofs.seekp(ios::beg);
                    hdr.write(ofs);
                    ofs.close();
                }
            }
        }
    }
    //----------------------------------------------------------------

    void Form::name(const char* s) { _formname = s;};
```

Creating a Form

Before you can use the Forms software, you will need at least one *definitions file* and a *data file* that can serve as the input for the form fill-up program—the software that you use to display a form and enter data into the fields. You can solve this problem by writing a small program that creates a form and its data. This is also a good exercise, because it lets you see how to use the facilities offered by the C++ classes in the *Forms software*.

Defining a Form

The first program is for creating the definition of a form. This will be the invoice form shown in Figure 13.1. The program is shown in the file formdef.cpp (Listing 13.22). As shown in the file, the text items and the lines representing the form's background are prepared in an array of structures. The main program first creates a Form. Then it creates each background element and calls the add function of the Form to add to the definition. The fields are also created and added to the form's definition. Finally, a single call to the write_defn function of the Form saves the form's definition in a file named invoice.def.

Listing 13.22. formdef.cpp—A program to define an invoice form.

```cpp
//---------------------------------------------------------------
//  File: formdef.cpp
//
//  Create a form and save its definition in a file.

#include "form.h"
#include "txtgraph.h"

struct text_item
{
    char*          text;
    unsigned short xpos, ypos;
};

text_item txt_list[] =
{
  {"I N V O I C E", 36,  1},
  {"From:",          2,  1},
  {"No:",           60,  1},
  {"Date:",         60,  2},
  {"To:",            2,  7},
  {"F.O.B.",         2, 15},
  {"Terms",         18, 15},
  {"Date Shipped",  34, 15},
  {"Shipped Via",   50, 15},
  {"Ordered",        2, 18},
  {"Shipped",       11, 18},
  {"Description",   33 , 18},
  {"Price",         59, 18},
  {"Per",           66, 18},
  {"Amount",        70, 18}
};

int numtxt = sizeof(txt_list) / sizeof(text_item);

#define FULL_HLINE 78
```

```
struct line_item
{
    unsigned short xpos, ypos;
    unsigned short length;
    unsigned short c;
};

static line_item hlines[] =
{
    { 1, 14, 77, HLINE_DL},
    { 1, 17, 77, HLINE_DL},
    { 2, 19, 76, HLINE_DL},
    { 1, 19,  1, LH_HDL_VSL},
    {17, 17,  1, INVT_HDL_VSL},
    {33, 17,  1, INVT_HDL_VSL},
    {49, 17,  1, INVT_HDL_VSL},
};

static int numhlines = sizeof(hlines) / sizeof(line_item);

static line_item vlines[] =
{
    {17, 15,  2, VLINE_SL},
    {33, 15,  2, VLINE_SL},
    {49, 15,  2, VLINE_SL},
    {78, 15, 11, VLINE_SL},
    { 1, 15, 11, VLINE_SL},
    {10, 18,  8, VLINE_SL},
    {20, 18,  8, VLINE_SL},
    {58, 18,  8, VLINE_SL},
    {65, 18,  8, VLINE_SL},
    {69, 18,  8, VLINE_SL},
    {10, 17,  1, T_HDL_VSL},
    {20, 17,  1, T_HDL_VSL},
    {58, 17,  1, T_HDL_VSL},
    {65, 17,  1, T_HDL_VSL},
    {69, 17,  1, T_HDL_VSL},
    {10, 19,  1, CROSS_HDL_VSL},
    {20, 19,  1, CROSS_HDL_VSL},
    {58, 19,  1, CROSS_HDL_VSL},
    {65, 19,  1, CROSS_HDL_VSL},
    {69, 19,  1, CROSS_HDL_VSL},
    {17, 14,  1, T_HDL_VSL},
```

```cpp
    {33, 14,   1, T_HDL_VSL},
    {49, 14,   1, T_HDL_VSL},
    { 1, 14,   1, TL_HDL_VSL},
    { 1, 17,   1, LH_HDL_VSL},
    {78, 14,   1, TR_HDL_VSL},
    {78, 17,   1, RH_HDL_VSL},
    {78, 19,   1, RH_HDL_VSL},
    { 1, 19,   1, LH_HDL_VSL}
};

static int numvlines = sizeof(vlines) / sizeof(line_item);

struct field_item
{
    char*           id;
    unsigned short x, y, field_width;
};

static field_item fields[] =
{
    {"From1",   7,   2, 39},
    {"From2",   7,   3, 39},
    {"From3",   7,   4, 39},
    {"To1",     7,   7, 39},
    {"To2",     7,   8, 39},
    {"To3",     7,   9, 39},
    {"To4",     7,  10, 39},
    {"Num",    65,   1, 10},
    {"Date",   65,   2, 10},
    {"FOB",     2,  16, 15},
    {"Terms",  18,  16, 15},
    {"Shipdate", 34, 16, 15},
    {"Shipvia",  50, 16, 20},

    {"OrdQty1",  2, 20,   8},
    {"ShpQty1", 11, 20,   8},
    {"Descr1",  21, 20,  36},
    {"Price1",  59, 20,   6},
    {"Per1",    66, 20,   3},
    {"Amt1",    70, 20,   8},

    {"OrdQty2",  2, 21,   8},
    {"ShpQty2", 11, 21,   8},
    {"Descr2",  21, 21,  36},
```

```
        {"Price2",    59, 21,    6},
        {"Per2",      66, 21,    3},
        {"Amt2",      70, 21,    8},

        {"OrdQty3",    2, 22,    8},
        {"ShpQty3",   11, 22,    8},
        {"Descr3",    21, 22,   36},
        {"Price3",    59, 22,    6},
        {"Per3",      66, 22,    3},
        {"Amt3",      70, 22,    8},
};

static int numfields = sizeof(fields) / sizeof(field_item);
//---------------------------------------------------------------
// m a i n

main()
{
    Form inv;
// Add background items . . .
    SingleLineBox box1(5, 6, 46, 11);
    inv.add(box1);

// Add text items . . .
    int i;
    for(i = 0; i < numtxt; i++)
    {
        TextLine t(txt_list[i].text, txt_list[i].xpos,
                   txt_list[i].ypos);
        inv.add(t);
    }

// Add the horizontal lines
    for(i = 0; i < numhlines; i++)
    {
        HLine l(hlines[i].xpos, hlines[i].ypos,
                hlines[i].length);
        l.drawing_char(hlines[i].c);
        inv.add(l);
    }

// Add the vertical lines
    for(i = 0; i < numvlines; i++)
    {
```

```
            VLine l(vlines[i].xpos, vlines[i].ypos,
                    vlines[i].length);
            l.drawing_char(vlines[i].c);
            inv.add(l);
        }

// Now add the fields . . .
        for(i = 0; i < numfields; i++)
        {
            Field f(fields[i].id, fields[i].x, fields[i].y,
                    fields[i].field_width);
            inv.add(f);
        }

// Set the name of the form
        inv.name("Invoice");

// Set the key field
        inv.key_field("Num");

// Save the form definition in a file
        inv.write_defn("invoice.def");
    }
```

Building FORMDEF

Because the FORMDEF program for defining a form uses most of the classes of the Forms software, you have to compile and link several files to build the executable. The *makefile* formdef.mak, shown in Listing 13.23, eases this task. With this makefile, you will be able to build the executable FORMDEF.EXE by entering the following command at the DOS prompt:

```
make -fformdef
```

Note that the makefile assumes you will use BCCX, the protected-mode version of the Borland C++ compiler. To use the protected-mode compiler, you have to install the protected-mode kernel as instructed by Borland International. Basically, you have to use a command such as:

```
tkernel hi=yes kilos=2048
```

where the number following kilos= indicates the number of kilobytes of memory that you will allow the kernel to control and use. You will find more information in the *User's Guide* of Borland C++ compiler.

Running FORMDEF

Run the FORMDEF program with the following command at the MS-DOS prompt:

    FORMDEF

This will create a file named `invoice.def` with the definition of an invoice form. The file is a text file, so you can look at it with an editor. It contains extended line-drawing characters that you can see with a command such as

    more <invoice.def

Figure 13.6 shows a portion of what you would see on the screen. You will find it instructive to study this file with a text editor.

```
LNBFORM
100
FDEF
invoice.def
1
1756

        52
SingleLineBox
46  6  1  ┐
5   6  1  ┌
5  11  1  └
46 11  1  ┘
6   6 40  ─
6  11 40  ─
5   7  4  │
46  7  4  │
TextLine
I N V O I C E
36 1
TextLine
From:
2  1
TextLine
```

Fig. 13.6. First few lines of `invoice.def`.

Listing 13.23. `formfdef.mak`—Makefile for building the FORMDEF application.

```
###############################################################
#  Makefile for building the "formdef" application.
#

CFLAGS =   -c
OBJECTS = formdef.obj form.obj formdefn.obj filehdr.obj \
```

```
                    fileindx.obj str.obj dllist.obj field.obj \
                    txtgraph.obj formbg.obj

# For Borland C++ compiler
CC = bccx

formdef.exe:  $(OBJECTS)
         $(CC) $(OBJECTS)

.cpp.obj:
         $(CC) $(CFLAGS) $*

dllist.obj: dllist.cpp dllist.h dlink.h

str.obj: str.cpp str.h

formdefn.obj: formdefn.cpp formdefn.h dlink.h dllist.h \
              field.h str.h

formbg.obj: formbg.cpp formbg.h txtgraph.h str.h dllist.h \
            dlink.h pcline.h

field.obj: field.cpp field.h str.h dlink.h

form.obj: form.cpp form.h filehdr.h fileindx.h formbg.h \
          formdefn.h dllist.h dlink.h indxitem.h txtgraph.h \
          field.h pcline.h

filehdr.obj: filehdr.cpp filehdr.h str.h

fileindx.obj: fileindx.cpp fileindx.h dlink.h dllist.h \
              indxitem.h str.h

txtgraph.obj: txtgraph.cpp txtgraph.h pcline.h str.h dlink.h \
              outdev.h

formdef.obj: formdef.cpp form.h txtgraph.h \
             filehdr.h fileindx.h formbg.h \
             formdefn.h dllist.h dlink.h indxitem.h \
             field.h pcline.h str.h outdev.h
```

Creating the Form's Data

After the invoice form's *definitions file* has been created, you should build a *data file* to test the form fill-up program. Once again, you can write a small program to create the *data file*. Listing 13.24 shows the file formdat.cpp, which prepares the data for the fields in an array, loads them into a Form object, and uses the Form's write_data member function to save the data in a file named invoice.dat.

Listing 13.24. `formdat.cpp`—Create a form's data file.

```cpp
//-----------------------------------------------------------------
// File: formdat.cpp
//
// Fill out a form and save data in file.

#include "form.h"

struct field_data
{
    char*  id;
    char*  data;
};

static field_data contents[] =
{
    {"From1",   "LNB Software, Inc."},
    {"From2",   "2005 Aventurine Way"},
    {"From3",   "Silver Spring, MD 20904"},
    {"Num",     "22750-1"},
    {"Date",    "02/06/91"},
    {"OrdQty1", "1"},
    {"ShpQty1", "1"},
    {"Descr1",  "Source code"},
    {"Price1",  "29.95"},
    {"Per1",    "ea"},
    {"Amt1",    "29.95"}
};

static int num_contents = sizeof(contents) / sizeof(field_data);
//-----------------------------------------------------------------
// m a i n

main()
{
    Form inv;
// Load form's definition . . .
```

```
    inv.read("invoice.def", "Invoice");

    int i;
// Add data for the fields . . .
    for(i = 0; i < num_contents; i++)
    {
        inv.add_data(contents[i].id, contents[i].data);
    }

// Save the "filed-up" form in a data file
    inv.write_data("invoice.data");
}
```

Building FORMDAT

Use the *makefile* formdat.mak shown in Listing 13.25 to build the executable FORMDAT.EXE. As you did with FORMDEF, you can build FORMDAT with the command:

```
    make -fformdat
```

When you run FORMDAT, it creates a file named invoice.dat with the data for a copy of the invoice form whose definition is in the file invoice.def. You can look at the data file with a text editor, because it is a text file. Figure 13.7 shows the first few lines of the file invoice.dat as it appears when you type it out on the screen.

```
LNBFORM
100
FDAT
invoice.def
1
524

            Invoice
31
From1
LNB Software, Inc.
From2
2005 Aventurine Way
From3
Silver Spring, MD 20904
To1

To2

To3

To4

Num
```

Fig. 13.7. First few lines of the data file invoice.dat.

**Listing 13.25. `formdat.mak`—Makefile for building the
FORMDAT application.**

```
################################################################
#  Makefile for building the "formdat" application.
#

CFLAGS =  -c
OBJECTS = formdat.obj form.obj formdefn.obj filehdr.obj \
          fileindx.obj str.obj dllist.obj field.obj \
          txtgraph.obj formbg.obj

# For Borland C++ compiler (protected-mode version)
CC = bccx

formdat.exe:  $(OBJECTS)
        $(CC) $(OBJECTS)

.cpp.obj:
        $(CC) $(CFLAGS) $*

dllist.obj: dllist.cpp dllist.h dlink.h

str.obj: str.cpp str.h

formdefn.obj: formdefn.cpp formdefn.h dlink.h dllist.h \
              field.h str.h

formbg.obj: formbg.cpp formbg.h txtgraph.h str.h dllist.h \
            dlink.h pcline.h

field.obj: field.cpp field.h str.h dlink.h

form.obj: form.cpp form.h filehdr.h fileindx.h formbg.h \
          formdefn.h dllist.h dlink.h indxitem.h txtgraph.h \
          field.h pcline.h

filehdr.obj: filehdr.cpp filehdr.h str.h

fileindx.obj: fileindx.cpp fileindx.h dlink.h dllist.h \
              indxitem.h str.h

txtgraph.obj: txtgraph.cpp txtgraph.h pcline.h str.h dlink.h \
              outdev.h

formdat.obj:  formdat.cpp form.h filehdr.h fileindx.h formbg.h \
          formdefn.h dllist.h dlink.h indxitem.h txtgraph.h \
          field.h pcline.h
```

Filling in Forms

Now that the machinery for representing and manipulating a form is available, you can build a sample application that displays a form and lets the user fill in the entries. Before creating such a program, you still have to address the following questions:

- How should the form be displayed?

- How does the user interact with the software?

An easy way to answer these questions is to adopt the Model-View-Controller (MVC) architecture for the application. Then, the display will be handled by a "View" and the user interactions are in the realm of a "Controller."

> The Model-View-Controller (MVC) architecture originated in Smalltalk-80. Consult Chapter 3 for more information on MVC.

The FormView *Class*

You can encapsulate the View layer of the MVC architecture in a C++ class named FormView, declared in formview.h (Listing 13.26) and implemented in formview.cpp (Listing 13.27). The FormView class has the following private data members:

Form& _form; is a reference to the Form of which this is a View.

TextWindow _w; is the text-mode window where the Form is displayed.

Field* _curfield; is a pointer to the current Field object with which the user is interacting.

Listing 13.26. formview.h—Header file for the FormView class.

```
//-------------------------------------------------------------
// File: formview.h
//
// Define the classes necessary to present a View of a form.

#if !defined(__FORMVIEW_H)
#define __FORMVIEW_H

#include "txtgraph.h"
#include "outdev.h"
```

```
class Form;
class Field;

class FormView
{
public:
    FormView(Form& form);
    int accept_char(int c);
    void repaint();
    void save() {};
    void backspace();
    void tab();
    int quit() { return 1;}
    void putcursor();
private:
    Form&          _form;
    TextWindow     _w;
    Field*         _curfield;
};
```

```
#endif
```

The member functions of the `FormView` class are designed to handle single characters that the user enters. The `EventHandler` class, described next, calls an appropriate function of `FormView` whenever the user enters a keystroke. Characters such as tab and backspace require special handling. However, most characters are processed by the `accept_char` function that simply inserts the character into the data area of the current `Field`.

Listing 13.27. `formview.cpp`—Member functions of the `FormView` class.

```
//------------------------------------------------------------------
//  File: formview.cpp
//
//  Display a "View" of the form.

#include <conio.h>
#include "formview.h"
#include "field.h"
#include "form.h"


//------------------------------------------------------------------
// F o r m V i e w ( F o r m & )
// Create a View for specified form . . .
```

```
FormView::FormView(Form& form) : _form(form), _w(1, 1, 80, 25)
{
    _curfield = _form.first_field();

// Display form in the window
    repaint();
}
//-------------------------------------------------------------------
// a c c e p t _ c h a r
// Process character received from event-handler

int FormView::accept_char(int c)
{
    char s[2] = { c, '\0'};
    if(_curfield->curwidth() < _curfield->numchars())
    {
        putcursor();
        _curfield->append(s);
        return 1;
    }
    else
        return 0;
}
//-------------------------------------------------------------------
// b a c k s p a c e
// Process backspace character

void FormView::backspace()
{
// Delete a character, provided there is something to delete
    if(_curfield->curwidth() > 0)
    {
        char s[1] = {'\0'};
        _curfield->replace(_curfield->curwidth()-1, 1, s);
        putcursor();
        putch(' ');
        putcursor();
    }
}
    //----------------------------------------------------------
    // t a b
    // Process tab character

    void FormView::tab()
```

```cpp
{
    _form.current_field(_curfield);
    _curfield = _form.next_field();
    if(_curfield == NULL) _curfield = _form.first_field();
    putcursor();
}
//------------------------------------------------------------
//  r e p a i n t
// Redraw the form's "View"

void FormView::repaint()
{
// Clear the text window (by default, a 80 x 25 one)
    clrscr();

// Draw form's background
    TextGraphics* p_g;
    for(p_g = _form.first_bg(); p_g != NULL;
        p_g = _form.next_bg())
    {
        p_g->draw(&_w);
    }

// Draw the contents of each field . . .
    Field* p_f;
    for(p_f = _form.first_field(); p_f != NULL;
        p_f = _form.next_field())
    {
// Create a TextLine graphics object with the field's data
        TextLine* tl = new TextLine(p_f->data(),
                                    p_f->xpos(), p_f->ypos());

        tl->draw(&_w);
    }
    putcursor();
}
//------------------------------------------------------------
//  p u t c u r s o r
// Place cursor at the end of current field

void FormView::putcursor()
{
    gotoxy(_curfield->xpos()+_curfield->curwidth(),
           _curfield->ypos());
}
```

The EventHandler *Class*

The remaining piece of the puzzle is the "Controller" layer of the MVC architecture. The EventHandler class declared in the file ev_hndlr.h (Listing 13.28) and implemented in ev_hndlr.cpp (Listing 13.29). The EventHandler class maintains a reference to the FormView object to which it delivers the events. In this case, the events are the keystrokes from the user.

Listing 13.28. ev_hndlr.h—Header file for the EventHandler class.

```
//-------------------------------------------------------------
//  File: ev_hndlr.h
//
//  Declare the EventHandler class.

#if !defined(__EV_HNDLR_H)
#define __EV_HNDLR_H

#include <stdlib.h>
#include <conio.h>    // For console I/O routines of Borland C++
#include "formview.h"

// This macro converts an ASCII character into a
// control character
#define  Ctrl(X)  (X-0x40)

const int maxchars = 128;

class EventHandler
{
public:
    EventHandler(FormView& fv);
    void start();
    void send_char()
    {
        if(_formview.accept_char(_saved_char))
            putch(_saved_char);
    }

    void quit() { if(_formview.quit())_done = 1;}
    void backspace() { _formview.backspace();}
    void tab() { _formview.tab();}
    void repaint() { _formview.repaint();}
    void save() { _formview.save();}
```

```
            void ignore() {}
        private:
            FormView&   _formview;

            typedef void (EventHandler::*action)(void);

            action      _xlat_table[maxchars];
            int         _saved_char;
            int         _done;
        };

        #endif
```

One innovative feature of the EventHandler class is the event-handling through a table of commands in which each entry has a character associated with a pointer to a member function of EventHandler. When the user presses that character's key, the member function is called through the associated pointer. By confining yourself to single character commands, you can use the character itself as the index into the table. The xlat_table array in the EventHandler class is the array of pointers to member functions that permits you to translate a character into an "action." The start member function of the EventHandler class takes care of processing the keyboard events. In there, you can see how a character is translated to a function call.

Listing 13.29. ev_hndlr.cpp—Member functions of the EventHandler class.

```
//------------------------------------------------------------------
//  File: ev_hndlr.cpp
//
//  Implement the event-handler class.

#include "ev_hndlr.h"

struct command
{
    int    c;   // Character key pressed
    action a;   // Function to be called
};

static command cmdtable[] =
{
    {Ctrl('X'),   EventHandler::quit},
    {Ctrl('Q'),   EventHandler::quit},
    {      '\b',  EventHandler::backspace},
```

```
        {     '\t',  EventHandler::tab},
        {     '\r',  EventHandler::tab},
        {Ctrl('L'),  EventHandler::repaint},
        {Ctrl('S'),  EventHandler::save}
};

static int numcmd = sizeof(cmdtable) / sizeof(command);
//------------------------------------------------------------------
// E v e n t H a n d l e r ( F o r m V i e w & )
// Constructor for the EventHandler class

EventHandler::EventHandler(FormView& fv) : _formview(fv),
                              _saved_char(-1), _done(0)
{
// Initialize translation table; used here to convert a keypress
// to an "action"
    int i;
    for(i = 0; i < ' ';  i++)
        _xlat_table[i] = EventHandler::ignore;

    for(i = ' '; i < maxchars; i++)
        _xlat_table[i] = EventHandler::send_char;

// Add commands defined in "cmdtable"
    for(i = 0; i < numcmd; i++)
    {
        int c = cmdtable[i].c;
        _xlat_table[c] = cmdtable[i].a;
    }
}
//------------------------------------------------------------------
// s t a r t
// Start processing events

void EventHandler::start()
{
    int c, i;

    while(!_done)
    {
        if(kbhit())          // Is there a keypress?
        {
            c = getch();     // Get character without echoing
            _saved_char = c;
            (this->*_xlat_table[c])();   // Call "action" routine
```

```
        }
        else                    // Handle other events if no keypress
        {
// You can look for mouse events in this block
            ;
        }
    }
}
```

The FORMFILL *Program*

Finally, you have all the machinery needed to create a form fill-in program. Listing 13.30 shows the file formfill.cpp, which constitutes the main function of the FORMFILL program. As you can see, the main function is short. This is because all the work is done by the FormView, EventHandler, and Form classes, which further delegate responsibilities to their component classes.

Listing 13.30. formfill.cpp—Main program of a form fill-in application.

```
//-----------------------------------------------------------------
//  File: formfill.cpp
//
//  Program to fill in a form.
//

#include "form.h"
#include "formview.h"
#include "ev_hndlr.h"

void main(int argc, char **argv)
{
    Form inv;
    if(argc < 2)
    {
        cout << "Use: Formfill <filename> <keyword>" << endl;
        exit(0);
    }
    char* filename = argv[1];
    char* key = NULL;
    if(argc > 2) key = argv[2];
// Load form's definition . . .
    inv.read(filename, key);
```

```
cout << "Read and set up form..." << endl;

    FormView view(inv);
    EventHandler events(view);

    events.start();
}
```

Building FORMFILL

The FORMFILL program was tested under Borland C++. Because of the large number of header files and source modules, it is best to create a makefile and use the make utility (described in the *User's Guide* for Borland C++) to build the program. Listing 13.31 shows the makefile named formfill.mak. With this makefile, you can build the FORMFILL program by entering the following command at the MS-DOS prompt:

```
make -fformfill
```

Make sure that the PATH environment variable contains the name of the directory where Borland C++ compiler and the make utility reside.

**Listing 13.31. formfill.mak—Makefile for building the
FORMFILL application.**

```
##############################################################
#  Makefile for building the DOS version of the
#  "Formfill" application.
#

CFLAGS =  -c
OBJECTS = formfill.obj form.obj formdefn.obj filehdr.obj \
          fileindx.obj str.obj dllist.obj field.obj \
          txtgraph.obj formbg.obj formview.obj \
          ev_hndlr.obj outdev.obj

# For Borland C++ compiler
CC = bccx

formfill.exe:  $(OBJECTS)
       $(CC) @formfill.lnk
```

```
.cpp.obj:
        $(CC) $(CFLAGS) $*

dllist.obj: dllist.cpp dllist.h dlink.h

str.obj: str.cpp str.h

formdefn.obj: formdefn.cpp formdefn.h dlink.h dllist.h \
        field.h str.h

formbg.obj: formbg.cpp formbg.h txtgraph.h str.h dllist.h \
        dlink.h pcline.h

field.obj: field.cpp field.h str.h dlink.h

form.obj: form.cpp form.h filehdr.h fileindx.h formbg.h \
        formdefn.h dllist.h dlink.h indxitem.h txtgraph.h \
        field.h pcline.h

filehdr.obj: filehdr.cpp filehdr.h str.h

fileindx.obj: fileindx.cpp fileindx.h dlink.h dllist.h \
        indxitem.h str.h

txtgraph.obj: txtgraph.cpp txtgraph.h pcline.h str.h dlink.h \
        outdev.h

outdev.obj: outdev.cpp outdev.h

ev_hndlr.obj: ev_hndlr.cpp ev_hndlr.h formview.h str.h \
        filehdr.h fileindx.h formbg.h formdefn.h \
        dllist.h dlink.h indxitem.h txtgraph.h field.h \
        pcline.h form.h outdev.h

formview.obj: formview.cpp formview.h form.h str.h outdev.h \
        filehdr.h fileindx.h formbg.h formdefn.h \
        dllist.h dlink.h indxitem.h txtgraph.h field.h \
        pcline.h

formfill.obj: formfill.cpp formview.h str.h form.h outdev.h \
        filehdr.h fileindx.h formbg.h formdefn.h \
        dllist.h dlink.h indxitem.h txtgraph.h field.h \
        pcline.h ev_hndlr.h
```

The Link File

The makefile formfill.mak needs another file that stores the names of the modules that have to be linked to build the FORMFILL application. This file, formfill.lnk, appears in Listing 13.32.

Listing 13.32. `formfill.lnk`—Input to the linker.

```
formfill.obj form.obj formdefn.obj filehdr.obj
fileindx.obj str.obj dllist.obj field.obj
txtgraph.obj formbg.obj formview.obj
ev_hndlr.obj outdev.obj
```

Running FORMFILL

You can test FORMFILL with the files invoice.def and invoice.dat that we had created earlier. To try it, enter the following at the MS-DOS prompt:

```
formfill invoice.dat 22750-1
```

The resulting screen should be the one shown in Figure 13.1. To exit the program, enter Ctrl-X or Ctrl-Q.

Summary

This chapter develops and implements a Forms software package for creating, filling in, and storing forms. The focus is on creating the classes that are the basis of the Forms software. Each form is thought of as a collection of background graphics objects and a collection of fields. The Form class uses two doubly linked lists to maintain the background objects and the fields. Each field, modeled by the Field class, is capable of holding a single line of data. A String object in the Field stores the line of data for that field. To keep the design simple, forms are drawn on the screen using the extended line-drawing characters available on MS-DOS PCs.

A major strength of the design is the facility for storing forms in a file and retrieving them later. A form's storage is divided into two files: one for the form's definition, the other for the data filled in by the user. Each file has a well-defined header and an index to allow retrieval of a specific form by its name or number. Each component class in the form is capable of saving an instance of itself to a disk file and retrieving the instance later. The iostream library (see Chapter 5) is used for file I/O.

The Forms software has been implemented and tested with Borland C++ on an MS-DOS PC, but most of the software, excluding the PC-specific line drawing modules, should compile under any C++ compiler with the `iostream` library.

## Chapter 14

Developing Programs for Microsoft Windows in C++

Microsoft Windows, or *Windows* for short, is a popular graphical windowing environment for MS-DOS systems. Although Windows can run existing MS-DOS applications, only programs especially designed for Windows can take advantage of all the features of the graphical interface. In particular, with Windows you can

- run multiple applications at once (multitasking).

- cut-and-paste text and graphics between applications.

- have a consistent appearance and nearly identical way of interacting with most applications.

Unfortunately for software developers, the ease of use of Windows applications comes at the expense of a complex programming interface. For example, the Windows library contains over 550 functions. Although you can get by if you master a small fraction of these functions, you are never quite sure if you are overlooking some function that does exactly what your application needs to do. In addition to the sheer volume of information, you have to follow an entirely different approach when you write Windows applications. Despite these drawbacks, software development in Windows does offer several advantages:

- Windows offers *device independence*. The same Windows program will display its output on any monitor from EGA to VGA and print on any printer from a dot-matrix to laser.

- For the developer, Windows offers a variety of predefined user-interface components such as pushbuttons, menus, dialog boxes, lists, and edit windows.

- Windows includes an extensive interface to the graphics device (called Graphics Device Interface, GDI) for drawing graphics and text. In particular, the GDI lets you draw in your own coordinate system.

Until now C has been the programming language of choice for writing Windows applications. Meanwhile, C++ has been steadily gaining in popularity, and many programmers are interested in writing Windows applications in C++. However, calling Windows functions from a C++ program is not as simple as calling, for instance, the functions from the standard C library. This is because the compiler has to generate special object code when calling Windows functions and Windows use a different method of passing arguments to its functions. In other words, the C++ compiler has to support the requirements imposed by Windows. As you will see shortly, there are already several choices for creating Windows applications in C++.

This chapter shows you how to write a Windows application in C++. The specific goal is to add a graphical interface to the FORMFILL program described in Chapter 13. Although the focus has been on creating a solution that works for the FORMFILL program, the framework developed in this chapter can be used for any Windows application.

An interesting feature of the project you are about to undertake is that you are required to reuse as much of the DOS version of the software as possible. Assume that your company had a successful Forms package (for instance, the FORMFILL program from Chapter 13) for MS-DOS systems that performs well but suffers from the drawback that it supports text-mode displays only. Your task is to add a Microsoft Windows-based user interface to the Forms package. This chapter describes the steps you might take to achieve your goal.

> This chapter shows how to use C++ to build a Microsoft Windows application, but it does not provide a thorough introduction to Windows programming. It assumes that you already know how to program Microsoft Windows in C. To learn about programming Microsoft Windows, consult a book such as *Programming Windows*, Second Edition, by Charles Petzold, published by Microsoft Press in 1990.

What You Need

Before writing Windows programs in C++, you will need some software development tools. Currently, you can use one of the following to write Windows programs in C++:

- Zortech C++ Version 2.1 with the Microsoft Windows Software Development Toolkit.

- Borland C++ Version 2.0 (it includes the header files and libraries needed for Windows programming). This chapter's example uses Borland C++.

Of course, in both cases, you will need a copy of Microsoft Windows as well. Additionally, you would want the following:

- A fast system (a 12-MHz 80286 system or, preferably, a faster 80386 or 80486 system)

- As much memory as possible (4MB or more)

- A large hard disk (over 100MB preferred)

The system should be fast because the Windows environment puts a lot of demand on the processor. The extra memory helps, because Windows can use it with the processor operating in what is known as *protected mode*. The hard disk is a necessity because all software development tools seem to require a large amount of storage.

C++ and Windows Callbacks

A window is the basic object in the Microsoft Windows graphical environment. Clearly, the first task is to see whether you can use a C++ class to encapsulate a window and its data. In Windows, each window is identified by a *handle*, which is a 16-bit number. In fact, the Windows header file, <windows.h>, defines the type HWND that you can use as the data type for a handle to a window.

You get a handle to a window only after you call the CreateWindow function to create the window. Before creating a window, you have to register it by calling the Windows function RegisterClass. When you call RegisterClass, you have to provide two important pieces of information:

- A unique name for all windows of this type (the *class* name, in Windows terminology)

- The address of a function that Windows will call whenever there is a message to be sent to any window of this class (Windows class, not C++)

Windows calls this callback function to "send messages" to your application. For instance, when a mouse button is pressed inside a pushbutton, Windows calls the pushbutton's callback function with information about the mouse event. In Borland C++, if the callback function for a class of windows is named WindowProc, then the declaration of WindowProc would be as follows:

```
LONG FAR PASCAL _export WindowProc(HWND hWnd, WORD message,
                                   WORD wParam, LONG lParam);
```

All capitalized words—LONG, FAR, PASCAL, HWND, and WORD—are defined in the header file `<windows.h>`. The `_export` keyword is required for all functions that are called by Windows. The arguments passed to the callback function have the following meaning:

`HWND hWnd` is a window handle. This is the window for which the message is intended.

`WORD message` is a 16-bit value representing the message being sent to the window specified in the first argument. The `<windows.h>` header file lists symbolic names for every message that Windows can send. There are several hundred messages, but most applications have to deal with only a handful of these messages.

`WORD wParam` is a 16-bit value passed by Windows to your application. Its meaning depends on the message.

`LONG lParam` is a 32-bit parameter containing information relevant to the message being sent. Its interpretation depends on the message.

When you think of encapsulating a window in a C++ class, give some thought to how you should handle the callback function for the window. One solution is the following:

- Define a single callback function that is declared as a `static` function of a class (for the sake of concreteness, call it `WindowsEventHandler` class) designed to take care of message processing.

- In the `WindowsEventHandler` class, maintain a `static` list of all windows of the application.

- Design the C++ class that encapsulates a window in such a way that after the window is created, it is added to the list in the `WindowsEventHandler` class. Also, that class should store the window handle and have a member function for processing messages.

- When Windows calls the `static` callback function, compare the HWND parameter with the window handle of the C++ classes in the list and call the message-handling function from the class with a matching handle. If there is no match, call the Windows function `DefWindowProc` to process the message.

Listing 14.1 shows the file `wevents.h`, which declares the `WindowsEventHandler` class that defines the static callback function `WindowProc`. Its member functions are defined in the file `wevents.cpp` (Listing 14.2).

Listing 14.1. `wevents.h`—Header file for the `WindowsEventHandler` class.

```
//------------------------------------------------------------
//  File: wevents.h
//
//  Declare the WindowsEventHandler class that handles the
//  events.

#if !defined(__WEVENTS_H)
#define __WEVENTS_H

#include "winlist.h"

class FormView;

class WindowsEventHandler
{
public:
    WindowsEventHandler(FormView& fv) : _formview(fv) {}
    ~WindowsEventHandler(){}

    WORD start();

//  The "window procedure" that Microsoft Windows calls
//  to deliver messages for windows in this application

    static LONG FAR PASCAL _export WindowProc(HWND hWnd,
                WORD message, WORD wParam, LONG lParam);

    static void add(PlainWindow& w) {_wlist.add(w);}

private:
    FormView&            _formview;
    static WindowList    _wlist;
};

#endif
```

The `WindowsEvent` class uses the services of the `WindowList` class to maintain a list named `_wlist` of windows. You will find the implementation of the `WindowList` class in Listings 14.3 and 14.4. Essentially, the `WindowList` class maintains a doubly linked list of `PlainWindow` objects that happen to be the base class for all user-defined windows.

The `WindowEventHandler` class maintains a reference to a `FormView` class, which will be described later in the chapter. At this point, all you need to know is that the `FormView` class takes care of displaying the form.

Among the member functions of WindowsEventHandler, the add function is for adding a PlainWindow to the list of windows _wlist. The other important function is the static function WindowProc, whose implementation appears in Listing 14.2. Note that the primary job of WindowProc is to find the PlainWindow with the matching window handle and call that PlainWindow's process_message function. If the search does not succeed and a window is in the process of being created, that window's process_message function is called. Otherwise, WindowProc passes the message to the DefWindowProc function as required by the programming guidelines for Microsoft Windows.

Listing 14.2. `wevents.cpp`—Member functions of the
`WindowsEventHandler` class.

```
//------------------------------------------------------------
//  File: wevents.cpp
//
//  The "window procedure" that handles all messages sent by
//  Windows.

#include "wevents.h"
#include "formview.h"

WindowList WindowsEventHandler::_wlist;
//------------------------------------------------------------
// W i n d o w P r o c
// The "window procedure" for the application; this function is
// a static member of the WindowsEventHandler class

LONG FAR PASCAL _export WindowsEventHandler::WindowProc(
            HWND hWnd, WORD message, WORD wParam, LONG lParam)
{
// Locate window (identified by hWnd) in the static list of
// windows maintained in the WindowsEventHandler class
    PlainWindow* p_w = _wlist.first();

    for(; p_w != NULL; p_w = _wlist.next())
    {
        if(p_w->hWnd() == hWnd)
        {
            return p_w->process_message(message, wParam, lParam);
        }
    }
```

```
    // If not handled, check whether Windows called this function
    // during the creation of an instance of the "PlainWindow" class
    // or one of the classes derived from PlainWindow)
        if(PlainWindow::_not_yet_created)
        {
            PlainWindow* p_w = PlainWindow::_window_being_created;
            p_w->hWnd(hWnd);
            return p_w->process_message(message, wParam, lParam);
        }


    // If still not handled, forward message to Windows
        return DefWindowProc(hWnd, message, wParam, lParam);
    }
    //------------------------------------------------------------
    // Other member functions . . .

    WORD WindowsEventHandler::start() { return _formview.start();}
```

Listing 14.3. `winlist.h`—Header file for the `WindowList` class.

```
//----------------------------------------------------------
//  File: winlist.h
//
//  Interface class for a doubly linked list of windows.

#if !defined (__WINLIST_H)
#define __WINLIST_H

#include "dllist.h"
#include "plainwin.h"

class WindowList
{
public:
    WindowList() {}

    PlainWindow* first() { return (PlainWindow*)_wl.first();}
    PlainWindow* last() { return (PlainWindow*)_wl.last();}
    PlainWindow* next() { return (PlainWindow*)_wl.next();}
    PlainWindow* previous() {return (PlainWindow*)_wl.previous();}
    unsigned count() { return _wl.count();}

    void add(PlainWindow& w) { _wl.append(w);}
```

```
private:
    doubly_linked_list _wl;
};

        #endif
```

The Window Classes

Once you have addressed the question of how to handle the callback function, you can start defining the C++ classes that will represent the various types of windows in Microsoft Windows. In particular, the classes have to handle the following:

- User-defined pop-up or child windows
- Modal dialog boxes
- Predefined windows such as *edit* and *listbox* windows

The difference between modal dialog box windows and predefined windows is in their handling of messages: Modal dialog boxes have a callback function, whereas predefined windows have their own internal message-handling mechanism. You do not have to provide any callback function for predefined windows. In this section, you will develop the C++ classes necessary for each type of window. As you read the description, consult Figure 14.1, which gives an overall view of the class hierarchy.

Predefined Window Types

The predefined windows such as *edit* and *listbox* are the easiest to encapsulate in a class. In the form fill-in software, an edit window is used for data entry. An *edit* window maintains one or more lines of text. You will see its use later on; in Listing 14.4, you can see the implementation of the EditWindow class, which encapsulates an *edit* window. The only data member of this class is the handle of the *edit* window.

The member functions are primarily for notational convenience. Each member function calls a Microsoft Windows function to do its job. Here is a summary description of the member functions of the EditWindow class:

void create(HWND hParent, WORD child_id); calls CreateWindow to create an *edit* window as a child of the window whose handle is hParent.

`BOOL is_visible();` returns TRUE if the *edit* window is visible.

`void settext(const char* s);` copies the string s into the *edit* window's internal buffer.

`void gettext(char* s, WORD numchars);` copies up to numchars characters from the *edit* window's buffer to the string s. Make sure string s is at least numchars bytes long.

`void textlimit(WORD numchars);` limits to numchars the number of characters that the user can type into the *edit* window.

`void move(POINT& origin, POINT& extent);` moves the *edit* window's origin (its upper left corner) to the x-y coordinates specified by the POINT origin and resizes the *edit* window to the width and height specified by extent.

`void show();` makes the *edit* window visible.

`void hide();` hides the *edit* window.

`void focus();` gives the keyboard focus to the *edit* window. This means all subsequent keystrokes go to the *edit* window.

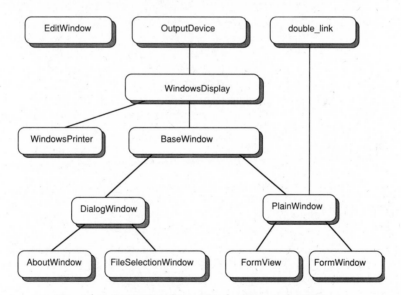

Fig. 14.1. C++ class hierarchy for Microsoft Windows.

Listing 14.4. `editwin.h`—Definition of the `EditWindow` class that represents an "edit" window.

```
//-----------------------------------------------------------
//  File: editwin.h
//
//  A class that encapsulates the "edit" class of Microsoft
//  Windows.

#if !defined(__EDITWIN_H)
#define __EDITWIN_H

#include <windows.h>

class EditWindow
{
public:
    EditWindow() : hWnd(0) {}
    ~EditWindow() { if(hWnd != 0) DestroyWindow(hWnd);}

// Function that actually creates the "edit" window
    void create(HWND hParent, WORD child_id)
    {
        hWnd = CreateWindow("edit", NULL,
                            WS_CHILD | WS_BORDER |
                            ES_NOHIDESEL,
                            0, 0, 0, 0,
                            hParent,
                            (HMENU) child_id,
                            BaseWindow::hInstance, NULL);
    }

    BOOL is_visible() {return IsWindowVisible(hWnd);}

    void settext(const char* s)
    {
        SendMessage(hWnd, WM_SETTEXT, 0, (LONG)s);
    }

    void gettext(char* s, WORD numchars)
    {
        SendMessage(hWnd, WM_GETTEXT, numchars, (LONG)s);
    }
```

```
        LONG textlength()
        {
            WORD w;
            LONG l;
            return SendMessage(hWnd, WM_GETTEXTLENGTH, w, l);
        }

        void textlimit(WORD numchars)
        {
            SendMessage(hWnd, EM_LIMITTEXT, numchars, 0);
        }

        void move(POINT& origin, POINT& extent)
        {
            MoveWindow(hWnd, origin.x, origin.y,
                             extent.x, extent.y, 1);
        }
        void show() { ShowWindow(hWnd, SW_SHOW);}
        void hide() { ShowWindow(hWnd, SW_HIDE);}
        void focus() { if(IsWindow(hWnd)) SetFocus(hWnd);}

private:
    HWND hWnd;   // Handle to this "edit" window
};

    #endif
```

BaseWindow *Class*

Both the user-defined windows and the modal dialog boxes have at least one data item in common: a window handle. Thus, we will start with the BaseWindow class (file basewin.h in Listing 14.5), which has a handle as the lone data member and which will serve as the base class for all types of windows. We derive the BaseWindow from the WindowsDisplay class, which, in turn, is derived from the OutputDevice class. This is necessary because we want to display output in a window. Recall from Chapter 13 that the OutputDevice class provides a device-independent way of displaying the graphics objects derived from the TextGraphics class. That claim is tested here because we will switch the output device from a text-display to a window. In fact, we will even print the form by drawing to a "printer" output device. Later sections provide the details of the output mechanism.

Listing 14.5. basewin.h—Header file for the BaseWindow class: basewin.h.

```
//-----------------------------------------------------------
//  File: basewin.h
//
//  Declare the abstract class from which all other windows
//  are derived.

#if !defined (__BASEWIN_H)
#define __BASEWIN_H

#include <windows.h>
#include "wdisplay.h"

class BaseWindow : public WindowsDisplay
{
public:
    BaseWindow() : _hWnd(0) {}

    BaseWindow(const BaseWindow& bw) : WindowsDisplay(bw),
        _hWnd(bw._hWnd) {}

    virtual ~BaseWindow() {}

    virtual WORD start() = 0;

// Some useful functions
    HANDLE hWnd() { return _hWnd;}
    void hWnd(HANDLE h) { _hWnd = h;}

    BOOL is_visible() {return IsWindowVisible(_hWnd);}

    void move(POINT& origin, POINT& extent)
    {
        MoveWindow(_hWnd, origin.x, origin.y,
                          extent.x, extent.y, TRUE);
    }
    void show() { ShowWindow(_hWnd, SW_SHOW);}
    void hide() { ShowWindow(_hWnd, SW_HIDE);}

    static HANDLE hInstance;
    static HANDLE hPrevInstance;
    static int    nCmdShow;
    static LPSTR  lpszCmdLine;
```

```
    protected:
        HWND    _hWnd;
    };

    #endif
```

The BaseWindow class includes four static member variables—hInstance, hPrevInstance, nCmdShow, and lpszCmdLine—used to store certain variables that are passed by Windows to a function called WinMain, which is the Windows counterpart of the main function of C and C++. The WinMain function of the form fill-in program appears later in this chapter.

Among the member functions of the BaseWindow class, the pure virtual function start serves a special purpose. For dialog windows, start should create the dialog and process messages until the user is through with the dialog. For other windows, start implements the message-handling loop of the Windows application. At this point, start is pure virtual because its implementation depends on whether a window is a dialog box or a regular window.

The other member functions of BaseWindow—is_visible, move, show, and hide—are similar to the identically named functions in the EditWindow class (Listing 14.4).

DialogWindow *Class*

The DialogWindow class, implemented in files dlogwin.h (Listing 14.6) and dlogwin.cpp (Listing 14.7), is the base class for all dialog boxes. A Windows dialog box needs a callback function just as any other window does. The static member function, DialogProc, serves as the sole callback function for all dialog boxes. As you can see from its implementation in Listing 14.7, the DialogProc function simply calls the process_message function of the currently active dialog, indicated by yet another static member variable of the DialogWindow class: _active_dialog. This variable is initialized by the constructor of DialogWindow.

Listing 14.6. dlogwin.h—Header file for the DialogWindow class.

```
//-----------------------------------------------------------
//  File: dlogwin.h
//
//  Declare the DialogWindow class. This is the base class for
//  all dialog boxes.

#if !defined(__DLOGWIN_H)
#define __DLOGWIN_H
```

```
#include "basewin.h"

class DialogWindow : public BaseWindow
{
public:
    DialogWindow(HWND owner);

    ~DialogWindow();

    void done() { FreeProcInstance(dproc);}

    virtual WORD start(); // Create and become modal

// Following function should return the name of the
// dialog (which should match the name of the dialog as
// it appears in the resource file)
    virtual LPSTR name() = 0;

protected:
    virtual BOOL process_message(HWND, WORD, WORD,
                                 LONG) { return FALSE;}

// Room for the value returned by a dialog
    WORD return_code;

private:
    static BOOL FAR PASCAL _export DialogProc(HWND hWnd,
              WORD message, WORD wParam, LONG lParam);

    static DialogWindow* _active_dialog; // Current active dialog
    FARPROC dproc;  // The exported dialog procedure
};

#endif
```

What makes the `DialogWindow` class work is the code in its `start` function (Listing 14.7). Following the requirements of Windows programming, it creates an instance of the `DialogProc` function. Then it sets up the modal dialog by calling the `DialogBox` function and installing the instance of `DialogProc` as the callback. The `DialogBox` function also needs a string that identifies the dialog box. This is the name you have used to define the dialog box in the resource file of the application. In this implementation, the name is returned by a virtual function called `name`. Every dialog box window derived from `DialogWindow` should define `name` so that it returns the name under which the dialog appears in the resource file.

Listing 14.7. `dlogwin.cpp`—Member functions of the `DialogWindow` class.

```cpp
//-----------------------------------------------------------
//  File: dlogwin.cpp
//
//  Define the member functions of the DialogWindow class.

#include "dlogwin.h"

// Initialize static variables
DialogWindow* DialogWindow::_active_dialog = NULL;


//-----------------------------------------------------------
// D i a l o g W i n d o w
// Constructor for a dialog

DialogWindow::DialogWindow(HWND owner) : return_code(0)
{
    if(_active_dialog == NULL)
    {
        _hWnd = owner;
        _active_dialog = this;
    }
}
//-----------------------------------------------------------
// ~ D i a l o g W i n d o w
// Destructor for a dialog

DialogWindow::~DialogWindow()
{
    if(_active_dialog != NULL)
    {
        _active_dialog = NULL;
    }
}
//-----------------------------------------------------------
// s t a r t
// Start processing messages
```

```
WORD DialogWindow::start()
{
// Create a modal dialog box
    dproc = MakeProcInstance(
                  (FARPROC)DialogWindow::DialogProc, hInstance);
    DialogBox(hInstance, name(), hWnd(), dproc);
    FreeProcInstance(dproc);
    done();
// Return the value stored in the member variable "return_code"
    return return_code;
}
//----------------------------------------------------------------
// D i a l o g P r o c
// Function called by dialogs to handle messages

BOOL FAR PASCAL _export DialogWindow::DialogProc(HWND hWnd,
                  WORD message, WORD wParam, LONG lParam)
{
// Send the message to the currently active dialog
      return _active_dialog->process_message(hWnd, message,
                                                wParam, lParam);

}
```

PlainWindow *Class*

The situation is somewhat different for windows that are not dialog boxes. At any time, there is only one instance of a modal dialog box, but there can be many user-defined windows. For these windows, the following rules apply:

- These windows have to reside in a linked list in the WindowsEventHandler class. Therefore, the base class must inherit from the double_link class.

- The start function has to provide a message loop that gets messages from Windows and calls a standard Windows function to dispatch them.

Listing 14.8 shows the file plainwin.h, which declares the PlainWindow class that meets these requirements. The member functions are defined in a file named plainwin.cpp (Listing 14.9). PlainWindow inherits from both BaseWindow and double_link. Because of inheriting from double_link, PlainWindow has to include the member functions clone, destroy, read, and write, which it leaves up to the derived classes to define.

Listing 14.8. plainwin.h—Header file for the PlainWindow class.

```
//-------------------------------------------------------------
// File: plainwin.h
//
// Declare an abstract base class "PlainWindow" that forms the
// basis of all user-defined windows.

#if !defined (__PLAINWIN_H)
#define __PLAINWIN_H

#include "basewin.h"
#include "dlink.h"

class istream;
class ostream;

class PlainWindow : public BaseWindow, public double_link
{
public:
    PlainWindow() {}
    PlainWindow(const PlainWindow& pw) : BaseWindow(pw) {}

    ~PlainWindow()
    {
        if(_hWnd != 0) DestroyWindow(_hWnd);
        _hWnd = 0;
    }

    double_link* clone() = 0;
    void destroy() = 0;

    void read(istream&) {}
    void write(ostream&) {}

    virtual WORD start();
    virtual LONG process_message(WORD message, WORD wParam,
                                 LONG lParam);
    virtual BOOL init(HWND hParent, WORD child_id);

protected:
    virtual BOOL register_class() = 0;
    virtual BOOL create_window(HWND hParent,
                               WORD child_id) = 0;
```

```
        static BOOL          _not_yet_created;
        static PlainWindow*  _window_being_created;
    };
```

```
    #endif
```

The PlainWindow class needs the static members _not_yet_created and _window_being_created to help process messages sent to a window during its creation. These static variables, as well as others from the BaseWindow class, are defined in the file plainwin.cpp.

PlainWindow's start function (Listing 14.9) provides the standard message-processing loop of a Windows application. Thus, after initializing all the windows in your application, you can start executing the message-handling loop by calling the start function for one of the windows. Note that this loop simply passes messages to a Windows function. Windows then calls the callback for the application, in this case, WindowsEventHandler::WindowProc (Listing 14.1) to deliver the message. WindowsEventHandler::WindowProc processes the message by calling the process_message function of the appropriate window. Each user-defined window class, derived from PlainWindow, has to define a process_message function to respond to the Windows message in a manner relevant to the application. In PlainWindow, process_message simply calls the default Windows message-handler: DefWindowProc.

To initialize a window, you have to call the init function (Listing 14.9). As defined in the PlainWindow class, the init function performs the following standard initializations:

1. It checks whether this is the first instance of the application (indicated by a zero value in the hPrevInstance variable) and if so calls the virtual function register_class to register this "class" of window with Microsoft Windows.

2. If all goes well, init calls another virtual function named create_window that actually creates the window. While the window is being created, init sets the static variable _not_yet_created to 1 and ensures that the PlainWindow* variable _window_being_created is set to the C++ keyword this (indicating the address of the current object).

All window classes derived from PlainWindow inherit the init function; they do not have to define init separately.

Listing 14.9. plainwin.cpp—Member functions of the PlainWindow class.

```
//------------------------------------------------------------
//  File: plainwin.cpp
//
//  Member functions of the PlainWindow class.
```

```
#include "plainwin.h"

// Initialize static members of BaseWindow and PlainWindow

HANDLE BaseWindow::hInstance = 0;
HANDLE BaseWindow::hPrevInstance = 0;
LPSTR BaseWindow::lpszCmdLine = 0;
int BaseWindow::nCmdShow = 0;
BOOL PlainWindow::_not_yet_created = 1;
PlainWindow* PlainWindow::_window_being_created = NULL;
//-----------------------------------------------------------
// s t a r t
// Start processing events

WORD PlainWindow::start()
{
    if(_hWnd != 0)
    {
        MSG m;
        while(GetMessage(&m, NULL, NULL, NULL))
        {
            TranslateMessage(&m);
            DispatchMessage(&m);
        }
        return m.wParam;
    }
}
//-----------------------------------------------------------
// p r o c e s s _ m e s s a g e
// Process messages from Windows

LONG PlainWindow::process_message(WORD message, WORD wParam,
                                  LONG lParam)
{
// In this case, simply call the "default" dispatcher . . .
    return DefWindowProc(_hWnd, message, wParam, lParam);
}
//-----------------------------------------------------------
// i n i t
// Initialize the window (register the class, if necessary; then
// create the window)

BOOL PlainWindow::init(HWND hParent, WORD child_id)
{
```

```
// Register, if this is the first instance (indicated by
// handle to previous instance being zero)
    if(hPrevInstance == 0  && !register_class()) return FALSE;

// If all's well, call create_window to create window
    _not_yet_created = 1;
    _window_being_created = this;
    if(! create_window(hParent, child_id)) return FALSE;
    _not_yet_created = 0;

    return TRUE;
}
```

Dialog Boxes for the Forms Package

Now that the abstract base classes are defined, you can begin creating concrete classes for the dialog boxes that are specifically meant for the Windows version of the FORMFILL program. Two dialogs come to mind:

- An About dialog box that displays a copyright notice and a short description of the software

- A File Selection dialog box that the user employs to choose the file to be opened

You will find these two dialog boxes in most Windows applications, and FORMFILL is no exception.

In Microsoft Windows, the layout and contents of dialog boxes are defined in a *resource file*, which is a text file that is compiled into a binary form by a *resource compiler* and appended to the executable program. During execution, when the program calls the DialogBox function (see Listing 14.7), Windows reads the description of a requested dialog from the executable file and displays it. Listing 14.10 shows the file formfill.rc, which lists the resources for the Windows version of the FORMFILL application. You should consult a book on programming Microsoft Windows or the documentation of the Microsoft Windows Software Development Kit for more information on the syntax of resource files. As you might surmise after studying Listing 14.10, the resource file defines the application's menus as well as its dialog boxes.

Note that you have to define the symbols such as IDM_OPEN, IDM_SAVE, and IDM_EXIT to have distinct values so that you can tell the menu selections apart. Listing 14.11 shows the file fwindef.h, which defines these symbols.

Listing 14.10. `formfill.rc`—Resource file for the `FORMFILL` application.

```
//--------------------------------------------------------------
// File: formfill.rc
//
// Resource file for the FORMFILL application.

#include <windows.h>
#include "fwindef.h"

// Icon for the application
FORMICON icon  FORMFILL.ICO

FormViewMenu MENU
BEGIN
    POPUP          "&File"
    BEGIN
        MENUITEM    "&Open...",         IDM_OPEN
        MENUITEM    "&Save",            IDM_SAVE,   GRAYED
        MENUITEM    "Save &As...",      IDM_SAVEAS, GRAYED
        MENUITEM    "&Print",           IDM_PRINT,  GRAYED
        MENUITEM    SEPARATOR
        MENUITEM    "E&xit",            IDM_EXIT
    END


    POPUP          "&Help"
    BEGIN
        MENUITEM    "A&bout FormFill...", IDM_ABOUT
    END
END

About DIALOG 22, 17, 144, 95
CAPTION "FormFill"
STYLE WS_POPUP | WS_DLGFRAME | WS_CAPTION | WS_BORDER
BEGIN
    CTEXT "Microsoft Windows"        -1,   0,  5, 144,   8
    CTEXT "Form Fill Program"        -1,   0, 14, 144,   8
    CTEXT "Version 1.00"             -1,   0, 34, 144,   8
    CTEXT "(C) 1991 LNB Software"    -1,   0, 54, 144,   8
    DEFPUSHBUTTON "OK"            IDOK,  53, 79,  32,  14,
WS_GROUP
END

FileSelection DIALOG 10, 10, 148, 112
CAPTION "Select File . . ."
```

```
STYLE WS_DLGFRAME ¦ WS_POPUP ¦ WS_CAPTION ¦ WS_BORDER
BEGIN
    CONTROL "File &Name:", -1, "static", SS_LEFT ¦ WS_CHILD, 4,
4,  60, 10
    CONTROL "",            IDC_FILENAME, "edit", ES_LEFT ¦ WS_BORDER
¦ WS_TABSTOP ¦ WS_CHILD, 4, 16, 100, 12
    Control "&Files in",  -1, "static", SS_LEFT ¦ WS_CHILD, 4, 40,
32, 10
    CONTROL "", IDC_FILELIST, "listbox", LBS_NOTIFY ¦ WS_BORDER ¦
WS_CHILD ¦ WS_TABSTOP ¦ WS_VSCROLL, 4, 52,  70, 56
    CONTROL "", IDC_PATHNAME, "static", SS_LEFT ¦ WS_CHILD, 40,
40, 100, 10
    DEFPUSHBUTTON "&OK",IDOK,        87, 60,  50, 14
    PUSHBUTTON "Cancel",IDCANCEL,    87, 80,  50, 14
END


END
```

Listing 14.11. `fwindef.h`—Resource and message IDs in `FORMFILL`.

```
//---------------------------------------------------------
//  File: fwindef.h
//
//  Define various IDs.

#if !defined(__FWINDEF_H)
#define __FWINDEF_H

// "File" menu items
#define IDM_OPEN      100
#define IDM_SAVE      101
#define IDM_SAVEAS    102
#define IDM_PRINT     103
#define IDM_EXIT      104


// Help menu
#define IDM_ABOUT     300
```

```
// Control IDs
#define IDC_FILENAME  400
#define IDC_PATHNAME  401
#define IDC_FILELIST  402

// Position of "File" menu
#define FILEMENULOC 0

// Application-specific messages
#define FORM_OPEN    WM_USER+1
#define FORM_SAVE    WM_USER+2
#define FORM_SAVEAS  WM_USER+3
#define FORM_PRINT   WM_USER+4

#endif
```

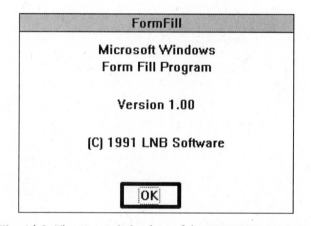

Fig. 14.2. The About dialog box of the FORMFILL program.

The About *Dialog Box*

In the formfill.rc file (Listing 14.10), the line that starts with About DIALOG defines a dialog box named About. Figure 14.2 shows the About dialog as it appears on the screen (later on you will see how this dialog is activated). A C++ class named AboutWindow, derived from DialogWindow (Listing 14.6 and 14.7), implements the dialog box. Listings 14.12 and 14.13 show the implementation of the AboutWindow class.

Listing 14.12. about.h—Header file for the AboutWindow class.

```
//------------------------------------------------------------
//   File: about.h
//
//   Class that displays the "About" box.

#if !defined(__ABOUT_H)
#define __ABOUT_H

#include "dlogwin.h"

class AboutWindow : public DialogWindow
{
public:

    AboutWindow(HWND owner) : DialogWindow(owner) {}

protected:
    LPSTR name() { return "About";}
    BOOL process_message(HWND hWnd, WORD message,
                         WORD wParam, LONG lParam);
};

    #endif
```

The AboutWindow class has two member functions—name and process_message—that are required of any dialog box window. The name function returns the string About, which is the name of the dialog box in formfill.rc (Listing 14.10).

The process_message function (Listing 14.13) implements a typical Windows message-handling code that consists of a switch statement. (Yes, this goes against an earlier assertion that object-oriented programming gets rid of switch statements, but the goal of switch-less programming proves somewhat elusive because of Windows' message-driven architecture.)

Listing 14.13. about.cpp—The process_message function of the AboutWindow class.

```
//------------------------------------------------------------
//   File: about.cpp
//
//   Implement the member functions of the "About" dialog box.

#include "about.h"
```

```
//-----------------------------------------------------------------
// p r o c e s s _ m e s s a g e
// Function that handles messages for the About dialog box;
// note that by convention the "process_message" function
// sends unprocessed messages to its base class

BOOL AboutWindow::process_message(HWND hWnd, WORD message,
                                     WORD wParam, LONG lParam)
{
    switch (message)
    {
        case WM_INITDIALOG: // Do any necessary initializations
            return TRUE;

        case WM_COMMAND:     // Return TRUE when "OK" is selected
            if(wParam == IDOK)
            {
                EndDialog(hWnd, TRUE);
                return TRUE;
            }

        default:
            return DialogWindow::process_message(hWnd, message,
                                                   wParam, lParam);

    }
}
```

The FileSelection *Dialog Box*

This dialog box is defined toward the end of the file formfill.rc (Listing 14.10). The description begins on a line that starts with FileSelection DIALOG (that means the name of the dialog is FileSelection). Figure 14.3 shows how the FileSelection dialog box appears to the user. Compared to the About dialog, FileSelection has many more components. You will get a rough idea of how the dialog's definition works by correlating the on-screen appearance of the FileSelection dialog with its definition in formfill.rc (Listing 14.10). You will see that the FileSelection dialog consists of an *edit* window, a *listbox*, two *pushbuttons* (labeled *OK* and *Cancel*), and several *static windows*. The listbox displays a directory listing from which the user can pick a file or change the directory. The *edit* box displays the current selection and also lets the user type in a file name. The user selects one of the OK or Cancel pushbuttons to terminate the dialog.

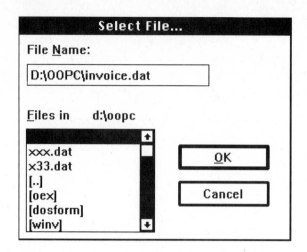

Fig. 14.3. The `FileSelection` dialog box of the `FORMFILL` program.

The C++ class named `FileSelectionWindow` (Listings 14.14 and 14.15) implements the functionality of the `FileSelection` dialog box. The `FileSelectionWindow` class has several `String` variables for storing various components of a file name.

Listing 14.14. `fselwin.h`—Header file for `FileSelectionWindow` class.

```
//------------------------------------------------------------
//  File: fselwin.h
//
//  Declare the FileSelectionWindow class. This class displays
//  and manages a dialog window for selecting files.

#if !defined(__FSELWIN_H)
#define __FSELWIN_H

#include "dlogwin.h"
#include "str.h"

class FileSelectionWindow : public DialogWindow
{
public:

    FileSelectionWindow(HWND owner, const char* title,
        const char* dirname, const char* filename,
        BOOL file_must_exist);

        LPSTR name() { return "FileSelection";}
```

```
    String pathname() { return _pathname;}

protected:
    BOOL process_message(HWND hWnd, WORD message, WORD wParam,
                    LONG lParam);
private:
    String  _title;
    String  _pathname;   // Complete path name
    String  _dirname;
    String  _filename;
    String  _idir;       // Initial directory
    String  _ifile;      // Initial file name
    BOOL    _file_must_exist;

    void    update_list(HWND hWnd);
    void    ok_selected(HWND hWnd);
    BOOL    list_selected(HWND hWnd, LONG lParam);
    BOOL    name_selected(HWND hWnd, LONG lParam);
};

#endif
```

FileSelectionWindow has the lone constructor with the prototype:

```
FileSelectionWindow(HWND owner, const char* title,
    const char* dirname, const char* filename,
    BOOL file_must_exist);
```

The arguments have the following meanings:

HWND owner is the window handle of the owner of the dialog.

const char* title specifies the text displayed in the title bar of the dialog window.

const char* dirname specifies the directory whose contents are initially listed in the *listbox* within the dialog window.

const char* filename is the initial file specification, such as *.dat or *.*. Files matching the specification will appear in the *listbox*.

BOOL file_must_exist is a flag that, when set to TRUE, forces the dialog to verify that the selected file already exists.

Here is how you might use the FileSelectionWindow:

```
#include <dir.h>  // For prototype of getcwd (Borland C++)
// . . .
// Get current directory
    const unsigned maxchr = 80;
```

```
      char dir_name[maxchr];
      getcwd(dir_name, sizeof(dir_name));

// Open a FileSelectionWindow to look for all files
// Assume hOwner is handle of owner
      FileSelectionWindow fdlog(hOwner, "Open a file", dir_name,
                               "*.*", TRUE);
      if(fdlog.start() == 0)
      {
// File name is valid . . .Call "pathname" to get it
          String file_selected = fdlog.pathname();
// . . .
      }
```

This code starts by getting the name of the current directory by calling the getcwd function from the Borland C++ library. Then, you create a FileSelectionWindow and start the dialog by calling its start function. If the start function returns a zero, you can assume that there is a selection from the user. You can get the selected file name by calling the pathname function of the FileSelectionWindow dialog.

**Listing 14.15. fselwin.cpp—Member functions of the
FileSelectionWindow class.**

```
//------------------------------------------------------------
//  File: fselwin.cpp
//
//  Implement the member functions of the FileSelectionWindow.

#include "fwindef.h"
#include "fselwin.h"

const unsigned maxlen = 80;

//------------------------------------------------------------
// F i l e S e l e c t i o n W i n d o w
// Constructor for the FileSelection dialog box

FileSelectionWindow::FileSelectionWindow(HWND owner,
    const char* title, const char* dirname,
    const char* filename, BOOL file_must_exist) :
        DialogWindow(owner),
        _title(title), _idir(dirname), _ifile(filename),
        _file_must_exist(file_must_exist)
```

```
{
// If missing, add a '\' to path name
    int len = _idir.length();
    if(_idir[len-1] != '\\') _idir = _idir + "\\";

    _dirname = _idir;
    _filename = _ifile;

// Append file name to path name
    _pathname = _dirname + _filename;
}
//-------------------------------------------------------------------
// p r o c e s s _ m e s s a g e
BOOL FileSelectionWindow::process_message(HWND hWnd,
                         WORD message, WORD wParam, LONG lParam)
{
    switch (message)
    {
        case WM_INITDIALOG:   // Do any necessary initializations

            SendDlgItemMessage(hWnd, IDC_FILENAME, EM_LIMITTEXT,
                maxlen, 0);   // Limit path names to "maxlen"
            update_list(hWnd);
            return TRUE;

        case WM_COMMAND:
            switch(wParam)
            {
                case IDCANCEL:
                    return_code = 1;
                    EndDialog(hWnd, TRUE);
                    return TRUE;

                case IDOK:
                    ok_selected(hWnd);
                    return TRUE;

                case IDC_FILELIST:
                    if(list_selected(hWnd, lParam)) return TRUE;
                    break;

                case IDC_FILENAME:
                    if(name_selected(hWnd, lParam)) return TRUE;
            }
```

```
            default:
                return DialogWindow::process_message(hWnd, message,
                                                      wParam, lParam);
        }
}
//------------------------------------------------------------------
// u p d a t e _ l i s t
// Update the list of files in the dialog box

#define LIST_DIRS      0x4000
#define LIST_SUBDIRS   0x0010

void FileSelectionWindow::update_list(HWND hWnd)
{
// Fill list box with names of files from specified directory
    char* t = new char[maxlen];
    strcpy(t, _pathname);
    DlgDirList(hWnd, t, IDC_FILELIST,
                IDC_PATHNAME, LIST_DIRS | LIST_SUBDIRS);
// Set the file name
    SetDlgItemText(hWnd, IDC_FILENAME, t);
    delete t;
}
//------------------------------------------------------------------
// o k _ s e l e c t e d
// This function is called when user clicks on OK button

void FileSelectionWindow::ok_selected(HWND hWnd)
{
// Retrieve the file name and see whether it's valid
    char fname[maxlen];
    GetDlgItemText(hWnd, IDC_FILENAME, fname, maxlen);

    _pathname = fname;
// If file name ends in ":" or "\\", append the initial file name
// in an attempt to make it a valid name
    int len = _pathname.length();
    char c = _pathname[len-1];
    if(c == ':' || c == '\\') _pathname = _pathname + _ifile;

// If file name has any wildcard character (* or ?), then
// the listbox has to be updated
```

```
        if(strchr(_pathname, '*') ||
           strchr(_pathname, '?'))
        {
            update_list(hWnd);
            return;
        }

// If necessary, verify that file exists
        if(_file_must_exist)
        {
            OFSTRUCT ofs;
            char buf[maxlen];
            strcpy(buf, _pathname);
            if(OpenFile(buf, (LPOFSTRUCT)&ofs, OF_EXIST) < 0)
            {
// File does not exist; display message and return
                char str[maxlen];
                strcpy(str, _pathname);
                if( MessageBox(hWnd, str, "File does not exist!",
                        MB_OK | MB_ICONEXCLAMATION) == IDOK)
                return;
            }
        }
        EndDialog(hWnd, TRUE);
}
//------------------------------------------------------------
// l i s t _ s e l e c t e d
// Called when user clicks in the list of file names

BOOL FileSelectionWindow::list_selected(HWND hWnd, LONG lParam)
{
    switch(HIWORD(lParam))
    {
        case LBN_SELCHANGE: // New item selected
        {
            char buf[maxlen];
            if(DlgDirSelect(hWnd, buf, IDC_FILELIST))
            {
// Selection is a new directory name
                _dirname = buf;
                }
                else
                {
```

```
// Selection is a file name
                _filename = buf;
            }
// Complete the path name
            _pathname = _dirname + _filename;
            const char* t = _pathname;
            SetDlgItemText(hWnd, IDC_FILENAME, (LPSTR)t);
            return TRUE;
        }

        case LBN_DBLCLK:     // Double click on an item
        {
            char buf[maxlen];
            if(DlgDirSelect(hWnd, buf, IDC_FILELIST))
            {
                _dirname = buf;
                _pathname = _dirname + _ifile;
// Update the list of files . . .
                update_list(hWnd);
            }
            else
            {
                _filename = buf;
                _pathname = _dirname + _filename;
                const char* t = _pathname;
                SetDlgItemText(hWnd, IDC_FILENAME, (LPSTR)t);
            }
            return TRUE;
        }

        default:
            return FALSE;
    }
}
//------------------------------------------------------------------
// n a m e _ s e l e c t e d
// Called when user interacts with the edit box for file name

BOOL FileSelectionWindow::name_selected(HWND hWnd, LONG lParam)
    {
    // If the edit box is empty, disable the OK button
        if(HIWORD(lParam) == EN_CHANGE)
        {
```

```
// First, get the count of characters
        LONG charcount = SendMessage(LOWORD(lParam),
                                        WM_GETTEXTLENGTH, 0, 0L);
// Enable or disable OK button based on count
        EnableWindow(GetDlgItem(hWnd, IDOK), (BOOL) charcount);
        return TRUE;
    }
    else
        return FALSE;
}
```

Windows for the Forms Package

To create the user interface for the FORMFILL program, you will need a window to display the form. In anticipation of a future version of FORMFILL that might open more than one form at once, we will start with a FormView class that will be the main window of the application, complete with menu bar, scroll bars, and borders. We will display the form in a separate window, called FormWindow, which will be a child window of FormView. Note that the complete class hierarchy is illustrated in Figure 14.1. Consult this figure as you read the description of the classes.

The FormView *Class*

The DOS version of the FORMFILL program also uses a FormView class, but this version of the FormView class is specific to Microsoft Windows. The FormView class (Listings 14.16 and 14.17) provides the main window of the application. This window includes a menu bar with pull-down menus and has scroll bars attached to it. The FormView class handles all user interactions. In fact, the start function of the WindowsEventHandler class (Listings 14.1 and 14.2) does its job by simply calling the start function of the FormView object associated with that WindowsEventHandler. Do not be alarmed if you do not see start declared in the header file for the FormView class—it inherits from the PlainWindow class (Listings 14.8 and 14.9).

Data in FormView

The FormView class is designed to handle one form at a time. The form is actually manipulated by an instance of a FormWindow class (to be described later) whose window is a child of the FormView window. Thus, the most significant private data in FormView is an instance of FormWindow named _fw. This is the object that will manipulate the form. The following are advantages of using a FormWindow to manage a form:

- You can easily support multiple forms by creating multiple instances of FormWindows. The variable _fwID can keep count of the instances.

- You can scroll by moving FormWindow's window around as the user interacts with the scroll bars. The POINTs _forigin, _fextent keep track of the origin and the extent of the child window where the form is displayed.

The _width and _height are used to store the current width and height of FormView's window. The other data members of FormView—_hmax, _vmax, _hpos, and _vpos—are used to support horizontal and vertical scrolling,

Listing 14.16. `formview.h`—Header file for the `FormView` class.

```
//-------------------------------------------------------------
//  File: formview.h
//
//  Declare a "form view window"--this is the shell window
//  around actual form display.

#if !defined (__FORMVIEW_H)
#define __FORMVIEW_H

#include "fwindef.h"
#include "str.h"
#include "formwin.h"

class FormView : public PlainWindow
{
public:
    FormView() : _hpos(0), _vpos(0) {}
    FormView(const FormView& w) : PlainWindow(w),
                                  _fw(w._fw) {}
    ~FormView() {}

    double_link* clone() { return new FormView(*this);}
    void destroy() { delete this;}

    LONG process_message(WORD message, WORD wParam,
                         LONG lParam);
    void process_command(WORD wParam, LONG lParam);
```

```
protected:
    BOOL register_class();
    BOOL create_window(HWND hParent, WORD child_id);

private:
    FormWindow  _fw;          // Window where form displays
    static WORD _fwID;
    POINT       _forigin;     // Origin and extent of form
    POINT       _fextent;     // window _fw
    short       _width;       // This window's width and
    short       _height;      // height
    short       _hmax, _vmax; // Scroll bar range and
    short       _hpos, _vpos; // positions

    static BOOL is_registered;// TRUE when class is registered

    enum {disable = 0, enable = 1};
    void adjust_menus(BOOL on);
    void adjust_scrollbars();
    void hscroll(WORD wParam, LONG lParam);
    void vscroll(WORD wParam, LONG lParam);
    short max(short a, short b)
    {
        return (a > b) ? a : b;
    }
    short min(short a, short b)
    {
        return (a < b) ? a : b;
    }
};

#endif
```

Initializing `FormView`

When using a `FormView` object in a program, you have to initialize it by calling its `init` function (defined in the `PlainWindow` class, Listing 14.9). This function will call the `register_class` function of `FormView` to register the *window class* of the window used in `FormView`. As you will see in Listing 14.17, the `register_class` function sets up the members of a `WNDCLASS` structure and calls the Windows function `RegisterClass` to do the job. Among the members of the `WNDCLASS` structure, the following assignments are noteworthy:

```
    WNDCLASS WndClass;
//  . . .
    WndClass.lpfnWndProc = WindowsEventHandler::WindowProc;
    WndClass.hInstance = hInstance;
    WndClass.hIcon = LoadIcon(hInstance, "FORMICON");
    WndClass.hCursor = LoadCursor(NULL, IDC_ARROW);
    WndClass.hbrBackground = GetStockObject(LTGRAY_BRUSH);
    WndClass.lpszMenuName = "FormViewMenu";
    WndClass.lpszClassName = "FormViewWindow";
```

The `lpfnWndProc` member specifies the callback function for the window. According to our design, you have to use `WindowsEventHandler::WindowProc` as the callback for all windows in the `FORMFILL` application. The `hIcon` field specifies the icon to be displayed when the application is minimized; here the icon is named `FORMICON`, which is defined in the resource file. Specify the background pattern in the `hbrBackground` field. `FormView` uses a light gray background.

You have to provide the name of the menu in the `lpszMenuName` field—this is the same name you used in defining the menu in the resource file (see `formfill.rc` in Listing 14.10). Finally, the class name of the window should be in the `lpszClassName` field of the `WNDCLASS` structure. Windows of the `FormView` class use the class name `FormViewWindow`.

After registration, the next step in initialization is to create the window by using the `create_window` function. The `create_window` function (Listing 14.17) handles window creation by calling the `CreateWindow` function from the Windows library. You have to provide the class name of the window, the title to appear in the window's title bar, and the style of the window. The style for the `FormView` window is

```
WS_HSCROLL ¦ WS_VSCROLL ¦ WS_OVERLAPPEDWINDOW ¦ WS_CLIPCHILDREN
```

This says that you want an *overlapped* window with horizontal and vertical scroll bars and you want Windows to exclude the area occupied by the child windows when drawing in the parent. When you say *overlapped window*, Windows automatically creates a standard-looking window with all the trimmings (minimize and maximize box, a standard system menu, and thick borders).

What `FormView` Does

You can determine what `FormView` does by studying its `process_message` function. That is where all messages are handled. The following summarizes the major messages handled in `FormView`'s `process_message`:

> `WM_CREATE` message indicates that the `FormView` window is being created. Here, you can determine the height (`yChar`) and average width (`xChar`) of characters (these are members of the `WindowsDisplay` class from which all

window classes are derived). These will be necessary to handle scrolling. At this point, you should initialize the FormWindow _fw by calling its init function so that the child window will be ready to display the form.

WM_SIZE message indicates that the user has resized the FormView window. The response is to store the current width and height in the member variables _width and _height, and call the adjust_scrollbars function. This function draws the scroll bars if the FormWindow's window is not entirely visible in the FormView window.

WM_COMMAND message reports the user's menu selection. This message is handled by a separate function—process_command—which is summarized later.

WM_HSCROLL and WM_VSCROLL messages report the user's interactions with the horizontal and vertical scroll bars, respectively. Scrolling is handled by three private member functions: adjust_scrollbars, hscroll, and vscroll. At the heart of the scrolling logic is the idea that the form is displayed in a full-page window (FormWindow's window), and it can be scrolled by moving the origin of this window with respect to its parent—the FormView window. You should study the hscroll and vscroll functions for details.

FORM_OPEN message is a user-defined message that FormWindow sends to FormView when the form is successfully opened and displayed. FormView's response to this message is to disable the Open... menu selection in the File menu so that no more forms can be opened. At the same time, it enables the Save, Save As..., and Print options in the File menu. The entire chore of adjusting menu items is handled by a private member function named adjust_menus.

By convention, all unprocessed messages are sent to the process_message function of the parent class that, for FormView, is PlainWindow.

Processing Commands

The process_command function in FormView handles the user's menu selection. Windows places the ID of the menu selection in the wParam argument. This ID is the same as the ones you use in the resource file to identify the menu entries (see formfill.rc in Listing 14.10 and fwindef.h in Listing 14.11). The specific menu options are as follows:

IDM_EXIT indicates that the user has selected the Exit option to quit the application. You can handle this message by sending a WM_CLOSE message to FormWindow's window.

IDM_OPEN means the user wants to open a form from a file. The code to handle this option resizes FormWindow's window to display a full-page form and sends a FORM_OPEN message to FormWindow.

IDM_SAVE indicates that the user wants to save the form in the current file. FormView handles this by sending a FORM_SAVE message to FormWindow.

IDM_SAVEAS implies that the user wants to save the form in a specified file. FormView handles this by sending a FORM_SAVEAS message to FormWindow.

IDM_PRINT is a user request to print. Again, the message is handled by delegating the job to the FormWindow (by sending it a message).

IDM_ABOUT indicates that the user has selected the About... option from the Help menu. This message is handled by creating an AboutWindow, as follows:

```
AboutWindow about_me(hWnd());
about_me.start();
```

This window displays the dialog box shown in Figure 14.2. The example just given demonstrates how the encapsulation by a C++ class helps us reduce the complexity of Windows programming.

Listing 14.17. `formview.cpp`—Member functions of the `FormView` class.

```
//------------------------------------------------------------------
//  File: formview.cpp
//
//  Implement the member functions of the application's
//  "form window."

#include <dir.h>
#include "fwindef.h"
#include "fselwin.h"
#include "formview.h"
#include "about.h"
#include "outdev.h"
#include "wevents.h"

WORD FormView::_fwID = 1;
BOOL FormView::is_registered = FALSE;

const chars_per_line = 80, lines_per_page = 65;
```

```
//-------------------------------------------------------------------
// r e g i s t e r _ c l a s s
// Register this class of window with Microsoft Windows

BOOL FormView::register_class()
{
    if(is_registered) return TRUE;

    WNDCLASS WndClass;

// Fill in the fields and register the class

    WndClass.style = NULL;
    WndClass.lpfnWndProc = WindowsEventHandler::WindowProc;
    WndClass.cbClsExtra = 0;
    WndClass.cbWndExtra = 0;
    WndClass.hInstance = hInstance;
    WndClass.hIcon = LoadIcon(hInstance, "FORMICON");
    WndClass.hCursor = LoadCursor(NULL, IDC_ARROW);
    WndClass.hbrBackground = GetStockObject(LTGRAY_BRUSH);
    WndClass.lpszMenuName = "FormViewMenu";
    WndClass.lpszClassName = "FormViewWindow";

    BOOL bStatus = RegisterClass(&WndClass);
    if(bStatus) is_registered = TRUE;
}
//-------------------------------------------------------------------
// c r e a t e _ w i n d o w
// Create a new window by calling the Windows function
// CreateWindow

BOOL FormView::create_window(HWND hParent, WORD child_id)
{
    int x = CW_USEDEFAULT;
    int y = CW_USEDEFAULT;
    int width = CW_USEDEFAULT;
    int height = CW_USEDEFAULT;

// If there is a parent, make the window's size match that of
// parent's
    if(hParent != 0)
    {
// Get parent's rectangle
        RECT r;
            GetClientRect(hParent, (LPRECT)&r);
```

```
            x = y = 0;
            width = r.right - r.left;
            height = r.bottom - r.top;
        }
        _hWnd = CreateWindow("FormViewWindow",    // Window class
                             "FormFill",          // Window name
                             WS_HSCROLL | WS_VSCROLL |
                             WS_OVERLAPPEDWINDOW |
                             WS_CLIPCHILDREN,      // Window style
                             x,                    // x position
                             y,                    // y position
                             width,                // Width
                             height,               // Height
                             hParent,              // Parent handle
                             (HMENU)child_id,      // Menu or child ID
                             hInstance,            // Instance
                             NULL);                // Additional data

        if (hWnd() == NULL) return FALSE;

// Save this window's handle in the list of windows
        WindowsEventHandler::add(*this);

        ShowWindow(hWnd(), nCmdShow);
        UpdateWindow(hWnd());
        return TRUE;
}
//----------------------------------------------------------------
// p r o c e s s _ m e s s a g e
// Process messages sent to the "form window"

LONG FormView::process_message(WORD message, WORD wParam,
                               LONG lParam)
{
    switch(message)
    {
      case WM_CREATE:  // Do any necessary initializations here
        hDC(GetDC(hWnd()));
            GetTextMetrics(hDC(), &tmFontInfo);
            xChar = tmFontInfo.tmAveCharWidth;
            yChar = tmFontInfo.tmHeight +
                    tmFontInfo.tmExternalLeading;
            yChar = (3*yChar)/2; // Leave room between lines
```

```
// Initialize the child window where the form is displayed
        if(!_fw.init(hWnd(), _fwID))
        {
            MessageBox(hWnd(),
                        "Error creating child window",
                        " Fatal Error!", MB_OK);
            PostQuitMessage(1);
        }
        _fwID++;

        ReleaseDC(hWnd(), hDC());
        return 0;

    case WM_SIZE:
        _width = LOWORD(lParam);
        _height = HIWORD(lParam);
        if(IsWindow(_fw.hWnd())) adjust_scrollbars();
        return 0;

    case WM_COMMAND:
        process_command(wParam, lParam);
        return 0;

    case WM_SETFOCUS:
        ShowCursor(TRUE);
        return 0;

    case WM_KILLFOCUS:
        ShowCursor(FALSE);
        return 0;

    case WM_VSCROLL:
        if(IsWindow(_fw.hWnd())) vscroll(wParam, lParam);
        return 0;

    case WM_HSCROLL:
        if(IsWindow(_fw.hWnd())) hscroll(wParam, lParam);
        return 0;

    case WM_QUERYENDSESSION:
        return 0;  // Don't quit, form may have changed

    case FORM_OPEN:
        adjust_menus(wParam);
        return 0;
```

```
                    default:        // Forward message to base class
                        return PlainWindow::process_message(message, wParam,
                                                            lParam);
                }
            }
            //----------------------------------------------------------------
            // p r o c e s s _ c o m m a n d
            // Process menu commands

            void FormView::process_command(WORD wParam, LONG lParam)
            {
                switch(wParam)
                {
                    case IDM_EXIT:
                        if(IsWindow(_fw.hWnd()))
                            SendMessage(_fw.hWnd(), WM_CLOSE, wParam,
                                                             lParam);
                        else
                            SendMessage(hWnd(), WM_CLOSE, wParam, lParam);
                        return;

                    case IDM_OPEN:
            // Size the window so it can display a full-page form
                        _forigin.x = _forigin.y = 0;
                        _fextent.x = chars_per_line * xChar;
                        _fextent.y = lines_per_page * yChar;
                        _fw.move(_forigin, _fextent);
                        adjust_scrollbars();

            // Now send the FORM_OPEN message to the window to load form
                        SendMessage(_fw.hWnd(), FORM_OPEN, wParam, lParam);
                        return;

                    case IDM_SAVE:
                        SendMessage(_fw.hWnd(), FORM_SAVE, wParam, lParam);
                        return;

                    case IDM_SAVEAS:
                        SendMessage(_fw.hWnd(), FORM_SAVEAS, wParam, lParam);
                        return;

                    case IDM_PRINT:
                        SendMessage(_fw.hWnd(), FORM_PRINT, wParam, lParam);
                        return;
```

```
          case IDM_ABOUT:  // Display the "About" dialog box
              AboutWindow about_me(hWnd());
              about_me.start();
              return;
      }
}
//----------------------------------------------------------------
// a d j u s t _ m e n u s
// Turn certain menu items on or off

void FormView::adjust_menus(BOOL on)
{
    HMENU hMenu = GetSubMenu(GetMenu(hWnd()), FILEMENULOC);

// For now allow only one form to be open at any time
    if(on)
    {
        EnableMenuItem(hMenu, IDM_OPEN, MF_GRAYED);
        EnableMenuItem(hMenu, IDM_SAVE, MF_ENABLED);
        EnableMenuItem(hMenu, IDM_SAVEAS, MF_ENABLED);
        EnableMenuItem(hMenu, IDM_PRINT, MF_ENABLED);
    }
    else
    {
        EnableMenuItem(hMenu, IDM_OPEN, MF_ENABLED);
        EnableMenuItem(hMenu, IDM_SAVE, MF_GRAYED);
        EnableMenuItem(hMenu, IDM_SAVEAS, MF_GRAYED);
        EnableMenuItem(hMenu, IDM_PRINT, MF_GRAYED);
    }
}
//----------------------------------------------------------------
// a d j u s t _ s c r o l l b a r s
// Adjust scroll bar range and position of thumbwheel for both
// scroll bars

void FormView::adjust_scrollbars()
{
    _hmax = max(0,chars_per_line - _width/xChar);
    _vmax = max(0,lines_per_page - _height/yChar);
    _hpos = min(_hpos, _hmax);
    _vpos = min(_vpos, _vmax);

    SetScrollRange(hWnd(), SB_HORZ, 0, _hmax, FALSE);
    SetScrollPos(hWnd(), SB_HORZ, _hpos, TRUE);
```

```
        SetScrollRange(hWnd(), SB_VERT, 0, _vmax, FALSE);
        SetScrollPos(hWnd(), SB_VERT, _vpos, TRUE);
}
//-------------------------------------------------------------------
// v s c r o l l
// Scroll form vertically

void FormView::vscroll(WORD wParam, LONG lParam)
{
    short incr = 0;

    switch(wParam)
    {
        case SB_TOP:
            incr = -_vpos;
            break;

        case SB_BOTTOM:
            incr = _vmax - _vpos;
            break;

        case SB_LINEUP:
            incr = -1;
            break;

        case SB_LINEDOWN:
            incr = 1;
            break;

        case SB_PAGEUP:
            incr = min(-1,-_height/yChar);
            break;

        case SB_PAGEDOWN:
            incr = max(1,_height/yChar);
            break;

        case SB_THUMBPOSITION:
            incr = LOWORD(lParam) - _vpos;
            break;
    }
// Some sanity checks . . .
    if(_vpos + incr > _vmax) incr = _vmax-_vpos;
    if(_vpos + incr < 0) incr = -_vpos;
```

```cpp
    if(incr != 0)
    {
        _forigin.y -= incr * yChar;
// More sanity checks . . .
        if(_forigin.x < _width - _fextent.x)
            _forigin.x = _width - _fextent.x;
        if(_forigin.x > 0) _forigin.x = 0;

// Move the form window to the new position
        _fw.move(_forigin, _fextent);
        InvalidateRect(_fw.hWnd(), NULL, TRUE);
        UpdateWindow(_fw.hWnd());

// Update the scroll bar position
        _vpos += incr;
        SetScrollPos(hWnd(), SB_VERT, _vpos, TRUE);
    }
}
//-------------------------------------------------------------
// h s c r o l l
// Scroll form horizontally

void FormView::hscroll(WORD wParam, LONG lParam)
{
    short incr = 0;

    switch(wParam)
    {
        case SB_TOP:
            incr = -_hpos;
            break;

        case SB_BOTTOM:
            incr = _hmax - _hpos;
            break;

        case SB_LINEUP:
            incr = -1;
            break;

        case SB_LINEDOWN:
            incr = 1;
            break;
```

```
        case SB_PAGEUP:
            incr = min(-1,-_width/xChar);
            break;

        case SB_PAGEDOWN:
            incr = max(1,_width/xChar);
            break;

        case SB_THUMBPOSITION:
            incr = LOWORD(lParam) - _hpos;
            break;
    }
// Some sanity checks . . .
    if(_hpos + incr > _hmax) incr = _hmax-_hpos;
    if(_hpos + incr < 0) incr = -_hpos;
    if(incr != 0)
    {
        _forigin.x -= incr * xChar;
// More sanity checks . . .
        if(_forigin.x < _width - _fextent.x)
            _forigin.x = _width - _fextent.x;
        if(_forigin.x > 0) _forigin.x = 0;

// Move the form window to the new position
        _fw.move(_forigin, _fextent);
        InvalidateRect(_fw.hWnd(), NULL, TRUE);
        UpdateWindow(_fw.hWnd());

// Update the scroll bar position
        _hpos += incr;
        SetScrollPos(hWnd(), SB_HORZ, _hpos, TRUE);
    }
}
```

The FormWindow *Class*

Although FormView acts as the "View" of the application, you can think of the FormWindow class as providing the "View" of a single Form object (see Chapter 13 for the listings of the Form class).

Most of the work of the FORMFILL application is done in the FormWindow class. These discussions do not describe the FormWindow class in detail; they provide an overview only. You will have to be familiar with Windows programming, read the source code (Listings 14.18 and 14.19), and try executing the program to understand it fully.

Data in `FormWindow`

Because the `FormWindow` class provides a "View" of a `Form` object (the `Form` class is described in Chapter 13), it has an instance of `Form` named `_form` as a data member. The other data members are as follows:

`String _fname;` is for storing the name of the file from which the form is loaded.

`BOOL _form_open;` is a flag that is set to TRUE when a form is open and on display.

`BOOL _changed;` is TRUE if the user enters any data into the form.

`static BOOL is_registered;` is used to indicate whether the `FormWindow`'s window class has already been registered.

`String _title;` is the title to be displayed in the title bar of `FormWindow`'s window.

`EditWindow ed;` is the *edit* window used for data entry.

`Field* _curfield;` points to the current field being edited. The `Field` class appears in Chapter 13.

Listing 14.18. `formwin.h`—Header file for the `FormWindow` class.

```
//-------------------------------------------------------------
//  File: formwin.h
//
//  Declare a "form window" — the window where the form is
//  displayed.

#if !defined (__FORMWIN_H)
#define __FORMWIN_H

#include "form.h"
#include "str.h"
#include "fwindef.h"
#include "plainwin.h"
#include "editwin.h"
#include "fselwin.h"
#include "outdev.h"
```

```
class FormWindow : public PlainWindow
{
public:
    FormWindow() : _title("untitled"), _changed(0),
                    _form_open(0) {}

    FormWindow(const FormWindow& w) : PlainWindow(w),
        _form(w._form), _fname(w._fname),
        _title(w._title), _curfield(w._curfield),
        ed(w.ed), _changed(w._changed),
        _form_open(w._form_open) {}

    ~FormWindow() {}

    double_link* clone() { return new FormWindow(*this);}
    void destroy() { delete this;}

    LONG process_message(WORD message, WORD wParam,
                            LONG lParam);
    void process_mouse(HWND hWnd, WORD message, POINT ptMouse);
    void process_key(HWND hWnd, WORD wParam, LONG lParam);
    void process_command(WORD wParam, LONG lParam);
    void query_save();
    void save() { _form.write_data(_fname);}
    void load() { _form.read(_fname);}
    void repaint(OutputDevice* od);
    BOOL print_form(HWND hWnd);
    void open_form();
    BOOL form_is_open() { return _form_open;}

    Field* field_at(unsigned short x, unsigned short y);

protected:
    BOOL register_class();
    BOOL create_window(HWND hParent, WORD child_id);
    BOOL get_fileselection(const char *title,
                            BOOL file_must_exist);
    void get_edittext(Field* p_f);
    void set_edittext(Field* p_f);
    void put_editwin(Field* p_f, POINT& org, POINT& ext);

private:
    Form        _form;          // Form being viewed . . .
    String      _fname;         // Name of data file
```

```
    BOOL        _form_open;     // TRUE = form open
    BOOL        _changed;       // Has form been altered?
    static BOOL is_registered;  // TRUE when class is registered
    String      _title;
    EditWindow  ed;             // An "edit" window for data entry
    Field*      _curfield;
};

#endif
```

Initializing FormWindow

You initialize a FormWindow by calling its init function, which in turn calls its register_class function, followed by create_window. As you can see from Listing 14.19, FormWindow's register_class function registers a window class named FormFillWindow. The background (hbrBackground) is white (WHITE_BRUSH) and the cursor is a cross-hair.

In create_window, the window style is

```
    WS_CHILD ¦ WS_VISIBLE ¦ WS_CAPTION ¦ WS_CLIPSIBLINGS
```

This says that the FormWindow's window is a child window (WS_CHILD) with a title bar and border (WS_CAPTION). The window will be initially visible (WS_VISIBLE), and the child windows will clip each other (WS_CLIPSIBLINGS).

Message Processing in FormWindow

As in FormView, all the action in FormWindow takes place in its message-processing function: process_message (see Listing 14.19). The following list describes how the most significant messages are handled in FormWindow's process_message function:

WM_CREATE message arrives when the window is created. The response is to set up the mapping mode and get the dimensions of characters. These items are important when you draw the form and are discussed further in a later section. As the window is created, you should initialize the *edit* window ed that will be used for data entry.

WM_PAINT message indicates that the window needs repainting. The application's architecture is such that you can repaint the form by setting up a DC, setting the mapping mode, and calling the private function named repaint, which expects a pointer to the OutputDevice as an argument. In this case, the `OutputDevice` is the `FormWindow` itself, so the call is of the form

```
repaint(this);
```

The `repaint` function (Listing 14.19) loops over all the background elements and fields and draws them on the `OutputDevice`.

`WM_CLOSE` indicates that the window is about to be closed. The processing involves calling the `query_save` function to ask the user whether the form should be saved and then sending a `WM_CLOSE` message to the parent window, which happens to be the `FormView` window.

`WM_LBUTTONDOWN`, `WM_RBUTTONDOWN`, and other mouse events are processed by the `process_mouse` function. Essentially, this function determines whether the mouse event occurred at a field and if so, the function moves the *edit* window to that field. The `process_mouse` function uses the functions `get_edittext` and `set_edittext` to copy data between a field and the *edit* window.

`FORM_OPEN` message is sent by the `FormView` window when the user selects the `Open...` option from the File menu. You can process this message by calling `open_form` which displays the `FileSelection` dialog box, gets the user's selection, and loads the form into the `Form` object named `_form`. Of course, the actual input operation is done by calling the `read` function of the `Form` object.

`FORM_SAVE` and `FORM_SAVEAS` messages come from `FormView`. These are handled by saving the form, if necessary. Once again, to save the form's data to a file, all you have to do is call the `Form` object's `write_data` function.

`FORM_PRINT` message tells `FormWindow` to print the form. The `print_form` function handles this chore. Disregarding the details, the basic idea is to create a `WindowsPrinter` object, get a handle to a Device Context (DC) for the printer, and "draw" the form to that device context. The actual drawing is done by calling the `repaint` function with the address of the `WindowsPrinter` object as its argument. The next section describes the output mechanism further.

Listing 14.19. `formwin.cpp`—Member functions of the `FormWindow` class.

```
//-----------------------------------------------------------
//  File: formwin.cpp
//
//  Implement the member functions of the application's
//  "form window."
```

```
#include <dir.h>
#include "formwin.h"
#include "wevents.h"

BOOL FormWindow::is_registered = FALSE;
//--------------------------------------------------------------
// r e g i s t e r _ c l a s s
// Register this class of window with Microsoft Windows

BOOL FormWindow::register_class()
{
    if(is_registered) return TRUE;

    WNDCLASS WndClass;
// Fill in the fields and register the class

    WndClass.style = NULL;
    WndClass.lpfnWndProc = WindowsEventHandler::WindowProc;
    WndClass.cbClsExtra = 0;
    WndClass.cbWndExtra = 0;
    WndClass.hInstance = hInstance;
    WndClass.hIcon = NULL;
    WndClass.hCursor = LoadCursor(NULL, IDC_CROSS);
    WndClass.hbrBackground = GetStockObject(WHITE_BRUSH);
    WndClass.lpszMenuName = NULL;
    WndClass.lpszClassName = "FormFillWindow";

    BOOL bStatus = RegisterClass(&WndClass);
    if(bStatus) is_registered = TRUE;

    return bStatus;
}
//--------------------------------------------------------------
// c r e a t e _ w i n d o w
// Create a new window by calling the Windows function
// CreateWindow

BOOL FormWindow::create_window(HWND hParent, WORD child_id)
{
    char* t = new char[_title.length()+1];
    strcpy(t, _title);

    int x = CW_USEDEFAULT;
    int y = CW_USEDEFAULT;
    int width = CW_USEDEFAULT;
```

```
        int height = CW_USEDEFAULT;
        if(hParent != 0)
        {
// Get parent's rectangle
            RECT r;
            GetClientRect(hParent, (LPRECT)&r);
            x = y = 0;
            width = r.right - r.left;
            height = r.bottom - r.top;
        }
        _hWnd = CreateWindow("FormFillWindow",    // Window class
                            t,                     // Window name
                            WS_CHILD ¦ WS_VISIBLE ¦
                            WS_CAPTION ¦
                            WS_CLIPSIBLINGS,       // Window style
                            x,                     // x position
                            y,                     // y position
                            width,                 // Width
                            height,                // Height
                            hParent,               // Parent handle
                            (HMENU)child_id,       // Menu or child ID
                            hInstance,             // Instance
                            NULL);                 // Additional data
        delete t;

        if (hWnd() == NULL) return FALSE;

// Save this window's handle in the list of windows
        WindowsEventHandler::add(*this);

        ShowWindow(hWnd(), SW_SHOW);
        UpdateWindow(hWnd());
        return TRUE;
}
//---------------------------------------------------------------
// p r o c e s s _ m e s s a g e
// Process messages sent to the "form window"

LONG FormWindow::process_message(WORD message, WORD wParam,
                                    LONG lParam)
{
    switch(message)
```

```
    {
        case WM_CREATE:
// Set up mapping mode, transformation, and character size
        hDC(GetDC(hWnd()));
            xv_extent = GetDeviceCaps(hDC(), LOGPIXELSX);
            yv_extent = GetDeviceCaps(hDC(), LOGPIXELSY);
            xw_extent = 1440;        // That's 1440 "twips"
            yw_extent = 1440;
            mapping_mode = MM_ANISOTROPIC;
            set_mapping();
            GetTextMetrics(hDC(), &tmFontInfo);
            xChar = tmFontInfo.tmAveCharWidth;
            yChar = tmFontInfo.tmHeight +
                    tmFontInfo.tmExternalLeading;
            yChar = (3*yChar)/2;   // Leave room between lines
        ReleaseDC(hWnd(), hDC());

// Initialize the"data entry" editor window
            ed.create(hWnd(),
                    ((LPCREATESTRUCT)lParam)->hInstance);
        return 0;

     case WM_PAINT:
            PAINTSTRUCT ps;
// Get a device context
            hDC(BeginPaint(hWnd(), &ps));
            if(_form_open)
            {
                set_mapping();
// Draw form's view
                repaint(this);
            }
            EndPaint(hWnd(), &ps);
        return 0;

     case WM_SETFOCUS:
            ShowCursor(TRUE);
            return 0;

     case WM_KILLFOCUS:
            ShowCursor(FALSE);
            return 0;
```

```
        case WM_KEYDOWN:                    // Process keyboard events
            process_key(hWnd(), wParam, lParam);
            return 0;

        case WM_LBUTTONDOWN:                // Process mouse events
        case WM_RBUTTONDOWN:
        case WM_LBUTTONUP:
        case WM_RBUTTONUP:
        case WM_LBUTTONDBLCLK:
        case WM_RBUTTONDBLCLK:
            process_mouse(hWnd(), message, MAKEPOINT(lParam));
            return 0;

    case WM_CLOSE:
        query_save();
        SendMessage(GetParent(hWnd()), WM_CLOSE,
                    wParam, lParam);
        return 0;

// Some application-specific messages

    case FORM_OPEN:
        open_form();
// Tell parent window whether form is open
        SendMessage(GetParent(hWnd()),
                    FORM_OPEN, _form_open, lParam);
        InvalidateRect(hWnd(), NULL, TRUE);
        UpdateWindow(hWnd());
        return 0;

    case FORM_SAVE:
        if(_changed) save();
        _changed = 0;
        return 0;

    case FORM_SAVEAS:
        if(get_fileselection("Save As:", FALSE))
        {
            save();
            _changed = 0;
        }
        return 0;
```

```
        case FORM_PRINT:
            if(!print_form(hWnd()))
            {
                MessageBox(hWnd(),
                            "Could not print form.",
                            "FormFill (PRINT ERROR)",
                            MB_ICONEXCLAMATION ¦ MB_OK);
            }
            return 0;

        default:  // Forward message to base class
            return PlainWindow::process_message(message, wParam,
                                                    lParam);
    }
}
//------------------------------------------------------------------
// p r o c e s s _ m o u s e
// Process mouse events occurring in this window

void FormWindow::process_mouse(HWND hWnd, WORD message,
                                POINT ptMouse)
{
    switch(message)
    {
        case WM_LBUTTONDOWN:
        case WM_RBUTTONDOWN:
// Convert point to "character position"
            hDC(GetDC(hWnd));
            set_mapping();
            DPtoLP(hDC(), &ptMouse, 1);
            unsigned short xMouse = ptMouse.x/xChar;
            unsigned short yMouse = ptMouse.y/yChar;
// Identify field at this location
            Field* p_f = field_at(xMouse, yMouse);
// Copy text from edit window into current field
            if(ed.is_visible())
                get_edittext(_curfield);
            if(p_f != NULL)
            {
                _curfield = p_f;
// Position the edit window
// First compute the new location in device coordinates
                POINT org, ext;
                org.x = p_f->xpos()*xChar;
```

```
                    org.y = p_f->ypos()*yChar;
                    LPtoDP(hDC(), &org, 1);
                    ext.x = p_f->numchars()*xChar;
                    ext.y = yChar;
                    LPtoDP(hDC(), &ext, 1);
                    put_editwin(p_f, org, ext);
                }
                else
                    ed.hide();
                ReleaseDC(hWnd, hDC());
        }
}
//------------------------------------------------------------------
// p r o c e s s _ k e y
// Process keyboard events delivered to this window

void FormWindow::process_key(HWND hWnd, WORD wParam, LONG)
{
    switch(wParam)
    {
        case VK_F1:    // Function key "F1"
            MessageBox(hWnd,
                "Help will be available in future",
                "No Help Yet",
                MB_ICONINFORMATION | MB_OK);
            break;

        case VK_TAB:   // Tab key (go to next field)
            break;
    }
}
//------------------------------------------------------------------
// q u e r y _ s a v e
// Save form if it has changed and user wants to save it

void FormWindow::query_save()
{
    if(_changed &&
        (MessageBox(hWnd(), "Save changes?", "Form modified",
                    MB_YESNO | MB_ICONQUESTION) == IDYES))
    {
        if(_fname.length() > 0)
            save();
        else
```

```
        {
            if(get_fileselection("Save in:", FALSE))
                save();
        }
        _changed = 0;
    }
}
//---------------------------------------------------------------
// g e t _ f i l e s e l e c t i o n
// Display the FileSelection dialog and get file name selected
// by user

BOOL FormWindow::get_fileselection(const char *title,
                BOOL file_must_exist)
{
// Get current directory name
    const unsigned maxchar = 80;
    char this_dir[maxchar];
    getcwd( this_dir, sizeof(this_dir));

// Open a FileSelection dialog box
    FileSelectionWindow fw(hWnd(), title, this_dir,
                            "*.dat", file_must_exist);
    if(fw.start() != 0) return FALSE;

// Get the path name from the selection window
    _fname = fw.pathname();
    return TRUE;
}
//---------------------------------------------------------------
// r e p a i n t
// Redraw the form's "View" in the window

void FormWindow::repaint(OutputDevice* od)
{
// Draw form's background
    TextGraphics* p_g;
    for(p_g = _form.first_bg(); p_g != NULL;
        p_g = _form.next_bg())
    {
        p_g->draw(od);
    }
```

```
// Draw the contents of each field . . .
    Field* p_f;
    for(p_f = _form.first_field(); p_f != NULL;
        p_f = _form.next_field())
    {
// Create a TextLine graphics object with the field's data
        TextLine* tl = new TextLine(p_f->data(),
                                    p_f->xpos(), p_f->ypos());
        tl->draw(od);
    }
}
//-------------------------------------------------------------
// o p e n _ f o r m
// Open a form

void FormWindow::open_form()
{
// If anything is on display, save it
    query_save();

// Get file name and load data . . .
    if(get_fileselection("Open file:", TRUE))
    {
        load();
        _form_open = 1;

// Set window's title to the file name
        const char* t = _fname;
        SendMessage(hWnd(), WM_SETTEXT, 0, (LONG)t);

// Set up some variables . . .
        _curfield = _form.first_field();
    }
    else
        _form_open = 0;
}
//-------------------------------------------------------------
// p r i n t _ f o r m
// Print the form

BOOL FormWindow::print_form(HWND hWnd)
{
    BOOL bError = FALSE;
    WindowsPrinter prn;
    if(prn.hDC() == NULL) return(FALSE);
```

```
// Change cursor to an hourglass shape
    HANDLE hSavedCursor = SetCursor(LoadCursor(NULL, IDC_WAIT));
    EnableWindow(hWnd, FALSE);

    char szPrntMsg[]="Printing Form";
    RECT rect;

    if(Escape(prn.hDC(), STARTDOC, sizeof(szPrntMsg)-1, szPrntMsg,
            NULL) > 0 &&
      Escape(prn.hDC(), NEXTBAND, 0, NULL, (LPSTR)&rect) > 0)
    {
        while(!IsRectEmpty(&rect))
        {
// Draw the form; first, set up mapping mode
            SetMapMode(prn.hDC(), MM_ANISOTROPIC);
            SetWindowExt(prn.hDC(), 1440, 1440);
            SetViewportExt(prn.hDC(),
                        GetDeviceCaps(prn.hDC(), LOGPIXELSX),
                        GetDeviceCaps(prn.hDC(), LOGPIXELSY));
            GetTextMetrics(prn.hDC(), &prn.tmFontInfo);
            prn.xChar = prn.tmFontInfo.tmAveCharWidth;
            prn.yChar = prn.tmFontInfo.tmHeight +
                        prn.tmFontInfo.tmExternalLeading;
            repaint(&prn);

// Go to the next band
            if(Escape(prn.hDC(), NEXTBAND, 0, NULL, (LPSTR)&rect)
< 0)
            {
                bError = TRUE;
                break;
            }
        }
    }
    else
    {
// Indicate that there is an error in printing
        bError = TRUE;
    }

    if(!bError) Escape(prn.hDC(), ENDDOC, 0, NULL, NULL);
```

```
// Change cursor back to normal
    SetCursor(hSavedCursor);
    EnableWindow(hWnd, TRUE);

    return(!bError);
}
//----------------------------------------------------------------
// f i e l d _ a t
// Return pointer to field at the location of button press or
// return NULL if no field at that point

Field* FormWindow::field_at(unsigned short x, unsigned short y)
{
    Field* p_f;
    unsigned short xf;
    for(p_f = _form.first_field(); p_f != NULL;
        p_f = _form.next_field())
    {
        xf = p_f->xpos();
        if(x >= xf && x <= xf+p_f->numchars() &&
            y == p_f->ypos())
        {
            return p_f;
        }
    }
    return NULL;
}
//----------------------------------------------------------------
// s e t _ e d i t t e x t
// Copy text from field to edit window

void FormWindow::set_edittext(Field* p_f)
{
    String s = p_f->data();
    ed.settext(s);
}
//----------------------------------------------------------------
// g e t _ e d i t t e x t
// Copy text from edit window into field

void FormWindow::get_edittext(Field* p_f)
{
    char* data = new char[p_f->numchars()+1];
    ed.gettext(data, p_f->numchars()+1);
```

```
        String s(data);
        p_f->data(s);
        _changed = 1;  // Mark form as "changed"
        delete data;
}
//-------------------------------------------------------------
// p u t _ e d i t w i n
// Place the edit window on a field

void FormWindow::put_editwin(Field* p_f, POINT& org, POINT& ext)
{
        ed.textlimit(p_f->numchars());
        set_edittext(p_f);
// Position the window and make it visible
        ed.move(org, ext);
        ed.show();
        ed.focus();
}
```

Output in Windows

Recall from Chapter 13 that the OutputDevice class enables you to display the TextGraphics objects in a device-independent manner. The drawing functions of the TextGraphics class (presented in Chapter 13) expect a pointer to an OutputDevice as an argument. The actual drawing is performed by calling functions such as draw_line and draw_text, which should be defined for any OutputDevice. Here we will capitalize on that idea and display the form on a window by ensuring that the window is also an OutputDevice. To do so, we start by deriving a WindowsDisplay class from OutputDevice. Then, as long as the PlainWindow class inherits from WindowsDisplay, we can display the TextGraphics objects from the DOS version of FORMFILL in a window by calling their draw function with a pointer to the window as argument. The repaint function of the FormWindow class illustrates how this is done.

The WindowsDisplay *Class*

The WindowsDisplay class (Listing 14.20) supports drawing in a window. For the FORMFILL application, we need two functions only:

- `draw_line` to draw a line

- `draw_text` to display a line of text

As Listing 14.20 shows, these functions are implemented using Windows drawing functions `MoveTo`, `LineTo`, and `TextOut`.

Device Context (DC)

If you have drawn graphics in Microsoft Windows, you know that you need a handle to a *device context (DC)* before you call the drawing functions. The DC is a data structure in which Windows stores the current graphics attributes, such as background and foreground colors, line style, and font. The private member variables of the `WindowsDisplay` class that handle the DC are

`HDC _hDC;` handle to the DC (HDC) where we store the current handle to DC. Note that you have to get a DC every time you draw.

`WORD mapping_mode;` to define how our coordinate system (the `logical` coordinates) maps onto the coordinate system of the display device (*device* coordinates). We will use the `MM_ANISOTROPIC` mapping mode in the `FORMFILL` program. You will find a good discussion of the mapping modes in Chapter 11 of Charles Petzold's *Programming Windows*, Microsoft Press (1990).

`WORD xw_extent, yw_extent;`, which are x- and y-extents of a rectangle in the logical coordinates that will be mapped to a rectangle in device coordinates with extents given by `xv_extent` and `yv_extent`.

`TEXTMETRIC tmFontInfo;` for storing information about the font. In particular, we need the height and width of characters.

`WORD xChar, yChar;` to express the width (average) and height of characters.

You can access the HDC through the member function `hDC()`. Also note, that the `is_text` function returns a zero, which triggers the graphics function calls in the draw functions of the `TextGraphics` class (see Chapter 13).

Output Strategy for FORMFILL

Remember that our goal is to create a Windows-based interface to the text-oriented `FORMFILL` application shown in Chapter 13. There, the form's coordinates were assumed to be character positions (see Figure 13.3). If you want to reuse most of the classes from the DOS version of `FORMFILL`, you have to support the same coordinate system in the Windows version. This can be best done by setting up the mapping mode for a `FormWindow` as follows:

```
// Assume handle to DC is valid . . .
        SetMapMode(hDC(), MM_ANISOTROPIC);
        xw_extent = yw_extent = 1440;
        SetWindowExt(hDC(), xw_extent, yw_extent);
        xv_extent = GetDeviceCaps(hDC(), LOGPIXELSX);
        yv_extent = GetDeviceCaps(hDC(), LOGPIXELSY);
        SetViewportExt(hDC(), xv_extent, yv_extent);
```

The number 1440 refers to an inch expressed in units of 1/20th of a printer's point measurement (a *point* being 1/72 of an inch). The unit *1/20th of a point* is also referred to as a *twip* in Windows terminology. The calls to `GetDeviceCaps` return the number of pixels along x and y coordinates that match one inch in logical coordinates. Thus, we are mapping a 1440 twips by 1440 twips rectangle in logical space onto a rectangle of similar size in the device coordinates. After setting up this mapping, you should get the information on the font and set up the xChar and yChar variables as follows:

```
GetTextMetrics(hDC(), &tmFontInfo);
xChar = tmFontInfo.tmAveCharWidth;
yChar = tmFontInfo.tmHeight +
        tmFontInfo.tmExternalLeading;
yChar = (3*yChar)/2; // leave room between lines
```

Once xChar and yChar are initialized in this manner, an (xc, yc) coordinate pair in character coordinates can be converted into logical coordinates (xl, yl) as follows:

```
xl = xc * xChar;
yl = yc * yChar;
```

This is how the character coordinates are handled in the draw_line and draw_text functions in Listing 14.20.

Listing 14.20. wdisplay.h—Definition of WindowsDisplay and WindowsPrinter classes.

```
//--------------------------------------------------------------
//  File: wdisplay.h
//
//  WindowsDisplay class (represents a Microsoft Windows
//  display).

#if !defined(__WDISPLAY_H)
#define __WDISPLAY_H
```

```cpp
#include <windows.h>
#include <string.h>
#include "outdev.h"

// A class for storing device context and mapping mode
// for a Microsoft Windows

class WindowsDisplay : public OutputDevice
{
public:
    WindowsDisplay() : _hDC(0) {}
    WindowsDisplay(HDC h) : _hDC(h) {}

    WindowsDisplay(const WindowsDisplay& wd) :
        _hDC(wd._hDC), mapping_mode(wd.mapping_mode),
        xw_extent(wd.xw_extent), yw_extent(wd.yw_extent),
        xv_extent(wd.xv_extent), yv_extent(wd.yv_extent),
        tmFontInfo(wd.tmFontInfo), xChar(wd.xChar),
        yChar(wd.yChar) {}

    void draw_line(unsigned short x1, unsigned short y1,
        unsigned short x2, unsigned short y2)
    {
        MoveTo(_hDC, x1*xChar, y1*yChar);
        LineTo(_hDC, x2*xChar, y2*yChar);
    }

    void draw_text(const char* str, unsigned short x,
                          unsigned short y)
    {
        TextOut(_hDC, x*xChar, y*yChar, (LPSTR) str,
                strlen(str));
    }

    HDC hDC() { return _hDC;}
    void hDC(HDC h) { _hDC = h;}

    unsigned is_text() { return 0;}

    void set_mapping()     // Set up mapping mode
    {
        SetMapMode(hDC(), mapping_mode);
        SetWindowExt(hDC(), xw_extent, yw_extent);
        SetViewportExt(hDC(), xv_extent, yv_extent);
    }
```

```
protected:
    HDC         _hDC;        // Device context for drawing
    WORD        mapping_mode;
    WORD        xw_extent;
    WORD        yw_extent;
    WORD        xv_extent;
    WORD        yv_extent;
    TEXTMETRIC  tmFontInfo;
    WORD        xChar;
    WORD        yChar;
};


// A class for printing under Windows

class FormWindow;

class WindowsPrinter : public WindowsDisplay
{
public:
    friend FormWindow;
    WindowsPrinter() : WindowsDisplay() {_hDC = GetPrinterDC();};
    WindowsPrinter(const WindowsPrinter& d) :
        WindowsDisplay(d) {}
    ~WindowsPrinter() { if (_hDC != NULL) DeleteDC(_hDC);}

    HDC GetPrinterDC();
};

#endif
```

The WindowsPrinter *Class*

In Windows, you use the same functions to draw on any graphics output device, whether it is a screen or a printer. In other words, you can send the output to a printer by getting the handle to a DC for the printer and calling the drawing functions such as LineTo and TextOut with that HDC as the argument. In the FORMFILL application, we create a WindowsPrinter class, derived from WindowsDisplay, to support printing. In FormWindow, when you want to print, all you have to do is call the repaint function with a pointer to a WindowsPrinter as argument.

The WindowsPrinter class is declared in Listing 14.20, but Listing 14.21 shows its most important member—the GetPrinterDC function, which returns the handle to a DC for the printer. The job of GetPrinterDC is to get information about the printer from the [windows] section of the WIN.INI file. In that section Windows stores a variety of setup parameters, including the printer that the user has selected using the Windows Control Panel. The printer is listed under the device keyword. For example, on a system with a PostScript printer connected to the first parallel port, this information reads

```
[windows]
```

```
device=PostScript Printer,PSCRIPT,LPT1:
```

In this case, the name of the printer is PostScript Printer, the driver is PSCRIPT, and the printer port is LPT1. The GetPrinterDC function calls GetProfileString to get the string following the device=. Then it parses the string looking for the commas that separate the three parts. Once the printer's name, the driver, and the port are found, GetPrinterDC returns the handle to the DC it obtains by calling the Windows function CreateDC. The print_form function in the FormWindow class (Listing 14.19) shows how the printing is done through the WindowsPrinter class.

**Listing 14.21. wdisplay.cpp—Implementation of the
GetPrinterDC function.**

```
//------------------------------------------------------------
// File: wdisplay.cpp
//
// Functions that help us send output to printer or a window
//  in Microsoft Windows.

#include "wdisplay.h"

//------------------------------------------------------------
// G e t P r i n t e r D C
// Get a "device context" for the currently selected printer

HDC WindowsPrinter::GetPrinterDC()
{
    char PrinterInfo[80];
    LPSTR p_tmp;
    LPSTR PrintDevice;
    LPSTR PrintDriver = NULL;
    LPSTR PrinterPort = NULL;
```

```
    // Get printer information from the win.ini file
        if (!GetProfileString("windows", "device", (LPSTR)"",
                              PrinterInfo, 80)) return (NULL);

    // Parse the retrieved printer info organized with the form
    // "PrintDevice,PrintDriver,PrinterPort"
        p_tmp = PrinterInfo;
        PrintDevice = p_tmp;
        while (*p_tmp)
        {
    // The strings are separated by comma
            if (*p_tmp == ',')       // Look for comma
            {
                *p_tmp++ = '\0';    // Mark end of string

    // Skip blanks
                while (*p_tmp == ' ') p_tmp = AnsiNext(p_tmp);

                if (!PrintDriver)
                    PrintDriver = p_tmp;
                else
                {
                    PrinterPort = p_tmp;
                    break;
                }
            }
            else
                p_tmp = AnsiNext(p_tmp);
        }

    // Create a DC for the printer
        return (CreateDC(PrintDriver, PrintDevice, PrinterPort,
                    (LPSTR) NULL));
    }
```

Windows FORMFILL Program

Now we have the classes needed to build the Windows version of the FORMFILL program. Listing 14.22 shows the file `formfill.cpp`, which provides the WinMain function—the entry point of all Windows applications. The WinMain function is declared in the manner required by Windows.

The WinMain function of the FORMFILL program first stores the arguments hInstance, hPrevInstance, lpszCmdLine, and nCmdShow into static variables of the BaseWindow class with identical names. Then, it creates a FormView object fv, which serves as the main view of the application. The fv.init() call registers and creates the FormView window. After the view is created, WinMain sets up a WindowsEventHandler named ev, which is given the view fv to control. Finally, WinMain gets the ball rolling by calling the start function of the WindowsEventHandler ev.

Listing 14.22. `formfill.cpp`—Windows version of the FORMFILL program.

```
//------------------------------------------------------------
//  File: formfill.cpp
//
//  Microsoft Windows version of a program to fill in a form.
//

#include "formview.h"
#include "wevents.h"

int PASCAL WinMain(HANDLE hInstance, HANDLE hPrevInstance,
                   LPSTR lpszCmdLine, int nCmdShow)
{
    BaseWindow::hInstance = hInstance;
    BaseWindow::hPrevInstance = hPrevInstance;
    BaseWindow::lpszCmdLine = lpszCmdLine;
    BaseWindow::nCmdShow = nCmdShow;

    FormView fv;
    if(!fv.init(NULL, 0)) return 1;

    WindowsEventHandler ev(fv);
    return ev.start();
}
```

Ancillary Files

Before you can build the FORMFILL program, you will need several more files:

- An icon to be displayed when the application's window is minimized

- A makefile to help you compile and link the application

- A link file that lists the object modules to be linked

- A module definition file as required by Microsoft Windows

You also need a resource file, but we already have the resource file for FORMFILL, `formfill.rc` (Listing 14.10).

Preparing the Icon

Because the icon is a small (32 pixels by 32 pixels) image, you have to use a special utility to create it. Borland C++ comes with the Whitewater Resource Toolkit, which enables you to create, edit, and modify resources such as bitmaps, icons, and cursors. Icons are stored in files with the `.ICO` extension. Figure 14.4 shows the icon editor in the Whitewater Resource Toolkit, editing the file `formfill.ico`, which will be the icon we will use in FORMFILL.

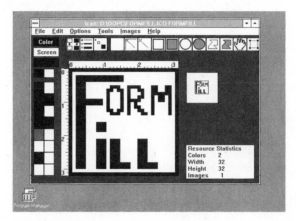

Fig. 14.4. The icon for FORMFILL in Whitewater Resource Toolkit's icon editor.

The Makefile for FORMFILL

Listing 14.23 shows the file `formfill.mak`, which is the makefile for building the Windows version of the FORMFILL application. This makefile uses the protected-mode versions of the Borland C++ compiler (BCCX) and linker (TLINKX). To use these protected-mode tools, you should have more than a megabyte of extended memory and you have to install Borland's protected-mode kernel with a command like this:

```
TKERNEL hi=yes kilos=2048
```

where the number following `kilos=` indicates the number of kilobytes to be used by the kernel.

The makefile also assumes that Borland C++ is installed in the directory D:\BORLANDC. If you have installed Borland C++ in a different location, you have to change all occurrences of D:\BORLANDC in formfill.mak (Listing 14.23) and formfill.lnk (Listing 14.24).

Many modules listed in the makefile do not appear in this chapter. All missing files, except str.h and str.cpp, are from Chapter 13. The str.h and str.cpp files appear in Chapter 8.

Listing 14.23. formfill.mak—The makefile for building FORMFILL.

```
###############################################################
# Makefile for the FORMFILL program (Windows version).

CC = BCCX
LINK = TLINKX
CFLAGS = -c -ms -W
OBJECTS = formfill.obj form.obj formdefn.obj filehdr.obj \
          fileindx.obj str.obj dllist.obj field.obj \
          txtgraph.obj formbg.obj wdisplay.obj \
          plainwin.obj formwin.obj formview.obj \
          dlogwin.obj fselwin.obj about.obj wevents.obj

formfill.exe: $(OBJECTS) formfill.def formfill.res formfill.ico
    $(LINK) @formfill.lnk
    rc formfill.res

.cpp.obj :
    $(CC) $(CFLAGS) $<

.rc.res :
    rc -r -iD:\BORLANDC\INCLUDE $<

# Dependencies

formfill.obj: formfill.cpp formview.h wevents.h fwindef.h \
              str.h formwin.h form.h plainwin.h editwin.h \
              fselwin.h outdev.h basewin.h \
              filehdr.h fileindx.h formbg.h formdefn.h \
              dllist.h dlink.h indxitem.h txtgraph.h field.h \
              pcline.h winlist.h wdisplay.h

form.obj: form.cpp form.h filehdr.h fileindx.h formbg.h \
          formdefn.h dllist.h dlink.h indxitem.h txtgraph.h \
          field.h pcline.h
```

```
formdefn.obj: formdefn.cpp formdefn.h dlink.h dllist.h \
            field.h str.h

filehdr.obj: filehdr.cpp filehdr.h str.h

fileindx.obj: fileindx.cpp fileindx.h dlink.h dllist.h \
            indxitem.h str.h

str.obj: str.cpp str.h

dllist.obj: dllist.cpp dllist.h dlink.h

field.obj: field.cpp field.h str.h dlink.h

txtgraph.obj: txtgraph.cpp txtgraph.h pcline.h str.h dlink.h \
            outdev.h

formbg.obj: formbg.cpp formbg.h txtgraph.h str.h dllist.h \
            dlink.h pcline.h

wdisplay.obj: wdisplay.cpp wdisplay.h outdev.h

plainwin.obj: plainwin.cpp plainwin.h basewin.h dlink.h \
            wdisplay.h

formwin.obj: formwin.cpp formwin.h wevents.h form.h str.h \
            fwindef.h plainwin.h editwin.h fselwin.h \
            outdev.h filehdr.h fileindx.h formbg.h formdefn.h \
            dllist.h dlink.h indxitem.h txtgraph.h field.h \
            pcline.h basewin.h winlist.h wdisplay.h

formview.obj: formview.cpp formview.h form.h str.h fwindef.h \
            plainwin.h editwin.h fselwin.h outdev.h \
            filehdr.h fileindx.h formbg.h formdefn.h \
            dllist.h dlink.h indxitem.h txtgraph.h field.h \
            pcline.h basewin.h wevents.h winlist.h wdisplay.h

dlogwin.obj: dlogwin.cpp dlogwin.h basewin.h wdisplay.h

fselwin.obj: fselwin.cpp fselwin.h dlogwin.h basewin.h \
            str.h fwindef.h wdisplay.h

about.obj: about.cpp about.h dlogwin.h basewin.h wdisplay.h
```

```
wevents.obj: wevents.cpp wevents.h winlist.h dllist.h \
             dlink.h plainwin.h basewin.h formview.h \
             form.h str.h fwindef.h wdisplay.h \
             editwin.h fselwin.h outdev.h \
             filehdr.h fileindx.h formbg.h formdefn.h \
             dllist.h dlink.h indxitem.h txtgraph.h field.h \
             pcline.h
```

Link File for FORMFILL

The input file for the linker is `formfill.lnk`. It appears in Listing 14.24. These are commands read and interpreted by the Borland C++ Linker. Consult the *User's Guide* of Borland C++ for an explanation of the options.

Listing 14.24. `formfill.lnk`—Linker input file for building FORMFILL.

```
/Tw /n /c D:\BORLANDC\LIB\c0ws formfill.obj form.obj +
formdefn.obj filehdr.obj fileindx.obj str.obj dllist.obj +
plainwin.obj formwin.obj formview.obj wdisplay.obj +
field.obj txtgraph.obj formbg.obj dlogwin.obj +
fselwin.obj about.obj wevents.obj
formfill,
D:\BORLANDC\LIB\cwins D:\BORLANDC\LIB\cs
D:\BORLANDC\LIB\import
formfill
```

Module Definition File

The linker also needs a module definition file to link a Windows application. The file `formfill.def` (Listing 14.25) is the module definition file for the FORMFILL application.

Listing 14.25. `formfill.ldef`—Module definition file for FORMFILL.

```
NAME          FORMFILL
DESCRIPTION   'Forms Package for Microsoft Windows'
EXETYPE       WINDOWS
CODE          PRELOAD MOVEABLE
DATA          PRELOAD MOVEABLE MULTIPLE
HEAPSIZE      0x9fff
STACKSIZE     10240
```

Building FORMFILL

Once the ancillary files—formfill.mak, formfill.rc, formfill.ico, formfill.lnk, and formfill.def—are ready, you can build the executable FORMFILL.EXE by using the make utility as follows:

```
make -fformfill
```

Running FORMFILL

After FORMFILL.EXE is successfully built, you can run the application under Microsoft Windows with the command:

```
win formfill
```

assuming that you have Windows properly installed and set up on your system. To test the program, you will need the files invoice.def and invoice.dat that were created in Chapter 13. To open a form, select the File option on the menu bar. Figure 14.5 shows what you will see on the screen. From the pull-down menu, you have to select the Open option. You will get the FileSelection dialog box shown in Figure 14.3. In that dialog box, choose the file invoice.dat and press the pushbutton labeled OK. At this point, you will see a display of the form's background. You can now move the cursor to a field and press any mouse button. An edit window will appear; enter your input in this window. Figure 14.6 shows a partially filled in form.

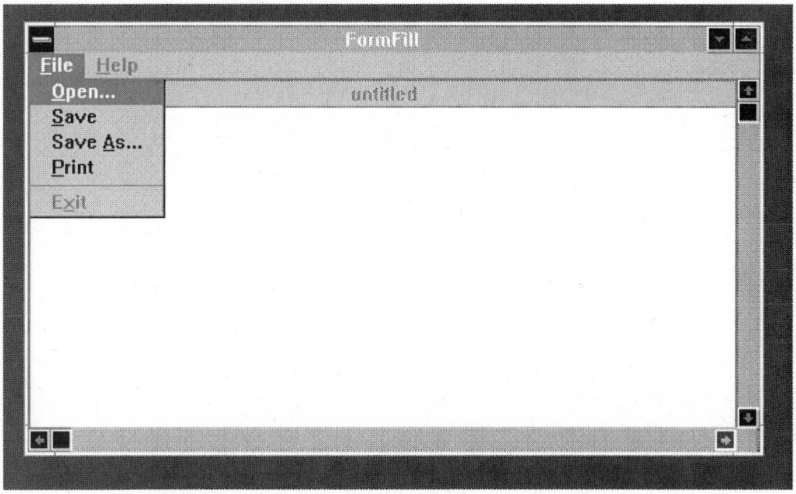

Fig. 14.5. The File menu in FORMFILL.

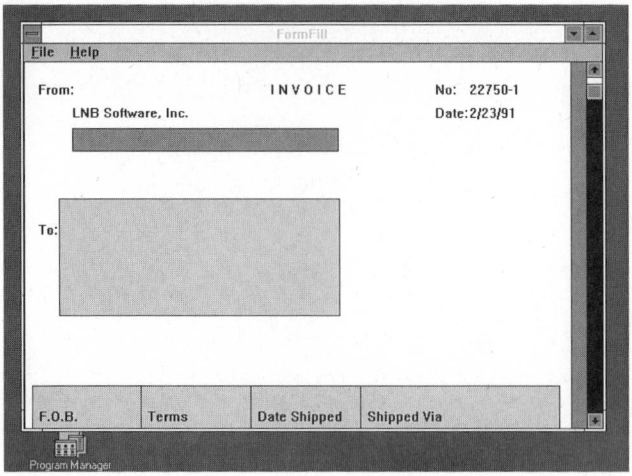

Fig. 14.6. Filling in a form in FORMFILL.

Minimizing FORMFILL

As with any other Windows application, you can reduce the FORMFILL application to an icon by clicking on the Minimize box on the upper right-hand corner of the frame. Figure 14.7 shows the appearance of the FORMFILL application when minimized. Notice that the icon is the same one shown in Figure 14.4.

Fig. 14.7. The FORMFILL icon on the Windows desktop.

Exiting FORMFILL

Select the Exit option under the File menu to terminate the FORMFILL application. If you make changes to the form and try to exit without saving the form, you will see a message box with a question as shown in Figure 14.8. This gives you a chance to save the form before exiting.

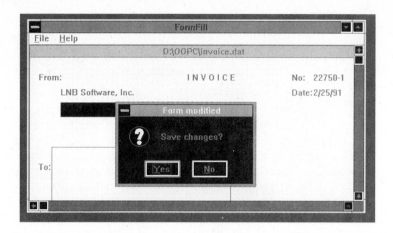

Fig. 14.8. The Save changes? message in FORMFILL.

Suggested Improvements

Although FORMFILL is a nearly complete Windows application, it is far from being a commercial-quality product. In particular, here are some of the ways in which you can enhance the application and the framework underlying the application:

- The WindowsDisplay class has two graphics primitives only (draw_line and draw_text). You might want to add some more graphics primitives to this class.

- The FormView class handles only one open form at a time. Consider adding the capability of opening several forms at the same time.

- From Chapter 13 you will recall that the *definitions* and *data file* include an index. After the FileSelection dialog box, you could display a *listbox* with the contents of the index so that the user can pick a specific form out of several that might be stored in a single file.

- FORMFILL does not have any help feature yet; you should add a facility that displays help information when the user presses the F1 key or selects the Help menu.

Summary

This chapter presents a framework of C++ classes that can accommodate the message-driven architecture of Microsoft Windows applications. Each window in the application is modeled by a C++ class. As far as Windows is concerned, there is a single message-handling function in the application. This message-handling function is a static member of a C++ class (WindowsEventHandler), which maintains a list of all window classes in the application. Windows calls this central function whenever there is a message for any window in the application. The central message-processing function takes care of calling the message-handling function of the appropriate window class. This chapter shows a similar scheme for using modal dialog boxes. Predefined Windows objects, such as the *edit* class of windows, are also encapsulated in a C++ class for ease of use.

The C++ classes developed in this chapter have been used to add a graphical interface to the form fill-in program of Chapter 13. You can easily extend the framework shown in this chapter to other Windows applications.

## Chapter 15

C++ and the X Window System

Chapters 13 and 14 show you how to use C++ and object-oriented techniques to create applications for MS-DOS and Microsoft Windows environments. This chapter introduces you to the task of writing C++ programs for another significant graphical environment—the *X Window System* (or *X* for short). Because X is not as common-place as MS-DOS and Windows, this chapter starts with an introduction to X. Next comes a discussion of the problems you face when trying to mix C++ and *Xlib*—the C language library for programming the X Window System.

For serious application development, you will need a well-designed set of C++ classes as well as a complete framework for applications. The *InterViews* toolkit, developed at Stanford University, provides a solution. It includes the necessary C++ classes and supports an application-development framework that is based on the *Model-View-Controller (MVC)* architecture. Additionally, InterViews is freely available (it is in the X software distribution from Massachusetts Institute of Technology), and you can use it in commercial applications as long as you acknowledge the source. Of course, you do have the problem of learning what InterViews offers and how to use the InterViews classes. To help you with this process, the latter part of this chapter gives you a brief introduction to the InterViews toolkit.

> This chapter shows how to use the InterViews toolkit to write C++ programs that use the facilities of the X Window System. Although the InterViews toolkit is summarized, the subject of programming the X Window System is not covered thoroughly. To learn about programming the X Window System, please consult a book such as this author's *X Window System Programming*, published by SAMS, a Division of Macmillan Computer Publishing, in 1991.

What You Need

Before the discussion of programming X and InterViews, review the following list of the tools you will need to write InterViews applications in C++:

- A graphics workstation with the X Window System or an X terminal connected to a host that runs X. A reasonable "workstation" would include an Intel 80386-based PC with a VGA monitor, at least 8MB of memory, and a 150MB hard disk running one of the commercially available UNIX System V systems and, of course, X.

- The InterViews toolkit. This toolkit is available on MIT's X distribution (in the contrib/toolkits directory).

- A C++ compiler. If you run Santa Cruz Operation's Open Desktop system, you can use SCO C++, which also includes the InterViews class library with complete source code.

All InterViews examples in this chapter were tested on an Intel 80386-based workstation running SCO Open Desktop Version 1.0, SCO C++ Version 3.0, and InterViews Version 2.6. The InterViews examples should compile and link on most UNIX systems, with a C++ compiler, where InterViews can run. Such systems include workstations from Sun Microsystems, Digital Equipment Corporation, and Hewlett-Packard, as well as 80386 PCs running UNIX System V from SCO and Interactive Systems Corporation.

X Window System

The X Window System is a device-independent, network-transparent, graphics windowing system for raster displays. This section explains what this means and briefly describe how X works, and what you gain by using X.

> **Bit-mapped or Raster Graphics Displays**
>
> Graphics displays have two distinct components:
>
> - Video monitor, the terminal where the output appears.
>
> - Video controller, the circuitry that causes the output to appear by sending the appropriate signals to the monitor.
>
> In a bit-mapped graphics display system, the monitor displays an array of dots (known as *pixels*), and the appearance of each pixel corresponds to the contents of a memory location in the video controller. For a black-and-white display on which each pixel is either bright or dim, a single bit of memory can store the state of a pixel. The term *bit-mapped* refers to this correspondence between each bit in memory and a pixel on the screen.
>
> *Raster graphics* is another name for bit-mapped graphics, because the graphics appearing on the monitor are constructed from a large number of horizontal lines known as *raster lines*. These raster lines are generated by an electron beam sweeping back and forth on a phosphor-coated screen. Because each dot of phosphor, corresponding to a pixel, glows in proportion to the intensity of the beam, each line of the image can be generated by controlling the intensity of the beam as it scans across the screen. By drawing the raster lines repeatedly, the illusion of a steady image is created.

Traditional Approach to Graphics Versus the X Window System

To understand how X works, you have to compare it with the conventional approach to graphics output. Until workstations came along, graphics terminals were the only way to get graphics output from a computer program. For the sake of concreteness, consider how a terminal such as the Tektronix 4107 is used and programmed. Typically, this terminal is connected to a computer through a serial RS-232 connection. Application programs that display graphical output call the appropriate functions from a graphics library. These functions do their job by sending a stream of bytes to the terminal, which interprets these bytes and produces graphical output. Figure 15.1 illustrates this approach to graphics output. Here are the salient points of the traditional approach to graphics output:

- A graphics terminal usually displays output from one system at a time.

- The graphics library is tied to a specific type of terminal—it is device-dependent.

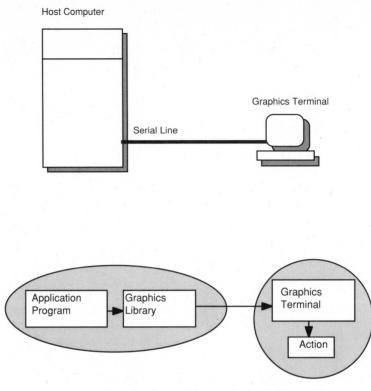

Fig. 15.1. Traditional host-based graphics.

Distributed Graphics with X

Graphics with X, illustrated in Figure 15.2, is similar to that done the traditional way, but X improves on the traditional approach in a number of important ways:

- An X-based application program is partitioned into two distinct components: an *X server* controlling the graphics workstation and an *X client* program that sends the drawing commands to the server.

- The X server uses a standard protocol called the *X protocol* to interpret the data stream sent by the X clients and perform the tasks requested by client applications.

- The client applications send graphics requests to the server via any 8-bit communication link such as TCP/IP, DECnet or AppleTalk. This allows the X clients running on a computer to display their output on a X server elsewhere in a network.

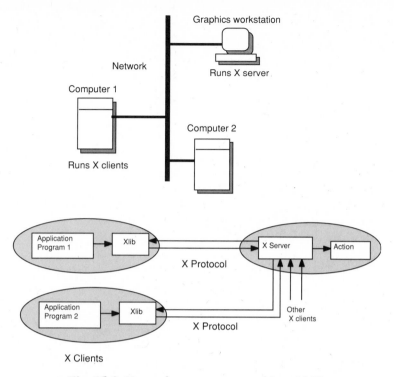

Fig. 15.2. Network-transparent graphics with X.

The X protocol is similar to the byte sequences necessary to program a graphics terminal like the Tektronix 4107. Just as bytes sent from the application control the Tektronix 4107 terminal, the X protocol byte stream controls the X display server.

However, there is a crucial difference between terminals like the Tektronix 4107 and X. Although the Tektronix 4107 is typically configured as a terminal that works over a serial connection, the X protocol will work over any 8-bit network connection. Also, the X protocol defines a more powerful set of capabilities than that available in the 4107. For example, X supports a hierarchy of windows and conceptual models of hardware display devices to achieve device independence.

What Is X?

As you can see from the brief comparison of X with traditional graphics, X has three basic components:

- The X server
- X clients

- The X protocol used by clients and servers to exchange messages

Additionally, there is a library of functions called *Xlib* that provides the C language programming interface to X. If you want to write X applications in C++, you will have to call Xlib functions from your C++ program. This can be troublesome, because prior to X Version 11, Release 4 the Xlib functions were not declared completely in the header files.

In a typical scenario, your workstation is connected to several other workstations and computers on a local area network. As shown in Figure 15.3, with X running at your workstation, you can interact with several processes—each displaying in its own window on the screen. Some of the processes may run locally at the workstation (provided your workstation's operating system is capable of handling multiple processes), and some may be executing at another system. For example, in Figure 15.3, window 1 is where you are interacting with your workstation. This window appears as a terminal to the workstation. Window 2 shows the output of an X application that is also running in the workstation. Window 3 is another terminal window where you may be interacting with computer A, and the output of another X application executing in computer B appears in the fourth window.

Process

In most operating systems, the term *process* refers to a program executing in memory and its associated environment. The environment usually includes the input and output files belonging to the program and a collection of variables known as *environment variables*. You create a process whenever you run a program. The command interpreter of the operating system (called the *shell* in UNIX) is also a process—one that creates processes at your command.

Clients and Servers

Behind the scene, in the scenario shown in Figure 15.3, is the *X server* running in the workstation, listening to the network connection at a specific port, and acting on the commands sent by the *X clients*, a term that refers to the applications that use the workstation's display.

This arrangement, shown in Figure 15.4, is known as the *client-server model*. As the name implies, the server provides a service that the client requests. Usually, clients communicate with the server through a network, and client and server exchange data using a protocol understood by both. You may have already seen this model in action. For example, a *file server* stores files and allows clients to access and manipulate the files. Another common application, the *database server*, provides a centralized database from which clients retrieve data by sending queries. Similarly, as illustrated in Figure 15.4, the *X display server* offers graphics display services to clients that send *X protocol* requests to the server.

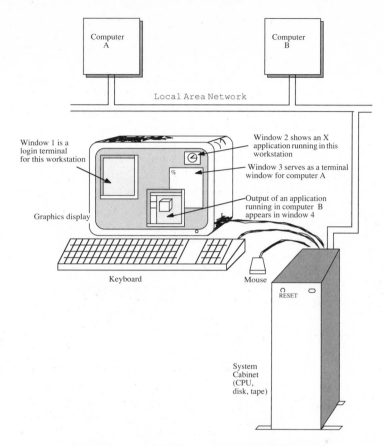

Fig. 15.3. A workstation with the X Window System.

In contrast to file servers and database servers—which are usually processes executing in remote machines—the X server is a process executing in your workstation while at the same time serving clients that may be running locally or on remote systems.

X Server

The functionality of the X Window System is in the X server—the process executing in your workstation and managing the graphics output and the inputs from the keyboard and mouse. Figure 15.5 provides a simplistic representation of what goes on in an X display server. It shows modules that read X protocol requests from clients over a network connection and process requests from each client. If a request is for graphics output, a device-dependent graphics module takes care of generating the output on your workstation's display.

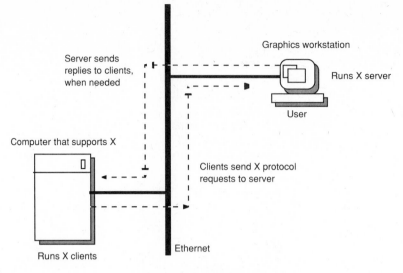

Fig. 15.4. Client-server model.

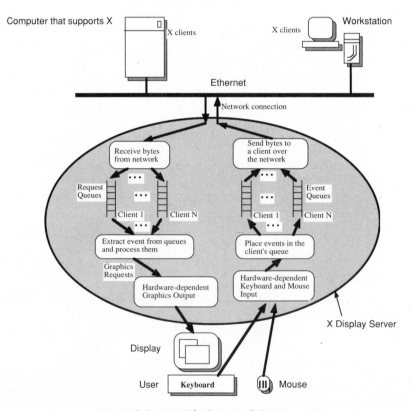

Fig. 15.5. Simplified view of the X server.

Hierarchy of Windows

Creating a window is one of the basic X protocol requests the X server handles. An X application often appears to have a single output window; in reality, however, most X applications use many windows to construct the user interface.

Consider the sample X text editing application shown in Figure 15.6. This text editor has a text entry area and two scroll bars for examining text that may not be visible in the window. Even at this basic level in the application, two windows are on the screen—the *root window*, which occupies the whole display screen, and the editor window inside it. On closer examination, the editor window turns out to be just a frame that holds three other windows: the document window where the text appears and the two scroll bar windows. Further, as shown in Figure 15.7, each scroll bar window contains three smaller windows: the thumbwheel in the middle and two arrows at the ends.

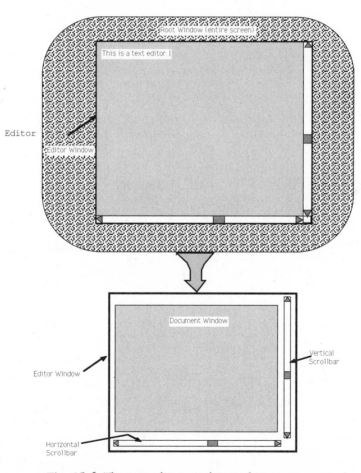

Fig. 15.6. The text editor window and its components.

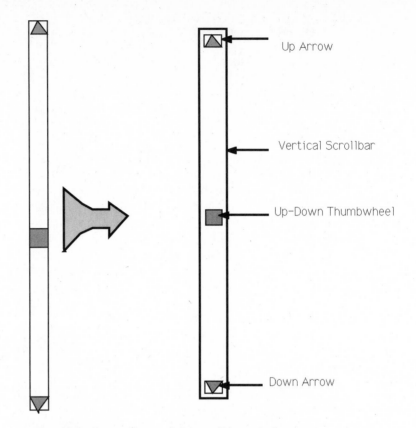

Fig. 15.7. Components of the scroll bar window.

Arrangement of windows in a parent-child hierarchy is the norm in X. Figure 15.6 shows the editor window as a child of the root. The editor window has three children: the document window and two scroll bar windows. Each scroll bar window, in turn, has three children: two arrow windows and a thumbwheel window. This results in a treelike hierarchy of windows for the text editor (Figure 15.8).

Event Delivery

The X server considers anything you do with the keyboard and the mouse as events to be reported to the clients. Typically, you move the mouse around the screen, and a small graphics shape (the *mouse pointer*) follows the motion on the screen. When you are running X applications, everything on the screen appears in windows, and each window is associated with a specific client. When you press and release a mouse button, the X server sends these input events to the client that originally created the window containing the mouse pointer. For *keyboard events*, the keypress always belongs to a designated window—one that has the *input focus*. You can control which window gets the input focus by using a window manager application.

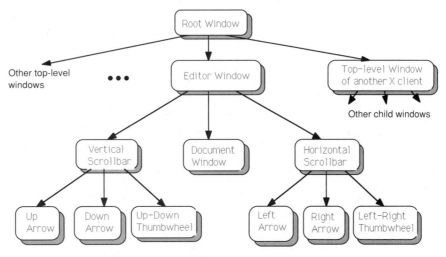

Fig. 15.8. Hierarchy of windows in the editor.

The X server sends another kind of event, an *expose event*, to clients. These events inform a client if anything happens to its window. For example, because windows overlay each other, when they are moved around previously obscured parts of a window may become visible again. In this case, the server sends an expose event to the client application, which must take care of drawing into the exposed area of the window. As with Macintosh and Microsoft Windows, the burden of maintaining the appearance of a window rests with the application that owns it, not with the X server. This is one aspect of X server that usually surprises newcomers: If your application's code does not handle expose events, nothing will be drawn in the window.

X Protocol: The Machine Language of X

Because X clients communicate with display servers using the X protocol, X protocol defines exactly what can be achieved with the X Window System. A *protocol* is an agreement between the server and the client about how they will exchange information and how that information will be interpreted. In the X protocol, data is exchanged in an asynchronous manner over a two-way communication path that allows transmission of a stream of 8-bit bytes. The X protocol also defines the meaning of the byte stream. By drawing an analogy with microprocessors, you might say that the X protocol is the machine language of the X Window System. Just as the logic circuitry in a microprocessor interprets the bit-patterns in instruction bytes and performs some simple task, the X display server interprets the X protocol byte stream and generates graphics output. Thus, the X protocol completely defines the capabilities of the X Window System.

Xlib: The Assembly Language of X

You can write an application that uses the X display server by directly sending bytes conforming to the X protocol, but doing so is very tedious—like programming a microprocessor using only machine language. Moreover, you do not have to do it. The X Window System comes with a library of C routines: Xlib. Xlib gives you access to the X protocol through more than 300 utility routines.

If the X protocol is the machine language of X, then Xlib is its assembly language. Programming in assembly language is not easy, but it is much easier than using machine language.

X Toolkits—The High-Level Languages of X

Although the Xlib library is very convenient, its capabilities are basic. For example, Xlib does not have a function that will display a menu with a selected list of entries. You can create a menu by calling a number of Xlib routines, but that takes some work. To solve this problem, you need another set of routines that implement objects such as buttons, lists, and menus, which can be used to build a graphical user interface.

This idea has been pursued by several groups. The X Window System comes with the *X Toolkit Intrinsics* (also known as *Xt Intrinsics*), which uses an object-oriented approach to implement basic building blocks called *widgets*. Some other toolkits, such as the Motif toolkit from Open Software Foundation, use a still higher level of abstraction. The Motif toolkit is built on the X Toolkit Intrinsics. Continuing with our analogy of microprocessor programming, these are the high-level languages of the X Window System.

The InterViews toolkit also falls in this category, except that it is for writing X applications in C++. Like Motif, InterViews also provides a set of high-level building blocks for creating the user interface of an application as well as for drawing text and graphics in windows.

X Protocol, Xlib, or Toolkit?

You might wonder when, if at any time, anyone uses the X protocol directly. The answer is this: You need to worry about X protocol only when you are implementing an X display server or writing a library of routines to be used in X applications as a programming interface to the X protocol. Of course, just as all C programs are ultimately translated to machine code, all calls to Xlib or X toolkit routines eventually get converted to X protocol requests.

If you plan to program in X, Xlib is a good place to start. It helps you learn what X can do and how to perform basic tasks such as opening a window, handling a keypress or button press, and drawing text and graphics in a window. When developing complete applications, you will find it more productive to use a toolkit. The penalty for using a toolkit is that toolkit-based applications generally require more memory than those based on bare-bones Xlib routines.

Figure 15.9 shows the general structure of an X application. The application primarily calls routines from a toolkit. The toolkit may call routines from the Xt Intrinsics, which, in turn, calls Xlib. The application may also make direct calls to some Xlib routines for generating text and graphics output in a window.

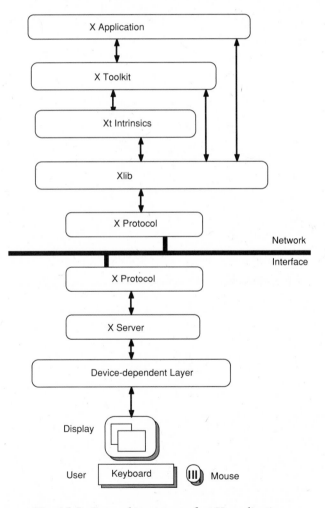

Fig. 15.9. General structure of an X application.

Dependence on the Operating System

The basic design of X does not depend on any operating system. All X needs is a reliable data path between the clients and the X server. So far, X implementations have used TCP/IP, DECnet, and STREAMS networking protocols for transferring data between the server and clients. The operating system sometimes becomes a factor because of its close ties to the networking software being used by a client application to transmit the X protocol requests to the X server. For example, in Berkeley UNIX (also known as BSD UNIX) systems, X communicates using TCP/IP, whereas in Digital Equipment Corporation's VAX/VMS machines, the X protocol bytes are sent using the DECnet networking protocol.

AT&T's implementation of X uses the STREAMS mechanism that is native to UNIX System V. Nevertheless, as long as there is a common networking protocol available for data transfer, the X server can display output from any client without regard to the operating system under which the client executes.

Where X Fits In

X is intended to handle a user's interaction with a computer through a bit-mapped graphics display. The basic mission of the X Window System is quite similar to that of a graphics terminal. Like a graphics terminal, X is capable of displaying graphical output. But, X is more than a graphics system—it is a windowing system capable of organizing graphical output in a hierarchy of windows on the screen. This capability and the ability to accept input from keyboard and mouse make X ideal for handling user interactions.

Graphics terminals are fine for displaying static information, such as plots and three-dimensional views of a solid object. But the biggest drawback of these terminals is their slow-speed connection (RS-232 at 9600 baud) to the computer. The relatively slow speed limits the terminals' ability to handle rapid changes to the display, such as those necessary for a graphical user interface where there should be immediate visual feedback when a window is moved or a mouse button is pressed.

Workstations solve this problem by integrating the CPU and display in a single unit, with a high-speed data path between the two. But each workstation manufacturer uses a different approach to displaying graphics. X solves both of these problems:

- It works over any communication channel. The speed limitations of a serial connection can be easily overcome by using the much faster Ethernet (10 million bits per second, a thousand times faster than a 9600-baud connection) as the channel.

- It defines a standard model for creating, manipulating, and displaying in windows. Thus, X is well-suited for implementing applications that need graphical user interfaces.

X Terminals: A New Breed of Terminals

The similarity between traditional graphics terminals and the X Window System has prompted the emergence of a new breed of terminals that are based on X. You can think of these terminals as stripped-down versions of a workstation, with a network connection and running the X server only. These X terminals are useful in facilities with minicomputers and mainframes that have to provide standard graphics capabilities to many users. The X terminals are much cheaper than full-fledged graphics workstations. Also, because they do not have any operating system (the CPU in an X terminal runs only one program—the X server), they do not need the attention and care that go with installing and maintaining an operating system.

The demand for X terminals is growing steadily. In anticipation of increased sales, almost every computer and workstation vendor has introduced (or has plans to introduce) X terminals. In some ways, the X terminals are bringing back the era of timesharing with the added twist of a single X terminal providing access to many computers.

MS-DOS PCs and Macintoshes as X Servers

Just as a stripped-down workstation can be configured as an X terminal, an MS-DOS PC or a Macintosh also can display output from an X application. Knowing the client-server model of X, you can guess that the main requirement is an X server at the PC or the Macintosh. Together with the server, you also need some form of networking software that will communicate with the machine on which the X application is running. Several vendors have developed X servers for MS-DOS PCs and Macintoshes.

Benefits of X

If you have programmed a window system, you do not need to be convinced that a standard window system is a good idea. You know that with a standard such as X, you do not have to learn a new window system for every new machine. With the widespread support X enjoys, once you learn X, you can write applications for a wide variety of workstations. There are several other benefits as well, as described next.

Network Transparency

The ability to display graphics across the network is what makes X versatile as a windowing system. To an X client it makes no difference whether the X display server is local or across the network. This ability is why X is described as a *network-transparent* windowing system.

Network transparency leads to what David Rosenthal, an expert on X, calls the *interoperability* of X clients and servers: If written properly, an X client can work with any X server. Interoperability is, by no means, guaranteed; the client application must be written properly. The existence of an X protocol request for a particular task does not guarantee that the server will successfully perform the task—it may fail and return an error. Treatment of color, for example, is an area that requires careful consideration (because workstations have varying color capabilities). To be able to interoperate with any server, your X application must handle all contingencies.

Separation of Computing and Graphics

In the X Window System, there is a clear separation of graphics and computing. Output from an X application is handled by sending X protocol requests to an X server. The rest of the application can perform its computations on a system that best suits its needs. For example, a computation-intensive simulation model can use a Cray supercomputer for its work while providing a visual representation of the results on a workstation or an X terminal.

Diverse Systems Under X

A consequence of the client-server model used by X and its network transparency is that you can mix and match computers and workstations from many different vendors, as long as they support X and they can be networked. This is an important benefit for people who have to select computer hardware and software. Picking a specific system does not have to mean that all future software and hardware upgrades must come from the same vendor. If the hardware and software support X, additions to the facility can be from any one of the many vendors that also support X.

Such heterogeneous computing environments already exist in universities and laboratories, and the trend toward mix-and-match computing is just beginning to appear in commercial environments as well.

Mechanism, Not Policy

"X provides mechanism, not policy." This quote from the architects of X states the underlying philosophy of X. The X protocol sets forth the basic tasks that an X server performs. There is no mention of menus, button, or labels in the X protocol. It is up to the application to construct the user interface using the primitive facilities of the X server. You can use X to build any type of user interface you want. For example, the much-publicized Motif toolkit is capable of producing the *look* and *feel* of Microsoft Windows, whereas the InterViews toolkit has its own look and feel. It is also possible to develop an X application that mimics the layout and behavior of Macintosh applications.

Room for Future Extensions

The architects of the X Window System realized that they could not envision all needs that an X server may have to fulfill. To account for unforeseen tasks, they left room for *extensions* in the X protocol. Already, there is much work being done in adding a three-dimensional graphics extension to the X server. This extension to the X protocol makes use of another standard, known as PHIGS, the Programmers Hierarchical Interactive Graphics System, that supports three-dimensional graphics. The new extended version of X is being called PHIGS Extended X, or PEX.

Versions of X

The development of the X Window System started in 1984 at Massachusetts Institute of Technology under the auspices of the MIT Laboratory for Computer Science and MIT/Project Athena. From the beginning, X had support from industry because of the involvement of DEC and IBM in Project Athena. By early 1986, DEC introduced the first commercial implementation of X running on the VAXstation-II/GPX under the Ultrix operating system. This was X Version 10 Release 3 (X10R3). Soon X attracted the attention of other prominent workstation vendors, such as Hewlett-Packard, Sun Microsystems, and Tektronix.

Feedback from users of X10 urged the project members to start a major redesign of the X protocol. As the design of what would become X Version 11 (X11) was proceeding, X10R4 was released in December of 1986. This was the last release of X Version 10.

In January 1987, during the first X technical conference, 11 major computer vendors announced a joint effort to support and standardize on X11. The first release of X11, X11R1, became available in September 1987. To ensure continued evolution of X under the control of an open organization, the MIT X Consortium was formed in January 1988. Under the leadership of Robert W. Scheifler, one of the principal architects of X, the consortium has been a major reason for the success of X.

In March 1988, Release 2 of X11, X11R2, became available. X11 Release 3, X11R3, appeared in late October 1988. Most recently, in January 1990, the M.I.T. X Consortium released X11R4. The X11 protocol has remained unchanged. Enhancements between releases have been in interclient communications that prescribe how X clients can coexist and exchange data. When this book was being written, the most prevalent versions of X were X11R3 and X11R4.

C++ and X

Now that you have an overview of X, let us consider what is involved in writing X programs in C++. At first glance, writing X applications in C++ appears to be straightforward. After all, Xlib is a set of C functions, and C++ programs can call C functions (see Chapter 10). Unfortunately, there are a few minor problems when you try to use the Xlib functions in a straightforward manner:

- C++ requires function *prototypes*—all functions have to be declared before they are used. Until X11R4, the header file <X11/Xlib.h> did not have function prototypes. This means that if you are using X11R3, you have to write your own prototypes for the Xlib functions. In X11R4, function prototypes are available, but other problems remain.

- In C++, class, delete, and new are reserved keywords that you cannot use as names of variables or functions in your program. Unfortunately, some X header files use class, delete, and new in a manner that C++ does not allow. This poses a problem, because you have to include these header files in your X programs. One way to fix this is to use the C preprocessor. For instance, the header file <X11/Xlib.h> uses the reserved keyword class. Were everything else fine, you could make this file acceptable to the C++ compiler by creating a new header file, called, for instance, Xlibcpp.h, in the following manner:

```
#if !defined(__XLIBCPP_H)      // Prevent multiple inclusion
#define __XLIBCPP_H

#if defined(__cplusplus)
extern "C" {                   // If C++ program, use extern "C"
#endif

#define class x_class          // Redefine "class"
```

```
#include <X11/Xlib.h>        // Include standard Xlib.h

#undef class                 // Undefine "class"

#if defined(__cplusplus)
}
#endif
```

Now you can use this header file in place of <X11/Xlib.h> in your C++ programs. Of course, this takes care of only one problem. You have to handle all reserved keywords in this manner and make sure that all functions have proto-types.

In addition to plain Xlib, if you want to access any of the X Toolkits, you will have to address similar problems for each header file.

Even if the header files were in a form acceptable to the C++ compiler, you may not want to call the Xlib functions as and when needed. Because C++ supports object-oriented programming, you might want a set of classes that provides the objects you need to build the user interface. This is where a toolkit like InterViews can help. The remainder of this chapter will give you an overview of InterViews, describe some of its capabilities, and show a simple example.

InterViews

InterViews, which stands for *Interactive Views*, is a collection of over 175 C++ classes for building graphical user interfaces using the facilities of the X Window System. All calls to Xlib functions are encapsulated in a small set of classes in such a way that an InterViews application does not have to call Xlib functions at all. Because of its design, InterViews provides a high degree of isolation from the underlying window system. Therefore, at least in theory, you can port an InterViews application to a new window system by rewriting the X-dependent classes so that they work with the new window system.

InterViews uses object-oriented techniques together with the model-view-controller (MVC) architecture (see Chapters 3 and 12) for its design. Objects through which the user can interact with the application are called *interactors*. In fact, a class named Interactor serves as the base class for all interactors. The interactors play the role of combined *view* and *controller*; the application-specific code is the *model*. In an InterViews application, you are supposed to create the user interface by arranging interactors and other graphical and text objects in a hierarchical fashion in a *scene*. You start with a top-level scene of type World into which you "insert" other interactors and scenes, which in turn can contain other interactors. Thus, the scenes create a hierarchy just as the windows in X do. When the scene is complete, you can get the application going by calling the Run function of the World. You will learn more about this process in the following sections.

Saying "Hello, World!" in InterViews

Before you study the InterViews class hierarchy, you would find it helpful to go over a small application, sayhello, that uses several InterViews classes to display a "Hello, World!" message in a window. This example will show you the typical structure of InterViews programs and give you a feel for the way in which InterViews classes are used.

Specifying sayhello

Let us first specify what we expect from sayhello. The program should do the following:

- Display the "Hello, World!" message in a window.

- In the same window, provide a pushbutton labeled Exit. The program should exit when the user presses on this button.

- Always center the message and the button in the window with the message displayed above the button.

- Allow users to specify as command-line options the font, foreground and background colors, and the size of the window in which the message appears.

Designing sayhello

The first step in designing an InterViews program such as sayhello is to determine the appropriate hierarchy of InterViews classes that will do the job. In this case, there are two basic objects that are immediately apparent:

- A message with the text "Hello, World!"

- A pushbutton

If you were to browse through the InterViews reference manual, you would find the following candidate classes that meet our needs:

- The Message class is an interactor that displays a line of text. Thus, you can use this to display the "Hello, World!" message.

- The PushButton class displays a line of text within a rectangle with rounded corners. The PushButton also needs a ButtonState object to hold the "state" (an arbitrary integer value) of the button. When the user "clicks" on the button (the user brings the mouse pointer inside the pushbutton, then presses and releases a mouse button), the PushButton copies a predefined value into that ButtonState object. You can use the PushButton class to create the button with the Exit message.

A Scene for the Components

Once you have identified these two primitive objects, you need a "container" to hold them together. In InterViews, you "compose" the user interface by placing interactors in a Scene. You can think of the Scene as a paste-up board on which you lay out the components to create the user interface. As you will see shortly, there are many types of Scene objects and a Scene can contain other Interactors (Scene is itself derived from the Interactor class). As illustrated in Figure 15.10, we will lay out the Scene for the sayhello application in the following manner (for ease of reference, we give a name to each object):

- We will define a HelloMessage class, derived from the MonoScene class, to hold a single Interactor—a VBox (vertical box) with the other components inside it. The definition of a HelloMessage class simplifies the way we will display the message and handle the user's inputs.

- The Message instance, named message, will display the "Hello, World!" message.

- The PushButton, quit_button, will be the button that the user presses to exit sayhello.

- To center message and quit_button, we will use two HBox (horizontal box) objects: top_hbox for message and bottom_hbox for quit_button. Inside each HBox, we will place HGlue (horizontal glue) objects on either side of the contained object. This will center the message and quit_button objects along the horizontal axis. The Glue objects stretch and shrink as needed to maintain a variable-sized open space between two adjacent interactors.

- Finally, an instance of the VBox class, named vbox, will hold the two HBox objects—top_hbox and bottom_hbox—centered vertically using three VGlue objects.

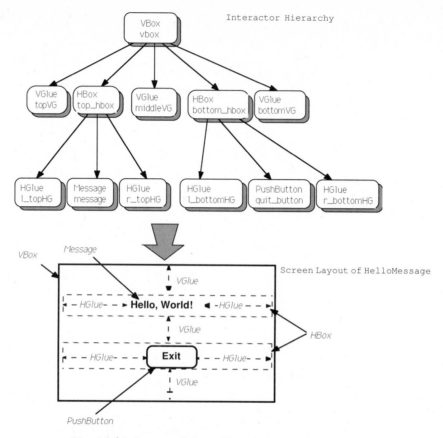

Fig. 15.10. Layout of the `HelloMessage` scene.

Once you have the layout of the `HelloMessage` interactor, you can declare the `HelloMessage` class, as shown in Listing 15.1. Notice the InterViews header files that you have to include before you can use the predefined classes such as `Message`, `PushButton`, `HBox`, and `VBox`.

Listing 15.1. `hello1.h`—The header file for the `HelloMessage` class.

```
//-------------------------------------------------------
//  File: hello1.h
//
//  An interactor class for displaying "Hello, World!".

#if !defined(__HELLO1_H)
#define __HELLO1_H

// Include InterViews header files
```

```
#include <InterViews/box.h>
#include <InterViews/button.h>
#include <InterViews/glue.h>
#include <InterViews/message.h>
#include <InterViews/world.h>

class HelloMessage : public MonoScene
{
public:
    HelloMessage();
    ~HelloMessage();

    ButtonState* quit() { return quit_now;}

private:
    ButtonState* quit_now;
    HGlue*       l_topHG;
    HGlue*       r_topHG;
    HGlue*       l_bottomHG;
    HGlue*       r_bottomHG;
    VGlue*       topVG;
    VGlue*       middleVG;
    VGlue*       bottomVG;
    HBox*        top_hbox;
    HBox*        bottom_hbox;
    VBox*        vbox;
    Message*     message;
    PushButton*  quit_button;
};

#endif
```

The HelloMessage class includes pointers to all its component objects. The HelloMessage constructor (see Listing 15.2) allocates these components and "composes" the entire interface using HBoxes and a VBox. Finally, the constructor inserts the Vbox into itself to complete the scene. In the next discussion, you will see how we use the HelloMessage class.

Listing 15.2. hello1.C—Implementation of the HelloMessage class.

```
//-------------------------------------------------------------
//  File: hello1.C
//
//  The HelloMessage class to display the "Hello, World!"
//  message in InterViews.
```

```
#include "hello1.h"

//------------------------------------------------------------
// H e l l o M e s s a g e
// Constructor for the HelloMessage scene
// The idea is to create an interactor with the "Hello, World!"
// message and a pushbutton; in the main program, this
// interactor will be managed by a dialog object

HelloMessage::HelloMessage()
{
// Create the Glue objects
    l_topHG = new HGlue;
    r_topHG = new HGlue;
    l_bottomHG = new HGlue;
    r_bottomHG = new HGlue;
    topVG = new VGlue;
    middleVG = new VGlue;
    bottomVG = new VGlue;

// A ButtonState to hold value returned by PushButton
    quit_now = new ButtonState(false);

// Create the Message and the PushButton
    message = new Message("Hello, World!");
    quit_button = new PushButton("Exit", quit_now, true);

// Create the HBox objects—one with the message and
// the other with a PushButton
    top_hbox = new HBox(l_topHG, message, r_topHG);
    bottom_hbox = new HBox(l_bottomHG, quit_button, r_bottomHG);

// Now place the two HBoxes in a VBox with VGlues in between
    vbox = new VBox(topVG, top_hbox, middleVG, bottom_hbox,
                    bottomVG);

// Insert this VBox into the HelloMessage Interactor
    Insert(vbox);
}
//------------------------------------------------------------
// ~ H e l l o M e s s a g e
// Destructor for the HelloMessage scene
```

```
HelloMessage::~HelloMessage()
{
// Delete all objects allocated by the constructor
    delete quit_now;
    delete l_topHG;
    delete r_topHG,
    delete l_bottomHG;
    delete r_bottomHG,
    delete topVG;
    delete middleVG;
    delete bottomVG;
    delete top_hbox;
    delete bottom_hbox;
    delete vbox;
    delete message;
    delete quit_button;
}
```

Handling Events

Like any X application, an InterViews application runs by repeatedly accepting events (such as mouse movements and mouse button clicks) and processing them. InterViews hides most of the details of event-handling in its classes. You only have to call the Run function of any Interactor to initiate a default event-processing loop. You are, of course, free to define a modified Run function in your derived Interactor classes. Typically, an application would define a Scene class of its own, just as we define HelloMessage for sayhello, and would provide a Run function to handle the event-handling. For sayhello, we will take the easy way out and let another built-in class called Dialog handle the events.

One of the constructors for the Dialog class has the following prototype:

```
Dialog(ButtonState* state, Interactor* internal,
        Alignment = Center); // Ignore "Alignment" for now
```

where the Interactor specified by internal defines the inside of the Dialog. The state argument is a pointer to a ButtonState that you provide. That ButtonState should be tied to a PushButton inside the interactor specified by the internal argument. The code that creates a PushButton in the HelloMessage constructor (Listing 15.2) shows how a ButtonState is tied to a PushButton. When you activate an instance of the Dialog class by calling its Accept function, the Dialog will keep processing inputs until the value in the ButtonState becomes nonzero.

In sayhello, we can use the Dialog class in the following manner:

1. Create a `HelloMessage`:

   ```
   HelloMessage* hello_msg = new HelloMessage;
   ```

2. Create a `Dialog` with this `HelloMessage` as the interactor. For the `Dialog`'s `ButtonState*` argument, provide a pointer to the `ButtonState` used by the `quit_button` in `HelloMessage`. The `quit` function of `HelloMessage` returns a pointer to this `ButtonState`. Thus, you can create the `Dialog` with the code:

   ```
   Dialog* dlog = new Dialog(hello_msg->quit(),
                   hello_msg);
   ```

3. Once this `Dialog` is inserted into the `World`, you can start the `Dialog` by calling its `Accept` function:

   ```
   dlog->Accept();
   ```

Listing 15.3 shows the file `sayhello.C` (in SCO C++, the names of C++ files end with an uppercase `.C`) which implements the main function of `sayhello`, the program that displays "`Hello, World!`". The form of the `main` function is about the same in most InterViews applications. You create a `World`, insert your scene into it, and start processing events. In most applications, event-processing is done by calling the `Run` function of the `World`. In `sayhello`, this step is replaced by calling the `Accept` function of the `Dialog`. Figure 15.11 shows the hierarchy and layout of the top-level interactors that is created by the `sayhello.C` program shown in Listing 15.3.

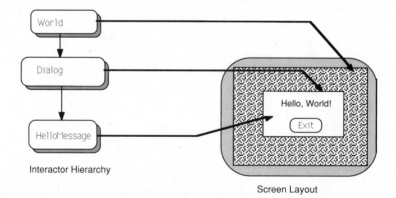

Fig. 15.11. Hierarchy and layout of the top-level interactors in `sayhello`.

Listing 15.3. sayhello.C—The main program to display "Hello, World!".

```
//---------------------------------------------------------------
//  File: sayhello.C
//
//  Main program that uses a dialog to display a HelloMessage
//  interactor, which, in turn displays the "Hello, World!"
//  message.

#include "hello1.h"
#include <InterViews/dialog.h>


//---------------------------------------------------------------
// m a i n

int main(int argc, char** argv)
{
// Create the World
    World* hello_world = new World("Sayhello", argc, argv);

// Create a HelloMessage scene
    HelloMessage* hello_msg = new HelloMessage;

// Create a Dialog to manage the HelloMessage, noticing how
// the pushbutton's state is passed to the Dialog. When this
// pushbutton is pressed, the dialog exits

    Dialog* dlog = new Dialog(hello_msg->quit(), hello_msg);

// Insert the dialog into the World
    hello_world->Insert(dlog);

// Let the dialog handle the events
    dlog->Accept();

// Clean up . . .
    delete hello_world;
    return 0;
}
```

Building and Testing `sayhello`

You have seen the source file for `sayhello`, but we have not yet shown you how to build the executable file. You know that `sayhello.C` has to be compiled and linked—the question is "With which libraries?" This section summarizes the procedure for building and testing `sayhello`.

Compiling and Linking `sayhello`

The steps involved in compiling and linking the `sayhello` application will depend on your C++ compiler. On most UNIX systems, you should be able to compile and link `sayhello` with a single `CC` command. The only problem is that the libraries necessary to complete the linking may differ from one system to another. On an SCO UNIX system running SCO C++ 3.0 (which is based on AT&T `cfront` 2.1) and InterViews 2.6, the following UNIX shell command builds `sayhello`:

```
CC -o sayhello sayhello.C hello1.C -lIViews -lX11 \
-lmalloc -lsocket -lm
```

Of the listed libraries, only the following libraries are needed on all systems:

- `libIViews.a` (indicated by the option `-lIViews`) for the InterViews classes

- The `-lX11` option for the Xlib functions called by InterViews

- The `-lm` option for the `sin` and `cos` functions that InterViews calls

The libraries specified by the options `-lmalloc` and `-lsocket` may not be needed on your system.

After building `sayhello`, you can run it from a UNIX shell in an `xterm` (the terminal emulator in X) window with the command:

```
sayhello&
```

This command produces the window shown in Figure 15.12. The frame around the window comes from the OSF/Motif window manager. You can close the window and exit the application by pressing and releasing any mouse button with the pointer inside the button labeled `Exit`.

Making Things Easy with `make`

A better way to build `sayhello` is to prepare a *makefile* and use the UNIX make utility. The makefile describes the names of files that make up a program and how they are interrelated. It also includes information about how to create the program. The make utility reads the makefile and, based on the time of last modification, decides which files need compiling. The utility follows any other specified steps to create an updated version of the program. With make you can avoid retyping long commands and, more importantly, avoid unnecessary recompilations (or get errors because you forgot to compile a file that was affected by your most recent changes).

Fig. 15.12. Hello, World! from sayhello.

The makefile for sayhello is quite simple, because it has only two source files. Listing 15.4 shows this file. For larger projects with many source files, the makefile will be similar looking, but with more entries.

Listing 15.4. Makefile for sayhello.

```
####################################################################
# Makefile for building "sayhello" with SCO C++ and InterViews  #
#                                                                #
# NOTE: The libraries are good for SCO C++ Release 3.0 and       #
#       InterViews Release 2.6 running under SCO Open Desktop    #
#       Release 1.0. You may have to change these for your       #
#       system.                                                  #
#                                                                #
####################################################################

# Some common definitions . . .
RM = rm -f
CC = CC

# Compiler flags and paths for include files and libraries
CFLAGS =
INCLUDES = -I.
LIBS = -lIViews -lX11 -lmalloc -lsocket -lm
```

```
OBJS = sayhello.o hello1.o

    # Targets . . .

all::     sayhello

sayhello:    $(OBJS)
    @echo "linking $@"
    $(RM) $@
    $(CC) -o $@ $(OBJS) $(LIBS)

sayhello.o: sayhello.C hello1.h
    @echo "compiling sayhello.C"
    $(RM) $@
    $(CC) -c  $(CFLAGS) sayhello.C

hello1.o: hello1.C hello1.h
    @echo "compiling hello1.C"
    $(RM) $@
    $(CC) -c  $(CFLAGS) hello1.C
```

Specifying Command-Line Options

One of our requirements for sayhello was to be able to specify parameters such as font, foreground and background colors, and geometry (the location and size of the application's window) from the command line. We ignored this requirement, because sayhello automatically gets this capability through its World object. For example, try using the following command to run sayhello:

```
sayhello -font "*helvetica*bold*-r-*180*"&
```

Figure 15.13 shows the resulting output from sayhello. Notice how the text appears in a different font. When you run sayhello without specifying any font, the output appears in the default font of the X server. In this case, the command line specifies an 18-point Bold Helvetica font (consult a book on the X Window System for information on specifying the font names). Accordingly, the output appears in this new font.

Fig. 15.13. Saying `Hello, world!` in 18-point Bold Helvetica font.

Here is how you can process the command-line options in an InterViews application. When you create the `World`, you should provide the command-line arguments to the `World`'s constructor like this:

```
int main(int argc, char** argv)
{
// Create the World
    World* hello_world = new World("Sayhello", argc, argv);

// . . .
}
```

The `World` constructor automatically interprets and removes from `argv` the command-line arguments shown in Table 15.1.

Table 15.1. Command-Line Options Processed by `World`.

Option	Meaning
-background	Next argument specifies the background color
-bg	Shorter version of -background
-display	Next argument identifies the X server where the output appears
-foreground	Next argument specifies the foreground color
-fg	Short form for -foreground
-font	Next argument is the name of the font to be used
-fn	Synonym for -font
-geometry	Next string specifies the position and size of the application's window
-iconic	Starts the application as an icon
-name	The next argument specifies the instance names of interactors

continues

Table 15.1. continued

Option	Meaning
-reverse	Displays output in *reverse video* (swaps foreground and background colors)
-rv	Same as -reverse
-title	The next string is used as a title to be displayed in the main window's title bar
-xrm	The next argument is passed to the X resource manager

The InterViews Class Hierarchy

Now that you have seen an example of InterViews programming and seen some of the InterViews classes in action, you can understand an overview of the entire class hierarchy. Although the InterViews toolkit comes with manual pages for most of the classes, there is no description of the overall class hierarchy. Even the manual page for a class does not indicate its base class. The only way to find this information is to go through the InterViews header files. Because this information can be very helpful in forming a mental picture of how the classes fit together, the next four figures reflect the class hierarchy of the header files in InterViews Release 2.6. Figures 15.14 through 15.17 show these diagrams. The following discussions briefly describe the hierarchies.

Breakdown of the Classes

If you were to count the classes declared in the header files of the InterViews toolkit, you should find 177 classes. Of these classes, 33 are stand-alone and 144 appear in six distinct hierarchies. Here is a breakdown of the classes:

1. The Interactor class hierarchy contains 59 classes (Figure 15.14). This class tree represents all interactive objects and includes the World, Box, and MonoScene classes that are commonly used in most InterViews applications.

2. Figure 15.15 shows the Resource class hierarchy with a set of 47 classes. The Resource hierarchy includes the obvious classes such as Font, Color, and Pattern, as well as the ButtonState class, which you have seen used in the sayhello program (Listings 15.1 through 15.3). A large number of classes in the Resource hierarchy are for supporting "rubber-banding," which refers to the way a drawing is animated in keeping with the mouse movements.

3. The third major hierarchy is rooted at a class named `Persistent` (Figure 15.16). If you look at the next level in this hierarchy, you will see the `Graphic` class, which is the base class for all graphical objects in InterViews. The significance of having the `Persistent` class at the root of this hierarchy is that all `Graphic` objects are *persistent* objects—they can be saved to the disk and retrieved later. There are 32 classes in this tree.

4. The remaining 39 classes (Figure 15.17) play a supporting role. Some of these classes are used internally by the other classes. A few are used directly in applications. For example, the `Event` class represents X events, `Damage` helps you manage exposed areas of windows, and `Cursor` models the mouse pointer.

The following discussions summarize some of the commonly used classes from the three major hierarchies: `Interactor`, `Resource`, and `Graphic`. (You might want to call this the `Graphic` subtree, because `Persistent` is the root class of this tree.)

Interactor *Classes*

If you browse through Figure 15.14, you will recognize classes such as `Button`, `Scroller`, `Menu`, and `Dialog` as commonly used components for user interfaces. On the other hand, the purpose of the classes `MonoScene`, `Tray`, and `Deck` might not be readily apparent to someone familiar with a windowing system such as X, Macintosh, or Microsoft Windows. These classes are, however, central to the idea of *hierarchical composition* in InterViews. As you have seen from the simple example program, `sayhello`, you have to create the user interface of an application by placing various components in a `Scene`, which is an `Interactor` capable of holding other `Interactors`.

The base class of this hierarchy, the `Interactor`, provides the basic member functions needed to support drawing, resizing, and event-handling. Specifically, here are some of the basic operations of the `Interactor` class:

`virtual void Draw();` displays the contents of the interactor, including the contents of any interactor it contains.

`void Read(Event& e);` reads the next event from the application's queue of events.

`virtual void Handle(Event& e);` handles the given event.

`virtual void Update();` redraws to reflect change in state that affects the interactor.

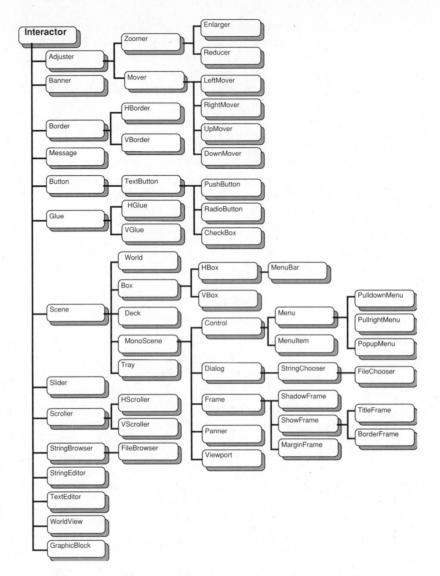

Figure 15.14. The Interactor class hierarchy in InterViews.

Scene

The Scene subtree in Figure 15.14 defines all the classes that are capable of holding one or more instances of interactors. You will need a Scene to compose the interface. Because a Scene is itself an Interactor, you can have a complex hierarchy of interactors in a Scene. Scene is an abstract base class—it only defines the operations that are to be supported by all derived classes. Here are some of the member functions of Scene (of course, anything available in the Interactor class is also a part of the Scene class, because Scene is derived from Interactor):

void Insert(Interactor* i); adds the Interactor specified by the pointer i to the Scene.

void Remove(Interactor* i); removes the Interactor specified by the pointer i from the Scene.

void Move(Interactor* i, Coord x, Coord y, Alignment = BottomLeft); moves the interactor to the specified location.

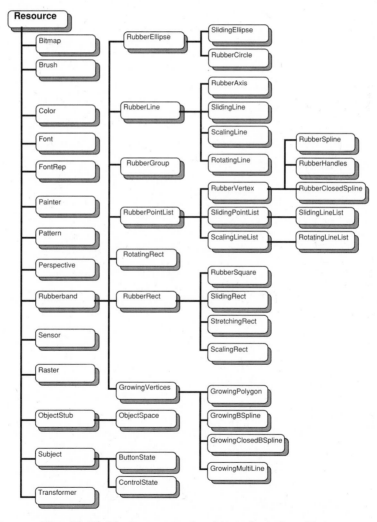

Fig. 15.15. The Resource class hierarchy in InterViews.

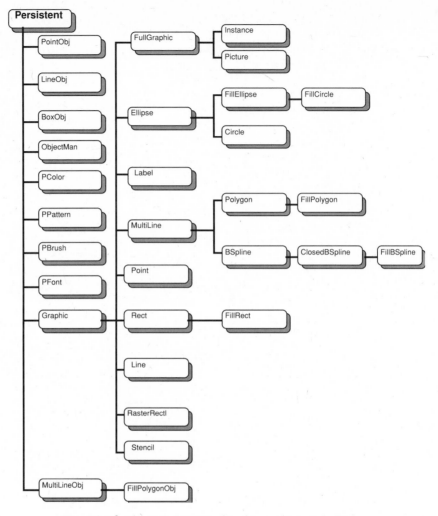

Fig. 15.16. The `Persistent` class hierarchy in InterViews.

World

`World` is the root scene for a display (this is like the root window in X). You must create a `World` object before any other interactors are created. You create the top-level window of the application by inserting into the `World` object a scene that composes the main window of the application. `World` takes care of reading in X resources from a resource file and handling command-line options.

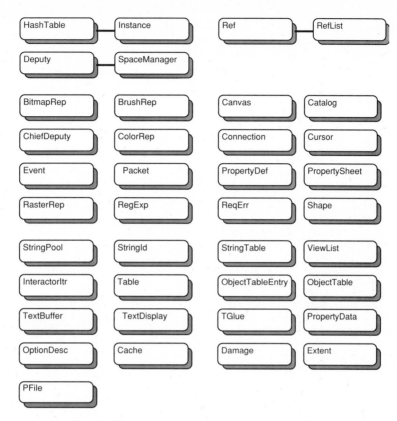

Fig. 15.17. Other supporting classes in InterViews.

MonoScene

A MonoScene is a Scene that can contain a single interactor. Usually, an InterViews application derives a class from MonoScene to serve as the container that holds the interactor hierarchy of the application. An example is the HelloMessage class used in the sayhello application (Listings 15.1 and 15.2).

Resource *Classes*

The classes in the Resource hierarchy (Figure 15.15) are primarily for storing graphics state parameters and geometry information and for supporting graphical output. This hierarchy includes classes such as the following:

- Painter is the object that interactors use to perform graphical output. A Painter provides drawing operations—such as Line, Rect, FillRect, and BSpline—and manages graphics states—such as foreground and background colors, font, and fill pattern.

- Transformer stores a transformation matrix for graphical output. It is used by the Painter.

- Color represents a color.

- Brush is used for line drawing.

- Font represents a font.

- Pattern specifies a pattern to be used for area fills.

Additionally, the Resource class hierarchy also includes classes for special purposes, such as the following:

- Sensor defines which input events are relevant to an interactor. Any interactor interested in input events (mouse or keyboard events) has a Sensor that defines the events of interest to that interactor.

- ButtonState represents the internal state of a Button. You can think of a Button as being the view of a ButtonState.

- RubberBand provides support for animating graphics objects, such as rectangles and circles. It has several subclasses, such as RubberRect, which lets a corner of a rectangle track the mouse movement; SlidingRect, which is a fixed-size rectangle that moves around with the mouse pointer; and RotatingRect, which is a rectangle that rotates to follow the mouse pointer.

Graphic *Classes*

InterViews provides two types of graphical output:

- *Immediate-mode* graphics, in which an Interactor uses a Painter to generate graphical output that appears immediately on the display, but the graphic is not available for any further manipulation

- *Structured graphics*, with which you treat graphical elements such as Line and Circle as objects that can be manipulated

The Graphic subtree of the Persistent hierarchy (Figure 15.16) provides a set of classes that support object-oriented structured graphics. The Graphic classes include the following graphical objects:

- `Point` represents a point.

- `Line` denotes a line.

- `MultiLine` is a number of connected lines.

- `Rect` and `FillRect` represent unfilled and filled rectangles.

- `Ellipse` and `FillEllipse` are unfilled and filled ellipses.

- `Circle` and `FillCircle` are unfilled and filled circles.

- `BSpline`, `ClosedBSpline`, and `FillBSpline` represent open, closed, and filled B-splines (a *B-spline* is a mathematical description of a smooth curve joining a number of points).

- `Label` is a text string.

- `Instance` refers to another `Graphic`.

- `Picture` contains a collection of `Graphic` objects.

Learning More About InterViews

The InterViews distribution package comes with a few short tutorials about the software. They are a good starting point for newcomers to the InterViews toolkit. In particular, you will get a good overview of InterViews, especially the way InterViews is envisioned to be used, from the paper by the authors of InterViews (Mark A. Linton, John M. Vlissides, and Paul R. Calder), "Composing User Interfaces with InterViews," *Computer* 22, No. 2 (February 1989), pages 8–22.

If you are adventurous enough, there is another source of information. InterViews comes with complete source code for the library, as well as the source for a number of sample applications. You can get accurate information about the Interviews classes by studying these source files. The sample applications are also helpful. After seeing how an application behaves, you can look at the relevant source files to see which InterViews classes are used to achieve that behavior.

The best way to learn more about InterViews is to start using the InterViews toolkit. In the beginning, you can get by with a few commonly used components. The InterViews reference manual provides adequate information for using these components. Once you are familiar with the basic style of InterViews—hierarchical composition of interface—you will not have any problem creating applications as powerful as any you could create with other X toolkits.

Summary

The X Window System is a network-transparent windowing system based on the client-server model. The X server process, running on a workstation with a bit-mapped graphics display, manages windows in which the output from X client applications appear. Whether the X clients run locally or on a remote computer, they send requests to the server using a communication channel. The bytes exchanged between a client and the server conform to the X protocol. X version 11 (X11) consists of the X server, X protocol, and Xlib—the library of C routines that programmers use to access the server. The designers of X sought to provide only primitive building capabilities necessary to support user interaction. They refrained from dictating how a user interface should look and feel. Thus, X can be used to build a variety of user interfaces.

C++ programmers wishing to use object-oriented programming techniques to create X applications can either incorporate Xlib functions into their own classes or use an existing toolkit such as InterViews. Calling Xlib functions in your C++ programs can be tricky if you are using X Version 11 Release 3 (X11R3), because the header files do not include function prototypes. X11R4 includes the prototypes, but there may be small incompatibilities stemming from the use of reserved keywords such as `class`, `new`, and `delete`.

Using InterViews may give you an easy way of writing X applications in C++, because InterViews provides a set of C++ classes that represent components of user interface and graphic objects. The philosophy of InterViews is that you compose the user interface by placing components in a scene in a hierarchical fashion. This chapter gives an overview of the InterViews class library and shows how to use some of these classes in a simple application.

## Chapter 16

Advanced Topics in C++

The previous chapters show what C++ and object-oriented programming techniques can do and how you can use these tools to build applications for environments such as MS-DOS and Microsoft Windows. Despite its well-known capabilities, C++ is relatively young, having been first released commercially in late 1985. In fact, features such as multiple inheritance and the iostream library were introduced in AT&T C++ Release 2.0, which became available only in 1989. The current release of AT&T C++ is 2.1, but AT&T is already working on Release 3.0. Two probable new additions to that release are

- Templates (also known as Parameterized types)

- Exception handling

Another ongoing development that affects the future of C++ is the work being done by the American National Standards Institute (ANSI) C++ Technical Committee, X3J16. The X3J16 committee is developing a draft proposal for a standard for the C++ programming language, starting with the following documents as the basis:

- The ANSI C standard (*ANSI X3.159-1989—Programming Language C*)

- The *AT&T C++ Language System Release 2.1 Reference Manual* (also available as *The Annotated C++ Reference Manual* by Margaret A. Ellis and Bjarne Stroustrup, published by Addison-Wesley in 1990)

The X3J16 committee has already decided to include templates in the C++ draft standard, and it is considering the inclusion of exception handling as well. The templates will be based on the experimental design presented in Chapter 14 of *The Annotated C++ Reference Manual*, or *ARM* as it is popularly known. When the X3J16 committee considers exception handling, the design will most likely be derived from the material in Chapter 15 of the ARM. Therefore, this final chapter of the book gives you an overview of templates and exception handling based on information available in the ARM and some recent articles in the *Journal of Object-Oriented Programming* (published bimonthly by SIGS Publications, New York).

> *Templates* enable you to define generic classes, and *exception handling* provides a uniform way to cope with errors in C++ programs.
>
> Because templates and exception handling are not yet a part of the C++ language, this chapter can only show a few hypothetical examples to illustrate how you might use these features. These examples are based on the proposed syntax for templates and the proposed mechanism for exception handling, but these may change in the future. If your C++ compiler supports templates and exception handling, you should consult the compiler's documentation for the latest information on using these features.

Templates

When it becomes available in C++, a *template* will define a family of classes or functions. For instance, a class template for a Stack class will let you create stacks of various data types such as int, float, and char*. Similarly, a function template for a sort function would help you create versions of the sort function for sorting, for instance, an array of int, float, or char* data. If you think about it for a moment, when you create a class or function template, you essentially want to define a class or a function with a *parameter*—a data type, for instance, that you would specify when the class or function is actually being used. This is why templates are often referred to as *parameterized types*.

Stacks for int *and* float

As an example of a class declaration with a parameter, consider the following simple declaration of a stack class, named intStack, that is capable of holding int variables:

```
const int MAXSIZE = 128;

class intStack            // Define a stack for int variables
{
public:
    intStack() { _stackptr = 0;}
    int push(int x) {return _array[_stackptr++] = x;}
    int pop() { return _array[-_stackptr];}
    int empty() const { return (_stackptr == 0);}
```

```
private:
    int _array[MAXSIZE]; // Internally, an array stores the
data
    int _stackptr;
};
```

The `intStack` class uses an array of `int` variables as the internal storage for the stack. Here is how you might use the `intStack` class:

```
    intStack i_stack;

  // Push an integer value
    i_stack.push(301);

  // Pop a number off the stack
    int last_val = i_stack.pop();
```

Now suppose you want to define a stack of `floats`, a `floatStack` class, that uses the same internal mechanism as `intStack`. If you think about it, you will realize that you can define the `floatStack` class simply by replacing every `int` in the `intStack` class declaration with `float`. What this tells you is that if you were able to define a single `Stack` class that accepted a data type as a parameter and if the C++ compiler permitted you to create new class definitions by invoking `Stack`'s definition with any data type, you could use a single definition to create stacks for any type of data. In other words, what you need is a way to define *parameterized* classes. The proposed templates mechanism will enable you to define classes and functions with parameters, but there is a way to define generic classes even now. The next discussion explains how to use preprocessor macros to do this.

Generic Classes Using Macros

Before describing the syntax of templates, let us go over an alternate way of defining generic classes using the macro facility of the C preprocessor. After all, a preprocessor macro can take parameters, so it should be possible to use the `#define` directive to create a class definition that is parameterized. You can indeed use macros to define generic classes. In fact, AT&T's `cfront` translator comes with a header file named `generic.h` that defines two macros to simplify declaration of generic classes:

- The macro `name2(a,b)` takes two arguments and "pastes" them together to create a new macro, `ab`. With ANSI standard C preprocessors, the `name2` macro can be defined using the token-pasting operator `##` as follows:

```
    #define name2(a,b) a##b
```

With this macro, if you write

```
name2(int,Stack)
```

the preprocessor expands it to the symbol `intStack`. Note that the `generic.h` file in the Borland C++ compiler does not define the `name2` macro; instead, it defines a macro named `_Paste2` that performs exactly like `cfront`'s `name2`.

- The `declare` macro takes two arguments and is defined as follows:

```
#define declare(x,y) name2(x,declare)(y)
```

The `declare` macro pastes the string `declare` to the first argument and passes the second argument to the resulting macro. Thus, if you were to write

```
declare(Stack,int)
```

the preprocessor would expand it and invoke the macro with

```
Stackdeclare(int)
```

Now that you know how the `name2` and `declare` macros work, let us see how you can use them to define a generic stack class. The following are the steps:

1. Define a macro `Stack` with a data type as an argument. Let this macro create a new macro name by concatenating the symbol `Stack` with the type. You can use the `name2` macro from `generic.h` to define the `Stack` macro like this:

```
#include <generic.h>
#define Stack(TYPE) name2(TYPE,Stack)
```

With this definition, `Stack(int)` will result in the symbol `intStack`.

2. Define another macro, `Stackdeclare(TYPE)`, that takes a data type as an argument and defines the class named `Stack(TYPE)`. Listing 16.1 shows how the `Stackdeclare(TYPE)` macro is defined.

Listing 16.1. `gstack.h`—A generic stack implemented using macros.

```
//------------------------------------------------------------
// File: gstack.h
//
// Macro to declare a generic stack.
// NOTE: This version is for AT&T cfront 2.1. If you are using
// Borland C++, change "name2" to "_Paste2" as noted later.

#if !defined(__GSTACK_H)
```

```
#define __GSTACK_H

#include <generic.h> // Define the macros "name2" and "declare"

const int MAXSIZE = 128;

// Borland C++ Users: Change "name2" on next line to "_Paste2"

#define Stack(TYPE) name2(TYPE,Stack)

// Skip the ending semicolon in the class declaration embedded
// in the following macro definition. The semicolon will be
// added when the macro is invoked. Also, every line must end
// with a backslash followed by a newline so that the
// preprocessor treats this as a single macro definition

#define Stackdeclare(TYPE)                              \
class Stack(TYPE)                                       \
{                                                       \
public:                                                 \
    Stack(TYPE)() { _stackptr = 0;}                     \
    TYPE push(TYPE x) {return _array[_stackptr++] = x;} \
    TYPE pop() { return _array[-_stackptr];}            \
    int empty() const { return (_stackptr == 0);}       \
private:                                                \
    TYPE _array[MAXSIZE];                               \
    int  _stackptr;                                     \
}

#endif
```

After defining the macros Stack(TYPE) and Stackdeclare(TYPE), as shown in Listing 16.1, you can declare and use a stack for int variables as follows:

```
// Declare a Stack for int types
declare(Stack,int);

main()
{
    Stack(int) id_stack;       // Define an instance of the stack


    id_stack.push(100);        // Push a value on to the stack
    int val = id_stack.pop(); // Pop a value from the stack
// . . .
}
```

Here is what happens. The invocation of the `declare(Stack,int)` macro expands to a call to `Stackdeclare(int)`, which declares a class named `intStack`— the name created by the macro `Stack(int)`. After this declaration, the statement

```
Stack(int) id_stack;
```

creates an instance of `intStack` named `id_stack`. You then can use the stack in the usual manner by calling its `push` and `pop` functions.

Listing 16.2 shows the file `gstack.C`, which is a complete program for testing the generic stack.

Listing 16.2. `gstack.C`—A test program for the generic stack.

```
//------------------------------------------------------------
// Main program to test the "generic stack."

#include "gstack.h"
#include <iostream.h>

// Declare a Stack for int types
declare(Stack,int);

int main()
{
    Stack(int) id_stack;

// Push some integers
    cout << "Pushing: " << endl;
    cout << id_stack.push(1) << endl;
    cout << id_stack.push(2) << endl;

// Pop one by one and display
    cout << "Popping: " << endl;
    cout << id_stack.pop() << endl;
    cout << id_stack.pop() << endl;

    if(id_stack.empty())
        cout << "Stack is now empty." << endl;

    return 0;
}
```

When compiled and run, this program correctly displays the following output:

```
Pushing:
1
2
Popping:
2
1
Stack is now empty.
```

Now if you need a stack for `float` variables, you can declare and use one as follows:

```
#include "gstack.h"
// Declare a stack for floats
    declare(Stack,float);
// . . .

// Create an instance of a stack of floats
    Stack(float) v_stack;

// Use the stack
    v_stack.push(29.95);
```

From this example, you can see that it is possible to create parameterized class definitions with the help of the C preprocessor, but the process is somewhat convoluted. Also, some preprocessors may not be able to handle the large macro definitions needed by some generic classes. Clearly, a simpler way of declaring parameterized classes would be a welcome addition to the C++ language.

Class Templates

In C++, the reserved keyword `template` is meant for defining class and function templates (the keyword is already reserved, even though templates are not yet a part of the language). With the proposed syntax, the template for a generic `Stack` class might look like this:

```
const int MAXSIZE = 128;

template<class T> class Stack
{
public:
    Stack(T)() { _stackptr = 0;}
    T push(T x) {return _array[_stackptr++] = x;}
    T pop() { return _array[--_stackptr];}
    int empty() const { return (_stackptr == 0);}
```

```
private:
    T     _array[MAXSIZE];
    int   _stackptr;
};
```

If you compare this with the approach based on the macros defined in `generic.h`, you will find that the class definition is very similar. Essentially, the `template<class T>` prefix in the class declaration states that you are going to declare a class template and that you would use T as a class name in the declaration. Thus, `Stack` is a parameterized class with the type T as its parameter. With this definition of the `Stack` class template, you can create stacks for different data types like this:

```
Stack<int>     istack;     // A stack for int variables
Stack<float>   fstack;     // A stack for float variables
```

You could similarly define a generic `Array` class as follows:

```
template<class T> class Array
{
public:
    Array(int n=16) { _pa = new T(_size = n);}
    T& operator[](int i);
// . . .

private:
    T*    _pa;
    int   _size;
};
```

You can then create instances of different `Array` types in the following manner:

```
Array<int>     iArray(128);    // A 128-element int array
Array<float>   fArray(32);     // A 32-element float array
```

Function Templates

Like class templates, function templates define a family of functions parameterized by a data type. For example, you could define a parameterized `sort` function for sorting any type of array like this:

```
template<class T> void sort(Array<T>)
{
// Body of function (do the sorting)
// . . .
}
```

This essentially declares a set of overloaded `sort` functions, one for each type of `Array`. When defining the sort function, you will need a comparison operator for the class T. Thus, one restriction on using the `sort` function template is that the class you provide in place of T must have a comparison operator defined.

You can invoke the `sort` function just like any ordinary function. The C++ compiler will analyze the arguments to the function and call the proper version of the function. For example, given `iArray` and `fArray`, the arrays of `int` and `float`, respectively, you can apply the `sort` function to each as follows:

```
sort(iArray);  // Sort the array of int
sort(fArray);  // Sort the array of float
```

Member Function Templates

When we declared the `Array` class template, we left the `operator[]` member function undefined. Each member function in a class template is also a function template. When the member functions are defined inline, you do not have to use any special syntax for the member functions of a template class; just use the template parameters as and when necessary in the function's body and in its argument list. When the member function of a class template is defined outside the body of the class, you have to follow a specific syntax. For instance, the `operator[]` function of the `Array` class template may be defined like this:

```
template<class T> T& Array<T>::operator[](int i)
{
    if(i < 0 || i >= _size)
    {
// Handle error condition. Assume that there is a function
// named "handle_error" available for this purpose.
        handle_error("Array: index out of range");
    }
    else
        return _pa[i];
}
```

Advantages of Templates

Templates will help you define classes that are general in nature (generic classes). Even though generic classes can be defined now, templates make the process simpler and safer. Here is how.

So far, you have seen two ways to define generic classes. Early in this chapter you saw how the macros defined in the generic.h header file can be used to declare parameterized classes. Although these macros work, they are cumbersome to define and use. The proposed syntax for templates will greatly simplify the process of defining parameterized classes.

The other approach to generic classes is explained in Chapter 8, which presents a way of creating a generic singly_linked_list class by starting with a singly linked list of a base class called single_link and making sure that any data type that needs to be stored in the list is also derived from the single_link class. The only problem with that approach is that the member functions of the singly_linked_list class return pointers to single_link and not pointers to the type of objects actually stored in the list. Thus, you have to cast each pointer returned by the singly_linked_list class to your data type before you use it. Such type casts defeat the type-checking facilities of C++ and increases the potential for errors. With class templates, you can eliminate the need for any type casts and define parameterized classes in a safe manner.

Exception Handling

Exceptions refer to unusual conditions in a program. They can be outright errors that cause the program to fail or conditions that can lead to errors. Typically, you can always detect when certain types of errors are about to occur. For instance, in implementing the subscript function (operator[]) of the Array class, you could detect whether the index is beyond the range of valid values. Such errors are called *synchronous exceptions*, because they occur at a predictable time—an error caused by the array index going out of bounds will occur only after executing a statement where that out-of-bounds index is used. Contrast this with *asynchronous exceptions*, which are caused by events beyond the control of your program. Therefore, your program cannot anticipate their time of occurrence. The proposed exception-handling mechanism for C++ is meant to cope with synchronous exceptions only.

Benefits of Exception Handling

Although it is easy to detect synchronous exceptions, such as failing to allocate memory or an array index going out of bounds, it is hard to decide what to do when the exception occurs. Consider the malloc function in the ANSI C library. When you call malloc to allocate a block of memory, you get back a pointer to the allocated block. If malloc fails, it returns a NULL pointer (a zero address). The burden of checking for this exceptional condition is on the caller. As a C programmer, you are probably quite familiar with blocks of code like this:

```
#define MAXCHR 80
char *line;


if((line = (char *) malloc(MAXCHR)) == NULL)
{
/* Failed to allocate memory; print message and exit */
    fprintf(stderr, "Failed to allocate memory.\n");
    exit(1);
}
```

Whenever you call `malloc` in your program, you essentially repeat similar blocks of code over and over again.

Now consider an alternative. Suppose `malloc` was written so that whenever it fails, it would *jump* (ANSI C's `setjmp` and `longjmp` functions provide the capability to jump from one function to another) to a function that you specify, perhaps with an error code as an argument—a code that indicates what went wrong. Such a function is typically called a *handler* or an *exception handler*. If you do not provide an exception handler, `malloc` could jump to a default handler that prints a message and exits. If you do provide a handler, you could handle the error condition any way you wish. In certain applications, you may not even have to terminate the application. Best of all, with such an exception handler installed, you could call `malloc` without worrying about an error return, because you know that, in case of any allocation failure, `malloc` will jump to the exception handler. Thus, if you know that there is an exception handler, you can eliminate all those extra lines of code that checks if `malloc` has returned a `NULL` pointer.

Like `malloc`, C++ class libraries will have many functions that will detect an error condition and will have to decide how to handle the condition. If exception handling is an integral part of C++, all class libraries will have a uniform way to cope with all "exceptional conditions." That is why there is an ongoing effort to provide exception handling in C++.

The Trouble with `setjmp` and `longjmp`

In ANSI C, the pair of functions, `setjmp` and `longjmp`, enables you to jump back from many levels of function calls to a specific location in your program. In this way, you abort what you were doing and get back to where you started. The `setjmp` function saves the "state" or the "context" of the process; `longjmp` uses the saved context to revert to a previous point in the program. The context (or "state") of a process refers to the information that will enable you to reconstruct exactly the way the process is at a particular point in its flow of execution. In ANSI C, an array data type named `jmp_buf` is available for storing information needed to restore a calling environment. This data type is defined in the header file `<setjmp.h>`.

To understand the exact mechanics of setjmp and longjmp, look at the following lines of code:

```
#include <setjmp.h>
jmp_buf saved_context;

main()
{
    if (setjmp(saved_context) == 0)
    {
// This is executed the first time set_jmp is called
        process_commands();
    }
    else
    {
// This block is executed when longjmp is called
        handle_error();
    }
}

process_commands()
{
    int error_flag = 0;
// When an error occurs, error_flag is set to 1
// . . .
    if(error_flag) longjmp(saved_context, 1);
}
```

When you call the setjmp function, it will save the current context in the jmp_buf variable named saved_context and return a zero. In this case, the first if statement in main is satisfied, and the process_commands function is called. If there is any error in process_commands, the error_flag will be set to a nonzero value, and we will call longjmp with the following arguments:

- The first argument is the jmp_buf variable, which contains the context to which longjmp should return.

- The second argument specifies the return value to be used during this return.

The longjmp function will first revert the calling environment to this saved state; this amounts to "unrolling" or "unwinding" the stack back to where it was when setjmp was originally called. After reverting to the saved context, longjmp returns. When the return statement in longjmp is executed, it will be just like returning from the call to setjmp that originally saved the buffer saved_context, except that the returned value will be what you provide as the second argument to longjmp. Thus, calling longjmp causes the program to "jump" into the else block of the first if statement in main. In this way, the setjmp and longjmp pair gives you the capability to jump unconditionally from one C function to another without using conventional return statements. Essentially, setjmp marks the destination of the jump and longjmp acts as a nonlocal goto that executes the jump.

When you first look at it, a combination of setjmp and longjmp appears to be the ideal way to handle exceptions in C++. This is indeed true and the proposed exception-handling mechanism (to be described later) can be implemented using setjmp and longjmp, but only because the proposed design also provides a solution to another problem.

The problem is the following. In C++, class instances have to initialized by calling class constructors and destroyed by calling the corresponding destructors. Because longjmp abruptly jumps back to a previous point in the execution of the program, there will be situations in which a constructor has been called, but a jump occurs before calling the destructor. In such cases, any memory allocated by a constructor will not be freed, because the call to the destructor is skipped. There may be other problems as well, because the internal state of some objects may be left in an unknown condition. Thus, if you use setjmp and longjmp to handle exceptions, there must be a way to call the destructors of all relevant objects before you call longjmp. Although this chapter will not provide the details, this is precisely what a setjmp/longjmp-based implementation of the exception-handling mechanism has to do in practice.

Proposed Exception-Handling Mechanism for C++

Andrew Koenig and Bjarne Stroustrup have proposed an exception-handling mechanism for C++, which they describe in their recent paper, "Exception Handling for C++," in the *Journal of Object-Oriented Programming* 3, No.2 (July-August 1990), pages 16–33. In this paper, the authors outline a portable implementation of the proposed design based on C's setjmp/longjmp mechanism. In particular, they describe a scheme to solve the problem of ensuring that the destructors are called correctly before you "unwind" the stack. The following sections summarize how you will see the proposed exception-handling features as a programmer.

An Example

Let us start with an example. Consider the Forms software of Chapter 13. That software uses a Form class to represent a form. Form has a member function, read, to read the definition of a form from a file. Suppose you are rewriting read to use the proposed exception-handling mechanism to cope with the exception caused by the failure to open a specified file. Here is how you would add exception handling to the read function of the Form class:

1. Define a class with a descriptive name, say `FormIOException`, representing the exception that can occur when you are trying to read or write forms. You might declare it as follows:

```
class FormIOException
{
public:
    FormIOException(char* filename) :
        _filename(filename) {}
private:
    char* _filename;
}
```

2. In the `Form::read` function, when the file cannot be opened, *throw* a `FormIOException` like this:

```
void Form::read(const char* filename)
{
// Open an input stream on the specified file
    ifstream fs1(filename);
    if(!fs1)
    {
// Throw exception if file could not be opened
        throw FormIOException(filename);
    }
// Continue with normal processing
// . . .
}
```

That's how you would throw the exception. The code that *catches* the exception will be provided by the programmer using the `Form` class. It would look like this:

```
// Create a form and read in its definition from a file
    Form invoice;

// Be prepared to catch any exceptions
    try
    {
// If an exception is "thrown," control will transfer to the
// catch block.
        invoice.read("invoice.def");
    }
    catch(FormIOException fio)
    {
// You can display a message or display a dialog box informing
// the user that the file could not be opened
        cout << "Error opening " << fio._filename << endl;
    }
```

This example illustrates the essential features of the proposed exception-handling mechanism. There are a few other important points that are summarized next.

Summary of Exception-Handling Mechanism

The general syntax of exception handling can be illustrated as follows:

```
// Exception classes
   class IOException;
   class MemAllocException;
   class MathError;

// Place inside a "try" block code that may throw exceptions
   try
   {
       process_commands();
   }

// Place the exception-handling code inside "catch" blocks--one
// for each type of exception

   catch(IOException io)
   {
// Errors in I/O
// . . .
   }
   catch(MemAllocException mem)
   {
// "Out of memory" errors
// . . .
   }
   catch(MathError math)
   {
// Handle math errors
// . . .
   }
   catch(...)  // Use ... to mean any exception
   {
// Handle all other exceptions here
// . . .
   }
```

As you can see, each `try` block can have a number of associated `catch` blocks that establish handlers for various exceptions. The `catch` blocks are tried in the order of appearance. You should place the `catch(...)` last, because this block is meant for any type of exception.

A function that detects errors and throws exceptions can indicate the specific exceptions that it might throw. Suppose a function named `setup_data` throws the exceptions `IOException` and `MemAllocException`. The function's declaration can indicate this as follows:

```
void setup_data() throw(IOException, MemAllocException);
```

The list of possible exceptions is called the *exception specification* of the function.

Special Functions

There are two special functions that are meant for handling exceptions that occur during exception handling itself:

- `void terminate();` is called when you do not provide an exception handler for a thrown exception or when an error occurs during the stack unwinding. The `terminate` function, by default, calls the `abort()` function from the ANSI C library. You can, however, have `terminate` call a function that you can set up by calling the `set_terminate` function which is declared as follows:

  ```
  typedef void (*PtrFuncVoid)();
  PtrFuncVoid set_terminate(PtrFuncVoid);
  ```

  If you write a function named `handle_termination` to handle the termination, you can have `terminate()` call it by doing the following:

  ```
  PtrFuncVoid old_term_handler; // To save old handler
  void handle_termination();       // New handler
  old_term_handler = set_terminate(handle_termination);
  ```

- `void unexpected();` is called if a function throws an exception that is not in its exception specification—the list of exceptions that the function is supposed to throw. The default action of `unexpected()` is to call `terminate()`, which in turn calls `abort()` to exit the program. Like `set_terminate`, there is a `set_unexpected` function with which you specify a function that `unexpected()` should call. You use `set_unexpected` in the same manner as `set_terminate`:

  ```
  typedef void (*PtrFuncVoid)();
  PtrFuncVoid old_unexpected;  // To save old handler
  void handle_unexpected();    // New handler
  old_unexpected = set_unexpected(handle_unexpected);
  ```

Summary

Even though C++ is already proving useful in many practical problems, it is still in its infancy and lacks certain features such as *exception handling* and *templates*. Exception handling will provide a uniform way to handle errors in C++ class libraries and programs. Templates will support the definition of parameterized classes and functions. The American National Standards Institute (ANSI) X3J16 committee, which is developing a draft standard for the C++ programming language, plans to add templates and exception handling to the C++ language. The X3J16 committee will define these features using the experimental designs presented in Chapters 14 and 15 of *The Annotated C++ Reference Manual* (ARM) by Margaret Ellis and Bjarne Stroustrup (Addison-Wesley, 1990). This chapter gives an overview of templates and exception handling based on the designs presented in the ARM.

Part Five

Appendixes and Index

Appendix A: Glossary

Appendix B: C++ Language Reference

Appendix C: C++ Compilers and Class Libraries

Appendix D: ANSI C Headers

Index

Glossary

abstract class   A class that cannot have any instance. Usually defined to specify the behavior of classes that will be derived from it.

analysis   In software development, the stage in which a problem is studied to understand the requirements.

anonymous union   An unnamed union in C++. All members of the union share the same storage, and the members are used just like ordinary variables.

base class   In C++, a class from which other classes are derived. The derived classes inherit from the base class.

call by reference   A function call mechanism that passes arguments to a function by passing the address of each argument rather than its value.

call by value   A function call mechanism that passes arguments to a function by passing a copy of each argument's value.

cfront   AT&T's C++ translator.

class   A group of objects that share common properties, common behavior, and common relationships. In C++, a class can be used to define a new data type.

client   An object that uses the services of another object. The object providing the service is the *server*.

constructor   In C++, a special member function with the same name as the class, which is called whenever an instance of a class is created. The constructor initializes a newly created instance of a class.

container class   A class that can store a collection of other objects and provides a way to iterate over the collection.

derived class   In C++, a class that inherits the data and functions of another class (the *base class*).

destructor   In C++, a special member function that is called immediately before an instance of a class is destroyed. The destructor should reverse the effects of the *constructor* and clean up. The destructor's name is constructed by adding a tilde (~) prefix to the name of the class.

DFD   An acronym that stands for *data flow diagram*. This is a diagramming notation that depicts the flow of data through a system and identifies the processes that manipulate the data.

dynamic binding   *Binding* refers to the association of a function name to the actual code to be executed. In dynamic binding, the code executed in response to a function call is not determined until run time (when the program is running). Dynamic binding is also known as *late binding*.

encapsulation   The technique of hiding internal details of an object from the outside world. In C++, encapsulation is achieved using the `class` construct together with the access control offered by the `public`, `private`, and `protected` keywords. Also known as information hiding.

free store   A pool of memory from which storage for objects is allocated (synonymous with *heap*).

friend   In C++, a friend of a class can access the private members of the class. The friend can be a function or an entire class.

generic class   See *parameterized type*.

heap   The pool of memory from which C and C++ programs allocate storage for new objects. C's `malloc` and C++'s `new` allocate objects on the heap.

implementation   In software, the source code that embodies a realization of the software design.

information hiding   See *encapsulation*.

inheritance   A mechanism that allows one class to share the structure and behavior of another class. In C++, a *derived class* inherits from one or more *base classes*. The derived class inherits all member functions of the base class.

instance   An object defined by a class.

instatiation   The process of creating an object from a class definition.

iostream   In C++, an object-oriented class library for I/O. Available in AT&T C++ Release 2.0 and later (and in many other C++ compilers).

late binding   See *dynamic binding*.

linkage   In C++, linkage specifies whether two names in different *scopes* refer to the same object or function. Linkage can be internal or external. All occurrences of a name with external linkage refer to the same object or function.

member function   In C++, functions defined inside a `struct` or a `class`. These functions define the operations that can be performed on the objects of that class.

method   In Smalltalk, an operation on an object. Similar to *member function* in C++.

module   In C++, a source file representing a unit of the program.

multiple inheritance   An inheritance mechanism that allows a class to inherit from more than one class. In C++, multiple inheritance allows a class to be derived from a number of base classes.

MVC   An acronym that stands for *Model-View-Controller*. This term denotes Smalltalk-80's architecture for applications. Each application is separated into three layers: the *Model* represents the application-specific code, the *View* takes care of the graphics that display the model to the user, and the *Controller* handles the user's interactions with the application.

object   An instance of a class.

object-oriented analysis   A method of analysis in which the requirements are determined in terms of real-world objects, their behavior, and their interactions.

object-oriented design   A method of transforming software requirements into specifications for objects and derivation of class hierarchies from which the objects can be created. Object-oriented design methods typically use a diagramming notation to represent the class hierarchy and to express the interactions among the objects.

object-oriented programming   Implementation of programs using objects, preferably in an object-oriented language such as C++.

overloaded function   A function with more than one definition. The multiple definitions differ only in the number and type of arguments. The compiler resolves calls to an overloaded function on the basis of the number and type of arguments.

parameterized type   In C++, a class definition that depends on one or more parameters. With parameterized types, a new class can be defined by setting the parameters in a single parameterized definition. The `template` keyword in C++ will support parameterized type. Also known as *generic class*.

persistence   The property of an object that allows it to outlast the execution of a program.

polymorphism   The program property in which the same operation may have different effects on different classes. In C++, polymorphism is supported through virtual functions and dynamic binding (available when virtual functions are invoked through a pointer to the base class).

private   In C++, an access specifier that delineates a section of a class so that only member functions of the current class can access the variables and functions in that section.

protected   In C++, an access specifier that delineates a section of a class so that only member functions of the current class and its derived classes can access the variables and functions in that section.

protocol   A specification of the ways in which operations may be performed on an object.

public   In C++, an access specifier that delineates a section of a class so that any function in the program can access the variables and functions in that section.

responsibility-driven design   A software design method that models software as a collection of collaborating objects, each with specific responsibilities. *Collaboration* refers to one class of objects using the facilities of another, and it is modeled by a *client-server* relationship where a client class makes a request to have a specific task performed by the server.

scope   In C++, a region of the source program in which an identifier can be used. In C++, names can have local scope, file scope, or class scope.

server   An object that provides services that are used by other objects. The objects that use the services are the *clients*.

single inheritance   A type of inheritance in which a class can inherit from another class only.

state   The values of the internal attributes of an object.

static binding   A type of binding that associates, at compile time, a function name with the code to be executed when that function is called. Contrast this with *dynamic binding*, in which the same association occurs while the program is executing.

storage class   In C++, the property of an object that determines how long the object's storage remains available to the program. The keywords `auto`, `register`, `static`, and `extern` specify the storage class of an object.

this   In C++, a pointer to the current object. May be used in member functions to refer to the current instance of the class.

virtual   In C++, a virtual function is one qualified by the `virtual` keyword. Usually, derived classes override the virtual functions of the base class. In practice, virtual functions are usually invoked through a pointer to the base class. The C++ compiler ensures that the overridden version of the virtual function from the derived class gets called even though the access is through a pointer to the base class. Because of this property, virtual functions support polymorphism in C++ programs.

Windows   Popular name for Microsoft Windows, a graphical user interface for MS-DOS systems.

X Window System   A network-transparent, device-independent graphical windowing system for bit-mapped displays. Popular on workstations running the UNIX operating system.

C++ Language Reference

This appendix is a concise reference manual for the C++ programming language as of June 1991. The current language definition is based on AT&T C++ Language System Release 2.1. Only selected features of the language are summarized. Many topics, such as the use of classes, are covered in the tutorial chapters (Chapters 4 through 9) earlier in this book. If you need a detailed reference manual for the C++ programming language, you should consult *The Annotated C++ Reference Manual* (ARM) by Margaret Ellis and Bjarne Stroustrup, published by Addison-Wesley in 1990.

Because C++ is based on ANSI standard C, many features of C++ are the same as those in ANSI C. Chapter 4 describes the differences between C++ and ANSI standard C.

When this appendix illustrates the syntax of language constructs, text typeset in `monospace` denotes keywords and punctuation marks that must be entered as shown. Words typeset in `monospace italic` represent placeholders that you can replace with actual symbols (such as names of variables, functions, or macros) of your program. Optional items are shown in square brackets and are monospace italic when they are also variable `[option]`. In the examples, missing lines of code are shown as follows:

```
// . . .
```

Character Set

One or more *source files* constitute a C++ program. Each source file is a text file consisting of letters, digits, underscores, punctuation marks, and whitespace characters as defined here:

letters	A B C D E F G H I J K L M N O P Q R S T U V W X Y Z
	a b c d e f g h i j k l m n o p q r s t u v w x y z
digits	0 1 2 3 4 5 6 7 8 9
underscore	_
punctuation	! # % ^ & * ( ) – + [ ] { } :; ' : " , . / < > ?
	\ ¦ ~
whitespace	space, HT (horizontal tab), VT (vertical tab), newline, form feed

Preprocessing

The compiler or translator processes a C++ source file in several phases, the first being *preprocessing*. The preprocessor reduces the program to a sequence of tokens, collectively known as a *translation unit*.

The preprocessor treats the source file as a sequence of distinct lines and processes each line separately. Lines beginning with a #, optionally preceded by white space, indicate the start of a preprocessor directive. The preprocessor interprets these directives and acts on them. Here are the steps that the preprocessor follows:

1. Replace each *trigraph sequence* (a sequence of three characters that start with two question marks) with its single character equivalent, as follows:

??(	[	??'	^	??>	}
??/	\	??<	{	??-	~
??)	]	??!	¦	??=	#

2. Splice lines by deleting all occurrences of a backslash immediately followed by a newline character. Thus, the following will be treated as a single line:

```
#define ReportError(zzz,emsg,eaction)            \
        {                                         \
            sprintf(ErrMsgBuf, "%s <—", zzz);  \
            strcpy(ErrMsgBuf, emsg);              \
            ErrorMessage(ErrMsgBuf, eaction);  \
        }
```

3. Replace each comment with a single space. A comment is anything enclosed in a /* and */ pair or everything on a line following a pair of slashes (//).

4. Separate each line in the source file into *preprocessing tokens* (these are C++ tokens, as defined later; a file name in an #include directive; or a single character other than white space) and whitespace characters.

5. Act on all directives and expand all macros.

6. Replace each escape sequence with its equivalent character.

7. Concatenate all adjacent string literals.

8. Convert the preprocessing tokens into C++ tokens, discarding all whitespace characters and creating the translation unit in the process.

Preprocessor Macros

You define a macro as follows:

```
#define macro_name token_sequence
```

This causes the preprocessor to replace all subsequent occurrences of *macro_name* with the *token_sequence*. Macros can take arguments, just like functions. You write a function-like macro as:

```
#define macro_name(arg1, arg2, ..., arg_n) token_sequence
```

with no space between the *macro_name* and the left parenthesis. When the preprocessor expands a function-like macro, it replaces any occurrence of the arguments (*arg1, arg2, ...*) in the *token_sequence* with the corresponding actual argument in the macro call. Here is an example:

```
#define square(x) ((x)*(x))
// . . .
c = square(a+b);        // This becomes: c = ((a+b)*(a+b));
pi2 = square(3.14159); // and this: pi2 = ((3.14159)*(3.14159));
```

The # Operator

The # operator, also known as the *stringizing* operator, works as follows. If the # precedes a macro argument, the preprocessor will replace that argument with a string literal created from the actual argument with which the macro is called. Thus, if you write

```
#define show(msg,x) sprintf(msg, #x " = %d", x)
show(buf, count);
```

the second line becomes

```
sprintf(buf, "count"" = %d", count);
```

which, after concatenation of adjacent string literals, results in

```
sprintf(buf, "count = %d", count);
```

The ## Operator

The ## operator concatenates two preprocessing tokens to create a third preprocessing token, which the preprocessor will further expand. For example, if you define

```
#define paste2(a,b) a##b
```

and write

```
class paste2(int,Stack);
```

the result will be

```
class intStack;
```

Furthermore, if you write

```
#define Stack(Type)          paste2(Type,Stack)
#define declare(Stack,Type)  paste2(Stack,declare)(Type)
#define Stackdeclare(Type)   class Stack(Type)
```

then the following macro

```
declare Stack(int);
```

will generate

```
class intStack;
```

The ## operator is also referred to as the *token-pasting* operator, because it creates new tokens by pasting together existing tokens. As you can see, the preprocessor always expands the tokens created by the ## operator.

Undefining a Macro

Use the #undef directive to remove the definition of a macro. Sometimes you have to undefine a macro so that you can define it differently than it is defined in a header file. For example, to remove the definition of the macro named DEBUG, you would write

```
#undef DEBUG
```

Note that nothing happens if the macro DEBUG is not currently defined.

File Inclusion

You can include the contents of a file into the translation unit with the #include directive. This directive starts with an #include followed by one of the following:

- A file name between angle brackets such as

  ```
  #include <filename>
  ```

- A file name inside a pair of double quotes:

  ```
  #include "filename"
  ```

- A previously defined macro name:

  ```
  #include A_MACRO
  ```

where *A_MACRO* must be defined to be a file name in an acceptable form (either in quotes or inside angle brackets).

The #include directives may be nested; an #include directive may appear in a file that is being processed by another #include directive.

Conditional Directives

The preprocessor provides #if, #elif, #else, and #endif directives for conditional compilation of source code. Conditional compilation blocks have the following structure (with optional items shown enclosed in square brackets):

```
#if if_condition
    if_part
 [#elif elif_condition_1
    elif_part_1
#elif elif_condition_2
    elif_part_2]
// . . .
[#else
    else_part]
#endif
```

The first line can be any one of these three: #if, #ifdef, or #ifndef. The conditions are expressions that evaluate to a constant and are assumed to be satisfied if the constant is nonzero. You can use the defined operator in a condition. For example, you can write

```
#if defined(DEBUG)
// This part compiled only when DEBUG is defined
// . . .
#endif
```

This is equivalent to writing

```
#ifdef DEBUG
// . . .
#endif
```

You can also use #ifndef to test whether a name is defined. Here is an example:

```
#ifndef TRUE
#define TRUE 1
#endif
```

You can equivalently write this code using the !defined operator as follows:

```
#if      !defined(TRUE)
#define TRUE 1
#endif
```

Other Directives

The #line directive enables you to alter the source file's name and the line number. The syntax is

```
#line line_number ["file_name"]
```

where *line_number* is an integer constant. This directive sets the predefined macros __LINE__ and __FILE__ to *line_number* and the string "*file_name*", respectively.

You can display diagnostic messages using the #error directive. The following is an example:

```
#if !defined(__cplusplus)
#error Please use the C++ compiler
#endif
```

A single # followed by whitespace characters constitute a *null directive*. A null directive does nothing.

Finally, the #pragma directive is available to support compiler-specific behavior. This directive is of the form

```
#pragma token_sequence
```

where the *token_sequence* as well as its meaning depends on the compiler.

Predefined Macros

The macros __cplusplus, __DATE__, __FILE__, __LINE__, __STDC__, and __TIME__ are already defined by the C++ preprocessor. Table 4.3 explains the meaning of all but the first macro. The __cplusplus macro is defined whenever a C++ compiler is compiling the program.

C++ Tokens

After preprocessing, the *translation unit* consists of C++ *tokens*, which can be one of the following:

- Identifiers
- Keywords
- Literals
- Operators
- Other separators

Identifiers

An *identifier* is a sequence of letters and digits. The sequence must start with a letter or an underscore.

Keywords

The following 48 identifiers are reserved for use as keywords of the C++ programming language:

```
asm     continue  float    new        signed    try
auto    default   for      operator   sizeof    typedef
break   delete    friend   private    static    union
case    do        goto     protected  struct    unsigned
catch   double    if       public     switch    virtual
char    else      inline   register   template  void
class   enum      int      return     this      volatile
const   extern    long     short      throw     while
```

They cannot be used for any other purpose. Additionally, identifiers starting with two underscores (__) are, by convention, reserved for use by the C++ compiler and the C++ libraries. You will find a short description of the keywords at the end of this appendix.

Literals

Literals are constants. There are four types of constants:

- Integer constant
- Character constant
- Floating-point constant
- String literals

Integer Constants

An *integer constant* consists of a sequence of digits. The starting characters of an integer constant determine the base of the integer value. Following are the rules:

- If the starting digit is not a zero (0), the digits are assumed to be *decimals*.
- If the digits start with a zero (0) followed by other digits, the value is treated as an *octal* integer. Note that the digits 8 and 9 cannot be a part of an octal integer.
- If the integer constant starts with 0x or 0X, the integer is interpreted as a hexadecimal number. The letters A through F (in both lowercase or uppercase) represent the decimal values ten through fifteen.

An integer constant can have a suffix to indicate one of the following types: `int`, `long int`, `unsigned int`, or `unsigned long int`. The suffix is interpreted as follows:

No Suffix: If there is no suffix, a decimal integer constant has the first of the following types that can hold the value: `int`, `long int`, or `unsigned long int`. Octal or hexadecimal constants without suffix get the first of the following types that can represent the value: `int`, `unsigned int`, `long int`, `unsigned long int`.

Suffix u or U: The constant is assigned the first of the following types that has a large enough range to represent the value: `unsigned int`, `unsigned long int`.

Suffix l or L: The constant's type is the first of the following that can represent the value: `long int`, `unsigned long int`.

Suffix (any combination of l *and* u *in lower- or uppercase)*: In this case, the constant is assumed to be of type `unsigned long int`.

Character Constants

A *character constant* is one or more characters enclosed in single quotes. Special characters such as newlines and backspace are represented by the following *escape sequences*:

\a	alert	
\b	backspace	
\f	form feed	
\n	newline	
\r	carriage return	
\t	horizontal tab	
\v	vertical tab	
\\	backslash	\
\'	single quote	'
\"	double quote	"
\?	question mark	?
\<*octal digits*>	octal constant	
\x<*hexadecimal digits*>	hexadecimal constant	

Each escape sequence specifies a single character. Thus, the escape sequence `'\x1b'` can be used to initialize a char variable to the hexadecimal value 1B.

Floating-Point Constants

Floating-point constants denote floating-point values. Several notations are allowed. Here are some examples:

> `29., 29.0, 29.95, 2.995e1, 2.995E1` are double floating-point constants.

> `29.0F` is a `float` and `0.32335678L` is a `long double`.

String Literals

String literals are sequences of characters enclosed in a pair of double quotes. Escape sequences can be embedded in a string literal. Also, adjacent string literals are concatenated. Each string literal defines a `static` array of `chars`. A null byte (a byte containing all zero bits) is automatically added at the end of a string literal.

Uses of Identifiers

You use identifiers as names for the following:

- Functions
- `class` and `struct`
- `union`
- `enum`
- Members of a `class`, `struct`, and `union`
- `typedef`
- objects

The syntax for declaring all of these is described later. An identifier has a *scope* and *linkage*, which are described next.

Scope of Identifiers

Each identifier or name has a *scope* that indicates the region of the program where that identifier can be used. C++ supports the notion of the following types of scope:

- *Local*: Names appearing inside a block statement (enclosed in a pair of curly braces {. . .}) have local scope. You can use these only within that block and only after the actual declaration. Note that you cannot define a function in a local scope. (This means you cannot define one function inside the body of another.)

- *File*: Names appearing outside all blocks and class declarations have file scope. These can be used within that file anywhere after the point where they are declared.

- *Class*: Names of data and function members of a `class` (or `struct`) have class scope. The rules for using names with class scope are discussed later under Classes.

Linkage of Identifiers

The linkage of an identifier is the property that determines whether a name appearing in two different scopes refers to the same object or function. There are two types of linkage:

- *Internal Linkage*: Names with internal linkage, appearing in different scopes, refer to distinct objects or functions. For instance, a name declared with the `static` keyword in a file scope has internal linkage; you can use the name for other functions or objects in another translation unit.

- *External Linkage*: Names in the file scope that are not explicitly declared to have internal linkage (with a `static` keyword) are global names with external linkage. All instances of a name with external linkage refer to the same function or object. You can use the `extern` keyword to indicate that a name has external linkage.

Names with Internal Linkage

Here are some names with internal linkage:

- A function name with the `inline` qualifier (this is why `inline` class member functions must have exactly one definition in a file).

- A name in the file scope that is qualified by the `const` keyword and not explicitly declared `extern`.

- Any name in the file scope that is declared `static`.

Names with External Linkage

Here are some names with external linkage:

- Any name that is explicitly declared `extern`.

- Names of class members that are declared `static`.

- Names of noninline member functions of a class.

Linkage to C

A name with external linkage that is *used* in a C++ program but *defined* in a C source file should be declared to have "C" linkage as follows:

```
extern "C" { declarations }
```

where `declarations` declare C functions. See Chapter 10 for further discussion of the linkage between C and C++.

Objects or Variables

An *object* is a block of storage with an associated identifier. Objects are also referred to as variables. An object has two basic attributes:

- *Storage class*: This determines how long the object exists.

- *Type*: This determines the meaning of the values contained in the object.

Storage Class

There are two basic storage classes:

- *Automatic*: Objects of this storage class exist only within a block statement (a pair of curly braces {. . .})—in local scope. You can specify automatic storage with the `auto` and `register` keywords. Because variables in a local scope are automatic by default, the `auto` keyword is almost never used. The `register` keyword, used to qualify an `auto` variable, is a hint to the compiler that the variable will be heavily used. The compiler may store this variable in a CPU register for faster access.

- *Static*: These objects exist throughout the life of the program. All objects with external linkage ("global objects") have static storage. You can use the `static` keyword to give static storage to local objects and class members.

> The `static` keyword has two different meanings. You can use it to specify internal linkage for a name and, at the same time, specify static (or permanent) storage for an object.

Type

Each name denoting an object or a function has a type, which can be one of the following:

- *Fundamental type*: This refers to the built-in data types, such as the integer types `char` and `int`, and to the floating-point types `float` and `double`.

- *Derived type*: These are types that you can define by combining fundamental types with operators and keywords of the language.

Fundamental Types

There are nine basic integer types:

- char is large enough to store any character from the character set of the language. A char must be able to hold values in the range 0 to 128. The size of a char is typically 1 byte.

- signed char is the same size as a char but can hold a minimum range of values –127 to 127.

- unsigned char is the same size as char, but holds only nonnegative values. The minimum range of values is 0 to 255.

- int is the most appropriate for the underlying CPU, but the size must be able to hold at least a 16-bit value. An int is at least as large as a short and must be able to store values in the range –32,767 to 32,767. Note that if a type is not specified in a declaration, the compiler assumes the type to be int. The signed int designation is equivalent to plain int.

- unsigned int is for storing nonnegative values that, at a minimum, range from 0 to 65,535. You can use the unsigned keyword alone to designate unsigned int.

- long is capable of storing at least a 32-bit signed integer (with values in the range –2,147,483,647 to 2,147,483,647). You can use the following equivalent designations for long: signed long, signed long int, or long int.

- unsigned long is for storing nonnegative 32-bit values (at least). The minimum range of its capacity is from 0 to 4,294,967,295. The designation unsigned long int is equivalent to unsigned long.

- short is equivalent to signed short, short int, or signed short int. A short has a minimum range of –32,767 to 32,767.

- unsigned short is the same size as short but is used to store nonnegative values only. The minimum range is 0 to 65,535. You can write unsigned short as unsigned short int.

There are three basic floating-point types:

- float provides at least 6 decimal digits of precision and can, at a minimum, represent floating-point values in the range -10^{38} to 10^{38}.

- double is capable of representing at least the same range as a float but with a minimum of 10 decimal digits of precision.

- long double is guaranteed to provide at least the same precision and range as a double.

The header files <limits.h> and <float.h>, respectively, specify the characteristics (smallest and largest values) of integer and floating-point data types.

Finally, C++ supports the void type, which is used to indicate the return type of functions that do not return a value.

Derived Types

You can derive an infinite number of derived types from the fundamental types in the following manner (the exact syntax is shown later in this appendix, in the Declarations section):

- Use the class keyword to define a new data type. A class has a number of objects of previously defined types, together with functions for manipulating these objects and rules for restricting access to these objects.

- Define a new type with struct, which is the same as a class but has different default access restrictions.

- Define an array of objects of a predefined type.

- Define a function returning an object of a given type.

- Define pointers to a function or an object.

- Define references to other objects.

- Define a union of objects of different types.

- Define pointers to class members.

Type Conversions

When conversions are needed, the C++ compiler automatically converts the value of an object from one fundamental type to another.

The compiler accepts a char, short, an enum type, or a constant from an enumerated list wherever an int value is expected. The compiler automatically converts the value to an int or, if the value is large enough to require it, an unsigned int.

The compiler performs the following conversions (in the sequence shown) in arithmetic operations involving two operands:

1. First, if one of the operands is long double, convert the other one to long double.

2. Else, if either one is double, convert both operands to double.

3. Else, if either one is `float`, convert both operands to `float`.

4. Else, convert each operand to an integer type (`int` or `unsigned int`, depending on the value).

5. After that, if either operand is `unsigned long`, convert the other to `unsigned long`.

6. Else, if one operand is `long`, convert the other one to `long`.

7. Else, if either operand is `unsigned`, convert the other one to `unsigned`.

8. Else, both operands are `int`.

For user-defined classes, the conversions, if needed, have to be supplied by the class definition.

Expressions, Operators, and Statements

In Tables 4.4 and 4.5, Chapter 4 covers operators and statements in detail. This section presents a few topics and terms that are not mentioned in Chapter 4.

An *lvalue* Expression

An *lvalue expression* (combination of names and operators) has a value that refers to an object or a function. Basically, lvalues can appear on the left-hand side of an assignment statement. For instance, in the following:

```
char buf[10];
buf[0] = 'N';
char* p_buf = buf;
int i = 1;
*(p_buf + i) = '\0';
```

buf, buf[0], p_buf, i, and *(p_buf+i) are lvalue expressions. The names of functions and variables are the simplest types of lvalue expressions.

Declarations

In C++, you have to declare the names (identifiers) of objects and functions before using them. Declarations specify how to interpret identifiers. You can use declarations to do the following:

- Specify the *storage class*, *type*, and *linkage* (these have been described earlier) of the object or function

- Define a function

- Provide initial value for an object

- Give names to enumerated constants (`enum`)

- Declare a new type (`class` and `struct`) or give a new name to an existing type (`typedef`)

Declarations do not always reserve storage for an object or a function—those that do are called *definitions*. For instance, the declaration of an object without an `extern` qualifier is a definition.

General Syntax of Declarations

The exact syntax of a declaration depends on whether you are defining an object or a function. In general, a declaration starts with one or more of the following:

- Storage class specifier: `auto`, `register`, `static`, or `extern`

- The keywords `friend` or `typedef`

- The keywords `const` and `volatile`

- `class` or `struct` when the type is new types

- Name of a type (a fundamental type such as `char`, `int`, and `double` or a `class`, `struct`, or a `typedef` name)

- The `enum` keyword when declaring enumerated types

- The `asm` keyword for assembly language statements

- For function declarations, the keywords `inline` and `virtual`

followed by a comma-separated list of declarations of individual objects, functions, or types. These individual declarations are expressions involving basic types (such as `char`, `int`, `float`, and `double`) and operators (such as `*`, `( )`, and `[ ]`).

Individual Declarations

The declarations of individual objects and functions use type names, pointers, references, and arrays. Additionally, you would use `typedef`s and enumerations in your declarations. The following discussions summarize the syntax of some important constructs.

typedef

You can use `typedef` to give a new name to an existing data type. Here are some examples of `typedef`:

```
typedef short BOOLEAN, WORD;
typedef char* P_CHAR;
typedef void (*PVF)();
```

The first statement defines BOOLEAN and WORD as synonyms for `short`; the second one enables you to use P_CHAR wherever you need a "pointer to a `char`"; and the third line defines PVF as the type "pointer to a function returning `void`." You can use these new names just as you would use any other type:

```
WORD message;              // Define a WORD variable
BOOLEAN all_done = 0;      // Define a BOOLEAN "all_done"
PVF funclist[10];          // Array of pointers to function
typedef P_CHAR *P_P_CHAR;  // Use in a new typedef
```

As the last line of code shows, you can use a `typedef` name in another `typedef`. By judiciously using `typedef`s, you can construct complicated type names easily.

enum

An enum (enumeration) can hold an integer value from a fixed set of named integer constants. You can use an enum variable anywhere an `int` type is used. The following is an example of enum:

```
enum boolean {false = 0, true = 1, no = 0, yes = 1,
              off = 0, on = 1};
enum boolean flag = off;
```

This example shows several properties of enum. The first line defines boolean to be an enumerated type. The enumeration list within the braces shows the names of the constants that are valid values of a enum boolean variable. Each constant can be initialized to a value of your choice, and there can be several constants that use the same value. In this example, the constants false, no, and off are set to 0, whereas true, yes, and on are all set to 1. The second line shows the definition of a boolean enumerated variable named flag, which is initialized to the constant off.

If you define an enumerator inside a class, the definition will be in the scope of that class. To use it outside the class, you have to qualify the names of the enumeration constants with the *class_name::* prefix, where *class_name* is the name of the class where the enumerator is defined.

Pointers

Pointers are declared using the unary * operator. The general form is

```
Type* qualifier_list object_name;
```

where *Type* is the name of a type, *object_name* is the object being defined, and *qualifier_list* is a list of qualifiers that apply to the pointer. The qualifiers can be const, volatile, or both. Here are some pointer declarations:

```
const int *p_i;       // *p_i is constant
int *const p_c_i;     // Pointer p_c_i is constant
const volatile long *p_rt_clock = 0x00000064;
char *title = "Object-Oriented Programming in C++";
```

Pointers to Class Members

You can declare a pointer to a class member as follows:

```
class_name::* optional_qualifier ptr_name;
```

where *class_name* is the name of the class and *ptr_name* is the name of the member-pointer variable. The *optional_qualifier* is const, volatile, or both. See Chapter 6 for a tutorial on pointers to class members.

References

References are declared using the unary & operator. The general form is

```
Type& qualifier_list object_name;
```

where *Type* is the name of a type (cannot be void), *object_name* is the object being defined, and *qualifier_list* is a list of qualifiers that apply to the reference. The qualifiers can be const, volatile, or both. Chapter 4 includes a tutorial discussion of references, which are a feature that ANSI C does not have.

Arrays

An array declaration is denoted by adding as suffix a pair of square brackets to one of the following:

- A fundamental type except void
- A pointer

- A class

- A pointer to a class member

- An enumeration

- Another array

The syntax for declaring an array is

```
a_type[integer_constant];
```

where `a_type` denotes one of the types for which arrays can be declared and `integer_constant` is an optional constant expression that specifies the dimension of the array.

Classes

In C++, you define new data types using the `class` or `struct` keyword. The term *class* refers to these user-defined data types created by `class` or `struct`. A class declaration specifies the variables in the class, the member functions that manipulate these objects, and a set of rules for controlling access to the member functions and member variables. Because `class` is at the heart of object-oriented programming, much of this book is devoted to explaining how to declare, define, and use classes. In particular, Chapters 6 through 9 cover basic class declarations, definitions of member functions, and the use of derivation and `virtual` functions. Therefore, detailed syntax of class declaration is not repeated here.

Keyword Summary

This section gives a summary description of each of C++'s 48 keywords arranged in alphabetical order.

asm is used to embed assembly language statements in C++ programs. The exact usage of the `asm` keyword is implementation-dependent.

auto is a storage class specifier for temporary variables. These variables are created on entering a block statement and destroyed on exiting. Local variables of a function have the `auto` storage class by default.

break enables you to exit the innermost `do`, `while`, or `for` loop. You can also use it to exit from a `switch` statement.

case is used to label the cases in a switch statement.

catch is reserved for future use in the exception-handling mechanism of C++. Chapter 16 describes the planned use of catch.

char is a built-in data type in C++. You can use char to declare character variables and arrays.

class is the basic building block of object-oriented programming in C++. A class contains member variables, member functions that operate on these variables, and a set of rules that control the access to the members of the class. The syntax for declaring a class is as follows:

```
class class_name
{
access_specifier_1:
    type item_1;
    type item_2;
    // . . .
access_specifier_2:
    type item_3;
    // . . .
};
class_name class_1, class_2;
```

where the first declaration defines a class with the name *class_name* and the second one defines two instances of that class: *class_1* and *class_2*. The access specifiers, *access_specifier_1* and *access_specifier_2* can be one of public, private, or protected. The members can be variables or functions. If you do not specify any access specifier, the default access to class members is private.

const is a type qualifier used to indicate that the variable following const may not be modified by the program. This means that you cannot assign a value to that variable, increment it, or decrement it.

continue lets you skip the execution of a loop. It is equivalent to executing a goto to the end of the loop. The continue statement affects the innermost loop in which it appears.

default is used as the label in a switch statement to mark code that will be executed when none of the case labels match the switch expression.

delete is used to deallocate objects that were allocated using new.

do is used with while to form iterative loops like this:

```
do statement while(expression);
```

where the `statement` is executed until the value of the `expression` becomes zero. The `expression` is evaluated after each execution of the `statement`.

double is a floating-point data type in C++. You use `double` to declare double-precision floating-point variables and arrays.

else is used with `if` to control the flow of execution with statements of the form:

```
if(expression) statement_1 else statement_2
```

where `statement_1` is executed if the `expression` is nonzero; otherwise, `statement_2` is executed.

enum defines an integer-valued data type that can take its values from a list of enumerated constants. The declaration has the following syntax:

```
enum etype { elist };
enum etype x1, x2;
```

where the first line shows the definition of an `enum` type named `etype` and the second line actually declares two variables, `x1` and `x2`, of type `etype`. Here `elist` is a comma-separated list of enumerated constants.

extern is used to inform the compiler that an object or a function is defined in another source file and that you want to use it in the current module. For successful linking, the object or function must be declared in one of the program modules without the `static` or the `extern` qualifier.

float is a basic floating-point data type in C++. You use `float` to declare single-precision floating-point variables and arrays.

for is used in iterative loops such as

```
for(expression_1; expression_2; expression_3) statement
```

In a `for` loop, `expression_1` is evaluated once at the beginning of the loop, and the `statement` is executed until `expression_2` becomes zero. The third expression, `expression_3`, is evaluated each time through the loop after executing `statement`.

friend identifies a function or a class that should have access to the `private` and `protected` members of a class.

goto enables you to jump unconditionally to a label in the current function.

if is used to test an expression and execute code only when the expression has a nonzero value. You can use `if` alone or with `else` with the following syntax:

```
if(expression) statement
```

or

```
if(expression) statement_1 else statement_2
```

where the `statement` following the `if` is executed if the `expression` is nonzero (true). When an `else` clause is present, `statement_2` is executed if `expression` is zero.

inline specifies that the body of the class member function should be replicated wherever the function is called. Inline functions may provide faster execution of code, but you get this speed at the expense of an increased storage requirement for code.

int is a basic data type in C++. You use `int` to declare integer variables and arrays. The size qualifiers `short` and `long` are used with `int` to declare an integer of desired size. The size of an `int` is implementation-dependent, but it is at least 2 bytes (capable of holding a 16-bit value).

long is a basic integer type in C++. You can use `long` as a size qualifier for `int` and `unsigned int` variables. Note that `long` alone means `signed long int`.

new is used to allocate objects on the *free store* (or the *heap*). In C++, you should use `new` in lieu of `malloc`.

operator indicates the start of the definition of an operator for a class. For example, a class `String` might define the `==` operator as follows:

```
class String
{
public:
// . . .
  int operator==(const String& s) const;
// . . .
};
```

private indicates that all subsequent members of the `class` or `struct` will have private access—these members are not accessible to any function other than the member functions of that class. The `private` block is indicated as follows:

```
class Form
{
private:
// These members are private
};
```

protected marks the start of a block of members functions and variables that can be accessed only by members of the class itself and by the member functions of all classes derived from it. The protected block is specified as follows:

```
class Form
{
protected:
// These members are protected (available to
// derived classes only)
};
```

public indicates that all subsequent class or struct members are accessible publicly—any function can access these members. The public block is specified as follows:

```
class Form
{
public:
// These members are available to all functions in or
// outside this class.
};
```

register is a storage specifier for integer data types, used to inform the compiler that the access to that data object should be as fast as possible. At its discretion, the compiler may use a CPU register to store that variable.

return is used to stop the execution of the current function and return control to the caller. If the function returns a value, use the statement

```
return expression;
```

to return the value represented by the *expression*.

short is a basic integer data type. You use short as a size qualifier for int and unsigned int variables. Note that short alone means signed short int.

signed is a qualifier used to indicate that data stored in an integer type (int or char) is signed. For example, a signed char can take values between –127 to +127, whereas an unsigned char can hold values from 0 to 255. The int, long, and short types are signed by default.

sizeof is an operator that returns the size of an object or a type in bytes.

static localizes the declaration of an object or a function to a source file (this is a use of static to denote internal linkage). You can use static to "hide" functions and data from other files. You can also use the static keyword to indicate storage class. If you declare a variable static, it will have permanent storage; it will retain its value throughout the life of the program.

struct is used to group the data items and member functions of a type of object and give that group a name by which you can refer to it later. The syntax is as follows:

```
struct structure_name
{
access_specifier_1:
    type item_1;
    type item_2;
    // . . .
access_specifier_2:
    type item_3;
    // . . .
};
structure_name struct_1, struct_2;
```

where the first declaration defines a structure with a name *structure_name* and the second one declares two instances of that structure: *struct_1* and *struct_2*. The access specifiers, *access_specifier_1* and *access_specifier_2* can be one of public, private, or protected. The members can be variables or functions. You can use struct just like class except that the default access to struct members is public, whereas for class the default access specifier is private.

switch is used to perform a multiway branch depending on the value of an expression. The syntax is

switch(*expression*) *statement*

Use case labels inside the *statement* to indicate what to do for each expected value of the *expression*. Use break to separate the code of one case label from another. A default label marks code to be executed if none of the case labels match the expression.

template enables you to declare generic classes. Chapter 16 discusses the proposed use of the template keyword.

this is a pointer to the current object. When inside a class member function, the this keyword refers to a pointer to the current instance of the class. Inside a member function, the C++ compiler automatically prepends a this-> to each reference to a member variable or function of the class.

throw is reserved for future use in the exception-handling mechanism of C++. Chapter 16 describes the planned use of throw.

try is reserved for future use in the exception-handling mechanism of C++. Chapter 16 describes the planned use of `try`.

typedef enables you to give a new name to an existing data type. The syntax is

```
typedef existing_type new_name;
```

For example,

```
typedef void (*P_VFUNC)();
```

will enable you to use P_VFUNC as a data type that means "pointer to a function returning `void`." You can use `typedef` to write complex declarations easily.

union is used to allocate storage for several data items at the same location. The declaration of `union` is identical to that of `struct`, except that in a `union` all data items in the declaration share the same storage location. You can also have an *anonymous union*, which is of the form

```
union { member_list };
```

where `member_list` denotes a list of member variables like the ones inside a `struct`. The members of an anonymous union can be used just like ordinary variables, except that you must be aware of the fact that they share the same storage area.

unsigned is a qualifier for the integer data types (`char`, `int`, `short int`, and `long int`) that informs the compiler that the variable will be used to store nonnegative values only. This effectively doubles the maximum value that can be stored in that variable. Another useful feature is that arithmetic involving unsigned integers can never overflow, because all operations are performed modulo, a number that is one greater than the largest value that can be represented by that unsigned type.

void is data type used to indicate the nonexistence of a return value or arguments in a function definition and declaration. You can also use `void*` to declare a pointer to any type of data object.

volatile is a type qualifier used to indicate that the variable that follows `volatile` may be modified by factors outside the control of the program. For example, the contents of a register in the real-time clock in your system will be such a variable. The `volatile` qualifier warns the compiler that actions performed on `volatile` data must not be "optimized out." You can use the qualifier `const` together with `volatile` to qualify objects that must not be changed by your program but that may change due to external factors.

while is used in loops such as

while (*expression*) *statement*

where the *statement* is executed until *expression* becomes zero (false). The expression is evaluated each time after executing the statement.

C++ Compilers and Class Libraries

This appendix provides a list of representative C++ compilers and class libraries. The list is by no means complete, nor does the appearance of an item in the list constitute an endorsement of the product. A summary description, address, phone number, and an e-mail address (if available) accompanies each entry.

This list is a condensed and edited version of a list posted monthly on the USENET (in the `comp.lang.c++` newsgroup) by Jean-Christophe Collet of Axis Design, Paris, France. Thanks to Jean-Christophe for indicating in the posting that the material may be used freely. If you have access to USENET news, check `comp.lang.c++` for a complete and latest version of the list.

Note that European telephone numbers contain a country code and city code, but you should precede the number with the international dialing code. This number is usually 011, so that number is included for the telephone numbers in this appendix.

C++ Compilers

Borland C++

The Borland C++ compiler for MS-DOS systems is two compilers in one: an ANSI standard C compiler as well as a C++ compiler that conforms to AT&T C++ Release 2.0. Additionally, the Borland C++ compiler enables you to create Microsoft

Windows applications (you do not need the Microsoft Windows Software Development Kit). Borland C++ includes Turbo Debugger, Turbo Assembler, and Turbo Profiler. Borland C++ was used to test the examples appearing in this book.

Borland International, Inc.
1800 Green Hills Road
P.O. Box 660001
Scotts Valley, CA 95067-0001
Telephone: (800) 331-0877, (408) 438-5300

Comeau C++

The Comeau C++ is Comeau Computing's port of AT&T's `cfront 2.1` to the following systems: Intel 80286 and 80386 MS-DOS systems, 80386-based systems running UNIX System V, AT&T UNIX PCs, and AT&T 3B1 and 3B2 systems.

Comeau Computing
91–34 120th Street
Richmond Hill, NY 11418
Telephone: (718) 945-0009
E-mail: attmail!csanta!greg

Glockenspiel C++

Glockenspiel C++ is a port of `cfront 2.0` for MS-DOS and OS/2 machines. The product requires Microsoft C version 6.0. The compiler is also available for many UNIX systems.

Glockenspiel
39 Lower Dominick Street
Dublin 1, Ireland
Telephone: 011-353-1-733-166
Fax: 011-353-1-733-034

GNU C++

The GNU C++ compiler is available in source code form. The latest version is `g++ 1.39.0`. This compiler has been ported to many UNIX systems.

Free Software Foundation
675 Massachusetts Avenue
Cambridge, MA 02139
Telephone: (617) 876-3296
E-mail: fsf@prep.ai.mit.edu

Green Hills C++

Green Hills provides C++ native and cross compilers for 680x0 and 88000 microprocessors.

Oasys
230 2nd Avenue
Waltham, MA 02154
Telephone: (617) 890-7889
Fax: (617) 890-4644

Guidelines C++

Guidelines C++ is a port of AT&T `cfront 2.0` for systems running MS-DOS and UNIX System V/386.

Guidelines Software, Inc.
P.O. Box 6368, Dept. UR
Moraga, CA 94570
Telephone: (415) 376-5527

InTek C++

InTek C++ is InTek's port of `cfront 2.0` to Intel 80386-based systems running MS-DOS and UNIX System V. The MS-DOS version supports Microsoft C 6.0 and Microsoft Windows.

Integration Technologies Inc. (Intek)
1400 112th Avenue S.E., Suite 202
Bellevue, WA 98004
Telephone: (206) 455-9935
Fax: (206) 455-9934
E-mail: mark@intek.com

NDP C++

NDP C++ is Microway's native C++ compiler (compatible with AT&T C++ 2.0) for DOS, UNIX, XENIX, and SunOS. The product supports Intel 80386, 80486, and i860 CPUs.

MicroWay
P.O. Box 79
Kingston, MA 02364
Telephone: (508) 746-7341
Fax: (508) 746-4678

Oregon C++

Oregon C++ is a native C++ compiler (compatible with AT&T C++ Release 2.0) for a variety of UNIX systems such as Sun-3, DEC VAX, 386 UNIX, NCR Tower 32, and Motorola Delta System V/68. The compiler includes a source-level debugger. Additionally, an AT&T C++ Release 2.1 compatible version is available for the Sun SPARCstations.

Oregon Software, Inc.
7352 S.W. Durham Road
Portland, OR 97224
Telephone: (503) 624-6883
Fax: (503) 620-6093
E-mail: support@oresoft.com

Saber C++ 2.0

Saber C++ version 2.0 is a complete UNIX programming environment for writing, browsing, and maintaining C++ programs on Sun, DEC, and HP workstations.

Saber Software, Inc.
185 Alewife Brook Parkway
Cambridge, MA 02138
Telephone: (617) 876-7636
Fax: (617) 547-9011

SCO/C++ 3.0

SCO/C++ version 3.0 is SCO's port of `cfront 2.1` for 80386 systems running SCO UNIX System V. It comes with the `dbXtra` source-level debugger, which can run on a terminal or as an OSF/Motif application. SCO C++ also includes InterViews 2.6 and the NIH Class Libraries, NIHCL (see C++ Class Libraries).

SCO Canada, Inc. (formerly HCR Corporation)
130 Bloor Street West, 10th Floor
Toronto, Ontario
Canada M5S 1N5
Telephone: (416) 922-1937
Fax: (416) 922-8397

Silicon Graphics C++

Silicon Graphics C++ ports `cfront 2.0` and includes a source-level debugger (dbx).

Silicon Graphics
2011 N. Shoreline Boulevard
Mountain View, CA 94039-7311
Telephone: (415) 960-1980

Sun C++

Sun C++ ports `cfront 2.0` to Sun-3 and Sun-4 systems running SunOS 4.0. It includes a source-level debugger (dbx), header files for standard SunOS libraries, and support tools such as `lex`, `nm`, `profiler`, `rpcgen`, and `yacc`.

Sun MicroSystems Inc.
2550 Garcia Avenue
Mountain View, CA 94043
Telephone: (415) 960-1300

Zortech C++ V 2.1

This is a native C++ compiler that conforms to AT&T C++ Release 2.0. Versions have been announced for MS-DOS, OS/2, 386 UNIX, and the Apple Macintosh. The DOS version was used to test certain examples that appear in this book.

Zortech Inc.
4-C Gill Street
Woburn, MA 01801
Telephone: (617) 646-6703
Fax: (617) 643-7969
In Europe:
Zortech Ltd.
106–108 Powis Street
London SE18 6LU
England
Telephone: 011-44-81-316-7777
Fax: 011-44-81-316-4138

C++ Class Libraries

C++/Views

C++/Views is a set of classes for Microsoft Windows programming. Includes a graphical class browser, an interface generator, and a documenter. The library works with Zortech C++ and Borland C++. See Chapter 12 for a more detailed description of C++/Views.

CNS, Inc.
1250 Park Road
Chanhassen, MN 55317-9260
Telephone: (612) 474-7600
Fax: (612) 474-6737

Classix

Classix is a library of Smalltalk-like classes for MS-DOS and UNIX systems. It is available in source code format only.

Empathy Inc.
P.O. Box 632
Cambridge, MA 02142
Telephone: (617) 787-3089

CommonView 2

CommonView 2 is a set of classes for Microsoft Windows 3.0 and OS/2 Presentation Manager (Versions 1.1 and 1.2). It requires Glockenspiel C++ 2.0 and Microsoft C 6.0.

ImageSoft, Inc.
2 Haven Avenue
Port Washington, NY 11050
Telephone: (800) 245-8840, (516) 767-2233
Fax: (516) 767-9067

InterViews 2.6

InterViews version 2.6 is a set of classes layered on top of Xlib for developing X applications. The library is intended for use with `cfront 2.0`. InterViews version 3.0 will be available soon.

SCO C++ 3.0 includes InterViews 2.6. The InterViews toolkit is also in the `contrib` directory of the X11R4 distribution tape. It is also available by anonymous FTP from the Internet site `interviews.stanford.edu` (IP address `36.22.0.175`). Look in the `pub` directory.

M++

M++ is a collection of classes that provides an array data type for use in C++ programs. The library requires an AT&T C++ 2.0 compatible translator or compiler. Versions are available for MS-DOS, 386 UNIX, and other UNIX systems such as Sun, DEC, and HP workstations. A source license is available. Chapter 12 further describes the M++ class library.

Additional modules are available for Least Squares Estimation, statistical utilities, and optimization.

Dyad Software Corp.
16950 151st Avenue S.E.
Renton, WA 98058-8627
Telephone: (800) 274-9739, (512) 343-5037
Fax: (512) 338-5599

Math.h++

The Math.h++ library is a set of mathematical classes that includes vectors and matrices with operations such as FFT. The full source code is available.

Rogue Wave Associates
P.O. Box 2328
Corvallis, OR 97339
Telephone: (503) 745-5908

NIHCL 3.0 (Formerly known as OOPS)

NIHCL version 3.0 is a set of Smalltalk-like classes for `cfront 2.0`. Available by anonymous FTP from `alw.nih.gov` (IP address `128.231.128.251`). The file name is

```
pub/nihcl-3.0.tar.Z
```

NIHCL is also available on MS-DOS 5¼-inch high density diskettes in the form of UNIX shell archives from John Wiley & Sons in Europe.

Customer Service Department
John Wiley & Sons
Shripney Road
Bognor Regis, West Sussex
PO22 9SA, England

Screens++

Screens++ is a set of classes for creating window-based user interfaces for applications running on MS-DOS and UNIX systems.

ImageSoft, Inc.
2 Haven Avenue
Port Washington, NY 11050
Telephone: (516) 767-2233

Windows++ 2.0

Windows++ version 2.0 is a set of classes for creating user interfaces for applications running on MS-DOS, XENIX, and UNIX systems.

Applied Intuition
5485 Beltline Road, Suite 225
Dallas, TX 75240
Telephone: (214) 458-7134

Zinc Interface Library

Zinc is a user interface class library for Turbo C++ that can work in either text or graphic mode. Source code is available.

ZINC Software Inc.
405 South 100 East, Suite 201
Pleasant Grove, UT 84062
Telephone: (800) 638-8665, (801) 785-8900
Fax: (801) 785-8996

ANSI C Headers

This appendix summarizes the contents of the header files in ANSI standard C.

Macros and Data Types Defined in ANSI C Header Files

Table D.1 provides a list of all macros and data types defined in the standard header files in ANSI C. The header files are then shown in alphabetical order. For each header file, you will find the prototype of each function together with a short description of the function.

Table D.1. Macros and Data Types in the ANSI C Library.

Macro or Data Type	Defined in	Description
_IOFBF	<stdio.h>	Constant for "full buffering"
_IOLBF	<stdio.h>	Constant for "line buffering"
_IONBF	<stdio.h>	Constant for "no buffering"
BUFSIZ	<stdio.h>	Size of buffer used by setbuf
CHAR_BIT	<limits.h>	Maximum number of in a char
CHAR_MAX	<limits.h>	Maximum value of a char
CHAR_MIN	<limits.h>	Minimum value of a char
CLK_TCK	<time.h>	Number of clock ticks per second returned by the clock function
DBL_DIG	<float.h>	Number of significant decimal digits in a double value

continues

Table D.1. continued

Macro or Data Type	Defined in	Description
DBL_EPSILON	`<float.h>`	Smallest positive `double` value `x` such that `1+x != 1`
DBL_MANT_DIG	`<float.h>`	Number of base `FLT_RADIX` digits in the mantissa of a `double` variable
DBL_MAX	`<float.h>`	Maximum representable `finite` value that can be stored in a `double` variable
DBL_MAX_10_EXP	`<float.h>`	Maximum integer such that 10 raised to that power can be stored in a `double` variable
DBL_MAX_EXP	`<float.h>`	Maximum integer such that `FLT_RADIX` raised to that power can be stored in a `double` variable
DBL_MIN	`<float.h>`	Minimum positive floating-point number that can be stored in a `double` variable
DBL_MIN_10_EXP	`<float.h>`	Minimum negative integer such that 10 raised to that power can be stored in a `double` variable
DBL_MIN_EXP	`<float.h>`	Minimum negative integer such that `FLT_RADIX` raised to that power minus 1 can be stored in a `double` variable
EDOM	`<errno.h>`	Constant to indicate invalid argument ("domain error")
EOF	`<stdio.h>`	A negative integer constant that indicates "end-of-file"
ERANGE	`<errno.h>`	Constant to indicate unrepresentable result ("range error")
EXIT_FAILURE	`<stddef.h>`	Status code that can be used with `exit` to indicate that the program ended with an error

Macro or Data Type	Defined in	Description
EXIT_SUCCESS	`<stddef.h>`	Status code that can be used with `exit` to indicate that the program executed successfully
FILE	`<stdio.h>`	A data type capable of storing all information necessary to perform file I/O
FILENAME_MAX	`<stdio.h>`	Maximum length of a file name string
FLT_DIG	`<float.h>`	Number of significant decimal digits in a `float` value
FLT_EPSILON	`<float.h>`	Smallest positive `float` value x such that 1+x != 1
FLT_MANT_DIG	`<float.h>`	Number of base FLT_RADIX digits in the mantissa of a `float`
FLT_MAX	`<float.h>`	Maximum representable finite value that can be stored in a `float`
FLT_MAX_10_EXP	`<float.h>`	Maximum integer such that 10 raised to that power can be stored in a `float` variable
FLT_MAX_EXP	`<float.h>`	Maximum integer such that FLT_RADIX raised to that power is representable in a `float`
FLT_MIN	`<float.h>`	Minimum positive floating-point number that can be stored in a `float`
FLT_MIN_10_EXP	`<float.h>`	Minimum negative integer such that 10 raised to that power can be stored in a `float`
FLT_MIN_EXP	`<float.h>`	Minimum negative integer such that FLT_RADIX raised to that power minus 1 can be stored in a `float`
FLT_RADIX	`<float.h>`	Radix of the exponent representation (usually 2 for binary exponent)

continues

Table D.1. continued

Macro or Data Type	Defined in	Description
FLT_ROUNDS	<float.h>	Constant to indicate how floating-point values are rounded (−1 = indeterminate, 0 = toward 0, 1 = to nearest representable value, 2 = toward positive infinity, and 3 = toward negative infinity)
FOPEN_MAX	<stdio.h>	Minimum number of files that can be open simultaneously
HUGE_VAL	<math.h>	A double expression that evaluates to a very large value (for use as return value by math functions when computed result is too large)
INT_MAX	<limits.h>	Maximum value of an int
INT_MIN	<limits.h>	Minimum value of an int
L_tmpnam	<stdio.h>	Size of char array large enough to hold temporary file names generated by tmpnam
LC_ALL	<locale.h>	Constant to indicate the program's entire locale (aspects that depend on the country or geographic region)
LC_COLLATE	<locale.h>	Constant to indicate behavior of strcoll and strxfrm
LC_CTYPE	<locale.h>	Constant to indicate behavior of all character-handling routines
LC_MONETARY	<locale.h>	Constant to indicate behavior of monetary formatting information returned by localeconv
LC_NUMERIC	<locale.h>	Constant to indicate behavior of decimal point format information returned by localeconv
LC_TIME	<locale.h>	Constant to indicate behavior of strftime function

Macro or Data Type	Defined in	Description
LDBL_DIG	`<float.h>`	Number of significant decimal digits in a `long double` value
LDBL_EPSILON	`<float.h>`	Smallest positive `long double` value x such that 1+x != 1
LDBL_MANT_DIG	`<float.h>`	Number of base `FLT_RADIX` digits in the mantissa of a `long double`
LDBL_MAX	`<float.h>`	Maximum representable finite value that can be stored in a `long double`
LDBL_MAX_10_EXP	`<float.h>`	Maximum integer such that 10 raised to that power is representable in a `long double`
LDBL_MAX_EXP	`<float.h>`	Maximum integer such that `FLT_RADIX` raised to that power minus 1 can be stored in a `long double`
LDBL_MIN	`<float.h>`	Minimum positive floating-point number that can be stored in a `long double`
LDBL_MIN_10_EXP	`<float.h>`	Minimum negative integer such that 10 raised to that power is representable in a `long double`
LDBL_MIN_EXP	`<float.h>`	Minimum negative integer such that `FLT_RADIX` raised to that power minus 1 can be stored in a `long double`
LONG_MAX	`<limits.h>`	Maximum value of a `long int`
LONG_MIN	`<limits.h>`	Minimum value of a `long int`
MB_CUR_MAX	`<stdlib.h>`	Number of bytes in a multibyte character for the current locale (always less than `MB_LEN_MAX`)
MB_LEN_MAX	`<limits.h>`	Maximum number of bytes in a multibyte character
NDEBUG	*not defined*	If defined, `assert` will be ignored

continues

Table D.1. continued

Macro or Data Type	Defined in	Description

NULL	`<locale.h>`
	`<stddef.h>`
	`<stdio.h>`
	`<stdlib.h>`
	`<string.h>`
	`<time.h>`
		Implementation-defined null pointer constant

RAND_MAX	`<stdlib.h>`	Maximum integral value returned by the rand function
SCHAR_MAX	`<limits.h>`	Maximum value of a `signed char`
SCHAR_MIN	`<limits.h>`	Minimum value of a `signed char`
SEEK_CUR	`<stdio.h>`	Constant to indicate "relative to current position"
SEEK_END	`<stdio.h>`	Constant to indicate "relative to end-of-file"
SEEK_SET	`<stdio.h>`	Constant to indicate "relative to start-of-file"
SHRT_MAX	`<limits.h>`	Maximum value of a `short int`
SHRT_MIN	`<limits.h>`	Minimum value of a `short int`
SIG_DFL	`<signal.h>`	Constant to indicate default handling of a signal
SIG_ERR	`<signal.h>`	Constant to indicate error return from the `signal` function
SIG_IGN	`<signal.h>`	Constant to indicate that a signal should be ignored
SIGABRT	`<signal.h>`	Signal to indicate abnormal termination
SIGFPE	`<signal.h>`	Signal due to divide by zero, overflow, or other floating-point errors
SIGILL	`<signal.h>`	Signal due to illegal instruction
SIGINT	`<signal.h>`	Signal raised when a specified attention key pressed by the user (for example, Ctrl-C)

Macro or Data Type	Defined in	Description
SIGSEGV	<signal.h>	Signal generated when a storage location is accessed at an invalid address
SIGTERM	<signal.h>	Signal sent to program to terminate it
TMP_MAX	<stdio.h>	Minimum number of unique names that can be obtained by calling the tmpnam function
UCHAR_MAX	<limits.h>	Maximum value of a unsigned char
UINT_MAX	<limits.h>	Maximum value of a unsigned int
ULONG_MAX	<limits.h>	Maximum value of a unsigned long int
USHRT_MAX	<limits.h>	Maximum value of a unsigned short int
clock_t	<time.h>	Data type capable of holding value of time returned by the clock function
div_t	<stdlib.h>	Data structure that can hold the value returned by div
errno	<errno.h>	Global variable to indicate the cause of the last error
fpos_t	<stdio.h>	A data type capable of recording all information necessary to specify each unique position in a file
jmp_buf	<setjmp.h>	An array type capable of holding information necessary to restore a calling environment
ldiv_t	<stdlib.h>	Data structure that can hold the value returned by the ldiv function
offsetof	<stddef.h>	Macro of the form offsetof(structure_type,member) that returns a size_t value, which is the offset in bytes of the member from the beginning of the structure

continues

Table D.1. continued

Macro or Data Type	Defined in	Description
ptrdiff_t	`<stddef.h>`	Signed integral data type which can hold the result of subtracting one pointer from another
sig_atomic_t	`<signal.h>`	A data type that can be accessed as a single entity even in the presence of hardware and software interrupts
size_t	`<stddef.h>` `stdlib.h>`	An unsigned integral data type that is the result of the `sizeof` operator
stderr	`<stdio.h>`	Pointer to FILE data associated with the standard error stream
stdin	`<stdio.h>`	Pointer to FILE data associated with the standard input stream
stdout	`<stdio.h>`	Pointer to FILE data associated with the standard output stream
struct lconv	`<locale.h>`	Structure to hold strings to be used in formatting numeric and monetary values
struct tm	`<time.h>`	Data structure for holding components of a calendar time
time_t	`<time.h>`	Data type capable of representing value of time returned by the `time` function
va_list	`<stdarg.h>`	Data type suitable for holding information needed by the macros `va_start`, `va_arg`, and `va_end`
wchar_t	`<stddef.h>` `<stdlib.h>`	An integral data type which can hold the entire range of values necessary to represent the largest extended character set supported by the compiler

Header Files in ANSI C

`<assert.h>`

```
void assert(<expression>);
```
Abort process if `expression` is false

`<ctype.h>`

```
int isalnum(int c);
```
True if c is alphanumeric

```
int isalpha(int c);
```
True if c is a letter

```
int iscntrl(int c);
```
True if c is a control character

```
int isdigit(int c);
```
True if c is a decimal digit

```
int isgraph(int c);
```
True if c is any printable character except space

```
int islower(int c);
```
True if c is a lowercase letter

```
int isprint(int c);
```
True if c is a printable character

```
int ispunct(int c);
```
True if c is a punctuation character

```
int isspace(int c);
```
True if c is a space character

```
int isupper(int c);
```
True if c is an uppercase letter

```
int isxdigit(int c);
```
True if c is a hexadecimal digit

```
int tolower(int c);
```
Convert c to lowercase if it is uppercase

```
int toupper(int c);
```
Convert c to uppercase if it is lowercase

`<errno.h>`

Define the macros EDOM, ERANGE, and `errno` (see Table D.1)

`<float.h>`

Define macros that specify various properties of floating-point data types: `float`, `double`, and `long double`. Consult Table D.1 for a complete list of these macros

`<limits.h>`

Define macros that specify various properties of integer data types: `char`, `int`, and `long`. Consult Table D.1 for a complete list of these macros

`<locale.h>`

```
struct lconv *localeconv(void);
```
Get information on formatting monetary and numeric values

```
char *setlocale(int category, const char *locale_name);
```
Set a new locale

`<math.h>`

```
double acos(double x);
```
Compute arc cosine of x

```
double asin(double x);
```
Compute arc sine of x

```
double atan(double x);
```
Compute arc tangent of x

```
double atan2(double y, double x);
```
Compute arc tangent of y/x

```
double ceil(double x);
```
Return the smallest integer value that is not less than x

```
double cos(double x);
```
Compute cosine of angle x (radians)

```
double cosh(double x);
```
Compute the hyperbolic cosine of x

```
double exp(double x);
```
Compute the exponential of x (e^x)

```
double fabs(double x);
```
Compute absolute value of x

```
double floor(double x);
```
Return the largest integer value that is not greater than x

```
double fmod(double x, double y);
```
Divide x by y with an integer quotient and return the remainder

```
double frexp(double x, int *expptr);
```
Break down x into mantissa and exponent of two

```
double ldexp(double x, int exp);
```
Reconstruct x out of mantissa and exponent of two (compute x*2^{exp})

```
double log(double x);
```
Compute the natural logarithm of x

```
double log10(double x);
```
Compute logarithm to the base 10 of x

```
double modf(double x, double *intptr);
```
Break x into fractional and integer parts

```
double pow(double x, double y);
```
Compute x raised to the power y (x^y)

```
double sin(double x);
```
Compute sine of angle x (radians)

```
double sinh(double x);
```
Compute the hyperbolic sine of x

```
double sqrt(double x);
```
Compute the square root of x

```
double tan(double x);
```
Compute tangent of angle x (radians)

```
double tanh(double x);
```
Compute the hyperbolic tangent of x

`<setjmp.h>`

`void longjmp(jmp_buf env, int value);`
　Return by restoring a saved context (nonlocal `goto`)

`int setjmp(jmp_buf env);`
　Save the current context for use by `longjmp`

`<signal.h>`

`int raise(int signum);`
　Create an exception condition corresponding to the specified signal number

`void (*signal(int signum, void (*handler)(int sigarg)))(int);`
　Set up the function named `handler` as the function to be called when the signal specified by `signum` occurs

`<stdarg.h>`

`void va_start(va_list arg_ptr, prev_param);`
　Set `arg_ptr` to beginning of argument list

`<type> va_arg(va_list arg_ptr, <type>);`
　Get next argument of specified type

`void va_end(va_list arg_ptr);`
　Reset `arg_ptr`

`<stddef.h>`

Define the macros and data types `NULL`, `offsetof`, `ptrdiff_t`, `size_t`, and `wchar_t`

`<stdio.h>`

`void clearerr(FILE *file_pointer);`
　Clear error indicator of stream specified by `file_pointer`

```
int fclose(FILE *file_pointer);
```
Close the file specified by `file_pointer`

```
int feof(FILE *file_pointer);
```
Check whether end of file occurred on a stream

```
int ferror(FILE *file_pointer);
```
Check whether any error occurred during file I/O

```
int fflush(FILE *file_pointer);
```
Write out (flush) buffer to file

```
int fgetc(FILE *file_pointer);
```
Get a character from a stream

```
int fgetpos(FILE *file_pointer, fpos_t *current_pos);
```
Get the current position in a stream

```
char *fgets(char *string, int maxchar, FILE *file_pointer);
```
Read a string from a file

```
FILE *fopen(const char *filename, const char *access_mode);
```
Open a file for buffered I/O

```
int fprintf(FILE *file_pointer, const char *format_string,...);
```
Write formatted output to a file

```
int fputc(int c, FILE *file_pointer);
```
Write a character to a stream

```
int fputs(char *string, FILE *file_pointer);
```
Write a string to a stream

```
size_t fread(void *buffer, size_t size, size_t count, FILE
*file_pointer);
```
Read unformatted data from a stream into a buffer

```
FILE *freopen(const char *filename, const char *access_mode, FILE
*file_pointer);
```
Reassign a file pointer to a different file

```
int fscanf(FILE *file_pointer, const char *format_string,...);
```
Read formatted input from a stream

```
int fseek(FILE *file_pointer, long offset, int origin);
```
Set current position in file to a new location

```
int fsetpos(FILE *file_pointer, const fpos_t *current_pos);
```
Set current position in file to a new location (use with `fgetpos`)

```
long ftell(FILE *file_pointer);
```
Get current location in file

```
size_t fwrite(const void *buffer, size_t size, size_t count, FILE
*file_pointer);
```
Write unformatted data from a buffer to a stream

```
int getc(FILE *file_pointer);
```
Read a character from a stream

```
int getchar(void);
```
Read a character from `stdin`; same as `fgetc(stdin)`

```
char *gets(char *buffer);
```
Read a line from `stdin` into a buffer

```
void perror(const char *string);
```
Print error message corresponding to last system error

```
int printf(const char *format_string,...);
```
Write formatted output to `stdout`

```
int putc(int c, FILE *file_pointer);
```
Write a character to a stream

```
int putchar(int c);
```
Write a character to `stdout`

```
int puts(const char *string);
```
Write a string to `stdout`

```
int remove(const char *filename);
```
Delete a named file

```
int rename(const char *oldname, const char *newname);
```
Rename a file

```
void rewind(FILE *file_pointer);
```
Rewind a file

```
int scanf(const char *format_string,...);
```
Read formatted input from `stdin`

```
void setbuf(FILE *file_pointer, char *buffer);
```
Set up a new buffer for the stream

```
int setvbuf(FILE *file_pointer, char *buffer, int buf_type,
size_t buf_size);
```
Set up new buffer and control the level of buffering on a stream

```
int sprintf(char *p_string, const char *format_string,...);
```
Write formatted output to a string

```
int sscanf(const char *buffer, const char *format_string,...);
```
Read formatted input from a string

```
FILE *tmpfile(void);
```
Open a temporary file

```
char *tmpnam(char *file_name);
```
Get temporary file name

```
int ungetc(int c, FILE *file_pointer);
```
Push back character into stream's buffer

```
int vfprintf(FILE *file_pointer, const char *format_string,
va_list arg_pointer);
```
Write formatted output to a file (allows variable length argument list)

```
int vprintf(const char *format_string, va_list arg_pointer);
```
Write formatted output to stdout (allows variable length argument list)

```
int vsprintf(char *p_string, const char *format_string, va_list
arg_pointer);
```
Write formatted output to a string (allows variable length argument list)

<stdlib.h>

```
void abort(void);
```
Abort a process by calling raise(SIGABRT)

```
int abs(int n);
```
Get absolute value of an integer

```
int atexit(void (*func)(void));
```
Set up function to be called when process terminates

```
double atof(const char *string);
```
Convert string to floating-point value

```
int atoi(const char *string);
```
Convert string to an integer value

```
int atol(const char *string);
```
Convert string to a long integer value

```
void *bsearch(const void *key, const void *base, size_t num,
size_t width, int (*compare)(const void *elem1, const void
*elem2));
```
Perform binary search

```
void *calloc(size_t num_elems, size_t elem_size);
```
Allocate an array and initialize all elements to zero

```
div_t div(int numer, int denom);
```
Divide one integer by another and return quotient and remainder

```
void exit(int status);
```
Terminate process after flushing all buffers

```
void free(void *pointer);
```
Free a block of memory

```
char *getenv(const char *varname);
```
Get definition of environment variable whose name is varname

```
long labs(long n);
```
Find absolute value of long integer n

```
ldiv_t ldiv(long numer, long denom);
```
Divide one long integer by another (return quotient and remainder)

```
void *malloc(size_t num_bytes);
```
Allocate a block of memory

```
int mblen(const char *s, size_t n);
```
Return the number of bytes in a single multibyte character

```
size_t mbstowcs(wchar_t *pwcs, const char *mbs, size_t n);
```
Convert a sequence of multibyte characters in mbs into a sequence of codes of wchar_t type

```
int mbtowc(wchar_t *pwchar, const char *s, size_t n);
```
Convert the multibyte character in s to wchar_t type

```
void qsort(void *base, size_t num, size_t width, int
(*compare)(const void *elem1, const void *elem2));
```
Use the quicksort algorithm to sort an array

```
int rand(void);
```
Get a random integer between 0 and RAND_MAX (also defined in <stdlib.h>)

```
void *realloc(void *pointer, size_t newsize);
```
Reallocate (adjust the size of) a block of memory

```
void srand(unsigned seed);
```
Set a new seed for the random number generator (rand)

```
double strtod(const char *string, char **endptr);
```
Convert string to a floating-point value

```
long strtol(const char *string, char **endptr, int radix);
```
Convert string to a long integer using a given radix

```
unsigned long strtoul(const char *string, char **endptr, int
radix);
```
Convert string to unsigned long using a specified radix

```
int system(const char *string);
```
Execute a command in `string` by passing it to the command processor of the underlying operating system

```
size_t wcstombs(char *mbs, const wchar_t *pwcs, size_t n);
```
Convert a sequence of codes of `wchar_t` type into a sequence of multibyte characters

```
int wctomb(char *s, wchar_t wchar);
```
Converts a character of `wchar_t` type into a multibyte equivalent

<string.h>

```
void *memchr (const void *s, int c, size_t n);
```
Search for first occurrence of a character in a buffer

```
int memcmp (const void *s1, const void *s2, size_t n);
```
Compare two buffers

```
void *memcpy (void *dest, const void *src, size_t n);
```
Copy the `src` buffer into the `dest` buffer

```
void *memmove (void *dest, const void *src, size_t n);
```
Move a number of bytes from one buffer to another

```
void *memset (void *s, int c, size_t n);
```
Set n bytes of buffer s to the character c

```
char *strcat(char *string1, const char *string2);
```
Append `string2` to `string1`

```
char *strchr(const char *string, int c);
```
Search string for the first occurrence of the character c

```
int strcmp(const char *string1, const char *string2);
```
Compare `string1` and `string2` according to alphabetical order

```
int strcoll(const char *string1, const char *string2);
```
Compare `string1` with `string2` using a locale-specific collating sequence

```
char *strcpy(char *string1, const char *string2);
```
Copy `string2` to `string1`

```
size_t strcspn(const char *string1, const char *string2);
```
Find first occurrence of a character from `string2` in `string1`

```
char *strerror(int errnum);
```
Get error message corresponding to specified error number

```
size_t strlen(const char *string);
```
Determine the length of a string (excluding the terminating null character)

```
char *strncat(char *string1, const char *string2, size_t n);
```
Append n characters from string2 to string1

```
int strncmp(const char *string1, const char *string2, size_t n);
```
Compare first n characters of two strings

```
char *strncpy(char *string1, const char *string2, size_t n);
```
Copy first n characters of string2 to string1

```
char *strpbrk(const char *string1, const char *string2);
```
Locate first occurrence of any character from string2 in string1

```
char *strrchr(const char *string, int c);
```
Find last occurrence of character c in string

```
size_t strspn(const char *string1, const char *string2);
```
Locate the first character in string1 that is not in string2

```
char *strstr(const char *string1, const char *string2);
```
Find the first occurrence of string2 in string1

```
char *strtok(char *string1, const char *string2);
```
Get tokens from string1 (string2 has the token separators)

```
size_t strxfrm(char *string1, char *string2, size_t maxchr);
```
Transform string2 to string1 using transformation rule appropriate for current locale

\<time.h\>

```
char *asctime(struct tm *time);
```
Convert time from struct tm to string of the form Sat Mar 30 10:15:55 1991

```
clock_t clock(void);
```
Get elapsed processor time in clock ticks

```
char *ctime(const time_t *time);
```
Convert binary time to string

```
double difftime(time_t time2, time_t time1);
```
Compute the difference between two times in seconds

```
struct tm *gmtime(const time_t *time);
```
Get Greenwich Mean Time (GMT) in a tm structure

```
struct tm *localtime(const time_t *time);
```
Get the local time in a `tm` structure

```
time_t mktime(struct tm *timeptr);
```
Convert time from `struct tm` to `time_t`

```
size_t strftime(char *str, size_t maxsize, const char
*format_string, const struct tm *timeptr);
```
Convert time from `struct tm` to string using specified format

```
time_t time(time_t *timeptr);
```
Get current time in a binary format

Index

Symbols

operator, 602
( ) operator, 354
<< operator, 139-141, 146-148
= operator, 218
== operator, 216
>> operator, 139-141
+ (plus) operator, 214-215

A

AboutWindow class, 481-482
access functions, 193-194
add function, 444
ADT, 14-15, 40
ADT (abstract data types), 4
ANSI (American National Standards Institute), 575
ANSI C
    escape sequences, 93-94
    header files, 633, 641-651
    keywords, 93
    library, 301-302
    macros, 633-640
    stream, 138
    trigraph sequences, 94

applications
    building for Microsoft Windows, 369-371
    in C++/Views for Microsoft Windows, 363-364
arguments, 127-128, 189-190
    default, 121
    passing to functions by references, 194
    reference types, 125-126
    to operator functions, 211
    variable-length lists, 308
    windows, 462
array classes/class objects, 350-351
    member functions, 356
array declarations, 616
array I/O, 354-355
array index operators, 352-353
arrays, 103, 346
    character initialization, 133
    filling, 351
    in M++ class library, 349-350
    multidimensional, 103
    using files as, 224-228
    vtable, 284
assemblers, 3
assembly languages, 3, 546
assignment operators, 342
AT&T C++ Release 2.0, 333

D

K-L

S

X

Z

Sams—Covering The Latest In Computer And Technical Topics!

Audio

Audio Production Techniques for Video	$29.95
Audio Systems Design and Installation	$59.95
Audio Technology Fundamentals	$24.95
Compact Disc Troubleshooting and Repair	$24.95
Handbook for Sound Engineers: The New Audio Cyclopedia	$79.95
Introduction to Professional Recording Techniques	$29.95
Modern Recording Techniques, 3rd Ed.	$29.95
Principles of Digital Audio, 2nd Ed.	$29.95
Sound Recording Handbook	$49.95
Sound System Engineering, 2nd Ed.	$49.95

Electricity/Electronics

Basic AC Circuits	$29.95
Electricity 1, Revised 2nd Ed.	$14.95
Electricity 1-7, Revised 2nd Ed.	$49.95
Electricity 2, Revised 2nd Ed.	$14.95
Electricity 3, Revised 2nd Ed.	$14.95
Electricity 4, Revised 2nd Ed.	$14.95
Electricity 5, Revised 2nd Ed.	$14.95
Electricity 6, Revised 2nd Ed.	$14.95
Electricity 7, Revised 2nd Ed.	$14.95
Electronics 1-7, Revised 2nd Ed.	$49.95

Electronics Technical

Active-Filter Cookbook	$19.95
Camcorder Survival Guide	$ 9.95
CMOS Cookbook, 2nd Ed.	$24.95
Design of OP-AMP Circuits with Experiments	$19.95
Design of Phase-Locked Loop Circuits with Experiments	$19.95
Electrical Test Equipment	$19.95
Electrical Wiring	$19.95
How to Read Schematics, 4th Ed.	$19.95
IC Op-Amp Cookbook, 3rd Ed.	$24.95
IC Timer Cookbook, 2nd Ed.	$19.95
IC User's Casebook	$19.95
Radio Handbook, 23rd Ed.	$39.95
Radio Operator's License Q&A Manual, 11th Ed.	$24.95
RF Circuit Design	$24.95
Transformers and Motors	$24.95
TTL Cookbook	$19.95
Undergrounding Electric Lines	$14.95
Understanding Telephone Electronics, 2nd Ed.	$19.95
VCR Troubleshooting & Repair Guide	$19.95
Video Scrambling & Descrambling for Satellite & Cable TV	$19.95

Games

Beyond the Nintendo Masters	$ 9.95
Mastering Nintendo Video Games II	$ 9.95
Tricks of the Nintendo Masters	$ 9.95
VideoGames & Computer Entertainment Complete Guide to Nintendo Video Games	$ 9.50
Winner's Guide to Nintendo Game Boy	$ 9.95
Winner's Guide to Sega Genesis	$ 9.95

Hardware/Technical

Hard Disk Power with the Jamsa Disk Utilities	$39.95
IBM PC Advanced Troubleshooting & Repair	$24.95
IBM Personal Computer Troubleshooting & Repair	$24.95
IBM Personal Computer Upgrade Guide	$24.95
Microcomputer Troubleshooting & Repair	$24.95
Understanding Communications Systems, 2nd Ed.	$19.95
Understanding Data Communications, 2nd Ed.	$19.95
Understanding FAX and Electronic Mail	$19.95
Understanding Fiber Optics	$19.95

IBM: Business

Best Book of Microsoft Works for the PC, 2nd Ed.	$24.95
Best Book of PFS: First Choice	$24.95
Best Book of Professional Write and File	$22.95
First Book of Fastback Plus	$16.95
First Book of Norton Utilities	$16.95
First Book of Personal Computing	$16.95
First Book of PROCOMM PLUS	$16.95

IBM: Database

Best Book of Paradox 3	$27.95
dBASE III Plus Programmer's Reference Guide	$24.95
dBASE IV Programmer's Reference Guide	$24.95
First Book of Paradox 3	$16.95
Mastering ORACLE Featuring ORACLE's SQL Standard	$24.95

IBM: Graphics/Desktop Publishing

Best Book of Autodesk Animator	$29.95
Best Book of Harvard Graphics	$24.95
First Book of DrawPerfect	$16.95
First Book of Harvard Graphics	$16.95
First Book of PC Paintbrush	$16.95
First Book of PFS: First Publisher	$16.95

IBM: Spreadsheets/Financial

Best Book of Lotus 1-2-3 Release 3.1	$27.95
Best Book of Lotus 1-2-3, Release 2.2, 3rd Ed.	$26.95
Best Book of Peachtree Complete III	$24.95
First Book of Lotus 1-2-3, Release 2.2	$16.95
First Book of Lotus 1-2-3/G	$16.95
First Book of Microsoft Excel for the PC	$16.95
Lotus 1-2-3: Step-by-Step	$24.95

IBM: Word Processing

Best Book of Microsoft Word 5	$24.95
Best Book of Microsoft Word for Windows	$24.95
Best Book of WordPerfect 5.1	$26.95
Best Book of WordPerfect Version 5.0	$24.95
First Book of PC Write	$16.95
First Book of WordPerfect 5.1	$16.95
WordPerfect 5.1: Step-by-Step	$24.95

Macintosh/Apple

Best Book of AppleWorks	$24.95
Best Book of MacWrite II	$24.95
Best Book of Microsoft Word for the Macintosh	$24.95
Macintosh Printer Secrets	$34.95
Macintosh Repair & Upgrade Secrets	$34.95
Macintosh Revealed, Expanding the Toolbox, Vol. 4	$29.95
Macintosh Revealed, Mastering the Toolbox, Vol. 3	$29.95
Macintosh Revealed, Programming with the Toolbox, Vol. 2, 2nd Ed.	$29.95
Macintosh Revealed, Unlocking the Toolbox, Vol. 1, 2nd Ed.	$29.95
Using ORACLE with HyperCard	$24.95

Operating Systems/Networking

Best Book of DESQview	$24.95
Best Book of DOS	$24.95
Best Book of Microsoft Windows 3	$24.95
Business Guide to Local Area Networks	$24.95
Exploring the UNIX System, 2nd Ed.	$29.95
First Book of DeskMate	$16.95
First Book of Microsoft QuickPascal	$16.95
First Book of MS-DOS	$16.95
First Book of UNIX	$16.95
Interfacing to the IBM Personal Computer, 2nd Ed.	$24.95
Mastering NetWare	$29.95
The Waite Group's Discovering MS-DOS	$19.95
The Waite Group's Inside XENIX	$29.95
The Waite Group's MS-DOS Bible, 3rd Ed.	$24.95
The Waite Group's MS-DOS Developer's Guide, 2nd Ed.	$29.95
The Waite Group's Tricks of the MS-DOS Masters, 2nd Ed.	$29.95
The Waite Group's Tricks of the UNIX Masters	$29.95
The Waite Group's Understanding MS-DOS, 2nd Ed.	$19.95
The Waite Group's UNIX Primer Plus, 2nd Ed.	$29.95
The Waite Group's UNIX System V Bible	$29.95
The Waite Group's UNIX System V Primer, Revised Ed.	$29.95
Understanding Local Area Networks, 2nd Ed.	$24.95

Understanding NetWare	$24.95
UNIX Applications Programming: Mastering the Shell	$29.95
UNIX Networking	$29.95
UNIX Shell Programming, Revised Ed.	$29.95
UNIX System Administration	$29.95
UNIX System Security	$34.95
UNIX Text Processing	$29.95
UNIX: Step-by-Step	$29.95

Professional/Reference

Data Communications, Networks, and Systems	$39.95
Gallium Arsenide Technology, Volume II	$69.95
Handbook of Computer-Communications Standards, Vol. 1, 2nd Ed.	$39.95
Handbook of Computer-Communications Standards, Vol. 2, 2nd Ed.	$39.95
Handbook of Computer-Communications Standards, Vol. 3, 2nd Ed.	$39.95
Handbook of Electronics Tables and Formulas, 6th Ed.	$24.95
ISDN, DECnet, and SNA Communications	$44.95
Modern Dictionary of Electronics, 6th Ed.	$39.95
Programmable Logic Designer's Guide	$29.95
Reference Data for Engineers: Radio, Electronics, Computer, and Communications, 7th Ed.	$99.95
Surface-Mount Technology for PC Board Design	$49.95
World Satellite Almanac, 2nd Ed.	$39.95

Programming

Advanced C: Tips and Techniques	$29.95
C Programmer's Guide to NetBIOS	$29.95
C Programmer's Guide to Serial Communications	$29.95
Commodore 64 Programmer's Reference Guide	$19.95
DOS Batch File Power	$39.95
First Book of GW-BASIC	$16.95
How to Write Macintosh Software, 2nd Ed.	$29.95
Mastering Turbo Assembler	$29.95
Mastering Turbo Debugger	$29.95
Mastering Turbo Pascal 5.5, 3rd Ed.	$29.95
Microsoft QuickBASIC Programmer's Reference	$29.95
Programming in ANSI C	$29.95
Programming in C, Revised Ed.	$29.95
QuickC Programming	$29.95
The Waite Group's BASIC Programming Primer, 2nd Ed.	$24.95
The Waite Group's C Programming Using Turbo C++	$29.95
The Waite Group's C++ Programming	$24.95
The Waite Group's C: Step-by-Step	$29.95
The Waite Group's GW-BASIC Primer Plus	$24.95
The Waite Group's Microsoft C Bible, 2nd Ed.	$29.95
The Waite Group's Microsoft C Programming for the PC, 2nd Ed.	$29.95
The Waite Group's Microsoft Macro Assembler Bible	$29.95
The Waite Group's New C Primer Plus	$29.95
The Waite Group's QuickC Bible	$29.95
The Waite Group's Turbo Assembler Bible	$29.95
The Waite Group's Turbo C Bible	$29.95
The Waite Group's Turbo C Programming for the PC, Revised Ed.	$29.95
The Waite Group's TWG Turbo C++Bible	$29.95
X Window System Programming	$29.95

For More Information,
Call Toll Free
1-800-257-5755

*All prices are subject to change without notice.
Non-U.S. prices may be higher. Printed in the U.S.A.*

Source Code Available On Disk

Complete source code for all the programs in *Object-Oriented Programming in C++* is available on an MS-DOS format 5-1/4" or 3-1/2" diskette. Simply fill in the order form below and mail it with your payment today. If you have a UNIX system, you can upload the code from an MS-DOS system to your UNIX system using a communications program.

The disk is available postpaid for $30 (foreign orders please add $6 for shipping and handling) from: LNB Software, Inc., 2005 Aventurine Way, Silver Spring, MD 20904.

Payment must accompany order. Send a money order or a check in U.S. funds drawn on a U.S. bank. Maryland residents please add sales tax.

Please send me ___ copies of *Object-Oriented Programming in C++ Code Disk* at $30 each .... _____

Maryland residents please add sales tax .... _____

Orders outside U.S. please add $6 shipping and handling .... _____

Total Amount Enclosed .... _____

SEND TO:

_____
Name

_____
Title   Company

_____
Address

_____
City   State   ZIP

_____
Telephone

IMPORTANT! Please indicate diskette size:

Diskette Size (check one):   5-1/4" _____   3-1/2" _____

Send order form and payment to: LNB Software, Inc., 2005 Aventurine Way,
Silver Spring, MD   20904

SAMS assumes no responsibility for this offer. This is solely an offer of LNB Software, Inc. and not of SAMS.